screen media

screen media
ANALYSING FILM AND TELEVISION

Jane Stadler with Kelly McWilliam

Routledge
Taylor & Francis Group
LONDON AND NEW YORK

First published 2009 by Allen & Unwin

Published 2020 by Routledge
2 Park Square, Milton Park, Abingdon, Oxon OX14 4RN
605 Third Avenue, New York, NY 10017

Routledge is an imprint of the Taylor & Francis Group, an informa business

Copyright © Jane Stadler and Kelly McWilliam 2009

All rights reserved. No part of this book may be reprinted or reproduced or utilised in any form or by any electronic, mechanical, or other means, now known or hereafter invented, including photocopying and recording, or in any information storage or retrieval system, without permission in writing from the publishers.

Notice:
Product or corporate names may be trademarks or registered trademarks, and are used only for identification and explanation without intent to infringe.

National Library of Australia
Cataloguing-in-Publication entry:

Stadler, Jane

   Screen media: analysing film and
   television /Jane Stadler; Kelly McWilliam.

   978 1 74175 448 3 (pbk.)

   Includes index.

   Motion pictures and television. Motion pictures and television–Social aspects. Motion pictures. Motion pictures–Social aspects. Television. Television–Social aspects. McWilliam, Kelly.

791.4

Text design by Kirby Stalgis
Set by Midland Typesetters, Australia.

ISBN-13: 9781741754483 (pbk)

contents

Acknowledgments	ix
Introduction: Thinking on both sides of the screen	xi
Digital technology and convergence	xiii
Organisation of the book	xvi
Outline of the book	xvii
1 By design: Art direction and *mise en scène* construction	1
Mise en scène	2
Costume	7
Setting	10
Action	17
Lighting	23
Camera position, framing and composition	26
Conclusion	28
Key skills	28
2 Cinematography: Writing in light and movement	31
Camera position	34
Camera movement	43
Lenses and focal properties	47
Conclusion	61
Key skills	62

3 Soundscapes: The invisible magic of sound — 65
- Distinctions between film and television sound — 66
- Ambience — 71
- Music — 71
- Dialogue — 75
- Sound effects — 80
- Conclusion — 89
- Key skills — 90

4 At the edge of the cut: Editing from continuity to montage — 93
- The role of the editor — 93
- Editing for multiple camera shoots — 97
- Television editing — 99
- Editing and narrative structure — 101
- Point of view — 102
- Continuity editing — 103
- Montage-style editing — 114
- Sound transitions — 117
- Editing action sequences — 119
- Conclusion — 121
- Key skills — 123

5 Plotting and planning: Storytelling and reviewing techniques — 125
- Synopses and scene breakdowns — 126
- Treatments — 130
- Scripts — 132
- Shooting scripts and storyboards — 139
- Film reviewing — 146
- Conclusion — 151
- Key skills — 152

6 Screen narratives: Traditions and trends — 155
- Contemporary film narratives — 155
- Classical narration — 157
- Story and plot — 160
- Structuralism — 161
- Complex narrative structures — 168
- Television and narrative structure — 172
- Digital game narratives — 179
- Narrative convergence — 180
- Conclusion — 182
- Key skills — 183

CONTENTS

7 Reality and realism: Seeing is believing — **185**
- Realism and codes of representation in film and television — 187
- Documentary — 190
- Mockumentary film and television — 196
- Realist film movements — 197
- Reality television — 205
- The ethics of style and the spectacle of the real — 210
- Conclusion — 213
- Key skills — 213

8 Genre: 'Something new based on something familiar'
  by Kelly McWilliam — **217**
- What is 'genre'? — 218
- Differences in medium: Genre in film and television — 228
- Key approaches to studying genre — 230
- Applying genre analysis: *Grey's Anatomy* — 239
- Conclusion — 242
- Key skills — 243

9 Star struck: Fandom and the discourse of celebrity
  by Kelly McWilliam — **245**
- History — 247
- What are 'stars' and 'celebrities'? — 249
- Audiences, identification and fandom — 256
- Key approaches to studying stars and celebrity — 261
- Conclusion — 268
- Key skills — 271

10 Skating the edge: Cult media and the (inter)active audience — **273**
- Approaches to cult media: Texts, audiences, industry — 275
- Cult film — 277
- Cult television — 279
- Theories of spectatorship — 286
- Audience research — 290
- Technological developments — 295
- Industry and institutions — 296
- Conclusion — 299
- Key skills — 300

11 The crowded screen: Transcultural influences and new directions in visual culture — 303
Hybridity: Theorising generic combination and transformation — 304
Characterisation, ideology, and social change — 307
Postfeminism and action cinema heroines — 310
Postmodern characteristics of screen culture — 316
Globalisation and screen culture — 325
New directions in screen culture — 330
Conclusion — 331
Key skills — 332

Glossary — 333
Bibliography — 354
  Film credits — 365
  Game credits — 370
  Television credits — 370
  Index — 375

acknowledgments

The inspiration for this book came from my time at the University of Cape Town in South Africa from 2002 to 2005, particularly from designing the Analysing Film and Television curriculum and working with students in the Screen Production programme. I dedicate my contribution to the book to my students, to my own teachers, and to the fabulous colleagues with whom I collaborated at UCT in the Centre for Film and Media Studies and the Centre for Educational Technology. Warmest thanks go to my co-author, Kelly McWilliam, for her friendship and collegiality as well as her wonderful ability to synthesise complex ideas and express them in a concise and accessible manner in her contribution to the book as a whole, and especially in the chapters on celebrity and genre for which she was primarily responsible.

Jane Stadler

I dedicate my contribution to Jane, with whom it has always been such a pleasure to work; to my Queensland University of Technology colleagues, but especially John Hartley, Brad Haseman and Paul Makeham, for their esteemed support and guidance; and to Sheona Thomson, who loves screen media almost as much as I do.

Kelly McWilliam

We would like to acknowledge the input of a number of people who have helped at various stages of the publication. First and foremost, we owe a debt of gratitude to Amanda Third who generously contributed to the development of ideas from an early stage, and whose excellent feedback on drafts of the *mise en scène*, sound, editing and realism chapters is deeply appreciated. We are also grateful for the expert advice and suggestions given by Lisa Bode, who read and commented on the editing and realism chapters and assisted in developing the cult media chapter; to Meg Rickards and Emma van der Vliet, who helped enormously with the storytelling and realism chapters respectively; to Melanie Rodriga, who was kind enough to give detailed input on a draft of the cinematography chapter; and to Becky Abbott who made valuable suggestions about the introduction and the manuscript as a whole. Meg Rickards, Emma van der Vliet, Melanie Rodriga and Becky Abbott all work in the film and television industries as well as in academia, so their experience in production has been extremely important in informing the integration of theory and praxis in the text. In addition, we are thankful for the insightful feedback by anonymous readers of the manuscript; for the sage advice of our colleagues Graeme Turner, Frances Bonner, Gillian Whitlock and John Hartley; for Angie Knaggs' assistance with copyright permissions; for Matt Campora's insights into multiform narrative; and for Rowena Grant Frost's suggestion of the GI Joe image and references to *The Virgin Spring*. We express sincere thanks for the expertise of our editor Lauren Finger and our publisher Elizabeth Weiss at Allen & Unwin, who have overseen the entire project and offered helpful input and guidance.

The research for this book was undertaken with the assistance of a University of Queensland research grant in 2007.

Jane Stadler and Kelly McWilliam
Brisbane, December 2007

introduction:
Thinking on both sides of the screen

This book is for those who like to think of slouching on the couch in front of the television as research, playing digital games and surfing the net as exercise, and going to the movies as an adventure. It speaks to screen enthusiasts keen to develop ways of articulating their responses to and ideas about film and television. While it is not a practical screen production guide, it does address the interests of those who intend to become involved in the screen media industries as directors, producers, writers, reviewers, researchers, educators, policy-makers, or any of the myriad collaborative roles that media production, distribution, circulation and regulation necessitate. Throughout, we emphasise the importance of 'thinking on both sides of the screen'. In other words, we encourage readers to develop the skills to understand and analyse how and why a screen text was shot, scored and edited in a particular way, and then to consider what impact those production choices might have on audience members' interpretation of the text. In this way, we emphasise the integral relationship between form—or how a subject is represented (whether through decisions about audio-visual style, casting, shot choice, editing, genre or other formal elements)—and content—or what the subject of the text is. The same content can be presented in many forms. For example, the *Lord of the Rings* trilogy takes the form of novels, feature films and digital games. Each form invites different modes of engagement with the content:

reading, listening and looking; or participating in the action. If *Lord of the Rings* were adapted for television, the form would alter again. The narrative would be organised into episodes, and each episode would follow a formal pattern in which the action builds to a suspenseful moment right before cutting to a commercial break. Different technologies, conventions and reception contexts characterise each medium, but in all screen texts the techniques of narrative organisation, set design, performance, lighting, cinematography, editing and sound are interrelated parts of an overall formal system. Film theorist David Bordwell argues that 'narration involves two principal formal systems, syuzhet [plot] and style, which cue the spectator to frame hypotheses and draw inferences' (1985: xiii). Following Bordwell, we explore how audiences interpret the story content, structure and style of screen texts and how meaning arises as much from the process by which these interconnected formal elements are organised and interpreted as from the content itself.

Ideally, form supports and enhances content. Sometimes the tension between form and content can give rise to ethical issues. For instance, the gruesome but beautifully filmed Australian movie *Wolf Creek*, directed by Greg McLean in 2005, begins as a road movie then segues into a slasher film when three young tourists become stranded in a remote area of the Australian outback. Titles at the beginning and end of *Wolf Creek* signal that it is based on actual events (the Ivan Milat backpacker murders in Belanglo Forest in New South Wales, where seven hitchhikers were killed). The terrifying story of the backpacker murders has been told in several forms, including an investigative journalism style book called *Sins of the Brother* (Whittaker & Kennedy 2001), which is based on real interviews and claims to offer a 'definitive account' of the murders. On television, the backpacker murders have been reported in the form of news broadcasts and documentaries. These realist forms are designed to be informative, hence they avoid dramatising events with special effects, chilling music or prosthetic gore. *Wolf Creek* employs the formal characteristics of horror films to titillate the audience, but it also incorporates some dialogue directly from *Sins of the Brother*—such as when Mick Taylor (played by John Jarratt) uses Ivan Milat's actual words to tell his victim: 'This little procedure is called making a head on a stick. Once your spine's severed, that's what you are' (Whittaker & Kennedy 2001: 150).

This incorporation of 'the real' into a formal system designed for the purpose of entertainment is problematic because the film has literally capitalised on real suffering, trivialising and sensationalising it within a genre geared to thrill the audience.

After setting up the relationships between different aspects of form in the first part of the book, we develop the ethical implications of form and content further in the chapter on realism, arguing that form itself makes a statement, and that some forms of representation may be more appropriate to convey particular content than others. We also stress the *relevance* of different approaches to screen analysis and the connections between screen theory and creative practice, drawing on familiar examples to illustrate the theoretical and applied concepts we discuss. The book covers screen terminology, providing a clear and accessible analytical and theoretical vocabulary supported by glossary terms and definitions. The technical terminology, theoretical approaches and analytical skills offered provide an important foundation for screen analysis, as well as opening up avenues of critical engagement, interpretation and insight. In addition, we investigate the processes of audience reception and issues of realism and context, and analyse the socio-cultural and political implications of audio-visual narratives. This textbook also contributes to understandings of narrative structure, genre, celebrity and stylistic techniques, and provides grounding in the first steps of scripting and storyboarding, enabling readers to develop links between screen theory and creative practice.

DIGITAL TECHNOLOGY AND CONVERGENCE

Instead of treating the move to digital screen technologies as something to be feared and avoided like James Bond avoids matrimony, we demystify technological developments. By showing the relationship between form and content, we try to make the topic interesting and accessible, as we do with other historical developments in screen media that are interwoven throughout the book. Often we discuss television as though it has marked similarities with film because developments in digital technology mean that the two media are experiencing **convergence**: image and sound quality, and even viewing contexts and audience experiences, are moving closer

> **Convergence** can refer to economic integration (business conglomerates and mergers) in the media industries, as well technical developments (like digital photography and editing, and broadband internet) that enable the provision of shared media content across different media formats and transmission systems.

together in many cases. Both feature films and television programs can still be made in a variety of formats—celluloid, videotape, high-definition video and high-definition television (HDTV); however, digitalisation is having a significant impact on all screen media. Analogue media differ from digital media in that analogue relies on mechanical or electrical modes of recording and transmitting audio-visual signals, whereas digital media use mathematical processes to record, represent, manipulate and transmit image and sound data. High-definition digital formats compress more data into a single audio-visual image than regular digital formats, giving a high-resolution image of similar quality to celluloid.

The advantages of high-definition digital video over celluloid are that it gives a premium quality image that is less expensive than film, as there are no processing costs. The production team can therefore experiment and work with a high shooting ratio (filming many more takes, shots and camera angles than end up in the finished production). They can immediately watch the footage and re-shoot shonky takes without waiting for film to be exposed, developed and processed. Legendary director David Lynch, who shot *Inland Empire* using minimum broadcast quality Sony PD150 digital cameras, used a shooting ratio so high he included 90 deleted scenes on the DVD, stating: 'The sky's the limit with digital. Film is like a dinosaur in a tar pit' (Lim 2006: n.p.).

In digital cinematography, a high-resolution digital image is similar to a high-gauge film (as discussed in Chapter 2) in that it contains concentrated information about the picture as measured in dots per inch, or **pixels**. High-definition digital images pack denser information into the picture area and can be enlarged, screened or printed without loss of image quality, whereas when a low resolution image is enlarged you can see the dots that make it up. Low-definition digital images, like

> **Pixels** are picture elements or the points of light that make up a photographic image. The pixel is a measure of the quality or resolution of an image, calculated in terms of the density of pixels in an area.

those recorded on webcams, stream low-resolution images (about 320 x 200 pixels) at a rate as slow as fifteen frames per second. This gives a stuttery look similar to old-fashioned silent film, which 'flickered' due to being projected at sixteen frames per second, but the small size of a computer monitor means the low-quality image is not as noticeable as it would be on a television or, worse, a cinema screen. High-definition digital television offers a higher resolution image, a faster frame rate and an overall better quality, smoother viewing experience compared with analogue television images.

With the increasing convergence of film and television technologies, the wide-screen format of HDTV is very close to that used for cinematic releases, and the popularity of large, wide plasma and LCD television screens and surround-sound systems in home viewing environments means watching television can increasingly be like a cinematic experience. Digital technologies have not yet been fully adopted as the industry standard worldwide, and convergence between film and television is incomplete, so processes like **telecine** and **pan and scan** have been developed to translate between different frame rates and screen shapes. Wide-screen productions are subjected to a pan and scan process so they can be viewed on a television screen without being 'letterboxed' with black strips at the top and bottom of the frame, and without cropping parts of the image at the sides of the frame. The advantage is that pan and scan offers selective control over what the audience sees. For example, if a text intended for a wide screen is watched in academy format, equipment like microphones that were meant to be outside the frame line may be visible. Similarly, if a text shot for a wide screen shows three people on a park bench, those on either side may each lose an arm, a leg and an ear if the image is reframed for a narrower screen unless the image is carefully cropped, perhaps panning right to frame the two characters central to the action in a two-shot, then panning left when the third character interjects. The disadvantage

Telecine is process that corrects for difference in frame rate when transferring movies or programs shot on celluloid from film to a format suitable for video or television.

Pan and scan is a means of copying footage shot in wide screen format and reframing it to fit on a squarer screen, by scanning the image for the most significant information and panning to the left or right to keep it in shot when the edges of the wide image are cropped. The process is much like using a scanner to copy a photograph, but with the added facility of being able to pan over the moving image and position the new frame line over the important part of the action.

of pan and scan is that it can't always keep everything of importance in shot, and it introduces camera movement or cuts unintended by the production team and unmotivated by the story.

High-definition digital television can be shot for and watched on wide screens, but because many people still have old sets and will continue to watch their outdated, box-shaped analogue television until the signal is switched off (which will happen in developed nations by 2015), the action must be framed with both possibilities in mind. Because of format differences and the constraints of hectic shooting schedules, tight budgets and being confined to the studio, much contemporary television still has a more restricted audiovisual style with more cramped composition, fewer moving camera shots and fewer layers of sound than feature films. This varies across genres and content providers, with high-budget American prime-time drama like *CSI* being shot in quite a 'cinematic' style, and local news and game shows sticking to a simpler style, as we discuss in the first section of the book.

ORGANISATION OF THE BOOK

In the chapters introducing screen aesthetics (Chapters 1–4), examples cover both film and television texts, comparing and contrasting the conventions of the two media forms. The purpose of this section of the book is to break complex, multi-modal screen texts down into elements that can easily be analysed by those willing to hone their powers of observation and acquire the vocabulary to analyse what they notice when critically engaging with screen texts. We then explore how each of these elements contributes to the construction of meaning and how they interrelate with one another to position the spectator, and to communicate character and theme. The detailed understanding of screen conventions and technical and analytic terms established in these early chapters is as valuable for readers who wish to move into screen production as it is for those who intend to pursue further interests in screen theory and analysis.

The middle section of the book (Chapters 5–8) relocates the building blocks of screen texts within the broader context of production and narration by introducing screenwriting, storyboarding and narrative structure, as well as the formulae and conventions of mainstream texts such as reality television and genre films. We consider how the conventions of representation in each case developed and emerged from earlier movements, and we investigate how fast-growing trends such as franchising and sequels that characterise contemporary cinema increasingly show the influence of television, even as television becomes more cinematic.

The final section (Chapters 9–11) broadens the scope of analysis further to consider the context of reception and the nature of audience responses to screen texts produced within different traditions and with different agendas in the global marketplace. We draw on the production and circulation of celebrity and the phenomena of cult media as interesting ways to engage with questions about audience reception of screen texts, and we close with an analysis of new directions in screen culture using Quentin Tarantino's *Kill Bill: Volumes One* and *Two* as a springboard.

OUTLINE OF THE BOOK

The first chapter, 'By design: Art direction and *mise en scène* construction', introduces the significance of four familiar elements of screen texts: setting, lighting, costume and action. By means of close textual analysis and detailed examples, we explore how these elements can combine to articulate meaning, convey atmosphere and emotion, invite character engagement, and express or undermine stereotypes. Particular attention is devoted to the analysis of lighting terminology and techniques, and the use of lighting to 'set the scene'. Performance, an aspect of screen studies which is often neglected, is analysed in terms of verisimilitude, casting choices, genre requirements, and the actor's range and emotional resonance. We also discuss the symbolic and cultural significance of setting, landscape and screen space.

Chapter 2, 'Cinematography: Writing in light and movement', grounds the terminology required to analyse mobile framing, composition, shot scale, depth of field, and so forth in a discussion of the narrative motivation for and impact of each technique, again stressing the relationship between form and content. This chapter links to the previous chapter, illustrating how lighting is integral to cinematography and how framing and composition are inseparable from a discussion of *mise en scène*—what is in the frame must be analysed in relation to *how* the shot is framed. In order to foreground the relevance of cinematographic techniques to an understanding of narrative significance and impact, our case study analyses the ways in which cinematography can function to communicate an experiential sense of the story world, situating the audience inside screen space and offering access to the protagonist's sensations and experiences. We also introduce contemporary research into the capacity of the moving image to communicate subjective and sensory experience and to evoke the tactility of vision, rather than distancing and objectification.

In Chapter 3, 'Soundscapes: The invisible magic of sound', we can't help but agree with David Lynch's claim that 'sound is half the picture'. This chapter offers the tools and techniques necessary to distinguish between diegetic and non-diegetic sound, off-screen sound, internal subjective sound, and so forth. As well as introducing the technical vocabulary associated with sound, we consider how sound undermines or enhances 'realism', and articulates screen space, time and movement. The emotive and imaginative qualities of sound, especially the musical score, are discussed in detail, along with the synaesthetic qualities of screen texts. This chapter also includes an analysis of a dialogue sequence and a discussion of how image and sound work together to create meaning by positioning the spectator, articulating the theme of the text, and contributing to characterisation.

Chapter 4, 'At the edge of the cut: Editing from continuity to montage', introduces editing terms and techniques such as the match on action, graphic match, jump cut, sound bridge and the concept of suture. The principles of continuity editing and the conventions of realism are contrasted with the rhythmic editing and 'collage' of imagery in contemporary music videos. Both are contrasted with Soviet Montage and the principle of juxtaposition, and the impact of each style on the audience is considered. Once again, connections are made to previous chapters to demonstrate the relationships between editing and sound, cinematography and elements of *mise en scène*.

Chapter 5, 'Plotting and planning: Storytelling and reviewing techniques', outlines the phases of screen production and introduces the skills needed to adapt a short text for the screen, working through the process of writing a treatment, a script and a storyboard. Storyboarding is an important part of pre-production that enables the director to communicate their vision to other members of the cast and crew. It is the first step in 'translating' ideas from words to images.

Storyboarding is also a creative way to apply what we have learned by mapping out how to shoot a short sequence, planning how lighting, sound, camera and action will work together, and deciding how the sequence will be structured and edited. The chapter also introduces film reviewing as an important vocational skill.

Chapter 6, 'Screen narratives: Traditions and trends', introduces narrative theory and identifies the binary oppositions that often underlie narrative structure and contribute to its ideological work. We contrast the traditional three-act narrative structure and its predominantly linear chronology with more unconventional narrative structures that communicate a meaning of their own. Using detailed examples, we investigate the significance of fragmented and multi-strand narratives in addition to more conventional mainstream examples. Finally, we explore the differences between the structures of television, film and digital game narratives, paying attention to television's distinctive seriality, lack of narrative closure, fragmentation and flow, and the domestic context of reception.

Chapter 7, 'Reality and realism: Seeing is believing', provides an outline of the main conventions and characteristics of reality television, documentaries, realist cinema movements, and film and television mockumentaries. We contrast the aesthetics of documentary style with the naturalistic conventions used to create an illusion of realism in mainstream cinema, which relies on techniques like continuity editing and three-point lighting. The chapter problematises the concepts of 'truth' and 'realism' in relation to the ethics of realist screen media, and explores the contemporary appeal of the 'ordinary' and the 'everyday' in the context of increasing technological manipulation and sophistication.

In Chapter 8, 'Genre: "Something new based on something familiar"', we overview genre as a way of categorising screen texts and of analysing textual features such as iconography, formula, setting and repetition. We also analyse genre as a discursive practice, a marketing strategy and marker of social attitudes, contextualising it within recent research and broader social and industrial contexts. This chapter prompts consideration of the economic imperatives of production and the power of industrial marketing mechanisms, drawing together an appreciation of audience expertise with a sophisticated understanding of socio-cultural contexts and ideological meanings.

Chapter 9, 'Star struck: Fandom and the discourse of celebrity', examines celebrity as a discursive construction generated by the production, distribution and reception of information about certain individuals in the media. We consider how stars and celebrities are produced, what role they play for the screen media industries, what they reveal about dominant cultural attitudes, and what the major differences are between stars and celebrities. We also discuss how audiences engage with celebrity, including what the impact of that identification might be.

In Chapter 10, 'Skating the edge: Cult media and the (inter)active audience', we compare and contrast cognitive understandings of film spectatorship and the semiotic, text-based analysis introduced in the first several chapters with empirical audience research and more contextual, ethnographic approaches to reception studies. Using cult media texts like *Æon Flux* and its fan base as examples, this chapter pits the power of fans and audiences against the power of the industry, looking at shifting conceptions of both in current debates about screen culture, drawing out connections between screen culture, subculture, cooption and commodification.

Chapter 11, 'The crowded screen: Transcultural influences and new directions in visual culture', is the final chapter. Here we explore emerging trends in screen culture including the influence of video games and the impact of digital media like computer-generated imagery and animation. We approach the topic of globalisation by analysing global media flows and the cultural influence of Asian cinemas, and use Quentin Tarantino's *Kill Bill* to illustrate transcultural media influences and genre hybridity, but also to consider the impact of postfeminism and postmodernism.

Each chapter in this book includes detailed examples and clear definitions of terms and concepts to illustrate key points. We conclude each chapter with a brief summary of the main points covered and a checklist of the key skills and learning objectives that have been addressed. These features, and the range of issues included, are designed to make the material accessible and to help you to think critically about film and television. We hope that you finish the text sharing our interest in and passion for screen culture, whether you're then ready to take the plunge into further studies, immerse yourself in the industry, or just return to the couch with renewed understanding.

1
by design:
Art direction and *mise en scéne* construction

Most people who use screen media in their everyday lives for entertainment or information evaluate what they see largely in terms of the storyline and the personalities on screen. This indicates the central importance of narrative and characterisation, but it also raises the following question: if all we are interested in is story and information, why not just read a novel, a newspaper or a film script? If all the meaning and impact is encoded in the script, then why does anyone ever bother to shoot and screen the film or television program? Thinking critically about film and television entails considering what makes screen media special, and what differentiates screen texts from literature, photography, theatre or opera, as well as examining the depth and significance added to a story when we see it staged, lit and performed.

Beginning by considering the relationship of screen media to theatre, and ending by pointing to the significance of photography and cinematography, this chapter aims to develop an understanding of the connection between a screen text's visual style and its meaning, mood and theme. Because style and content are intrinsically interconnected, we explore the relationships between subject matter and aesthetic components like composition, performance, costume, setting and lighting. In arguing that style can convey meaning, we suggest that the fictional world constructed on the screen can express, dramatise, add to or distract from a story's atmosphere and thematic content. Assessing the interplay between form, content, style and meaning also requires an appreciation of the roles and responsibilities of the cast and crew members responsible for crafting the visual style of a production and analysing their decisions about what to include in, or exclude from, the frame. Such decisions govern the design and placement of all the ingredients that create the fictional world inhabited by the protagonists, and the ingredients that lend the story world an aura of authenticity and vibrancy.

MISE EN SCÈNE

Mise en scène is a French theatrical term meaning to place on a stage, or to stage an action. In film and television, the stage equates to the screen, and *mise en scène* refers to the organisation of the elements that can be seen within the borders of the frame in any shot. *Mise en scène* can be broken down into four key components:

- costume (wardrobe, accessories, prosthetics and makeup);
- setting (architecture, décor, scenery and props);
- action (figure movement, object movement, performance); and
- lighting (including coloured light and shadow).

Mise en scène refers to everything that can be seen on the screen, including four key elements: costume, performance, setting and lighting.

Together, these four elements are central to constructing the story world and determining *where* the action takes place (on a set or location), *when* the action takes place (signalled by lighting that cues time of day, or sets and costumes that indicate period), and *how* and *why* the action takes place (as communicated via performance). These components of the fictional world express and dramatise the mood and thematic content of the storyline, conveying meaning through visual style.

In early films featuring only *mise en scène* and static camera (without synchronised sound or editing), and in contemporary studio-based television shows, the close relationship between the art of *mise en scène* construction and theatrical stage design is particularly evident: performers often face the camera and address the audience as though they are on a stage. As the following examples demonstrate, even screen texts that are not intended to look 'staged' often draw on traditions of symbolism, allusion and metaphor developed in theatre and literature. Consequently, the analysis of *mise en scène* incorporates terminology and techniques developed in literary criticism and theatre and drama studies.

When an element of the *mise en scène* alludes to or acts as a visual metaphor for something else, it can be described as allusive or metaphoric *mise en scène*. For example, the images of the black widow spider and the moth in the room during Pete's whispered phone conversation with Alice in the David Lynch film *Lost Highway* indicates Alice is a dangerous, man-eating femme fatale and Pete is irresistibly attracted to her like a moth to the light.

Metonymic *mise en scène* is another way in which elements of visual design can be interpreted. A metonym is a relationship of symbolic substitution when one part represents or stands for something larger. For instance, one might say 'I'll take the wheel', thereby using part of the car—the steering wheel—as a metonymic representation of the whole car and the act of driving and taking charge (steering). The American flag is a metonymic signifier or symbol for patriotism and all that the nation represents. When the flag is turned upside down, this signifies subversion or disrespect for America itself. In Oliver Stone's *Natural Born Killers* (1994) and the earlier road movie that influenced it, Dennis Hopper's 1969 classic *Easy Rider*, the American flag is hung upside down in certain scenes, as when the motorcyclists Wyatt and Billy ride through a small town during a Fourth of July parade, and when Mickey and Mallory kill the Indian in the desert. The inverted flag represents a challenge to authority and a rejection of the American dream by the films, the filmmakers and the characters.

The art department

The art department's role is best described as the art of forgery and illusion, since its purpose is to fake the existence of an entire narrative world. The art director, also known as the production designer, is in charge of the art department. This involves managing a team of set designers and decorators, illustrators and draftspersons, and liaising with wardrobe, makeup artists and researchers, as well as working closely with the director, producer and cinematographer. (We use the terms 'art director' and 'production designer' interchangeably, but where separate individuals are credited for each role, the production designer is largely responsible for envisioning the look and feel of the production, while the art director takes responsibility for executing the design.) Crew members working in wardrobe and the art department research the era and locale in which the story is set, sourcing, creating and constructing sets, props and costumes, prosthetics and makeup effects, as well as scouting locations and dressing sets for different scenes.

Wryly describing his experience upon entering the Hollywood film industry and beginning work in the art department, Ward Preston writes that the production designer is responsible for 'the enhancement of communication by visual means'—or, more frankly, 'for everything you see on the screen that doesn't move and is usually out of focus' (1994: x). Of course, some elements of the *mise en scène do* move, and frequently they *are* in focus—even if popular and critical acclaim is generally 'focused' on storylines, stars and directors. Sometimes the work of the art department steals the show, as in the lush costume and set design of Sophia Coppola's 2006 extravaganza *Marie Antoinette*. The range of skills a production designer requires in order to effectively manage the art department may include training in fine art, architectural drafting and interior design; the ability to undertake or oversee historical and cultural research; budgeting, business acumen and managerial expertise; inventiveness and a keen sense of style; insight into the practicalities of lighting, textiles, construction and cosmetics; and even legal expertise.

The production designer often commences work by doing preliminary sketches and working through a script breakdown, highlighting all references to the visual impact of the story and factoring in figures in the budget to achieve the required look, as discussed in a concept meeting with the director. Together, the production manager and the director brainstorm details like the **colour palette**, mapping out signature colours that might be associated with particular characters, locations or moods. Sometimes a visual timeline is created to chart the different scenes and plot points in the script, with fabric swatches and paint samples attached to signify shifts in the colour palette. The colour palette expresses the unique 'personality' of a production and the changing moods associated with different scenes and characters.

> The **colour palette** of a screen text is a colour scheme for lighting, décor and costume devised by the production manager to express and chart the shifting moods of characters and scenes over the course of the story.

The colour scheme of a film or television program has a significant impact on viewers and is closely linked to the expression of theme and characterisation. This is evident in a comparison of the grimy, earthy aesthetic that extends throughout the television series *Deadwood*'s Wild West setting versus *Ugly Betty*'s bright primary colours, and further variations between the warm tones of Betty's home versus the cold, stark whites of her work environment. Another revealing contrast is found between two contemporary Spanish films, *Pan's Labyrinth*, directed by Guillermo del Toro, and Pedro Almodóvar's *Volver*. The use of a verdant green aesthetic running throughout the lighting and setting in *Pan's Labyrinth* signifies the ancient forces of nature that the faun Pan embodies, and the shadowy browns and greens of the woods and the costumes express the darkness of the protagonists' lives under Franco's fascist rule in 1944. Eugemio Caballero, the production designer for *Pan's Labyrinth*, won an Oscar in 2007 for best art direction based on the creation of intricate puppetry and prosthetics, and the moody, mystical visual style that brought the fairytale world to life. A superb gallery of conceptual sketches, models and images of the development of costumes and props are displayed on the official website, www.panslabyrinth.com. In comparison with the deep greens pervading *Pan's Labyrinth*, *Volver*'s lush, bold colour palette, with its vivid reds, floral patterns and stark contrasts of light and dark, establishes an impassioned tone. Discussing the texture and atmosphere of *Volver*, Almodóvar has pointed out in his online production diary that pastel colours couldn't possibly capture the vivacious characters, nor could a muted aesthetic do justice to the surreal quality and dramatic extremes of a film that swings from comedy through musical numbers and domestic melodrama to the kind of action usually found in a thriller (www.clubcultura.com).

Colour can also be used to express and create emotion. Director Todd Haynes recreated the visual style of 1950s melodrama in his film *Far From Heaven* (2002), paying homage to the influence of earlier films like *All That Heaven Allows* (1955), directed by Douglas Sirk. Sirk's films had very complex colour palettes. In an interview with Anthony Kaufman, Haynes observes contemporary films are comparatively 'dumbed down' in terms of colour:

> A whole movie will be honeycomb gold colors if it's set in the past or all icy blue if it's a suspense thriller. But [Sirk's] films use complex interactions of warm and cool in every single scene. And emotions are multi-colored. Color, lighting, costume, all the visual elements are supplementing what can't be said in these films. (www.indiewire.com)

A range of different elements must work in concert to create a colour palette that supports both script and character. Members of the art department work closely with the director in designing the overall look and feel of a production. In addition, they liaise with the camera and lighting crew, and with actors regarding makeup and wardrobe. The art department also coordinates with the producer and production assistants regarding location permissions and copyright clearances. These last two tasks are little-known blights on the production process which are as important as they are onerous.

Permission must be sought to use any location outside the studio. The copyright clearance process is often difficult and costly, and subject to restrictions imposed by local bureaucrats and residents. Other than agreed product placement, any signs, logos, brands, containers or products associated with a known trademark or business presence are subject to copyright law. They may not be used indiscriminately in screen productions for fear of compromising brand identity, thereby giving rise to lawsuits and damages. For example, a television broadcaster once refused to air a public service announcement produced by university students because the shape of a Ponds cold cream jar was visible in shot. Even though the logo and label were turned away from the camera, the distinctive shape of the jar was considered enough to create an unwanted association between Ponds and the social issue in the advertisement. Frequently, copyright permission will be refused because a corporation does not want to be associated with the storyline of a production, or with the politics of the director or stars involved, or even with the demographic to whom the production is marketed. As Preston points out, in the television industry the problem is more pronounced due to the economic importance of advertising revenue derived from product tie-ins, product placements, sponsorship and commercial breaks: the television production itself cannot feature goods and services that might be seen to compete with those its sponsors advertise (1994: 35). This means the art department must frequently Photoshop fake business signs, billboards and labels, and mock up bogus brands (like the fictitious Ka-Boom! breakfast cereal box used when Vernita Green shoots at Beatrix Kiddo in *Kill Bill*).

COSTUME

In Michel Gondry's film *Eternal Sunshine of the Spotless Mind*, when the character of Clementine (Kate Winslet) impulsively introduces herself to the unlikely romantic lead, Joel (Jim Carrey), he comments on the vivid hue of her hair. Clementine, who dyes her hair 'blue ruin', 'red menace', 'green revolution' and 'agent orange' in the course of the narrative, flippantly replies: 'I apply my personality in a paste.' While this may have some truth for a character like Clementine, who boldly exhibits herself like a walking artistic statement of individuality and eccentricity, it applies equally well to all screen performers. Furthermore, it is the job of the crew in wardrobe to carefully mix and artfully apply that 'paste' by laboriously fixing the makeup and hair, wigs and prosthetics, faux tattoos, accessories and costumes that define the screen persona of each performer and lend credibility to the narrative.

In the recent Australian horror film *Wolf Creek*, the techniques used by the makeup artists were central to making the horror of the film believable by devising prosthetic gore and fake cadavers, as illustrated in Figure 1.1.

Costume and cosmetics also make statements about the image a person wants to project, and they make subtler statements about that individual's identity. For example, consider the screen tests for the different tattoos that were designed to be appropriate for the age, social class and personal style of the two male leads as shown in

Figures 1.2 and 1.3. The villain has a faded old fashioned rose tattoo and a knife, whereas the young backpacker sports a Celtic tattoo of a stylised dragon coiling back on itself in an infinity symbol.

Social class is often evident in the cut of clothing and hair, and the quality of accessories; a person's profession can be signalled through tan lines, rough hands, work boots, suit and tie, stethoscope or stilettos; and values and beliefs can be encoded in adornments like a cross, a head scarf, a wedding ring or piercings. Think about how film characters like Eliza Doolittle in *My Fair Lady*, Tom Ripley in *The Talented Mr Ripley* and Chris Wilton in *Match Point* adopt the signifiers of social status to pass in upper-class circles. In all three instances, this involves cultivating an appreciation of high culture like opera and wine, and changing their hair, attire and deportment. Costume, makeup and style also locate characters in a particular culture (e.g. a sari or a hijab), subculture (e.g. an asymmetrical Emo fringe hiding one eye), or climate (shorts or woollens).

Similarly, each decade or historical era is associated with fashions that vary for people of different ages and for dwellers in urban, rural and suburban areas. Careful research into the cultural milieu in which the story is set is necessary to get such details right for each character. The ornate, pastel, girlish garments in *Marie Antoinette* make actress Kirsten Dunst resemble a delicious piece of frosted confectionery. These garments express the frivolity and excess for which Marie Antoinette was well known, whereas the tight corsets and unwieldy hoops under the heavy, dark woollen clothing worn by Holly Hunter in Jane Campion's film *The Piano* provide a visual metaphor for the stifling constraints of Victorian femininity in the colonies.

Changes in costume, lighting and setting can also establish changes of emotion and atmosphere, as illustrated in British filmmaker Peter Greenaway's *The Cook, The Thief, His Wife and Her Lover*, where costumes actually change colour as characters pass from one room to another. This device enables full accentuation of the atmospheres associated with each room, from the bilious greens of the kitchen in which unspeakable things are cooked to the stark, sterile space of the white bathroom, or the opulent reds of the main dining room.

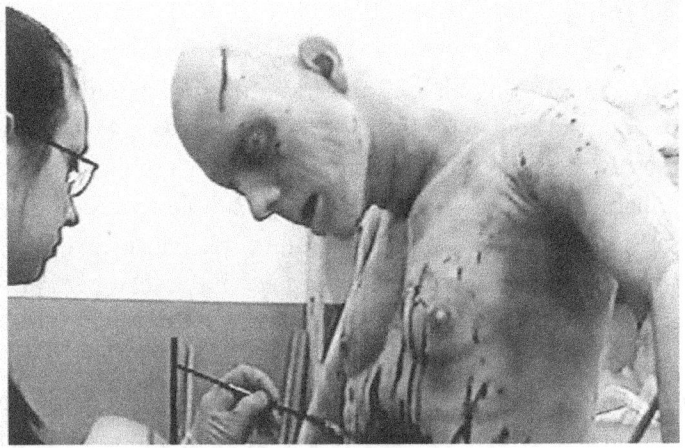

Figure 1.1 *Wolf Creek*'s DVD extra features show the art department creating prosthetic gore and fake cadavers

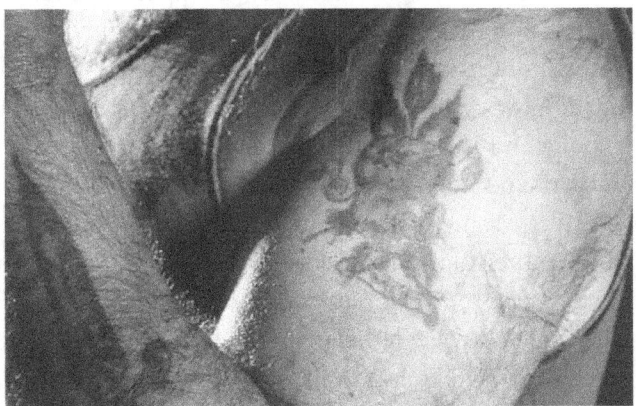

Figure 1.2 Old-fashioned, working class tattoos in *Wolf Creek*

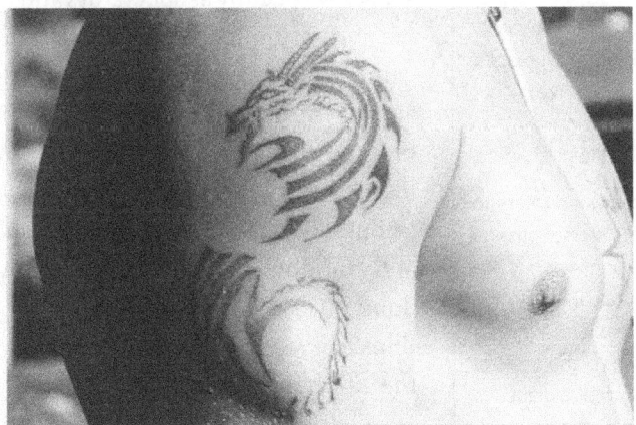

Figure 1.3 *Wolf Creek* tattoos signifying contemporary youth culture

SETTING

Like costume, setting also establishes atmosphere, indicates genre and period, and conveys information about class and culture. Setting includes the geography, architecture and décor visible on the screen and inhabited by the characters. At its simplest, setting refers to the environment, scenery or background space in which the action takes place. However, given that no aspect of the set design or scenic backdrop is ever left to chance in a screen production, setting can also be loaded with much more significance. In *Reading Hollywood: Spaces and Meanings in American Film* (2001), Deborah Thomas distinguishes between different types and functions of cinematic space, including what she terms dramaturgical space, physical space, cinematic aspects of space and, finally, the space occupied by the audience. Physical space is, as indicated above, the geographical and architectural setting. Dramaturgical space refers to the ways in which locations in a screen text can become dramatised and encoded with symbolic and social meanings, such as the public and private spaces of work and home, each of which defines characters' actions within certain parameters. Cinematic aspects of space are largely inaccessible to the characters themselves, and include elements like composition, background and foreground, on-screen and off-screen space. Although we will not be analysing it in this chapter, it is also worth remembering the importance of the spaces of set construction and screen production, projection and reception, including the spaces we occupy as spectators and the way we are positioned according to where the camera is located. In television **diegetic** and **extra-diegetic** spaces are commonly bridged. For example, in the Australian talk show *Rove Live*, Rove McManus frequently addresses the studio audience and the domestic audience directly, as is done on *Letterman* and similar shows. In films like *Layer Cake* and *Eternal Sunshine*, the production space is used in uncanny ways—for instance, when Jim Carrey runs *behind* the camera as it pans from left to

> The **diegesis** is the fictional reality of the story world, including places, sights, sounds and events that occur within it which are accessible to the characters.
>
> The **extra-diegetic** world refers to actions, spaces and events outside the story world and includes the reception context in which the audience is located and information like subtitles, credits and the musical score of which only the audience is aware (see also diegetic and non-diegetic sound).

right he seems to inexplicably move from one side of the frame to the other side in a continuous shot, thereby denaturalising the spectator's experience of screen space and setting. Such manipulations of screen space are as aberrant as they are fascinating, and in what follows we focus on established spatial and design conventions, considering not only the narrative function of setting, but also its contribution to defining character and conflict, and its aesthetic and experiential significance.

The first major distinctions between different types of settings are to do with the physical location of the camera and the action in interior or exterior spaces: studio-based shoots and location shoots. The decision to shoot on location or in the studio can be governed by considerations including budget, genre, storyline, the degree of control that is required over variables like sound and weather, and the medium itself. Television series tend to be shot in the studio because, with ongoing shooting costs and a tight production schedule, it is important to have a small number of reusable props and sets, and a controlled environment. Many dialogue heavy productions set mostly indoors are shot in the studio, and many action-related storylines and documentary-style productions require authentic locations, but these are not hard and fast rules. Some high-budget, action-packed film productions like *The Matrix* require a studio environment for many scenes, whereas *Lost* is a television series that relies on locations in Oahu, Hawaii.

Particular settings enable certain storylines, and become associated with their own characters, events and genres. Hospitals, high schools and courtrooms are favourite settings for soap operas and television dramas because those environments can credibly stage a crisis situation on a daily or weekly basis, as well as providing endless opportunities to introduce new characters to fuel the storyline. Horror films necessitate a terrible place—an isolated space where no one can hear you scream, a monster's lair or a familiar space rendered frightening by the unnatural forces that invade it. The narrative structures of certain genres are therefore often themed around particular landscapes and settings. Melodramas have domestic settings in which private relationship crises unfold; road movies are journey narratives set on the highways and back roads; and Westerns are located on the frontier. Notions of social inclusion and exclusion (insiders and outsiders) are also frequently derived from culturally defined narrative spaces. Consider how Chino and Orange County in *The OC* are shot with different film stock in order to accentuate the differences of class and culture, and how postcodes (the 09ers) in *Veronica Mars* signify social standing, just as they did in *Beverly Hills 90210*. In these television series, we also see how environment shapes character. For instance, a hard life lived in underprivileged conditions is likely to build a character quite different from a sheltered life in a McMansion.

Atmospheric elements of setting and décor can mirror, amplify or express a character's emotional or psychological state (Gibbs 2002). A bland, scrupulously neat little room or a claustrophobic environment can constrain possibilities for expressive action, as well as indicating something of the psychology and taste of the characters inhabiting those spaces. Thomas Elsaesser describes this function of *mise en scène* as the 'sublimation of dramatic conflict into décor, colour, gesture, and composition of frame' (1995: 521). He gives the example of melodramas like Sirk's *Written on the Wind* (1956), in which emotions rise to fever pitch and then crash down in dramatic scenes often staged on a sweeping staircase.

Specific spaces within domestic settings can also accrue symbolic meaning in certain genres, or in the work of individual directors. For instance, the attic, the basement and the bathroom are encoded as uncanny spaces in the horror genre and are linked to themes of the subconscious and the emergence of repressed material. Mick Broderick (2001) demonstrates that in many Stanley Kubrick films (notably *The Shining*), bathrooms are prime sites for horrifying and disturbing incidents to unfold because characters are often alone and vulnerable, with the door locked and running water muffling other sounds. The bathroom setting allows filmmakers to work with powerful contrasts, staging the desecration and defilement of the human body in a space designed for ablutions and purification. The stark décor of bathrooms is perfectly suited to invoking abject terror as the boundaries of the self are violated, reflected and distorted in mirrored surfaces while bright blood splatters against clean white tiles.

On location shoots, certain sites also have significance for national and cultural identity, as is the case with landmarks like the Sydney Harbour Bridge and Uluru, (formerly Ayer's Rock) which signify aspects of nature and culture symbolising Australian national identity. Martin Lefebvre describes the depiction of such iconic geography as moments when the location transcends its function as the setting, scenery or stage for action to unfold: it momentarily becomes the *subject* of the narrative, with symbolic and aesthetic significance in its own right (2006: 22). The relevance of certain iconic places to national and personal identity signals that space is also socially and culturally defined. Settings are associated with experiences of embeddedness, belonging, habit, habitat and home, or dislocation and alienation.

Lefebvre, who is interested in the function screen landscapes play in identity formation by way of **ideology** or cultural traditions, theorises how screen texts anchor symbolic aspects of landscapes in human life and tie them to particular belief systems (2006: xix). For example, the 'white picket fence' of American suburbia is 'obviously meant to convey settings representative of the ordinary, good and happy life in America' (Lefebvre 2006: xix). However, as represented in films like *American Beauty*, *The Chumscrubber*, *Far From Heaven* and *Blue Velvet*, and in television programs such as *Weeds* and *Desperate Housewives*, the symbolism of the setting and the 'apple pie' ideal of American suburbia are deconstructed, subverted and revealed to be a myth. Interestingly, each of these texts denaturalises the American dream and the ideologies of freedom, individualism and capitalism with which it is associated by defamiliarising the space and setting. Either through the use of technicolour or by opening with an aerial shot that shows the uniformity of the houses, these suburban stories all reveal that the ideal of private property to which the American dream is anchored really has little basis in freedom or individualism, as all the houses look the same—like tokens on a Monopoly board. Further, all the white picket fences constrain the people who inhabit the houses, and all the neighbours pry into each other's business.

Another example of the symbolic character of setting involves the significance of the landscape in Westerns and in television series like *Deadwood*. These texts are layered with historical and social constructs such as the myth that the Western frontier was an unclaimed land of opportunity, to be

> **Ideology** refers to a system of assumptions, beliefs, attitudes, values, practices and images that form a naturalised or 'commonsense' world-view. This belief system can be illusory (as in false consciousness) or characteristic of a particular class or group (as in bourgeois ideology, capitalist ideology or feminist ideology).

explored, tamed and cultivated. Such myths frame our understanding of the landscape as a setting for narratives of confrontation, when civilisation clashes with the harshness of nature and the savagery of its inhabitants. Without this myth, which Westerns simultaneously constructed and validated, the frontier landscape may have been interpreted as a space occupied by indigenous nomadic people for whom it was invested with spiritual significance, rather than as 'savage' territory awaiting white settlement, colonisation and cultivation. Such mythologies are not restricted to American texts. A similar dynamic exists in the way the landscape is represented in Australian films like *The Proposition*.

In recent films set in South Africa, a different set of ideological tensions comes into play. *Red Dust* and *In My Country* are two films about the Truth and Reconciliation Commission (TRC), in which the relationship between people and the land is articulated in terms of a narrative of contested ownership and occupancy, a retelling of the truth of events that unfolded during the apartheid era, and a journey charting progress towards a better future. In the images of the TRC convoy travelling across the South African landscape, 'transit' literally equates to a symbol of 'the transition' to democracy, away from a past defined by forced removals, the *Group Areas Act*, colonialism and displacement (see Figure 1.4). Thus the landscape itself is framed by filmmakers in a certain way, and at the same time it provides a

Figure 1.4 *Red Dust*: The road to truth and reconciliation

frame within which particular forces collide, characters develop and stories unfold.

Finally, setting can also express sensory elements like heat and cold, and convey cultural information that provides a context for the narrative action. This is evident in Pedro Almodóvar's description of the setting of *Volver* in his childhood homeland as roasting in a 'crucible of white walls' and dusty streets:

> I remember the red earth, the yellow fields, the ash green olive trees and the patios, blooming with life, plants, neighbours, secrets as deep as wells and loneliness ... In the patio, the women making lace would work on, catching the sun's last rays with her bundle of bubbly wood bobbins. Plants were watered, women sewed, and time passed while sitting on rocking chairs in the shade. (www.clubcultura.com)

While *Volver* worked with the authentic settings so central to Almodóvar's vision of the look and feel of the film, sometimes the set designer will need to manipulate the setting extensively to create the right sense of space, proportion or depth to support the storyline or create a desired impression of scale. **Forced perspective** is the technique used in *Eternal Sunshine of the Spotless Mind* to manipulate the relationship between the foreground and background by exaggerating or diminishing the size of props or causing the floor to slope away. This technique makes the fridge and table in Joel's childhood kitchen seem normal sized when adults stand next to them in the foreground, and appear as gigantic as it would to a three-year-old boy from where Joel is positioned (see Figure 1.5).

Symbolic spaces in road movies

Further to our discussion of symbolic spaces and significant props, consider how the car, the road and the mythic destination of 'the border' are central to the narratives of road movies. Road movies are narratives of transition and change, often featuring rebellious characters who, like the road movie's target audience, are caught up in a journey of self-discovery and the transition from adolescence to adulthood. Like the adolescent, the anti-hero is 'in transit,'

> **Forced perspective** is a technique used in set design to manipulate the size of elements in the foreground and background of the set in order to create an illusion of depth, distance or distorted spatial relations.

asserting individuality in the act of rebelling against authority and rejecting responsibility. The road itself is a signifier of freedom from the constraints of civilisation the protagonists seek to escape. Road movies typically celebrate individualism and liberty, but they also contain the threat of what could happen if taken to the extremes of nihilism, existentialism and hedonism. The fact that many road movies end in a crash, or the death of the protagonists, signals that the genre—particularly the sub-genre featuring an outlaw couple on the run—is inherently conservative, warning that life on the road is unsustainable. Ultimately, we need houses, mortgages, jobs and rules to survive.

The cars driven in road movies are significant because automobiles represent both autonomy and mobility. Frequently, convertibles or motorbikes are used to invoke the freedom of the open road. The type of vehicle is also an expression of personal style and identity, an extension of the self. Cars are 'symbolic signs, defining the priorities of their owners, and to a certain extent their owners' identities' (Orr 1993: 127), as is evident in Sean Penn's character's narcissistic relationship with his red 1964½ Mustang convertible in Oliver Stone's low-mileage road movie *U-Turn*.

Figure 1.5 Baby Joel in the giant kitchen, illustrating forced perspective in *Eternal Sunshine of the Spotless Mind*, courtesy of Universal Studios Licensing LLLP.

This analysis of the symbolic significance of spaces, settings and props in road movies demonstrates how *mise en scène* analysis can reveal the social function of screen texts, showing how road movies are often narratives of transgression, set in the transitional space of the road where protagonists negotiate the contested ideologies that underpin society. For instance, characters in road movies reject elements of the suburban setting of the American dream founded on 'truth, justice and the American way', while embracing the ideals of liberty and individualism that also inform American national identity and are in fact sustained by the institutions of truth and justice, law and order. As this example indicates, costume, setting and props—and even certain performers—can signal the iconography of a genre and invite an ideological reading of a text. We will return to this point in Chapter 8, but now we consider action and performance.

ACTION

Action, the third component of *mise en scène*, can include the intentional movement of all significant objects in shot, from cars driving by or tree branches falling, through dogs chasing intruders, to the figure movement and expression of performers. For our purposes, the most significant of these types of action is acting itself. Supplemented by an awareness of the significance of costume and makeup, an analysis of performance is central to understanding how film and television construct, represent and reproduce social categories like gender, class, ethnicity and sexuality. Since acting is the interface between characters and the actors who play them, we need to consider character types and functions as well as ways to critique performance styles.

Stereotypes

Stereotypes are a kind of cinematic or televisual shorthand based largely on a character's physical appearance, costuming, hair and makeup. They enable filmmakers to communicate with the audience efficiently by drawing on cultural assumptions and expectations. We all form assumptions about people in everyday life—nobody is immune to being stereotyped, or to stereotyping others. Similarly, the deployment of stereotypes is unavoidable in film and television texts, which consciously harness preconceptions about culture, class and gender in the service of dramatic tension and humour.

Some screen texts deliberately denaturalise stereotypes in an effort to avoid reinforcing hierarchies and assumptions. For example, the comedy series *My Name is Earl* playfully reworks stereotypes in each episode. In fact, the first words spoken in the pilot relate Earl's own experience of being stereotyped as we see a nice-looking family in a new car pull up outside a store, watching nervously as they wait for a dishevelled, unshaven man in shabby clothing to leave:

> You know that guy you see going into the convenience store when you stop off in that little town on the way to Grandma's house? Sorta shifty looking fellow who buys a pack of smokes, a couple of lotto scratchers and a tall boy at ten in the morning? The kind of guy you wait to come out before you and your family go in? Well, that guy is me. My name is Earl. And if you took the time to really get to know me, find out what kind of a person I truly am instead of just stereotyping me because of the way I look, well, you'd be wasting your time. 'Cos I'm exactly who you think I am.

In the study of film and television, it is important to become aware of stereotypical representations constructed through the *mise en scène* in order to work out what assumptions they are based on, and what function they perform in the narrative. Stereotypes are very useful in the media industry because they contribute to narrative economy, but they may have problematic implications for audiences because 'types and typing play into our everyday notions about people and identities, and our tendency to read people in terms of their age, sex, race, gender, region, nationality, class, or other categories, whether insidiously in racial profiling or in less sinister but no less stereotypical ways of assessing persons' (Robertson Wojcik 2004: 166). We habitually make assumptions about people based on the 'type' to which they seem to belong, but people are not 'types': we are individuals. Projecting assumptions on to people often implicitly situates them in a hierarchical relation to ourselves, and to others. This process can frequently lead us to jump to hasty conclusions about what they may be capable of feeling, thinking or doing. Frequently, filmmakers will knowingly harness the audience's assumptions about certain characters and encourage our tendency to make predictions about how those characters will behave, thereby setting us up for a comic payoff, or preventing us from foreseeing a twist in the plot. This happens when we fail to expect Verbal, the cripple in Bryan Singer's film *The Usual Suspects*, to be the arch-villain, or we fail to suspect that the sensitive, creative art dealer in D.J. Caruso's *Taking Lives* could be the killer. Often, as the cultural theorist Homi Bhabha points out, rather than labelling representations as positive or negative, stereotypical or multi-dimensional, we should consider how representations and characterisations construct subject positions and invite or preclude identification in ways that inform 'practices of racial and cultural hierarchization' (2004: 96).

Sometimes it is inappropriate to critique a screen text for including one-dimensional characters, as their role in the script does not warrant development. For instance, **stock characters** such as a waitress at a roadside diner, or a mechanic at a service station in a road movie, lack character development as they are only required to play limited, predictable roles, functioning like part of the setting. In this sense, stock characters are related to and may draw on stereotypes in order to function effectively in a supporting role. Like stock characters, **extras** tend to feature more as part of the scenery (for example, anonymous figures in a crowd scene) than in terms of performance. Nonetheless, such characters are a crucial part of the *mise en scène*, as Almodóvar's statement about the extras in *Volver* attests:

> **Stock characters** are minor characters whose function in the story is limited to, and often determined by, their job and their costume.

> **Extras** are members of the cast who do not have a speaking part or a prominent individual role and whose presence on screen serves to give the story world an authentic 'lived-in' feel.

> All they are supposed to do in front of the camera mirrors their own lives. Their presence has given depth and truth to those sequences where they participate. Women from this land know well what it is like to clean a tombstone, to pray at a wake, greet the neighbours, etc. And the faces of the men, slowly weathered by the sun and the wind, have a weight and an expressiveness that would be impossible to improvise. (www.clubcultura.com)

Performance

When evaluating the performance of actors playing more developed roles than those of stock characters or extras, the following factors should be considered: casting, range, depth, **verisimilitude**, figure movement and expression, and the role technology plays in screen performance.

Casting decisions are influenced by an actor's physical characteristics, such as gender, skin colour, attractiveness, age and build. The preconceptions audiences and casting agents form based on appearance can be as indicative of cultural value systems as they are of an actor's suitability for a role. Casting is also determined in part by the actor's previous experience and roles; therefore we can ask questions that help us evaluate performance, such as: 'Is Robin Williams miscast as a villain, or just extending his range?'

> **Verisimilitude** is the appearance or semblance of truth or realism.

Range refers to whether an actor can be convincing in a variety of roles, performing sentimental scenes as well as comical or aggressive roles. Many actors alternate roles in mainstream television or genre films with roles in more 'artistic' projects to prove their skill by playing against type and extending their range. Typecasting is an institutional practice that restricts a performer's range by casting an actor in a certain role throughout their career, due to acting style, range or physical characteristics.

The depth actors bring to a role is partly a function of the script: it is difficult to deliver a stunning performance if a character is underwritten. Nevertheless, it is important to assess lead actors in terms of whether they embody complex or cardboard characters. Depth of performance may not come from a character's dialogue, or even from their actions, but emerges from subtle movements and expressions that indicate emotional and psychological reactions stirring beneath the surface. Assessing emotional resonance is an important but deeply subjective way of evaluating performance. In asking whether the performance evokes the emotion that the role demands, critics must consider the reactions of other members of the audience in addition to relying on personal responses.

Depending on genre, historical context and the degree to which a text attempts to depict a realistic milieu, another measure of good acting is whether the performance appears credible and has verisimilitude—whether it seems 'very similar' to the way a real person would behave. Noteworthy studies of screen acting, including James Naremore's *Acting in the Cinema* (1988), and anthologies by Baron et al. (*More than a Method*, 2004), Alan Lovell and Peter Krämer (*Screen Acting*, 1999) and Pamela Robertson Wojcik (*Movie Acting*, 2004), distinguish early melodramatic and Vaudeville styles of acting derived from theatrical performance from later, more naturalistic performances. Acting in early cinema was literally 'theatrical'—that is, based on stage acting, mime and the bold style necessary to project to the back of the theatre. Technological changes such as synchronised sound and the use of close-ups affected acting techniques, introducing layers of subtlety such as projecting emotion from the eyes and emphasising aspects of vocal performance like cadence, tone and accent. Dialogue is not an aspect that can be considered in an analysis of *mise en scène*, since it is not part of visual style, but when assessing performance it is worth considering points such as whether an actor's accent is convincing if they are playing a foreign or regional character.

Like many of the tools and techniques used to critique performance, verisimilitude partly depends on the script, the set, casting decisions and costuming choices, but a lot still rides on the acting. It is hard to assess verisimilitude because the best acting frequently seems completely natural. In genres that call for naturalistic performance, the presence of the actor is erased to the extent that we completely believe in and engage with the character they embody. The problem here lies in divining whether the performers are acting extremely well, or simply playing themselves. This distinction helps differentiate between film and television performances. Television often requires performers to appear as themselves (Oprah Winfrey or Jerry Seinfeld, for instance), or to *personify* a particular character over successive seasons (as Hugh Laurie might be said to personify Gregory House in *House*) rather than *impersonating* a range of characters over many different screen appearances (King 2002: 150). Some performance styles, such as the Stanislavski Method, work to erase distinctions between actor and character, and between personification (playing oneself) and impersonation (imitating another). The naturalistic style emphasised in Method acting rests on the belief that good acting is 'true to life' and at the same time expressive of the actor's authentic, 'organic' self—hence the typical movie advertisement: 'Clint Eastwood *is* Dirty Harry' (Naremore 1988: 2). The Method, practised widely in the United States and made famous by stars such as Marlon Brando and Dustin Hoffman, requires actors to immerse themselves in the character and encourages 'a downgrading of the importance of the script, an emphasis on emotional memory and sense recall, and an upgrading of the role of the director, working closely with and on the actor' (Lovell & Krämer 1999: 6).

Movement and posture, expressivity and gesture, and all the performative elements of character action are central to the craft of acting, as Andrew Klevan details in *Film Performance* (2005). The way actors develop these skills depends in part on the tradition in which they are trained, but also on the genre and medium, and the ways in which actors react to their environment, other performers and aspects of film or television style such as camera position, lighting, costume and sound. Television actors working on a multi-camera studio shoot with a tight schedule are often required to memorise screeds of dialogue and nail a scene in a small number of takes, sometimes before a live audience. By contrast, film actors frequently endure long waits while fine adjustments are made to lighting and sound, only to have to deliver the same small snippet of dialogue in nuanced ways for dozens of takes, adjusting performances for subtle close-ups and using bolder movement and expression for long shots or moving shots as the scene is covered in a variety of ways. As Sharon Carnicke writes: 'Since the camera eye can change the apparent spatial distance from spectator to actor easily and quickly, film actors adjust their means of expression from theatrical full-body gestures in long-shots to subtle facial motions in the close-up' (1999: 77).

The unique challenges of screen acting include shooting scenes out of order, which makes it difficult to build up to an emotional climax, shooting one actor at a time so the other performers are not present to cue appropriate reactions, and circumstances 'when the actor must respond in a vacuum to sound and special effects that will be spliced in later' (Carnicke 1999: 84). These difficulties are balanced by certain advantages of screen technology. For instance, editing also affects the impression a screen performance makes. Scott Powell notes that 'performance depends a great deal on the editor's creative choices. Actors realise pretty quickly that the editor is their best friend, able to make them look good and ramp up the emotional impact by playing on reaction shots and building the best takes together, sometimes word by word' (2007: n.p.). Indeed, 'good cutting can make a good actor out of a donkey' (Hardwick cited in Carnicke 1999: 76).

LIGHTING

Lighting is the final element of *mise en scène* to be considered here. Light, shadow and colour can communicate themes and tell a story, but the significance of each is culturally and contextually specific: red can mean anger, danger, passion or luck. In *Jungle Fever*, a Spike Lee drama, green light is used to show Samuel Jackson's character as an unhealthy, squalid junkie, and symbolic lighting is also used to show divisiveness in Wesley Snipes' character's inter-racial relationship. In a scene where the inter-racial lovers quarrel, Snipes, cast entirely in shadow, expresses prejudice against 'half-white, half-black babies' as his white partner is brightly lit. The scene ends with a shot in which she points out that his view is racist. We see that there is light in the darkness and vice versa, and the two characters are seen together in the same frame for the first time as they approach mutual understanding. Because lighting can play such an important role in film and television, it is worth learning the technical terminology that will enable you to describe and analyse the different techniques.

Three-point lighting is the dominant code of lighting in most mainstream film and television productions. It looks natural but is in fact highly contrived, and even natural sources of light like the sun are modified by the use of reflectors and silk canopies to reduce shadows, control brightness and adjust for changing conditions like cloud movement that might create inconsistencies between takes. At least three light sources are required to create the illusion of everyday illumination:

> **Three-point lighting** is a system that balances the main light source (the key light) with fill light to soften shadows and back light to separate foreground from background.

1. key light (the main light source, often frontal);
2. fill light (usually a side light that softens shadows cast by the key light);
3. back light (which gives a sense of depth to the scene).

Often filmmakers will supplement available light or redirect the light provided by the three key sources by using reflective surfaces to bounce light on to an object. For instance, a fill lighting effect can be achieved in broad daylight without using any electrical lights at all, simply by angling a silvery reflector (like those used on car windscreens) to bounce sunlight into the shadowy area.

High-key illumination is a lighting technique based on the three-point lighting system. It produces a fairly bright image with high visibility, graduated shadows and gentle light that reveals expression and detail within shadows. Usually high-key lighting produces low **contrast** between the brightest and darkest areas of the image. High-key illumination is a very common technique and is used widely in drama, comedy and action.

Low-key illumination is a technique that often relies on a single light source to produce an image where much of the screen is in shadow because the level of the key light is too low to properly illuminate everything on screen. Very little fill or no fill light is used, which generates a chiaroscuro effect with patterns of light and shade, often producing a harsh effect with sharp contrast between light and dark areas, together with deep, stark shadows and hard light. Low-key illumination is often used in horror films, film noir and thrillers.

Shadow, light's inseparable partner, also deserves analysis. Attached shadow is a term that refers to shading on the surface of an object, whereas cast shadow occurs when an object blocks out light, and the shadow falls along the ground or is cast upon other objects. Together, light and shadow affect our perception of shape, texture and importance: we can't feel the objects on the screen, but light can give us the sense that something is hard and shiny, or soft and velvety.

Aspects such as the source, colour, intensity and direction of the light provide clues for the audience about where and at what time of day the action takes place. The light source is whatever motivates the light in the scene. The source may be the

---

High-key illumination employs the three-point lighting system to create a naturalistic effect with graduated shadows and gentle illumination that reveals expression and detail, even in scenes set at night.

Contrast refers to the degree of difference between the darkest and lightest areas of an image. High-contrast lighting always shows a distinct difference between light and dark areas, whereas low-contrast images are characterised by mid-tones of light and shade.

Low-key illumination relies on a single light source with little or no fill light, producing sharply contrasting areas of hard light and dark shadows.

sun, a window, firelight or a lamp, and it may originate from light naturally present on location, or from artificial light sources. The crew will select what types of light to use according to the implied source and required effect. Fluorescent lights produce a cold, greenish hue, and incandescent halogen lamps create a softer, warmer tone more suitable for indicating sunlight shining through a window, whereas ordinary household tungsten bulbs look somewhat orange on film. In addition to the colour of different light sources, the colour of light can be augmented or distorted using coloured gels (gelatine filters which look like cellophane, but are heat resistant). Coloured light is often used to create a particular atmosphere or emotion. Intensity indicates the quality and degree of contrast in a lighting set-up. **Hard light** has a strong intensity and creates distinct shadows whereas **soft light** is weaker in intensity and creates diffuse illumination.

The direction of light determines which aspects of a face or object it will highlight, and which will be cast in shadow. For instance, frontal light eliminates shadows, flattens the form, and smoothes imperfections whereas a side light or cross light is used to sculpt the form, enhancing textured surfaces. When used as the main light source, side light can create a sinister shadow over half a face. Back light separates subject from background when used as part of a three-point lighting setup, but it can also function to create a halo effect or to illuminate smoke or mist. This is the case in the comedy *Legally Blonde* which uses back light to romanticise the heroine and make her look angelic (see Figure 1.6). When used alone, back light creates silhouettes.

Hard light originates from an intense source and casts dark, sharp-edged shadows.

Soft light originates from a low-intensity light source and casts soft-edged, graduated shadows, or produces shadowless, diffuse illumination.

As the name suggests, top light comes from directly overhead. When trained on an actor, the effect can be quite unsettling as the performer's eyebrows cast shadows over eyes, obscuring expression as seen in Figure 3.2. Under light is even more sinister since it is unusual, or even unnatural, for light to come from below. For this reason, under light is most often used in horror films, to create a strange distortion of facial features. An unnatural, eerie effect of low-key under lighting and side lighting is shown in Figure 1.7 which features a scene from *Wolf Creek*.

Figure 1.6 When used as part of the high-key, three-point lighting system, back light creates a halo effect in *Legally Blonde*.

Figure 1.7 Low-key under-lighting and side-lighting in *Wolf Creek*

CAMERA POSITION, FRAMING AND COMPOSITION

While theatre and drama are important influences on *mise en scène* construction and analysis, cinematography is the aspect of *mise en scène* that distinguishes screen texts from plays. *What* appears in the frame is inseparable from *how* it is framed, as we will discuss further in Chapter 2. Here it is enough to note that where the camera is placed corresponds to where the audience is located in screen space, and affects our perception of the salience of elements of the *mise en scène*. For instance, a shard of broken glass framed in extreme close-up looms large in our visual field, captures our attention and seems loaded with potential to impact on the forthcoming action, whereas in medium close-up it is barely noticeable, and in a long shot it will be overlooked or considered completely insignificant. Similarly, whether an object is centred or marginalised in the frame, highlighted or shadowed affects perceptions of its meaning and value.

In the classic Italian film *The Bicycle Thief* by Vittorio de Sica (1948), we see the main character looking through a narrow window into a pawn shop where he must hock his most precious possessions in order to obtain a bicycle to get a job and provide for his family. The tight framing conveys a sense of the oppressive constraints of the socio-economic circumstances in Italy near the end of World War II. Subsequent shots inside the pawn shop show that *The Bicycle Thief* is not the story of one individual's misfortune: behind our protagonist, we see a long line of other impoverished people hocking their possessions, and behind the weary pawnbroker we see towering shelves of goods and endless racks of bicycles piled from floor to ceiling. This composition, which cages the characters and uses layers of similar figures and objects to show the extent of misfortunes shared by many people, drives home the message that unemployment and poverty are not individual problems but rather widespread social issues.

Figure 1.8 *The Bicycle Thief*

CONCLUSION

We can understand *mise en scène* as the art of 'making a scene' using costume, performance, lighting and setting to construct and describe the narrative world, to cue audience response and emotion, and to express theme or atmosphere. All elements of the *mise en scène* work together, contributing layers of meaning to a story.

The strengths of *mise en scène* analysis in revealing the symbolic and thematic content encoded in the visual style of film and television productions are also sometimes considered to be limitations. These elements of screen texts can be analysed using techniques developed by literary critics and theatre critics, working with symbols and approaches which are not specific to film or television and which ignore the unique contexts of production and reception, and aspects like technological innovation. It is therefore essential to enhance and complement the strategies for analysing *mise en scène* outlined in this chapter with an appreciation of the other aspects of film and television production and reception detailed in the chapters to follow.

KEY SKILLS

Having read this chapter, you should now be able to:

- identify the four components of *mise en scène* and explain the importance of each in terms of establishing era, location, atmosphere and character;
- analyse the type and function of lighting in any given shot, defining techniques such as three-point lighting, side lighting, back lighting, under lighting, top lighting, high-key and low-key lighting and the narrative purposes they may serve;
- critique screen performance using terminology that reflects an understanding of verisimilitude, an actor's dramatic range, and the ways in which cultural stereotypes can be signalled and deployed via costuming, makeup, movement and mannerisms;

- apply your knowledge of the significance of landscape, studio sets, locations and props in the analysis of any scene;
- critically reflect on the ways in which the construction of a narrative world enables or limits the possible action and characterisation, as well as the ideological and thematic content of a screen text.

2
cinematography:
Writing in light and movement

If you have ever wondered why people at the *Mode* magazine office in *Ugly Betty* appear strangely distant even when in close proximity to each other, what makes them seem to rush as they move from the background to the foreground of a shot, and how the stylish office space is sometimes weirdly distorted, you may have an eye for **cinematography**. Each of these features of the visual image is determined by the use of a special camera lens, deliberately selected to subtly warp the picture in ways that help to communicate Betty's experience of alienation and displacement in the glamorous and superficial world of fashion. This chapter focuses on the artistic and technical choices made with regard to camera position and movement. It also introduces techniques of image control using different lenses and adjusting light and focus to manipulate depth and movement through space, and to convey a psychological or experiential point of view. Understanding the decisions involved in cinematography and the technical terminology used to describe how a moving image has been photographed will enable you to express your interpretation

> **Cinematography** involves the use of a motion picture camera to record images on celluloid, video tape or a digital format that can subsequently be edited and viewed on a screen.

of film and television texts. It will also sharpen your creative and critical appreciation of screen aesthetics.

Tracing the term to its Greek origins, cinematography literally means 'moving photography', or the art of 'graphing' movement by recording light:

cinematography = kinetic (motion) + photo (light) + graph (to write, draw, or record).

Acclaimed cinematographer Dion Beebe says the role of the **director of photography** (the DP) 'is about interpreting and communicating the director's intentions. Our tools are lighting, camera composition and camera movement. We need to understand the language of filmmaking in order to take these often abstract ideas and then communicate them to the crew' (Scott 2006). Each aspect of cinematography contributes to a film or television text's meaning by recording *what* happens on the set or location as well as framing *how* audiences perceive and interpret the meaning, impact, point of view, and aesthetic qualities of those images. Without adequate light, there can be no photograph; hence the cinematography also involves lighting the image. Lighting was covered in Chapter 1 as a component of *mise en scène*, and will only be revisited here in terms of exposure and aperture settings that determine how much light is let into the camera. Other factors affecting the nature and quality of the visual image will be dealt with later in this chapter, including the type, quality and format of the medium (celluloid, video or digital), the size and shape of the screen or frame, variations in the speed of motion, and the use of special effects.

> The **director of photography** (also called the DP or the cinematographer) is the head of the photography department, responsible for designing and organising camerawork and lighting, as per the director's vision.

Cinematography requires technical expertise, artistic vision, and the ability to work collaboratively with a team of specialised crew members. The role of the DP or cinematographer is to actualise the way a film or television scene plays out in the imagination of the director by capturing the images and translating them to the screen. To this end, the DP works closely with the director and the art department, and gives instructions to the technicians in the camera, lighting and **grips** departments who are responsible for setting up and operating the camera, for lighting and for gripping equipment. Depending on the scale and budget of a production, the camera crew includes the DP, camera operator(s) and camera assistants who load the film or tape, move and operate the camera, adjust focus, and use the clapper board to identify and log each take. These roles are changing with the move to high-definition digital cinematography, where the image is recorded straight to a hard drive and electronic clapping takes the place of an old-fashioned clapper board. The crew members responsible for lighting are the **gaffer**, who is the chief electrician, and an assistant called the **best boy**. The grips are the crew members who heft or 'grip' the camera, setting tracks, dollies, jibs and cranes to enable camera movement.

Cinematographic techniques involve telling a story using conventions of camera position and movement, and subtle manipulation of the photographic image using different lenses, focus or special effects. Before introducing these techniques, we should clarify some terminology. Familiar terms like frame, shot, sequence and scene have specific uses in film and television. A **frame** refers to one still photographic image, like a single negative on a film strip. Film is projected at the rate of 24 frames per second to give the illusion of motion, and in video there are 25–30 frames per second. The term 'edge of frame', or **frame line**, can also refer to the borders of the camera viewfinder or the borders of the screen on which the image is projected, in which case it is often used to describe the boundary that separates the image from everything remaining out of shot. Members of the crew in the camera department sometimes refer to the frame line when they instruct the **boom** operator to keep the microphone out of shot and ensure it is not visible on screen. A **shot** is one continuous recording of any length. On set, the shot duration is the length of time between the director calling 'action' and 'cut'.

> **Grips** are production crew members who work with the photography unit, helping to move and set up equipment.
>
> The **gaffer** is the head electrician for a film or television production who is responsible for lighting. The term 'gaffer' means electrician and derives from the use of electrical tape called gaffer tape or duct tape for gaffing down electrical cables and cords so nobody trips over them when moving about a set or location.
>
> The **best boy** is an assistant electrician who helps with film and television lighting.
>
> A **frame** is a single complete photograph, one still image out of a series projected in sequence to give the illusion of motion.
>
> The **frame line** (also called the 'edge of frame') is the line defining the borders of the frame in the camera viewfinder that corresponds to the borders of the image on the cinema or television screen, separating what is visible from what is out of shot or off screen.

During editing, the original shot length may be trimmed if only part of the footage is needed; hence in a finished screen text, a shot is defined as the length of continuous footage between two edit points—a little like a sentence in a novel. For example, if a script involves two characters going on a dinner date, a single shot might show a person eating a bite of cake. A **scene** is a series of shots filmed in one continuous time and location, then edited together to form a narrative unit somewhat like a paragraph, or even a short chapter. When the action moves to a new location, the scene ends. In the dinner date example, a scene would include all the action at the restaurant from the time the couple sits down and peruses the menu to when the bill is paid and they leave. The term **sequence** refers to a semi-autonomous segment of narrative that can be shorter or longer than a self-contained scene. For example, a short shot sequence within the restaurant scene might show the couple squabbling about the bill, whereas a lengthy sequence might extend from the dinner invitation through to the journey home and the goodnight kiss.

> The **boom** is a long pole to which a microphone can be attached. It is used like an extended arm to reach into the action and hold the microphone close enough to record clear sound, while ensuring the crew and equipment remain out of shot.
>
> A **shot** is one uncut continuous recording of film, video or digital footage.
>
> A **scene** is a section of a film or television text set in one time and shot in one location, edited to form a self-contained dramatic or informative unit.
>
> A **sequence** is a series of connected shots that form a semi-autonomous section of the screen text, such as the credit sequence.

CAMERA POSITION

Camera position is a fundamental aspect of cinematography that affects the camera's proximity to the action, and determines the angle, level and point of view from which a shot is perceived and framed. Perhaps most importantly, camera position affects where the spectator is positioned in screen space by determining the vantage point from which audiences see the action. Early films framed the action so that the whole human figure could be seen at all times from a frontal position—much as spectators would watch a play on stage. It was only when technological and industrial developments enabled a shift towards psychologically motivated stories that variable camera positions were used and tighter framings were

Shot size

Shot size, or shot scale, is the most crucial aspect of framing and composition, as the distance of the camera from the subject in shot determines the scale of the screen image and affects the implied proximity of the spectator to characters (see Figure 2.1). While there are infinite variations in shot scale, industry conventions use the size of the human body on screen as a guide for categorising shot sizes. The most frequently used shots and their abbreviations are the **extreme long shot** (ELS), **long shot** (LS), **medium long shot** (MLS), **medium shot** (MS), **two shot** (2 shot), **medium close-up** (MCU), **close up** (CU) and **extreme close-up** (ECU).

Long shots dominated early cinema. Today, a long shot is often used to 'establish' a scene by giving a wide view of the overall space in which the action will unfold, or to showcase big action set pieces like explosions, fights or dances wherein movement is more important than detail. Also known as a ¾ shot, a knee shot, or Plan Américain (American shot), medium long shots only became more popular than long shots around 1910, some fifteen years after the birth of cinema. It is not by chance that this coincided with the emergence of stars in the cinema industry, and the corresponding fascination with movie actors and characters (Cousins 2004: 44). Two shots framing people very close together in conversation became prominent when synchronised sound was introduced and dialogue became important from 1926 onwards. Close-ups can frame any small detail like a book or a gun, but are most often used to film faces because bringing the audience close to the subject connotes intimacy or intimidation, enhancing emotion, identification or impact. Close-ups were not introduced to draw the audience into an intimate relationship with screen characters.

Shot size or shot scale, such as close-ups or long shots, refers to the relative size of a subject on screen, the distance of the subject from the camera, and the implied distance of the audience from the subject.

Extreme long shot: a shot scale using very distant, wide framing to display setting and landscape, rather than figure expression or movement.

Long shot: a shot scale framing the whole human body in the context of their environment.

Medium long shot: a shot scale framing a person from the knees up.

Medium shot: a shot scale framing a person from the middle half of their body, such as from the waist upwards.

Two shot: a shot depicting two people together, usually tightly framed in closer proximity to each other than would be comfortable in everyday life.

Medium close-up: a shot scale framing a person's chest and head.

Close-up: a shot in which a person's head and shoulders, or an object or detail of equivalent size takes up the whole screen. A shot of the human face alone is sometimes called a 'big close-up' or a 'choker close-up', whereas a shot of the head, neck and shoulders is a standard close-up.

Extreme close-up: a shot scale that shows a very small detail, like a person's eyes filling the frame.

widely used until narrative dramas starring individualised protagonists became popular. Extreme close-ups do not need to feature part of the body; they can frame details such as lips or lipstick marks on a wine glass.

Certain shot sizes are best suited to particular types of *action*. For example, filming dialogue in extreme long shot would seem artificial because we must be within a few metres proximity to hear someone clearly. Furthermore, certain shot sizes are appropriate for particular *media*. The cinema screen is huge by comparison with the human body, so it can showcase the grandeur of vast landscapes as well as offering a larger-than-life view of intimate emotional scenes. Because television and computer screens are far smaller, tight framing is best as long shots lose detail on small screens. Indeed, most televisions are ideally sized and shaped to frame a person in close-up, as screens correspond roughly to the size of a person's head and shoulders. Television cinematographers are more likely to use 'singles', or individual close-ups, rather than framing people in long shots or two shots because many television screens are still narrower and squatter than cinema screens.

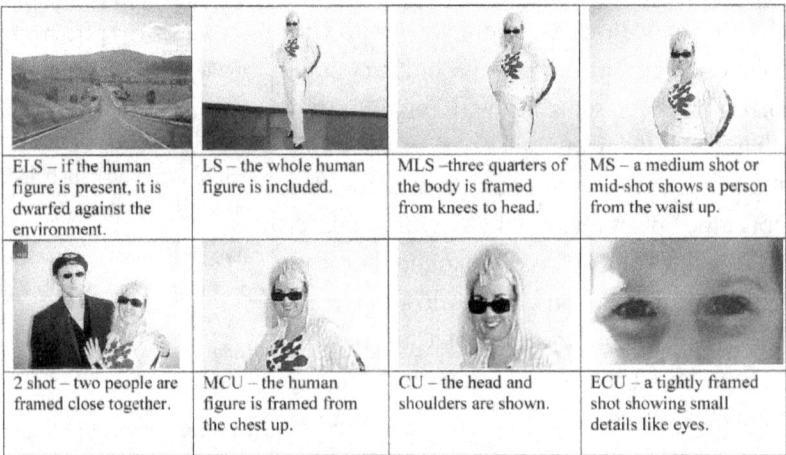

Figure 2.1 Shot size table

One of the biggest factors to impact on camera position is whether a scene is filmed with single or multiple cameras. Multi-camera shoots occur in both film and television, but are more common in television, as discussed later in relation to editing. In television production there will often be three or more cameras on the studio floor or at an event like a sports match. A vision mixer selects which image to use at a given point, switching between different points of view. Film productions often use multiple cameras to record unrepeatable action (difficult stunts like the crash in *Death Proof*) from a range of angles. With multiple cameras, camera operators must plan carefully to avoid getting each other in shot. Achieving high-quality sound and lighting while concealing the equipment from the view of any of the cameras is complicated. If, for instance, camera one films a two shot of an interview, while camera two holds on a close-up of the interviewer and camera three moves around to add visual dynamism to the scene, the frame line for the first camera will be much wider than for the close-up, and the frame for camera three varies; hence the boom or the movements of the third camera may intrude in the shot. It is also difficult to set lighting for all three views at once.

Camera angle

After shot size and framing, the next most significant aspect of camera placement involves camera angle. The camera can be directed at its subject from any angle, but the four main angles are neutral, high, low and oblique. When filming from a **neutral angle**, or a 'straight angle', the camera is positioned straight on, facing the subject at eye level without tilting upwards or downwards. When the camera is positioned higher than the subject being filmed, from a vantage point that looks down on the subject, it is called a **high-angle** shot. The effect of a high angle is to diminish the subject in screen space, which can imply that one character is shorter than another, is sitting, or is disempowered. In a **low-angle** shot (see Figure 2.2), the camera is positioned lower than the subject and is tilted to look upwards, allowing the subject to dominate screen space and sometimes giving the impression of aggrandisement.

Neutral-angle shots position the camera at eye level, without tilting.

High-angle shots are those in which the camera is positioned at a higher level than the subject on screen, tilted downwards to view the subject.

Low-angle shots film the subject from a position below eye level, tilting the camera upwards.

In Figure 2.2, the low-angle shot loosely aligns the viewer with the detective from *In the Cut*, using shallow focus to shoot over his shoulder as he looks up at Frannie (Meg Ryan). Because she is the heroine, the high angle reverse shot (Figure 2.3) locates the viewer *as* Frannie, shooting directly from her point of view.

Figure 2.2 Low-angle shot looking up over the detective's shoulder (*In the Cut*, Jane Campion, 2004)

Figure 2.3 High-angle reverse shot looking down at the detective from the window

When the camera is at an **oblique angle** (sometimes termed a 'Dutch tilt' or a canted frame), the image and the horizon line lean to one side as though the camera cocks its head. Conventionally, oblique angles indicate the world is off kilter, or show that a character is unbalanced, or perceives the world from an unusual perspective, as in *Touching the Void* (see Figure 7.2).

> **Oblique-angle** shots tilt the camera to one side so that the horizon line is not level and the world is represented from a skewed perspective.

Camera level

Level refers to the elevation of the camera. The main camera levels are **eye level**, **bird's eye** and **dog's eye**. Normally, camera position is at eye level with the subject in the frame: unless otherwise specified, when camera level is described it is assumed that the camera shoots from a straight angle or level position. If the camera is high above the subject looking straight down (perhaps viewing a person sleeping), it is termed a bird's eye shot. If the camera is low down near the floor, perhaps under the table filming ankles and knees, it is termed a dog's eye shot. Different combinations of camera level and angle are possible. Figure 2.3 from *In the Cut* is a high level *and* high angle shot.

Camera positions can have ideological implications when used to represent the power relations between screen characters rather than simply representing spatial relationships between characters. For example, if one character is consistently framed in low angle close-ups, it makes them seem important or dominant in comparison with a character on whom we consistently look down, from farther away.

> **Eye level** refers to a camera position that matches the eye level of the cinematographer with the eye level of the character being filmed.
>
> **Bird's eye** refers to an elevated camera position, situated high above a subject, usually looking straight down.
>
> **Dog's eye** level shots are filmed with the camera positioned at a low level, near the floor, showing the action unfold from an eye level similar to that of a dog.

Point of view

Another critical component of camera position is the perspective from which the camera and the viewers see the action. Screen texts are shot mostly from the perspective of the central protagonists, but this can be done in ways that offer varying degrees of insight into their experiences or subjectivity. An important question to ask when analysing the power relations inherent in cinematography is 'Who has visual agency?' Some characters in a narrative are active viewing subjects, whereas others may be objectified. In other words, question through whose eyes and whose world-view the audience is invited to see the story. For example, if women are frequently objectified from the point of view of male characters, the text may be communicating a patriarchal ideology.

The camera's position can be aligned with a character's optical **point of view** (**POV**), which implicitly places the audience in the character's shoes, showing events from their physical standpoint and conveying their personal (subjective) perception of events from a 'first-person perspective' as though we *are* the character. The camera can also view the action over the shoulder of a character (as in Figure 2.2, filmed over the detective's shoulder), giving a semi-subjective point of view which allows us to see part of a character's body (their shoulder or the side of their head) as well as showing us what they see from the position and angle that they see it. The camera can also offer deeper involvement with a character's experience by depicting internal perception, using **subjective imagery** to show what a person sees in their mind's eye, such as the sepia images of a young couple figure skating in *In the Cut* which depict the protagonist imagining her parents' relationship. The use of subjective imagery like dreams, fantasies, hallucinations, imagination or memory sequences gives the audience access to a point of view that can be described as psychological or internal subjective imagery. This is not a viewpoint other characters in the narrative can access: subjective imagery is only seen by the audience and the character whose inner world we enter.

> **Point of view (POV)** refers to the perspective from which the camera is positioned to view the action in a shot. In a POV shot, the camera position is aligned with the viewing position of a character on the screen.
>
> **Subjective imagery** shows what a character sees in their imagination or their mind's eye (such as flashback, fantasy or dream sequences).

At the other end of the scale, the camera can be positioned to show an **omniscient point of view**, shot from the perspective of a fly on the wall rather than from the perspective of any screen character. This point of view is a 'third-person perspective' or a 'god's eye perspective', as the camera is like an all-seeing invisible entity. We avoid using the term 'objective point of view' because it may imply that the camera can be placed in a neutral or impartial location, or that omniscient shots don't involve thoughtful decisions. The camera always implicates the audience in the act of viewing and aligns us with a particular point of view. A seemingly 'objective' shot may elide the point of view of the filmmaker, making it seem natural and unmotivated, but every single camera position meaningfully inflects how the audience perceives and interprets a shot. Omniscient shots can show the audience things in the story world that none of the characters sees (like an empty room), or they can simply capture the action from a vantage point that is not physically occupied by a character. For example, the opening sequence of *American Beauty* features omniscient aerial shots of Lester Burnham's neighbourhood, and of him waking up, rolling out of bed and going to the bathroom. Nothing in the film suggests that any character is airborne or that someone is spying on Lester at the time. Instead, the camera locates the audience in an omniscient point of view that works with Lester's retrospective voiceover narration to suggest he is looking back on his life as a disembodied soul. When we 'come down to earth' and cut to a dog's eye view under the bed, it suggests Lester has a pretty low opinion of his own life at the beginning of the story.

> **Omniscient shots** are filmed from the viewing perspective of an invisible observer, not a character in the narrative.

The final camera position to note is one in which the camera is at eye level, facing a person staring straight into the lens. Normally, even with a shot sequence filmed in first-person point of view, the reaction shot shows a person directing their gaze just to one side, rather than seeming to meet the eyes of the audience by looking into the camera. When a performer looks at or addresses the camera directly, it is termed **direct address**, or 'looking straight down the barrel' as though the camera 'shooting' the subject is a gun. This technique either functions to situate the audience directly inside the point of view of the character towards whom the performer's gaze is directed (as in Figure 2.4 which locates the audience in the position of Sarah Goldfarb being examined by a doctor in *Requiem for a Dream*), or it breaks illusion of reality and signals the character's awareness of an audience. Direct address is far more common in television than

> **Direct address** is where a person looks straight into the lens of the camera.

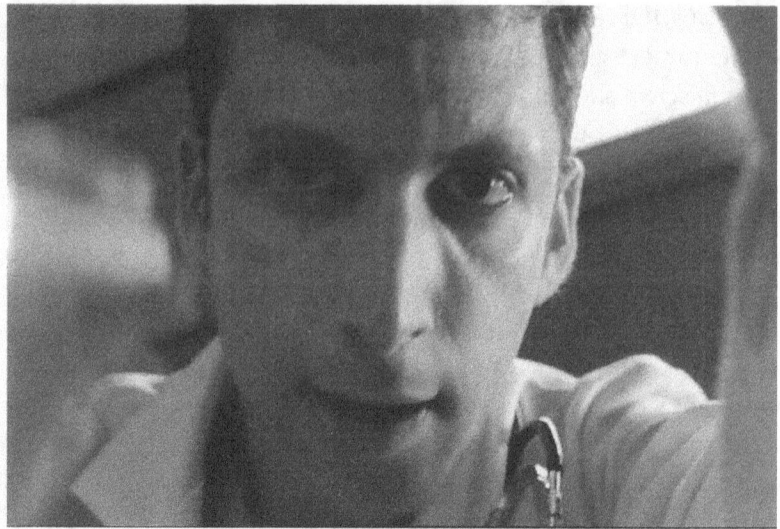

Figure 2.4 Direct address to camera in *Requiem for a Dream* provided through courtesy of Lionsgate

in film because television is a 'live' medium that frequently recognises the presence of an audience. Except in narrative drama, television is frequently filmed with a studio audience, and features familiar television presenters and personalities who face the camera and speak to us as though they are really in our homes. Film actors typically maintain the illusion that they are in their own world, and nobody is watching them.

Direct address to camera is also termed breaking the fourth wall, which is derived from theatre performances in which a set has only three walls and the audience is seated behind the imaginary fourth wall. In film and television, there are six zones of **off-screen space** beyond each of the four borders of frame, behind the set, and behind the camera where the viewer is located. As we have seen, the frame defines the limits of the image and every act of framing and composing a shot involves selection. Instead of cutting to a new shot from a different position, cinematographers may reframe the image within the shot (without cutting) to bring off-screen space on to the screen, revealing elements that were previously out of shot. Sometimes this

Off-screen space is the space of the story world that the audience imagines to extend beyond the four sides of the screen, as well as into the background behind the screen and into the foreground, where the camera is located and beyond.

can be used for surprise effect, controlling the moment something is revealed to screen characters and/or to the audience. There are other reasons a cinematographer might reframe a shot using camera movement, and there are many different mobile framing techniques, which we discuss below.

CAMERA MOVEMENT

The first cameras were big, bulky and difficult to move, so early films featured static shots taken with the camera on a tripod. It was the motion *in* the picture rather than the motion *of* the camera that was fascinating. The first attempts at mobile framing were tripod mounted pans and tilts.

Panning is a horizontal camera movement that gives a sense of surveying the width of screen space or following a moving object with one's eyes. 'Pan' comes from the word panorama, meaning to look all around, and the movement resembles the camera turning its head left or right. When panning, the camera can be on a tripod or handheld, and the pan can be executed at different speeds such as a 'whip pan,' which is so fast the panning movement blurs the image.

Tilting is a vertical camera movement used to suggest the camera tips its head to look a subject up and down or perhaps follow a falling object. Confusingly, the term 'tilt' also refers to a static camera position tipped to one side so the horizon line is not level, or tipped up or down in a fixed position in order to give a high or low angle view of the subject in shot.

In a **tracking shot** (also termed a **travelling shot** or a **dolly** shot) the camera moves through space, usually mounted on tracks or wheels. The cinematographer can track in, reverse track, track sideways, and perform diagonal or circular tracking movements. The first tracking shot literally strapped the camera to the front of a train rushing through a tunnel in 1898, one year before the first purpose-built tracks or dollies were devised (Cousins 2004: 25–9). There was a

Panning is a camera movement that scans screen space along the horizontal plane, moving right or left to give the impression of a head turning, often to follow a moving figure.

Tilting can be used for both static and mobile framing. A static camera can be tilted up, down or at an oblique sideways angle and locked in position on a tripod to shoot from a high, low or oblique angle. As a camera movement, tilting is a vertical motion, surveying up or down.

period in the early 1930s just after the introduction of sound when tracking shots virtually vanished because cameras had to be inside soundproofed boxes to prevent their noisy mechanical sound being recorded. As directional microphones and multi-layer soundtracks were introduced, cameras were liberated from the tripod once again. In television studios, cameras are often mounted on mobile pedestals or wheeled tripods that function as dollies and can also be raised or lowered smoothly to adjust camera level (a motion described as 'ped up' or 'ped down') to follow figure movement such as a person standing up or sitting down. This action can be approximated using a height-adjustable office chair with wheels. Today, professional dollies are sophisticated and expensive, such as the panther dolly which provides a stealthy, smooth gliding motion on low-friction tracks. Lower budget productions improvise by putting the cinematographer in a wheelchair, car or truck (this last technique gives a clue as to why travelling shots are also sometimes called 'trucking shots'). Car-mounted travelling shots are a staple of road movies and chase scenes.

> A **tracking shot**, also known as a **travelling shot**, is a mobile framing technique mounting the camera on tracks, wheels or any device that allows it to move through space and follow the action. 'Travelling shot' is the best term if it is not evident how the movement was achieved, or if it is unlikely tracks were used.
>
> A **dolly** is a camera mount with a wheeled base, enabling smooth, quiet camera movement.

The handheld camera is another form of mobile framing that allows cinematographers to execute travelling shots and other camera movements when literally holding the camera by hand. Handheld has a rough, unsteady feeling connoting immediacy and presence in screen space, rather than detached observation. This can lend a dangerous or documentary feel because the jolting of the camera operator's body walking over uneven surfaces, or the movement of their chest as they breathe is palpable in the unsteadiness of the image. Handheld cinematography only became common in the 1960s when lighter, portable 16mm cameras were introduced and a method of recording sound separately from the camera was developed, thereby freeing up camera movement. Interestingly, the radical politics of the youth movement in 1960s and the reaction against the social constraints of the 1950s, with its emphasis

> A **handheld camera** is a mobile framing technique in which the cinematographer carries the camera instead of using a tripod, producing a wide range of movements with a jerky look.

on consumerism and conservative conventions, coincided with technological advancements to popularise a new 'unconventional' style of rawer handheld cinematography that literally had a more 'liberated' aesthetic.

A **steadicam** is a shock-absorbent rig harnessed to the cinematographer's body which supports the camera on a mechanical arm to ensure a smooth travelling shot while the cinematographer walks, runs or follows the action. Footage shot with a steadicam has the freedom and presence of handheld footage, but looks smoother and more professional, following the action and freeing actors to improvise without worrying about moving out of shot or out of focus. The steadicam gives a more experiential feel than handheld camerawork because we don't notice the instability of the cinematographer's movement any more than we normally notice jerkiness in our own bodily movements.

Crane shots mount cameras on a wheeled platform with a mechanical arm that can be raised, lowered and shifted around to provide height and movement in a shot. Like many road movies *The Adventures of Priscilla, Queen of the Desert* uses a crane to shoot high angle travelling shots of the highway landscape (see Figure 2.5). The opening shot of Orson Welles' stylish film noir *Touch of Evil* uses a sophisticated crane shot to travel high over buildings and wind through the streets, tracking the movement of a car with a ticking bomb and introducing the detective who will investigate the explosion. Small cameras can also be secured on a jib arm or boom, then moved smoothly over the action, or raised and lowered like a crane.

> A **steadicam** is a contraption that allows the camera to be steady while also giving the freedom of movement permitted with handheld cinematography.

Aerial shots are characterised by extreme height and gliding or swooping movements, usually filmed from a helicopter. Aerial shots are expensive, and rarely found in television except as reusable establishing shots in the introductory credit sequence, such as flying over Newport beach in opening shots of *The O.C.* Except when in a plane or a crane, people seldom occupy elevated mobile positions so such flashy techniques are reserved for special

> **Crane shots** enable a wide and sophisticated range of camera movement by mounting the camera on a vehicle with wheels as well as an elevated mechanical arm that can move the camera, up, down or sideways.
>
> **Aerial shots** mount the camera on a device that can fly or move through the air in any direction.

Figure 2.5 Crane mounted reverse travelling shot in *The Adventures of Priscilla, Queen of the Desert*.

moments in film and television. They are often associated with hallucinations, dreams or other out-of-body experiences, or used to lend visual flair and an experiential thrill to dramatic, momentous events.

A **zoom** is not a camera movement because the camera is actually still; however, zooming gives the illusion of movement as the lens elements change to magnify or reduce the scale of a subject in the frame while the camera is rolling. The cinematographer can zoom in or out, and zooms can be executed at various speeds. A crash zoom is very fast, whereas a creep zoom reframes the image slowly and is often used to creep up on a character in order to generate suspense or draw the audience into their emotional experience.

This overview of camera movements shows the camera is an active agent in the narrative. Decisions about camera movement are typically motivated by the storyline, rather than being arbitrary or purely aesthetic. When analysing film and television, it is therefore important to move beyond describing *how* the camera moves to question *why* it moves, and what effect the movement has on the spectator with

> A **zoom** is a mobile framing technique in which the image is enlarged or reduced in scale without moving the camera, but by using the camera lens to create the effect of magnification and apparent movement.

respect to the meaning or experience conveyed in a shot. Camera movement enables complex, lengthy shots rather than short takes. This affects the duration and rhythm of shot sequences, sustaining attention on performance and sometimes using dynamic camera movement to compensate for a lack of figure movement or action in a scene. Mobile framing can also support the narrative by generating suspense (creep zoom) or surprise (reframe to reveal . . .) or drawing attention to a particular detail (track in to close-up).

LENSES AND FOCAL PROPERTIES

The choice of lens and the photographic properties of the shot determine what is in focus, how light is controlled, and how depth and space are represented. For the purpose of screen analysis, it is not essential to learn technical details such as **focal length** and **depth of field** (though we provide glossary definitions for interested readers), but you do need to develop the ability to recognise the effects particular lenses and lighting conditions have on the screen image. When a camera's **aperture** is wide open, the film or digital light sensor gets **exposure** to too much light, and the resulting image is often too bright (over-exposed), whereas if inadequate light is let into the camera the image will be under-exposed, or dark and indistinct. Lighting levels and camera settings therefore have a significant impact on picture quality and focus. The choice to use a particular lens also impacts on the focal properties and spatial relationships of an image by affecting whether a figure will remain in focus while moving between the background and foreground planes of a shot. This in turn influences the representation of perspective or depth, determining whether the audience has a wide or a cramped view of the setting.

Focal length is the distance from the centre of a lens to the point where the light rays converge to focus the image on the film stock, video tape or digital light sensor.

Depth of field refers to the range of distances in front of the camera lens in which an image is in focus. If a lens has a limited depth of field (e.g. a telephoto lens), objects in the foreground and background may be blurred when a narrow area of the middle ground is in focus.

Aperture is the size of the adjustable iris opening that allows light into a camera. Aperture is measured in f-stops (the smaller the number, the bigger the opening, and the shallower the focal range or depth of field).

Exposure is the amount of light entering the camera through the aperture. **Over-exposed** images are too bright and light, while **under-exposed** images are dim and dark.

The feeling of scorching heat and endless space in the Australian outback is created in *The Proposition* by over-exposing footage filmed with a normal lens in bright conditions. A **normal lens** has a middle focal length which causes virtually no distortion of the image on screen and offers a close approximation of normal human vision. If you do not notice anything unusual about the horizontal or vertical spatial relations in a shot—that is, if it looks 'normal'—odds are it has been filmed with a normal lens.

> A **normal lens** has a medium focal length (from 35–50 mm) which corresponds to normal perception without distorting depth or perspective.
>
> **Wide-angle lenses** have a short focal length (from 12.5–30 mm) and are good for showing width and depth in a long shot. The wider the angle, the more exaggerated spatial relations become, until objects in the background and foreground seem very far apart on screen and straight lines appear to bend or lean.

A **wide-angle lens** is a lens with a short focal length and, correspondingly, a greater depth of field than a normal lens—which means that the wide-angle lens can hold everything in sharp focus, even those areas close to and far from the camera. Perspective is deepened and elongated when a wide-angle lens is used, so subjects in the foreground and those in the background appear further apart than they actually are. A wide-angle lens is also capable of capturing a wider view of the space to either side of the camera, showing a broader expanse of the setting and background in shot. The shorter the focal length of a lens, the more you may notice distortion across the width of the frame, as a wide-angle lens warps straight lines so that they appear to bow slightly. A wide-angle lens is best for long shots. A close-up shot with a wide-angle lens will distort the human face. A wide-angle lens is used to create the effects in *Ugly Betty* described at the very beginning of this chapter (see Figure 2.6). Prominent parts of Betty's face, like her nose, braces and glasses, bulge forward unattractively when she is filmed in close-up using a wide-angle lens. Betty's co-workers seem abnormally distant from one another and always seem to be in a tearing hurry because the wide-angle lens exaggerates perspective and makes people moving at a normal speed appear to rush from the background into the foreground.

A **fish eye** lens (see Figure 2.7) is an extreme wide-angle lens creating a warped fishbowl effect, much like the peephole on a door which enables a person to check who is standing outside. This lens bends space to the extent of showing an almost panoramic, wrap-around view, making the elements in the middle of the frame unnaturally large and those at the sides of the frame unnaturally bowed.

Fish eye lenses are extreme wide angle lenses (with a focal length of 8mm and below), creating a warped fishbowl effect that bulges the image.

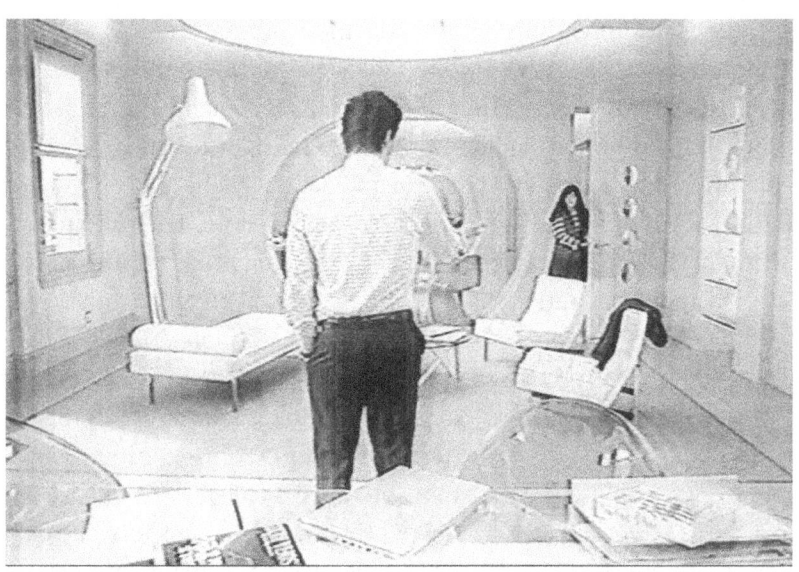

Figure 2.6 The wide-angle lens used in *Ugly Betty* exaggerates the distance between Betty and Daniel and makes the walls tilt

Figure 2.7 Fish eye lens in *Requiem for a Dream* (provided through courtesy of Lionsgate)

The **telephoto lens** is also called a long lens because it has a long focal length. You may have noticed that telephoto lenses are literally 'long' lenses that jut out like a telescope beyond the camera, extending the focal length (the distance in millimetres between the lens and the film when an image is in focus). The use of a telephoto lens flattens the planes of space in the image, apparently bringing the background and foreground closer together to cramp or compress the shot, narrowing what can be seen of the setting and limiting what is in focus. An effect of the telephoto lens is its ability to reframe the rhythm and tempo (alluded time) of what is happening on screen. Contrasting the rushing effect of a wide-angle lens, a telephoto long shot of an approaching subject 'suspends' time. For example, the slow-paced opening shot of a car approaching through the snow in *Fargo* augments anticipation of what comes next. Telephoto is rarely used for handheld footage, as it registers the movement of the camera to a greater extent, and the shallow depth of field makes areas of the image lose focus with movement. The telephoto lens is good for tightly framed stable shots like close-ups, as it conveys the quality of a personal encounter as though we could almost reach out and touch the character.

The **telephoto lens**, also known as a long lens, has a long focal length of 75–500 mm which is suitable for close-ups that are filmed from a distance. Telephoto lenses enlarge the subject while narrowing the field of view and flattening the image, making elements in the background and foreground of a shot seem closer than they actually are.

A **zoom lens** has variable focal length ranging from far away to close-up, combining a wide, normal and long lens in one. The appearance of motion produced by zooming in or out is an optical effect: it is not created by moving the camera. You can distinguish between a shot that moves closer to a subject using a zoom from a shot that dollies in by watching what happens at the edges and background of the frame. In both cases, the subject of attention appears to become larger, but with a dolly shot the spatial relations of subjects in the frame do not vary much: the background still seems distant while the object in the foreground occupies more of the frame. With a forward zoom, the surrounding space is progressively excluded from the frame and often loses focus or becomes flattened as the image is magnified.

Zoom lenses have an adjustable focal length like an 'all in one' wide angle, normal and telephoto lens which can magnify a subject in the background of a wide angle long shot until it is framed in telephoto close-up.

A **zolly shot**, also known as a 'vertigo shot', the 'big squeeze' or an 'American track', is a disorienting combination of zooming and tracking movements in opposing directions. It illustrates the experiential power of cinematography. In *Vertigo*, Hitchcock famously directed the cinematographer to crane up while simultaneously zooming in to represent the experience of a man frightened of heights. As Scottie (James Stewart) feels in danger of falling, his attention rushes towards the ground (the downward-zooming motion), and he physically pulls away from the sheer drop in fear (the upward-craning or back-tracking motion). Another example of this technique occurs in Mathieu Kassovitz's exquisitely photographed *La Haine* (*Hate*), a film about marginalised youths living on the urban periphery of Paris, railing against social disadvantage, prejudice and police brutality. When the disenchanted protagonists travel into the city centre, their sense of social exclusion from Parisian culture is expressed in the cinematography. As they enter Paris, the camera zooms forward, magnifying the buildings and causing them to blur and crowd in towards the camera, while the feeling of being physically repelled from the space is communicated by a reverse track. The visceral sense of dislocation and alienation that the characters feel is also experienced by the audience as the unsettling cinematography simultaneously pulls us in and pushes us out of the screen space. The story content reinforces film form to indicate the protagonists are outsiders, showing them being locked out of an acquaintance's apartment and evicted from a gallery.

> A **zolly shot** is executed using simultaneous zoom and dolly movements that create a disorienting feel.

The challenge of executing a zolly shot is keeping the subject in focus while the two opposing movements are happening. Sometimes a cinematographer will deliberately leave certain areas of an image out of focus. This is called shallow focus if only one plane of the image is sharp and other areas are blurry (see Figure 2.2), and it is called soft focus if the subject of the shot itself is slightly unclear.

Soft focus is an aesthetic strategy once commonly used to make a leading lady look romantic, and still popular when filming older actors in a manner that makes wrinkles and skin imperfections less noticeable. **Racking focus**, also known as pulling focus or shifting focus, is a technique that deliberately shifts the audience's attention from one

Racking focus, pulling focus or shifting focus redirects the audience's attention from an object in the foreground of a shot to an object in the background (or vice versa) by changing what part of the image is clear and what part is out of focus.

plane of space to another, literally directing us to focus on a different part of the image. For instance, a cinematographer can pull focus from a character speaking in the background to someone listening in the foreground, thereby redirecting the audience's attention (see Figures 2.8 and 2.9).

Figure 2.8 Rack focus from Mark Ruffalo (background) . . .

Figure 2.9 . . . to Meg Ryan (foreground) as she listens to him, then redirects her attention to the person he is talking about in *In the Cut*

In the Cut and cinematographic style

In the Cut, directed by Jane Campion in 2004, is a murder mystery filmed like a love story. Meg Ryan plays Frannie Avery, a withdrawn English teacher with tragic fashion sense and lank hair, who is questioned by a homicide detective about a murder in her Manhattan neighbourhood. As the erotic charge between Frannie and Detective Molloy (Mark Ruffalo) heats up and it appears Frannie herself may be in danger, she goes to stay with her sister Pauline, played by Jennifer Jason Leigh. Crime fiction from *film noir* through gangster films and serial killer movies has traditionally been a 'masculine' genre, filmed from an almost clinical distance in alienating urban environments with hard-edged, dark shadows. It is perhaps the popularity of female detectives, spies and forensic investigators on television that has caused a shift in the way the subject matter is treated. *In the Cut* is written, produced and directed by women, as well as featuring two female protagonists and a killer who romances his victims, giving them an engagement ring before beheading them and disarticulating their limbs. Despite this gruesome storyline, it is difficult to respond to the film as a chilling thriller because of the way it is shot.

Dion Beebe, the Brisbane born DP who won an Oscar for *Memoirs of a Geisha* in 2005, often uses a handheld camera and a **shift tilt lens** (see Figure 2.10), with the capacity for subtle differential focus to suffuse *In the Cut* with an aura of intimacy and authenticity—particularly in scenes showing the sisters. Much of the story plays out at close range in warm, domestic interiors, and the affection between the sisters is captured in shallow-focus, soft lighting, and handheld footage that deflects attention from everything except facial expression.

The use of close, handheld camerawork with a long lens not only makes the imagery more personal, it also gently softens the background and foreground into indistinct, dappled colours that take the edge off what would otherwise be a much coarser documentary feel. The effect is a beguiling, sensual, textured image blending a dreamlike quality with a raw,

> A **shift tilt lens**, developed from the swing tilt lens used in still photography, has a shallow depth of field and is used to produce areas of the image that are soft or out of focus while maintaining sharpness in another part of the frame. This draws attention to parts of the image that the filmmaker wishes to emphasise. The optical axis of the lens is normally parallel to the film plane. With this lens, it can be tilted to move it from the perpendicular and rotated on its axis, allowing a subject to be isolated within a particular depth of field.

Figure 2.10 Differential focus using a shift tilt lens foregrounds emotion in *In the Cut*

emotional honesty that expresses the characters' romantic longings, as well as harsher elements like fear and carnal desire. Campion wanted the camera to follow the rhythms of performance despite the challenges of shooting handheld footage with a lens that has such a shallow depth of field, so the film is characterised by constantly shifting focus which subtly draws the audience into the characters' emotional lives, inviting us to tune in to expressive nuances.

In contrast to the softness characterising the affection between the women, the harsh reality of Frannie's grief when her sister dies is captured with stark side light, hard-edged shadows and sharp focus against a brick wall (see Figure 2.11).

Speed of motion

Although it is not used in *In the Cut*, another technique that cinematographers use to give experiential impact to a scene, communicate story information or create an aesthetic effect involves manipulating the speed of motion by varying the speed at which footage is shot and screened. A slow-motion effect is achieved by shooting at high speed (filming over 24 frames per second, so when the footage is replayed at normal speed the action in a single second plays out over an extended time). A fast-forward effect is created when action is shot at a slow

Figure 2.11 *In the Cut* uses harsh shadows on Meg Ryan to accentuate her shock and grief

speed and played back at a faster rate. An exaggerated example is the accelerated motion of time-lapse photography, which occurs when footage filmed at a rate as slow as one frame per hour is played back at the normal rate of 24 frames per second, such as when seeds germinate and grow into leafy plants in David Attenborough's natural history television documentaries. By contrast with this temporal compression, the technique known as flow-mo (flow-motion, or bullet-time) extends and slices up time and space by joining together a number of still frames taken in extremely swift succession at different points around a moving subject. In *CineTech: Film, Convergence and New Media*, Stephen Keane describes bullet time in *The Matrix* as 'a slight freezing of time as the action is presented through a full panoramic turn' (2007: 153). Other techniques such as speed ramping and skip framing are defined and discussed in Chapter 4, since they can be contrived in postproduction to manipulate the speed of motion perceived on screen.

Because slow-motion and accelerated-motion techniques manipulate time, they are appropriate for storylines in which the passage of time is integral. For instance, time is distorted in *Donnie Darko*, which is a circular narrative about time travel. One particular shot combines and manipulates camera movement and speed of motion masterfully in a way that supports the theme of the film and conveys Donnie's personal experience of failing to keep pace with the changes he is experiencing, or of failing to connect with people. Early in the film, soon after a jet engine first lands in Donnie's bedroom, the Darko children catch the bus to school. When they arrive, a circular camera movement shows the bus tilting and rotating on its axis. This shot can be understood to represent Donnie's unbalanced state. As Donnie walks up the steps and enters the school, time seems to warp. It alternately hurries forward, lingers on certain characters, and speeds away as the camera moves in a continuous travelling shot through the school, observing but not engaging with the people encountered en route.

Special effects

For film and television analysis, it is more important to think about the impact and meaning of the image than to know how it is achieved. Although special effects (abbreviated as FX or SPFX) are part of the image we see on the screen, few are directly controlled by the cinematographer. Most special effects are now created on computers during post-production. Originally, **composite shots** using techniques like masking, matte shots, double exposure, superimposition and rear projection were used to allow more than one image to be recorded on the same frame, creating special effects that could not easily be achieved with live actors in real situations. For example, double exposure can give the illusion that an actor is talking to their doppelganger or twin if a section of the film is masked off and exposed separately, effectively joining two 'takes' of the same actor together in a single shot. Superimposition layers separate shots so they appear to form a single image, such as a ghost appearing in a scene. Rear projection is a technique that makes action shot in a studio seem to be taking place in a different setting—for example, moving footage can be projected behind a car or cockpit scene to give the appearance that a character is driving or flying a vehicle which is actually stationary at the time of the shoot. Chromakey and virtual sets have now superseded rear projection.

Composite shots use techniques like mattes, superimposition and double exposure to create special effects, usually by masking or blocking out areas of the frame, or filming two aspects of the image (such as the actors and the background) separately, then combining the images in post-production.

Chromakey, also known as blue-screen or green-screen, involves shooting actors in front of an entirely blue or green studio screen, then 'keying out' the background colour and replacing it with another background. The action can be mapped on to computer-generated virtual sets or footage of actual locations or scale models. If the actor's costume includes something like a tie that is the same colour as the blue screen, the actor will appear to have a tie-shaped hole in their chest when all blue is removed from the image. *Sky Captain and the World of Tomorrow* and *Sin City* are films shot entirely in front of blue screens and, in the ice skating sequence in *Big Love*, the mountainous background is 'keyed in' to give the illusion of being shot on location.

Since the 1990s, special effects have been executed using computer-generated imagery (CGI). CGI is versatile enough to be used for futuristic effects (in films like *The Matrix* trilogy and *Terminator 2*), and to create a sense of historical realism (in films like *Titanic*), as well as being used extensively in fantasy films and superhero comics or graphic novel adaptations. CGI is sometimes hard to spot as it is used for 'visible' and visually spectacular special effects like bullet time as well as 'invisible' effects that involve erasing or substituting story details, settings and even characters (Keane 2007: 56–61). For instance, *CSI: Crime Scene Investigation* uses CGI environments for difficult and expensive locations such as Las Vegas casinos. In *Lord of the Rings*, parts of the setting are CGI, while Gollum himself and many of the extras in the battle scenes are **virtual actors** that are brought to life during the post-production process, and live on in the digital game based on the film. The popularity of CGI and SPFX techniques, which are often judged in terms of the seamless integration of the virtual and the real, is just one indicator of the impact of the digital revolution and the increasing convergence between screen media industries.

> **Chromakey** is a visual effects technique that involves photographing actors in front of a blue or green screen which can later be substituted for a different background or setting.

> **Virtual actors**, also known as 'vactors', or 'synthespians', are digital characters created using CGI techniques.

Image quality, aspect ratio, framing and formats

The convergence of film and television due to digital media technologies was discussed in the Introduction. Here we consider the implications that differences between digital and analogue shooting formats have for cinematography. The quality of a screen image is determined by the recording medium, the **frame rate**, the mode of projecting or playing the image, and the size and shape of the screen. Cinematographers can work with a variety of recording media: film, video, high-definition video and high-definition television (HDTV).

When shooting on celluloid, cinematographers choose between **film stocks** differentiated by colour, dimensions and sensitivity to light. Film stock can be black and white, or colour. Footage shot in colour can be changed to black and white in postproduction, and black and white footage can be digitally colourised, or hand tinted. Colour and black and white film stock both come in different **speeds**—that is, film stocks have variable degrees of photosensitivity, or responsiveness to light. Film is described as fast when it is highly sensitive and can be used in dim light to produce a high-contrast image, and slow stock that is less sensitive to light can be used in brighter conditions to produce a lower-contrast image. Film also comes in a range of different dimensions, or **gauges**. Smaller gauges such as Super8 (stock that is 8 millimetres wide) are narrower and produce a lower quality, grainy image like an old home movie, and bigger formats such as Cinerama and IMAX produce an extremely high-quality image with a fine grain that can be projected on to a massive screen without loss of clarity or definition. The gauge of film stock used in most films screened in the cinema is 35 mm.

Depending on the budget, television can be shot on celluloid—for example, the first two seasons of *Buffy* were shot using 16 mm film stock and are discernibly grainier than the subsequent seasons,

> **Frame rate** refers to the number of frames screened per second to create the illusion of fluid motion. Frame rates differ for different media: film has a normal rate of 24 frames per second (fps), the Australian industry standard PAL video is 25 fps and the North American standard NTSC is 30 fps, whereas HDTV can range from 25–60 fps.
>
> **Film stock** refers to the physical properties of a strip of celluloid, including whether it is colour or black and white, its dimensions, and how sensitive to light it is.
>
> The **speed** of film refers to how the film stock responds when exposed to light: fast film is highly photosensitive and can be used when very little light is available, whereas slow film stocks are more suitable for bright conditions.
>
> The **gauge** of film stock refers to the width of the film strip in millimetres, which affects the definition and quality of the image. Video tape also comes in different gauges, but in addition the video image itself is made up of hundreds of horizontal lines of picture information which also affects the perceived quality of the image when it is screened.

which used 35 mm. Television programs can also be taped on analogue or digital video, or utilise high-definition digital production and transmission, as is the case with *Alias*. Differences in film gauges and grains are in some ways comparable to differences in image resolution in video and in digital photography.

The difference between the image quality and resolution of regular digital video footage and high-definition digital video can be seen in the stills from *Wolf Creek* (see Figures 2.12 and 2.13), which was shot in high-definition video, then transferred to film. According to Scott Kirsner: 'Digital cinematography, during its formative years, had much in common with kryptonite: It was mysterious and dangerous' (2006: n.p.). But this has changed since talented directors like David Fincher (*Zodiac*) and Michael Mann (*Collateral*), and cinematographers like Dion Beebe, have produced excellent features, defining digital as the way of the future in both film and television.

Whatever recording medium is used, **aspect ratio** is important, as it determines the shape of the image. When television was introduced, it adopted the same standard aspect ratio then used by feature films: a squarish frame about four units long by three units high. The adoption of wider screens for film was an attempt to claw back some of the audience share lost to television by enhancing the grandeur and scale of the cinematic viewing experience. *Kill Bill Vol. 2* alters

Figure 2.12 High-definition video still from *Wolf Creek*

Figure 2.13 MiniDV still from *Wolf Creek* DVD special features

Aspect ratio is the width-to-height ratio of a screen which affects image framing, size and scope. Television and video is typically 1.33:1, which is modelled on the 'academy ratio' of 1.37:1 that was standard in feature films when television was introduced. The contemporary widescreen standard is 1.85:1 for cinema and 1.77:1 for HDTV. Cinerama format and CinemaScope's anamorphic widescreen format has an ultra-wide aspect ratio of 2.35:1.

aspect ratio to give a sense of claustrophobia when Budd buries Beatrix alive and we see her trapped inside a coffin (see Figure 2.14).

Aspect ratio determines whether the image is boxy like an old television, or elongated and rectangular like a cinema screen. The shape of the screen in turn determines how cinematographers frame an image. We mentioned above that the television screen is well suited to display close-ups, but this is changing with the increasing convergence of film and television technologies. The wide screen ratio used in HDTV is very close to that used for cinematic releases. This widescreen aspect ratio saves set-up time and coverage, as two or three actors can be filmed conversing together in one shot. Digital technologies have not yet fully become the industry standard, and convergence between film and television is incomplete, so processes like telecine and pan and scan have been developed to translate between different frame rates and aspect ratios, as discussed in the Introduction.

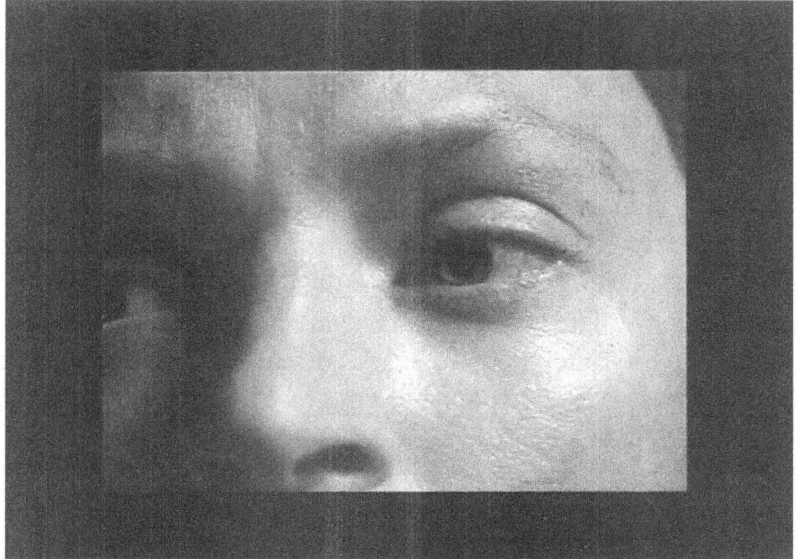

Figure 2.14 Beatrix's face is in academy aspect ratio when she is trapped inside a coffin in *Kill Bill Vol 2*. The black area of the surrounding frame shows the widescreen format characterising the rest of the film, showing the difference in film and television framing

CONCLUSION

In summary, the key things to know about cinematography in order to analyse a screen text are the terms describing the ways in which camera position and movement, lens choice and focus affect what elements of the image are included and emphasised in the frame, and how the viewer experiences or interprets the image. It is also important to think critically and curiously about differences in screen technologies and the increasing convergence of film and television, considering what informs choices about the recording medium, format and aspect ratio, and how such factors affect the picture and the viewing experience. Because of format differences, shooting schedules, budgets and the constraints of the studio environment, most contemporary television has a more limited visual style with tighter, less mobile framing than feature films. This varies across genres and content providers, with high-budget subscription television drama like Showtime's *Dexter* being shot in a sophisticated 'cinematic' style, and local broadcast news and reality television sticking to normal lenses, neutral camera angles, and simple, unobtrusive mobile framing like pans and zooms.

Cinematography does not, and cannot, exist in isolation from other aspects of the production and reception of screen texts. As cinematography's relationship to narrative strategies such as point of view is intimately connected with the design of the story and the *mise en scène*, and interlinked with the way filmmakers plan to edit a scene, manipulate the image in post-production, and transmit it to the audience, it is crucial to analyse camera work in conjunction with other aspects of the visual image and the overall communication of information about story and character. Also, consider how technical and stylistic choices can change and challenge conventions and norms as boldly as content that features rebellious characters, taboo subject matter or radical narrative structures.

KEY SKILLS

Having read this chapter, you should now be able to:

- describe the cinematography in a short sequence from any screen text, labelling shot scale, camera angle, camera movement and focus;
- explain differences in composition and impact between images filmed from high and low camera positions, and images with deep or shallow focus;
- define the following terms, noting what effect each camera technique has and when it might be used: panning, tilting, craning, zooming, tracking, handheld, steadicam;
- give examples of shots using a wide-angle lens and a telephoto lens, explaining how to tell the difference;
- think critically about differences between film and television cinematography, stating whether you think the two media will experience increasing convergence, or will diverge for the purpose of product differentiation when television becomes fully digital;

CINEMATOGRAPHY

- apply what you have learned by analysing five shots from the opening sequence of a screen text, noting the effect each aspect of cinematography has on the audience, and the meaning or importance it gives plot or character.

3
soundscapes:
The invisible magic of sound

Sound above 150 decibels packs enough punch to rupture an eardrum and cause permanent hearing damage, and a decent stereo cranked right up can exert enough pressure to trigger the car alarms on neighbouring vehicles. On a more insidious level, when the Nazgul's scream travels through the surround sound system in *Lord of the Rings*, it slithers over our flesh like an icy draft, creeping up from behind and sidling alongside until the presence of evil is palpable all around. As Karen Lury writes in *Interpreting Television*, 'sound's encroaching, overwhelming, even terrifying properties may well be related to the fact that we do not have "earlids" in the same way that we have "eyelids"' (2005: 58). Although we cannot see it, and are rarely as attentive to it as to movement and image, these examples show that sound has both powerful and subtle properties, and a physical dynamism that reaches right through the screen to touch the audience. In what follows we probe the technical secrets of sound's tactile force, and investigate the different dimensions in which it conveys meaning and sensation by working through the various types and properties of screen sound.

In this chapter, we consider the main varieties of screen sound: ambience, music, dialogue and noise (sound effects). While it is useful to distinguish between different types of sound for the purpose of clarification and analysis, the aim is not to listen to a film or television text and label everything you hear. Some sounds can be ambiguous or can belong to more than one category. We will explore the interplay of different forms of screen sound and their effects on the audience. For instance, sound can establish atmosphere and location, situate us within the story world, extend screen space, cue audience expectations, aid interpretation of the narrative, elicit visceral reactions, create suspense and provoke emotional responses.

Our main objective in this chapter is to help you fine-tune your skills in analysis by working through cinematic and televisual examples in order to tease out the varied functions of the soundscape. We use the term 'audience members' instead of referring to 'spectators' or 'viewers' because even though much film and television theory and analysis is geared to an appreciation of the moving image, it is important to remember that we listen to as well as watch screen texts. Most of the terms and techniques introduced in this chapter relate to both film and television, and can be used to analyse both kinds of screen texts—though there are important differences between the two media. In the course of this chapter we will distinguish between television sound and the use of sound in the cinema, and evaluate how technological developments are changing the ways in which sound designers manipulate sound and use effects to influence audience perceptions and responses to the narrative.

DISTINCTIONS BETWEEN FILM AND TELEVISION SOUND

Because sound was introduced many years after film had already established itself in popular culture, people tend to think of it primarily as a visual medium. The role of sound has often been considered secondary to the role of the image, or it has been overlooked entirely. It is only recently that sound has begun to receive critical attention, which is strange because motion pictures were never truly silent. Before **synchronous sound** was introduced in 1926, enabling the production of 'talking pictures' with integrated dialogue and music, film screenings would typically feature live musical accompaniment such as an organ playing along, speeding up the tempo at climactic moments and moving to a slower, minor key for sad scenes. The musical *Singin' in the Rain*, directed by Stanley Donen and Gene Kelly in 1952, is set at the time of the first 'talkies'. It offers a humourous take on the introduction of sound, and shows how this technical development led to the birth of new genres and new stars. *Singin' in the Rain* also shows how the camera was confined to a soundproof booth in the early days of sound, to avoid recording the noisy whirring of the camera along with the dialogue. Since Dolby stereo and surround sound emerged in 1974, sound has become increasingly sophisticated, situating audiences in a multi-dimensional soundscape. Unlike film, which initially used intertitles and mime to convey meaning, television piggybacked on the popularity of both radio and cinema, and was introduced in the 1950s with synchronised sound. As a consequence, sound has been central to television content.

> **Synchronous sound** is sound recorded simultaneously with the image.

In *Film Sound: Theory and Practice* (1985), Mary Ann Doane specifies three aspects of the spatial experience of film sound: sounds occurring anywhere in the space of the story world (including off-screen sound); sound emanating from sources that are framed on screen; and the acoustical space of the cinema or venue in which the film is screened. Here, one of the significant differences between film sound and television sound becomes evident: unless audience members are fortunate enough to have a lavish home entertainment system with surround-sound, the experience of televised sound will be impoverished by comparison with film sound. This is also true for films which are watched at home on DVD or video. Even though the recorded soundtrack on a DVD may be much more sophisticated than the soundtrack for television, most domestic speakers and amplifiers—not to mention ordinary television sets—lack the richness of cinema sound. By contrast with film, the soundscapes of television are therefore brasher, and lacking in layers, dimensionality or texture. This is because of the different conditions of production and reception, as well as the different technologies used in each medium. For instance, feature films have a larger budget for sound and a less hectic production schedule, and they are screened in a quiet cinema auditorium. When viewing television, the bustle of the domestic environment competes with screen sound as we contend with constant background noises like the air conditioner, the washing machine and our housemates.

Whatever television may lack in terms of layers of subtle sound, it makes up for with speech. Television is known as a 'dialogue-driven' medium, as it constantly features the use of dialogue and voiceover narration by fictional characters, commentators, announcers and advertisers. Television dialogue is often delivered using a more personalised, familiar mode of address than film dialogue. In addition to showing characters' conversations, prime-time dramas and comedies like *Grey's Anatomy*, *Desperate Housewives* and *My Name is Earl* open and close each episode with **voiceover narration** which gives the illusion that the protagonists are confiding in the audience as they would their dearest friend, or their private journal. Reality shows like *Big Brother* take this one step further, using the 'diary room' to stage confessional chats with Big Brother and, implicitly, the audience. News anchors and television presenters even go so far as to wish the audience goodnight and urge us to drive safely. In this manner, television recognises that it is situated in people's homes and uses sound to evoke an inclusive, familiar relationship with the audience rather than attempting to recreate the sonic experience of screen characters, or to inflect listener identification and influence emotional responsiveness.

Voiceover narration is speech that does not originate from a visible source on screen, and that cannot be heard by other screen characters. It is dialogue to which only the audience is privy, and which often seems to emanate from an unseen narrator or from a protagonist's thoughts.

Television caters to the domestic listening environment not only by privileging dialogue and minimising other sounds, but also by using bold cues like the laugh track in sit-coms to make the domestic audience laugh along with the 'studio audience'. As Lury writes, 'the laugh track is one of television's most explicit attempts to promote the illusion of sociability, to suggest that television viewing is a social rather than an individual encounter' (2005: 83). Interestingly, the presence of the sound of the audience is peculiar to television. Film creates the illusion that we are invisible observers *inside* the story world along with the screen characters, yet it rarely acknowledges that an off-screen audience exists. On television, the sound of the studio audience both prompts and confirms the responses of audience members at home, indicating that audience sounds are an important part of perpetuating television's aura of familiarity and camaraderie. Yet, as Lury's work indicates, although we hear and respond to the sound of the audience, we rarely actively listen to it, nor do we interpret it as contributing to the meaning of the television text (2005: 83).

Even though we may not have 'earlids', the above examples illustrate that audiences are accustomed to tuning out competing sounds in the domestic environment as well as tuning out aspects of television sound, so that we can focus on what we really *want* to hear. For this reason, television producers tend to amplify the sounds to which *they* want us to listen. For example, you may have noticed that the volume, pitch and pace of sound increases during advertisements. Whereas filmmakers want audiences to listen to sounds that guide interpretation of the narrative, television producers often also want us to listen to sounds that guide us to be good consumers. Indeed, a large component of the television soundscape serves commercial purposes and functions as a branding mechanism. Most broadcasters use sonic 'channel idents'—that is, short musical phrases that identify or brand the channel and let viewers know what station they are watching, even if they can't see the logo in the corner of the screen (Lury 2005: 75). Sound also works in a similar way to brand individual programs and advertisements—consider the 'fanfare' music used to signal the start of the news report.

The repetition of musical interludes in television is a common way of establishing the acoustic brand identity of particular programs (Lury 2005: 74–5). For instance, *Prison Break* combines a short phrase of music just three notes long accompanied by an accelerated burst of images when the show returns after a commercial break. This creates a signature rhythm, conveys the experience of being 'on the run,' and tunes the audience back in to the tense emotional charge of the show, thereby reinforcing its brand identity and luring our attention back to the screen for the next segment of the narrative.

In general, music is often used for commercial purposes on television. Some series encourage the consumption of tie-in merchandise such as their own soundtracks—for example, Ryan and Marissa's song 'Forever Young' became a hit single due to *The OC's* promotional efforts, and the obtrusive music underscoring *Grey's Anatomy* led to Snow Patrol becoming known as 'that *Grey's* band' after the Season Two finale aired complete with its own music video. Although feature films market their soundtracks too, the pervasive reliance on theme songs, jingles and musical transitions for branding purposes, as well as to signal scene changes or programming shifts, is derived from radio—a medium with which television has strong historical connections.

Television theorist Patricia Holland points out that 'the flow of sound holds television programs together' (1997: 79). The acoustic presence of familiar jingles, dialogue and voiceover lends a sense of continuity to what is often a disrupted viewing experience. Even when we are distracted from the television screen, it is still easy to recognise what is on and follow the storyline. In these ways, the purposes and technologies of television sound differ from those of cinema sound and must be taken into account when analysing screen sound.

Diegetic and non-diegetic sound

It is helpful from the outset to make a broad distinction between two types of sound: **diegetic** and **non-diegetic**. Diegetic sound refers to all kinds of sounds that are made by a physical source inside the story world, and that are audible to characters, including dialogue, background noises like traffic or wind, and sound effects like footsteps, doors creaking and dogs barking. Other than the use of sound to brand and punctuate different types of programming, television sound overwhelmingly comprises simple diegetic noises, designed not to detract attention from the dialogue. The term non-diegetic (also termed extra-diegetic sound, or sound over) means that the sound is heard 'over' the images on screen rather than seeming to come 'from' the images: it is produced by a source outside the story world. The characters can't hear non-diegetic sounds such as mood music or voiceover commentary spoken by an external narrator; hence voiceover is usually referred to as non-diegetic. In some screen texts, this distinction is blurred, as in the conversations between Tyler Durden and 'Jack', the protagonists in *Fight Club*. On first screening, we

Diegetic sound emanates from the diegesis, which means that its source is in the story world and it is audible to screen characters.

Non-diegetic sound such as the musical score emanates from an unspecified source external to the world of the screen narrative and cannot be heard by screen characters.

take the dialogue to be diegetic; however, by the end of the film we realise that Durden is a voice inside 'Jack's' mind, and other characters in the story world would not actually be able to hear him speak as a separate entity. A similar blurring of the boundaries is evident in the ironic inner musings of *Dexter*, television's favourite serial killer, whose private thoughts often bleed seamlessly into his conversations. This necessitates a further distinction between the external diegetic sounds that all characters can hear, and internal diegetic sound of which only one character is aware. Internal diegetic sound can best be described as **subjective sound**, and it refers to sounds accompanying dreams, memories, hallucinations and fantasies that a screen character experiences in flashbacks and so forth.

> **Subjective sound**, also known as internal diegetic sound, refers to sounds that are heard in a screen character's inner world, such as audible thoughts, memories, dreams and imaginings.

AMBIENCE

Ambient sound (also called 'atmos' or the 'buzz track') is what a space sounds like when it is silent. An empty room with a slate floor in the country sounds different from a small, cosy, carpeted urban apartment, and sound travels differently in a room with people and furniture in it than it does in an empty space. A good sound recordist will always ask everyone to hold their positions and observe a moment's silence while she records ambient sound. This track will then be used to create the sense of space and the general atmosphere behind all of the other sounds and actions in the scene. Without the ambient soundtrack, the diegetic dialogue and noise will sound unnatural, as it does for low-budget melodrama shot in a studio. Generally, even if a scene is shot in a studio, the sound technician will capture atmospheric background sounds to situate the space in a rural or urban environment, or wherever it is meant to be located in the narrative. In this way, ambient sound gives a naturalistic feel to a scene, it helps to establish the 'reality' of the scene, irrespective of where it is actually shot.

> **Ambient sound** or atmos (atmospheric sound) is also known as the 'buzz track' and it consists of sound that naturally occurs in the environment of a scene or the location in which the scene is meant to be set.

MUSIC

The musical score often functions to unify a film or television narrative in terms of theme, character or other motifs. Music can be either diegetic or non-diegetic. The musical score is from the non-diegetic soundtrack: only the audience can hear the music. Diegetic music, on the other hand, comes from inside the story world, and includes music that is playing on the radio or in a club, or performed by characters playing an instrument on screen. Such diegetic music is often called **source music**.

> **Source music** is diegetic background music that comes from tangible sources in the story world, such as radios, or songs that are performed by musicians on screen.

There is an extensive body of literature about film music, much of which also applies to television. Key texts include *Overtones and Undertones* (Brown 1994), *Film Music* (Donnelly 2001), *Movie Music* (Dickinson 2003), *Unheard Melodies* (Gorbman 1987) and *Film Music: A Neglected Art* (Prendergast 1992). Here we focus on two important functions of the musical score in film and television: the way music and sound design can facilitate identification with characters by articulating their subjective experience; and eliciting an emotional reaction from listeners. Music is a powerful way of articulating emotion, and as such it can encourage audience members to engage with the affective experiences of screen characters. For example, music literally functions as the emotional voice of Ada, the mute heroine in Jane Campion's film *The Piano*. In *Hearing Film* (2001), Anahid Kassabian argues that different types of music facilitate identification with screen characters in various ways: the **underscore**, or composed score (usually music without vocals created especially for the film or television series), which prompts *assimilating identifications*; and the **compiled score** (usually consisting of familiar songs already circulating in popular culture), which prompts *affiliating identifications*. The term 'assimilation' implies that a person is immersed in something that tends to overwhelm their individuality. In the case of film and television, music can work as a mechanism to facilitate identification with protagonists via integration or 'assimilation' with the subject positions offered in the story world. In other words, artfully composed music can influence or even manipulate us to feel caught up in the

> The **underscore** is non-diegetic music, usually composed specifically for the production in order to enhance the emotional impact or support the action in a scene.
>
> The **compiled score** is a compilation of popular music that features on a movie soundtrack. Such music can consist of diegetic and non-diegetic songs that have usually had quite a bit of radio exposure independently of the film.

experience of Calamity Jane in the TV series *Deadwood*, even though the identity position of an androgynous, sharp-shooting, tough-talking cowgirl in the American West in the 1890s is alien to contemporary audiences. Music thus helps auditors to construct a relationship with unfamiliar situations and characters.

Kassabian points out that, in the case of the compiled score, 'perceivers bring external associations with the songs into their engagements with the film' or television narrative (2001:3), which means that they might have personal connections or 'affiliations' with songs they have heard before, perhaps in romantic or sad contexts, or perhaps through the connotations of familiar lyrics and favourite musicians. 'Songs', Kassabian says 'choreograph good and bad times, serving as cues for memories of specific times of your life' (2001: 79). Kassabian's description of music's 'affiliating' properties can be understood as a reference to its intertextual dimensions. For instance, audience members who were in high school in the late 1980s may find themselves readily able to identify with the characters in *Donnie Darko* (made in 2002, but set in the '80s) because the compiled score triggers memories of the Joy Division posters that once adorned our bedroom walls, the songs playing at our first unsupervised parties, and our own experiences as awkward adolescents. The music can therefore function to reconnect adult audience members with their adolescence, and hence with the teenage characters in the narrative. For younger audience members, *Donnie Darko*'s soundtrack might have associations with '80s retro parties, thereby supporting the 'time-travelling' themes of the film itself. Some films like *High Fidelity* and television texts such as *Grey's Anatomy* rely heavily on compiled scores, and give music a central role in the narrative. Other television game shows such as *Don't Forget the Lyrics* test contestants' abilities to recall lines of dialogue from popular songs throughout the ages, capitalising on the power of the music to take the audience on a trip down memory lane and participate in the competition as they watch, listen and feel the urge to sing along. In these ways, film and television music plays a prominent role in situating texts historically as well as facilitating identification and encouraging participation or consumption. Kassabian suggests that composed music is often manipulative, intended to control audience identification and assimilate us into the narrative in specific ways, whereas the compiled score opens on to a wider range of affiliations and identifications due to the personal connections it makes (2001: 3).

Music can also be used to support characterisation and establish a sense of atmosphere and locale by giving the audience cues about place, culture, subculture, class and value systems. For instance, the compiled score in the Academy Award-winning South African film *Tsotsi*, directed by Gavin Hood in 2005, includes *kwaito* music, hip-hop and traditional tribal rhythms that establish an authentic local feel and a strong connection to black and coloured working-class cultures and musical traditions. This is particularly important as hip-hop lyrics have been used to express perspectives about race relations, gender dynamics and HIV/AIDS (Haupt 2001). Michael O'Shaughnessy (2004) points out that music can covertly communicate ideological positions and value systems, as when an orchestral European underscore pervades the Australian film *Walkabout*, taking precedence over the use of traditional Aboriginal instruments such as the didgeridoo and conveying the dominance of white culture.

In many narratives, characters are associated with a theme tune that communicates messages about their role and their personality. The TV series *Dirty Sexy Money* does this overtly as Nick's cell phone has a signature ring tone for each of his employers: 'Pretty Woman' plays when Karen Darling calls, 'Hallelujah' plays when Reverend Brian Darling phones, and so on. Higher pitched instruments like flutes may suggest that a character is elevated and refined, whereas the lower pitch of a saxophone is moody, sexy and dangerous. Kassabian even goes so far as to suggest that differences in musical **tempo**, **pitch** and genre are *gendered*—for example, the 'fallen woman' is often accompanied by jazz or blues saxophone music, whereas the 'virtuous woman' is associated with melodic flutes (2001:19). The quick tempo of the theme song of the TV series *Miami Vice* has more masculine associations: listeners who did not recognise the tune reported imagining 'aggression, speed and urban environments' when they heard the music (Kassabian 2001: 18–19).

The lyrics of music can also articulate the meaning of a scene, explaining what is taking place, such as when the

Tempo relates to the speed or slowness of sound or music: accelerated tempos can generate anxiety or adrenaline, whereas a slow tempo can be monotonous or relaxing.

Pitch refers to whether a sound is high or low.

Jane's Addiction song 'Been Caught Stealing' plays in the opening scene of the pilot episode of *My Name is Earl*. We hear the song as Earl tells us he will steal just about anything that isn't nailed down, while snatching a handful of kiddie CDs and an American flag from a car parked outside a convenience store. Music is often used quite simply in television, with many television genres using only the theme tune of the intro and outro, a short musical phrase for transitions, and only diegetic music (if any) within scenes. For instance, *Friends* has its familiar signature song 'I'll Be There for You' at the beginning of the program, and a particular refrain to cue scene changes, shifts in location, **temporal ellipsis** or the end of a commercial break.

Temporal ellipsis is when time passes in the story world that is not shown to elapse on screen.

Musicals have made a comeback recently with *Moulin Rouge*, *Sweeney Todd*, *Hairspray* and *Chicago* winning critical acclaim, and musical biopics like *Ray*, *8 Mile* and *Walk the Line* emerging as an increasingly popular variation. On television, music programs are perennially popular, ranging from MTV-style shows that function as extended advertisements for CDs and concerts through to talent quests like *Australian Idol*. Joss Whedon even wrote two musical episodes of *Buffy the Vampire Slayer*: 'Hush' and 'Once More with Feeling'. Musicals typically incorporate dance sequences in which diegetic music is used to articulate the central emotional thrust of the narrative. In the cult musical horror film *The Rocky Horror Picture Show*, the music catches the audience up in a spirit of participation in the narrative world that few other cinematic experiences can rival. More recently, films like *High Fidelity* and *Juno* have marketed their soundtracks aggressively for precisely this reason. A key point to remember is that we feel the rhythm of music in our bodies—music moves us not only by lifting our mood or bringing us down, but also by physically affecting us. For instance, at a loud concert bass notes reverberate in your thoracic cavity and you can literally feel the sound *doof doof doof doofing* in your body.

DIALOGUE

As noted above, dialogue is a core feature of virtually all film and television texts, but depending on the program or genre, television dialogue frequently has a more direct, explanatory, familiar mode of address than film dialogue. Television characters often tend to discuss their lives rather than enacting them. While a film character might communicate volumes with a meaningful glance, a character in a soap opera will spell out exactly what they feel in agonising detail and walk around wringing their hands while they do it. Television dialogue also tends to use 'dialogue hooks', whereby one character will pick up on what another person said and repeat key elements to recap the story, or use it as springboard to indicate where the next scene or episode is headed. In contrast with television, film tends to avoid articulating the meaning via dialogue alone, and does not use dialogue hooks as extensively to reinforce meaning or set up narrative transitions. There are also differences in the use of voiceover narration in each medium. On television, voiceover narration is often delivered in present tense as though the television screen provides a window into the lives of the characters unfolding in real time as we watch, whereas in feature films it is more often delivered in past tense, as part of a flashback that explains causal events and motivating factors that occurred earlier in the narrative (Lury 2005: 59–60).

The chatty, explanatory functions of speech, and the sense of uncontrived immediacy and presence that it can convey, mean that in some ways the introduction of sound to film inhibited the creativity of filmmakers in figuring out how to tell a story by using images, not words. Dialogue became the solution to explaining psychological motivation, creating a back-story and advancing the plot. But in other ways, sync sound added another dimension to cinema, enabling a greater degree of sophistication and complexity in the sorts of stories that could be told, and spawning the creation of several genres such as musicals and the witty word-play comedies of the 1940s. In addition, dialogue is important because it gives crucial clues about characterisation via accent, inflection, emphasis, tone and the connotations inherent in spoken words. Consider, for instance, the different ways that a single sentence is delivered by the felons in the lineup in Bryan Singer's film *The Usual Suspects*. Each character has a distinctly different way of saying 'Hand me the keys, you motherf***er.' From their speech, we infer that Keaton is of a higher class than Hockney, that McMannis is impulsive and aggressive, that Fenster's accent bespeaks his Latino origins and, in retrospect, that Verbal's sinister tone and the emphasis he places on the word 'me' are key signifiers of the power he holds and the pivotal role he plays in the narrative.

Personality traits and power relations between characters can be indicated not only in the way dialogue is spoken, but also the way in which it is shot and edited. Even though television typically uses slightly different conventions for shooting dialogue (often capturing dialogue in two shots, long takes or a multi-camera shoot rather than using a shot-reverse-shot pattern), some TV shows are as sophisticated as high-budget films. Action, fantasy, crime and science fiction programs typically liberate the camera and use more mobile framing and more sophisticated sound than shows like sit-coms.

Dialogue and power dynamics in *Silence of the Lambs*

During the course of Clarice Starling's first conversation with Hannibal Lecter in *Silence of the Lambs*, directed by Jonathan Demme in 1991, the audience gleans a lot of information about both characters. When analysing dialogue, consider how the power relations between characters are communicated by dialogue and by the way in which a conversation is filmed. For instance, Starling addresses Lecter as Doctor. He speaks French, talks easily about Europe, and humiliates Starling by describing her accent as 'one step away from poor white trash'—all of these dialogue clues are signifiers of class and power. As you analyse the dialogue extract transcribed below, ask who dominates the frame, and when the balance of power alters. Shot scale, camera angle and point of view are important cues that work in conjunction with the tone, content, emphasis, accent and inflection of speech to help to situate the audience inside screen space and align us with the experience of a particular character. Each scene has a dramatic narrative structure within which the audience is positioned and led towards the emotive climax. In the transcribed dialogue sequence, note that the changes in shot scale and angle correspond directly with the turning points, obstacles and climaxes in the scene itself.

As the scene begins, we are aligned with Starling's experience, following her sound perspective and her optical point of view as she passes by the other inmates and walks towards Lecter. Initially, Lecter looms larger in the frame, filmed in medium close-up while Starling

Image	Shot Description	Vocals
	1. Over-the-shoulder shot. Back of Starling's head in foreground, Lecter framed in MCU. Hard top and side lighting.	*Lecter:* May I see your credentials?
	2. Over-the-shoulder shot. Back of Lecter's head out of focus in foreground. Starling removes and extends badge (MS softer light).	*Starling:* Certainly. *Lecter:* Closer please.
	3. CU Lecter, looking directly at Starling.	*Lecter:* Closer (singsong voice).
	4. CU Starling, moves forward through shadow.	
	5. Lecter approaches the glass, moving into Choker CU.	
	6. Choker CU, Starling returns his stare.	
	7. Choker CU, Lecter, dropping his eyes to her badge.	*Lecter:* That expires in one week. (Winks) You're not *real* FBI, are you?
	8. Over Lecter's shoulder, Starling in CU	*Starling:* I'm still in training at the academy.
	9. Over Starling's shoulder, Lecter framed in CU.	*Lecter* (astonished): Jack Crawford sent a trainee to me?
	10. Over Lecter's shoulder, Starling in CU.	*Starling:* Yes sir, I'm a student. I'm here to learn from you. Maybe you can decide for yourself whether or not I'm qualified to do that.
	11. Over Starling's shoulder, Lecter framed in CU.	*Lecter:* Hmmm. That is rather slippery of you Agent Starling.
	12. Over Lecter's shoulder, Starling silently returns his gaze, framed in CU.	

	13. Over Starling's shoulder, Lecter framed in CU.	*Lecter:* Sit, please.
	14. Over Lecter's shoulder, Starling in MS. As Starling sits camera tilts down to a high angle, from Lecter's POV.	
	15. Choker CU of Lecter, direct address to camera.	*Lecter:* Now then, tell me. What did Miggs say to you? Multiple Miggs in the next cell. He hissed at you. What did he say?

Figure 3.1 Dialogue from *Silence of the Lambs*: Clarice Starling meets Hannibal Lecter

is framed in a mid-shot for shot two. Shots three to seven are tightly framed to reflect increased physical proximity as she accedes to his request to move closer. Although the characters remain in much the same physical position for the remainder of the scene, changes in shot scale express the emotional drama of the conversation and depict varying degrees of insight, absorption and dominance. For instance, shot seven is the point at which Lecter has successfully manipulated Starling into breaking the prohibition and approaching the glass, and it is also the moment that he scores his first point in dialogue: 'You're not *real* FBI'. He belittles her by placing emphasis on the word 'real' to stress her lack of professional experience and using the diminutive term 'trainee' in contrast with the more active connotations of 'in training'. His verbal dominance is mirrored in the cinematography, which makes Starling appear smaller than Lecter by framing her in a mid-shot (shot 8) while he is filmed very close up (shot 7). Shot scale signifies that he has more importance or more power at that point in the conversation, and the tight framing connotes forced intimacy or intimidation. Starling and Lecter are not actually that close in physical space: a telephoto lens has been used. The direct address to camera (shot 15, see Figure 3.2) puts the spectators directly in the line of fire, in Starling's position. This feels menacing, especially as she has been warned not to approach the glass. The closest shot (15) occurs when Lecter uses dialogue to dominate Starling and invade her most private space, humiliating her by making her repeat Miggs' crude remark about her personal odour. The high angle in shot 14 which looks down

Figure 3.2 Hanibal Lecter in *Silence of the Lambs*. Direct address to camera; hard top light casts a shadow obscuring eyes.

on Starling, making her appear belittled, is motivated by her being seated, but it also occurs at a point in the narrative when Lecter literally has 'the upper hand' and she feels diminished and degraded. Analysis of this sequence demonstrates how crucial dialogue is, and how important it is to consider sound in conjunction with content, characterisation, cinematography and other formal elements.

SOUND EFFECTS

Usually the noises or **sound effects** in a screen text function to reinforce the image because they correspond to elements in the *mise en scène* and help to make the story world seem real. For example, if we see a person being kicked by a kung-fu master on screen, we need to hear the whoosh of the swift movement and the thwack of impact to believe the fight is real. The term **fidelity** describes the degree to which sound coincides, or is incongruous, with the image. High-fidelity sound recordings match the source of the sound in the real world almost perfectly, with no audible distor-

> **Sound effects** refer to noise other than dialogue or music. Sound effects like footsteps and background traffic noise typically enhance realism by focusing attention, establishing location, developing atmosphere, and so forth.
>
> **Fidelity** is to sound what verisimilitude is to image: the term refers to the degree of realism or similarity that a recorded sound has when compared with its source.

tion, decay or manipulation. Low-fidelity sound is not faithful to its source: the images on screen do not match the accompanying sounds. For instance, the opening sequence of the film *Memento* is played in reverse motion with a murder 'un-happening' before our eyes to illustrate the short-term memory loss of the protagonist, Leonard (played by Guy Pearce). We hear the sound of the blood slurping back into the murder victim's wound when the scene plays in reverse. In actuality, there would have been no audible sound of blood seeping from Teddy's wound to record in the first place. Similar instances of low-fidelity sound are found throughout *Requiem for a Dream*. For example, when the pupil of an eye dilates, it does not make a rushing noise; the sound effect has been added to communicate the feeling of the sudden surge of drugs through the bloodstream.

Sound does not always reinforce the image. Sometimes we experience a disjunction between the signifier and signified as our expectations about the relationship between sound and image are actively undermined. For example, when Buffy's mother dies in the TV series *Buffy the Vampire Slayer*, the dialogue is dubbed out of sync, not matching what the actor's lips appear to be saying. Buffy asks the doctor whether her mother's death was quick and painless, and when his lips move in response the signifiers we see on screen (his reassuring, sympathetic body language and compassionate expression) suggest that this was indeed the case. However, what we hear (the signified meaning attached to the words he utters) is this: 'No, I just said that to make you feel better.' This could be interpreted as an instance of subjective sound, the sound that Buffy hears in her imagination. However, since that doesn't fit the narrative context (Buffy is at her most vulnerable and least cynical in this episode), we can also interpret the use of sound as evidence that the show's creator, Joss Whedon, is toying with the audience. The disjunctive sound undercutting the image reminds us that we are watching a fiction and it breaks the emotional grip of the scene, saving it from teetering over into melodrama.

Editing is extremely important to the relationship between sound and image in both film and television. Scott Powell has claimed that 'marginal' or mediocre images 'can really come to life when sound effects such as gunfire make you feel as though you are really there, caught up in the action' (2007: n.p.). Powell illustrates how 'creative sound work can really change the meaning and feel of a scene' (2007: n.p.) by laying a fart track over a scene in which a character in the TV series *24* is critically wounded, making his grimaces of pain read as flatulence.

Another important function of the soundscape is that it directs attention. Sound can be used to focus the audience's attention on the important action in a scene. In crowd scenes at sports stadia or in nightclubs, an omni-directional microphone would pick up the background noise just as much as the dialogue of the central characters, so it would be hard for the audience to hear the conversation. Such a situation calls for a uni-directional microphone (such as a shotgun microphone that only picks up sound from the direction in which it is pointed). Additionally, the extras would mime talking or cheering while the dialogue was being recorded, or the actors would repeat their lines in the studio using looping or automated dialogue replacement (ADR) to dub them in during post-production. Either way, the crowd noise is recorded on a separate track so that it can be layered behind the dialogue and faded out when the key characters exchange important information. The background noise in a scene will often become less audible when the audience needs to focus attention on lines of dialogue. This kind of sound fade can be termed **selective diegetic drop-out**. Unlike the human ear, microphones can't sort and filter noise, automatically screening out insignificant sounds. The presence of a human voice overrides other sounds—a perceptive quality that directors replicate with selective diegetic drop-out to simulate the movement of attention as we tune in to dialogue and screen out background noise from the environment.

> **Selective diegetic drop-out** is a technique whereby one element of the diegetic soundtrack, such as background noise, is faded out after the scene is set in order to direct attention to dialogue or other important elements.

Sound effects can also be used to cue the audience's response. For example, many television sit-coms such as *Friends* use a laugh track to prompt affective mimicry in the audience. The laugh track cues the domestic audience to laugh along with the 'studio audience'. Similarly in television game shows, whenever a contestant gives a wrong answer the disappointment shared by the contestant, the studio audience and the home viewer is cued by the low, blaring tone of a buzzer.

The Coen brothers' 2008 Academy award winning film *No Country for Old Men* has sparse dialogue and eschews non-diegetic music. It relies almost exclusively on sound effects like wind whistling, footsteps approaching and the sound of a gun being cocked to powerfully evoke atmosphere and emotion.

Sound speed, space and physicality

There are many ways in which sound establishes spatial relations and lends a sense of physicality and dimensionality to the flat screen, extending the world of the film beyond the borders of the frame and situating the audience inside screen space. Film director Philip Noyce says that up until the 1970s, when Dolby stereo sound was introduced: 'Everything came from the centre, behind the screen, and you changed audience perceptions by altering the volume or by using bass, treble and reverb' (Noyce 2001: 20). Loudness is still used to indicate the magnitude of a sound's source (a huge explosion or an insignificant one), and its proximity (near, or far away). With contemporary sound systems, off-screen sound can also seem to come from behind or in front of the screen, or from the top, bottom, left or right, thereby encouraging the audience to believe that there is a world beyond the frame that we cannot see. This enhances credibility, as well as creating a three-dimensional effect that situates the audience in the midst of the action. *Kill Bill, Vol. 1* uses surround sound in this way: when a mosquito circumnavigates the hospital room in which the Bride lies comatose, the high, whining *buzzzzzzzzz* moves from speaker to speaker, giving audiences the impression the mosquito is flying around the cinema.

Using sonic space to very different effect, Martin Scorsese harnesses music in *Bringing Out the Dead* to draw the audience into the frenzied adrenaline surges of the hero, Nick Cage, who plays a strung-out ambulance driver. A sense of covering great distances at high speed is conveyed by the rushing of air, the squealing of tyres and the warping of sound that happens when the speeding ambulance approaches then recedes into the distance. (Because of the Doppler effect, when the siren is closer it sounds higher pitched than when it moves away.)

Stanley Kubrick's *2001: A Space Odyssey* manipulates the speed of sound to produce the effect of dehumanisation and death. As

HAL, the sadistic computer controlling the spaceship, malfunctions and 'dies', it sings a song called 'Daisy' as its voice is played at slower and slower speeds, gradually sounding lower and more moronic. Conversely, speeding up the rate at which dialogue is played can make an actor sound like a chipmunk on amphetamines because it also distorts the pitch, making it higher and more childlike.

Alison Walker analyses how sound articulates space, physicality and feeling, creating an other-worldly dimension inhabited by the Ring Wraiths in *Lord of the Rings*. The 'in-between' (neither living nor dead) existence of the Ring Wraiths is articulated via the 'sliding movement of sound through the cinema' and the use of moving sound channels to suggest a presence that is not fixed in space (2004: 90). The surround-sound speakers are crucial to the evocation of a sense that the Wraiths are everywhere and nowhere, and when the Wraith is searching for Frodo, 'the atmos fades out to be replaced by a slow, deep metallic pulsing. This aural shift represents Frodo moving into a zone where he struggles against the "pull" of the ring' (Walker 2004: 90).

Digital sound manipulation

Advances in sound technology mean that even low-budget productions are now able to manipulate the directionality, dimensionality and pitch of sound to condition audience responses in new ways, using sound to propel the narrative. Sound design often begins with **spotting** (annotating the script to highlight particular sound effects that will need to be recorded and places where music will be required) and devising a sonic atmosphere that is in tune with the narrative, the characterisation and the composed score. Sound designer Tim Prebble points out that, like the musical score, sound effects also have a certain pitch, and these two sound elements should ideally work in complementary ways. Despair, anxiety and elation translate into different sonic registers, and composers working on the musical score of the film will try to make the soundscape evoke the emotion and atmosphere of particular scenes in order to facilitate spectatorial identification and enhance the impact of the film.

> **Spotting** involves careful annotations on the film or television script to identify and place the sound effects and music that need to be recorded and added in post-production. For sound mixers and designers, spotting sheets serve a function similar to that of log sheets for an editor.

Discussing the New Zealand feature *Fracture*, Prebble writes of using software that enabled him to break the sound of a train shriek into its composite parts and recombine them (retaining the feel of the sound but uncoupling it from its referent, thereby generating an affective response rather than cognitive recognition—'oh, it's a train'). Prebble says: 'These train shrieks grew to reflect the protagonist's state of mind as his world began to close in on him . . . As these tones grew to become the strongest pitch-based elements I developed for the film, I was dumbstruck to discover during our first run through that they were again perfectly in key with the score' (2004: 76).

Sonic perspective

Subjective perspective in film and television is not limited to expressing a character's optical point of view. For instance, French director Gaspar Noe's rape revenge film *Irreversible* distorts sound and uses a pulsing frequency designed to nauseate audiences so they experience the characters' visceral reaction to events. Anna Hickey-Moody and Melissa Iocco discuss how sound recording technology is used to augment bodily noises such as chewing and slurping, pissing and breathing in order to cue disgust via enhanced sound perspective in Rolf de Heer's film *Bad Boy Bubby*: 'Crafting the listener's disgust becomes an art form. It is a practice mastered primarily through the use of binaural microphones, which work to increase audience identification, and, alternatively, to provoke a corporeal response' (2004: 78).

Binaural microphones in *Bad Boy Bubby* 'created an intense, claustrophobic soundscape where the listener is (literally) aurally positioned between Bubby's ears' (Hickey-Moody & Iocco 2004: 79). In this way, sound is clearly related to the experience of space: a microphone worn on the performer's left ear must play back through the speaker or sound channel by the listener's left side, otherwise it feels like the listener has his or her 'back to the actors or the dialogue' (Hickey-Moody & Iocco 2004: 81). Binaural technology captures particularly visceral, emotive sound: 'When Bubby fastens glad wrap around his skull, the viewer's aural hemisphere is drawn into the muffled, uncomfortable soundtrack of refracted breathing. The corporeal effect this sound creates is palpable. Indeed, if fear is a sound, it is the billowing, crackling, subterranean noises associated with being enfolded in glad wrap' (Hickey-Moody & Iocco 2004: 80).

Subsonics and synaesthesia

Director Phillip Noyce reminds us that sound is a sensation felt as a physical vibration. Our bodies respond even when we can't consciously identify the source or meaning of a noise because the sound mix includes **subsonic** sound that registers below human perception. Discussing his use of digital sound technology to generate virtually inaudible subsonic effects, Noyce argues that sound manipulation is moving into an era where the audience can be affected emotionally without being consciously aware of it because 'sound goes directly to the central nervous system. It doesn't need to be decoded' (Noyce 2001: 20). For example, Noyce uses a bass rumble to make the audience subconsciously uneasy:

> **Subsonics** are very low-pitched sounds that reverberate beneath the register that is consciously audible to human perception.

People get a disturbed feeling in their guts, they know something's up but they can't hear it. They just feel it. For music too, you now have a much more elaborate, dynamic range possible, and high-pitched notes can affect an audience in a very, very emotional way. (2001: 20)

Because touch and other senses necessarily play a part in audio-visual experience, our perception of cinema is inflected with a rich physicality. According to Laura Marks, the intersensory links in film, video and television can be termed **synaesthesia**, which is 'the perception of one sensation in terms of another, such as the ability to distinguish colors by feel' (2000: 213). Synaesthesia was a symptom experienced by a pilot who had the disorienting sense of 'seeing' vivid sound while in a flight simulator in season three of *House*.

In order to understand what synesthesia means kinesthetically, and to grasp how sound can communicate texture, listen attentively as someone runs their fingernails over the rough rasp of sandpaper, silken fabric or a classroom blackboard. It is likely that your body will *feel* the sound, that you will hear it not only with your ears but with your own fingertips. Marks writes that 'by appealing to one sense in order to represent the experience of another,' audiovisual images evoke associations with touch, taste and smell (2000: 222). For example, in Darren Aronofsky's mathematical

> **Synaesthesia** refers to the evocation of intersensory links, where one kind of sensory experience is perceived, expressed or translated in terms of another sensation.

thriller *Pi*, the protagonist suffers from severe migraines. Through the use of intense subjective sound, the film literally enables audiences to *hear* the pain he experiences. Pain itself is silent, yet migraines are often accompanied by photosensitivity and acute sensitivity to sound. The skull-splitting experience of a migraine is communicated by means of a dull, throbbing, pulsing *doight-doight-doight* noise that feels like blood pumping through constricted vessels. This noise is then punctuated by a searing, high-pitched electronic shriek that attacks with sonic ferocity equivalent to a dagger piercing an eyeball. As a result, audience members not only hear the protagonist's headache, but may develop one of their own. This experiential use of sound to generate an embodied, sensory response can be termed synaesthetic sound.

It is interesting to compare tactile aurality and synaesthesia with **timbre**. In *Audio in Media*, Stanley Alten describes timbre in the following way: 'Timbre is the characteristic tonal quality of a sound. It not only identifies a sound source—reedy, brassy, tympanic—but also sonic qualities such as rich, thin, edgy, or metallic' (1999: 179). Bordwell and Thompson explain that 'the harmonic components of sound give it a certain colour, or tone quality' and timbre is 'indispensable in describing the texture or "feel" of a sound' (2008: 267–8).

> **Timbre** is the tonal quality of a sound. It relates to the ways in which a sound resonates in space and is associated with a characteristic colour, texture or feel.

The soundscape of *Lost Highway*: Sound is half the picture

'Half the film is picture, the other half is sound. They've got to work together,' David Lynch states in an online interview titled 'About the Music of *Lost Highway*' (Lynch & Reznor 2005). Lynch is a sound virtuoso who is centrally involved in designing the soundscape and score of all his projects. Trent Reznor, of Nine Inch Nails fame, worked as the soundtrack producer of *Lost Highway* and is credited with designing 'various ominous drones' for the film. Reznor says Lynch works with sound in a very associative, imaginative way: 'He'd say: "I've got a chase scene, and I'm picturing insects swarming around." Then he'd scribble on pieces of paper and say: "This is what I want it to sound like"' (Lynch & Reznor 2005). Lynch often exaggerates conventional techniques and makes us notice them, thereby making them mean something else.

In the convoluted narrative of *Lost Highway*, the protagonist Fred Madison (Bill Pullman) mysteriously morphs into a younger man named Pete Dayton (Balthazar Getty) after his wife Renee is murdered. Subsequently, Pete—who seems to be haunted by memories of Fred's life—encounters a woman called Alice Wakefield, who is the spitting image of Renee (both played by Patricia Arquette).

This case study is restricted to one pivotal scene, although the soundtrack of the entire film is fascinating. The compiled score encompasses a wide sonic spectrum from the magnetic, mysterious quality of David Bowie's 'Funny How Secrets Travel' at the beginning and end of the film and Lou Reed's sensuous 'This Magic Moment', which plays when Alice and Pete first set eyes on each other, to the discordant industrial menace of Rammstein and Marilyn Manson as the film makes a nightmarish descent into pornography and murder. In fact Lynch harnesses musical terminology to describe the film itself as a 'psychogenic fugue' (Herzogenrath 1999). A fugue is a term for music that begins in one way, changes into something completely different, and finally returns to where it began. A psychogenic fugue is a psychological disorder that involves amnesia and the adoption of an alter ego with a completely new identity and life.

In the scene when the jazz musician Fred Madison first meets the ghoulish Mystery Man (Robert Blake) at a party, sound establishes space and time in the story world. Smooth jazz music defines the space as sophisticated and urban, and it locates us in the late twentieth century as effectively as an ABBA song would place us in the 1970s, or sitar music would locate us in India. The music playing at the party fades into the background after it has 'set the scene'. The selective diegetic drop-out functions to signify the importance of the meeting, to align the audience with Fred's experience, and to denaturalise cinematic conventions and render the soundscape uncanny. When Fred is talking to the Mystery Man, his attention is entirely absorbed in the conversation: his words dominate the soundtrack and his face invades the entire screen. In this sense, we could call what Fred is hearing 'subjective sound' because the other characters in the story world continue to hear the jazz music. This makes us wonder whether the conversation with the ghoulish figure only took place in Fred's mind. *Lost Highway* repeatedly uses dialogue and other aspects of sound to undermine trust in Fred, who openly states: 'I remember things the way I want to, not necessarily the way they happened.'

When Fred calls home and, impossibly, the Mystery Man answers, the Mystery Man's voice sounds different when it comes from the other end of the phone, from inside Fred's house. It has a tinny sound and added reverberation that locates its source in a place with different acoustics from the party. The ghoulish laughter also sounds disembodied and inhuman. The soundscape creates the sense of the supernatural; it makes us feel the creepy undercurrents of the scene. One final thing to notice about the sound in *Lost Highway* is the ominous drones filling the moments of dark screen time and space. Fred and Renee's house is quiet and empty, but it seems to be occupied by something sinister due to the ambient soundtrack and the ominous drones.

CONCLUSION

Most audience members get upset if the dialogue is indistinct, and some with an interest in music may remark on the score, but few people are aware of the dynamic range of functions and layers of screen sound. Now that you are familiar with the terminology and techniques of sound design, you are likely to tune in and notice more dimensions of the soundscape, its source, its texture and its purpose in both film and television. To summarise, the key elements to listen for include distinctions between sounds emanating from a source in the story world and those audible only to the audience or the subjective perception of one character; subtle and obtrusive uses of music to establish mood and emotion or brand identity; sound effects that seem laughable when you realise how unabashedly contrived they are; and the ways in which important lines of dialogue are often cleverly accompanied by strategic camerawork and the absence of competing sounds. This last point is crucial, because sound does not operate in isolation from other aspects of the production process. We have briefly explored the relationship between sound and cinematography here, and significant connections between sound and editing are taken up in Chapter 4 in relation to sonic transitions and rhythmic editing.

KEY SKILLS

Having read this chapter you should now be able to:

- distinguish between diegetic and non-diegetic sound;
- define and give examples of ambient sound, sound effects, timbre, tempo, pitch, fidelity, underscore, compiled score, source music, subjective sound, synaesthesia, subsonics and diegetic drop-out;
- compare and contrast the use of sound in film and television texts;
- apply your understanding by analysing the functions of dialogue, music, ambient sound and sound effects in a screen text;
- think critically about the manipulative and commercial functions of screen sound, particularly music.

4
at the edge of the cut:
Editing from continuity to montage

THE ROLE OF THE EDITOR

What is it that locks us into the hero's point of view, accelerates the pace and pushes us to the edge of our seats as the screen explodes in frenzied motion during the climax of an action film? What keeps the secrets on Wisteria Lane, makes the foot tap in time to a music video, and leaves us teetering between life and death in the operating theatre when *Grey's Anatomy* cuts to a commercial break? What aesthetic element is unique to film and television? The answer to all these questions is, of course, the art of **editing**.

Editing is an intensely creative process that requires an excellent sense of rhythm and pace, and the capacity to make ruthless decisions and be shamelessly manipulative. The edit suite is both a time machine and a space invader,

Editing is the final process of determining the order in which events unfold on the screen and what information is revealed to the audience. It involves decisions about what to include, what to discard, and how to join individual shots to create sequences, scenes, stories, affect and associations. It is also a process of structuring the text, usually using continuity conventions to enable the audience to navigate through the space of the story world and follow the temporal and causal sequence of events.

an instrument that allows instantaneous transportation from one moment or location to another with every single cut. The editor situates the audience in first one, then another, point of view, shifting perspective from hero to victim to villain. Perhaps most importantly, the editor drives the vehicle of the plot. The screenwriter creates a map of the terrain over which a story will travel and the director rides shotgun—giving directions—but in the final cut it is the editor who skids into a spin at turning points in the story, throws us into reverse with a flashback, and shifts up a gear, then floors the accelerator to make our hearts race through the major obstacles and suspenseful moments of a narrative. Editing also requires great modesty. Like the magicians in *The Prestige*, an editor's craft demands that most of their work remains invisible to the audience. This chapter trains you to watch closely, revealing hidden secrets of the post-production process, which is the last act of magic in every screen text.

Screen production has three stages: scriptwriting, casting, budgeting, location scouting, planning and rehearsing consitute pre-production; the actual shoot is production; and editing happens during the post-production phase. Post-production includes everything between the time the director yells 'that's a wrap!' on the last day of a shoot until the television program is ready to be broadcast or the film is ready for marketing, distribution and screening. While post-production often involves compositing, CGI and other elements, this chapter focuses on editing itself. The main functions of editing include selecting, trimming and arranging shots into sequences and scenes, thereby establishing associations and relationships between shots and determining the dynamics of a screen text's structure, space, pace, continuity, rhythm and point of view.

As Tarantino says on *Death Proof* DVD extras, 'The final draft of the script is actually the first cut of the movie and the final cut of the movie is the last draft of the script.' Editing is fundamental to screen narratives.

Coverage refers to the number of set-ups (various takes of each shot from different angles and distances, with static or moving camera) that are needed to cut the scene together effectively. Virtually all shoots require coverage of more than one shot scale and angle, and more than one take so the editor has adequate footage from which to choose.

Even though editing is one of the last things to happen, filmmakers need to plan for editing to ensure adequate **coverage** before they even begin shooting. During pre-production, a **shot list** is created by the director (often in conjunction with the cinematographer and the editor). The filmmakers work through the script, painstakingly mapping out what shots are needed for each scene, including establishing shots and different angles and camera movements. Since feature films may have over 3000 shots, many shots that are not indicated in the script need to be planned so the editor will have enough material to work with. Another aspect of pre-production that pertains to editing is the creation of a detailed storyboard visualising a sequence of shots pictorially (see Chapter 5).

The structure of this chapter loosely follows the process of editing itself, moving from the building blocks of narrative to refining the detail. Editing involves a number of phases, beginning with discarding unusable takes, importing usable footage into the edit suite and labelling every take of each shot (called logging and capturing the **rushes**). Typically, the editor then roughly blocks out individual scenes and the overall structure of the narrative according to the script in an assembly edit or a **rough cut**. In most contemporary editing programs, this is done by inserting thumbnail images of each shot into place on a filmstrip or timeline representing the video and audio tracks of the finished story. Usually the picture edit and dialogue are **cut** separately from the majority of the sound mix, as visual cutting points frequently differ from audio cutting points. Scott Powell, editor of the TV series *24*, first lays down what he terms a 'radio cut', including dialogue and temporary music, to establish the narrative thread and emotional tenor, then he 'paints the images over the top' to illustrate the words (Powell 2007). The soundtrack is later 'tuned' by the sound designer and composer, who rework and master those layers of sound. The story is often condensed and restructured as decisions about shot choices, transitions and ways of manipulating pacing and impact are made. Editors progressively refine the cut by

> A **shot list** is a detailed breakdown of the type and style of shots required to give adequate coverage of each scene. Prepared in the pre-production process, it lists every shot that is needed to cover the action in each scene of the script, often planning the order in which they will be shot.

> **Rushes**, also known as 'dailies', refer to the raw footage shot on set each day, before certain takes are discarded or selected and edited into scenes. For film, the rushes are the first prints made from the processed negatives. Video and digital video does not require processing, so the rushes can be viewed immediately.

> The **rough cut**, also termed the assembly edit, is like a first draft. It is an early phase of the editing process in which the scenes and narrative structure are roughly blocked out in the manner indicated in the script and shot list.

> The term **cut** is used in filmmaking to signify the end of a shot or a take (on set) or the edit point (in post-production), and it can also refer metonymically to a complete edited sequence or story (as in the 'director's cut'). Note that one shot or one take on set may actually be cut up into several different shots in the editing process.
>
> The **fine cut**, also termed the final cut, is the finished product of the last phase of editing when the text takes the form that audiences see and hear on screen.

trimming the in and out points of individual shots and working with the audio tracks, which appear as visible sound waves spiking up and down under the images on the timeline. This phase is time consuming: editing a television hour ideally takes one working week for narrative drama (over 40 hours, cutting about one minute of screen time per hour, as for film). In the process of creating the **fine cut** (the final cut), the sound mix and visual effects must be adjusted, the music is added, and text like titles and credits is added on a simultaneous video track. Colour grading, and inserts like television station logos or text banners, are also done in post-production.

Editing is becoming more rapid and sophisticated. David Bordwell's research indicates that, during the classical Hollywood studio era (up until the 1960s), the average feature film contained roughly 600 shots, cut about every 10 seconds, whereas contemporary movies have an average shot length of three to six seconds (2002a: 16–17). A particularly fast-paced feature like *Dark City* has an average shot length of 1.8 seconds and *Moulin Rouge* is blindingly fast, containing over 4000 shots (Bordwell 2000, 2002a). Music videos and commercials are cut faster still. In this sense, television editing has influenced film, as many directors like Spike Jonze, Michel Gondry, Guy Ritchie and David Fincher began their careers in advertising and music videos. The transition to editing on non-linear digital editing suites and shooting on high-definition digital video has contributed to 'intensified' editing.

Non-linear editing was introduced in the 1990s. The term refers to editing packages like Avid, Final Cut Pro and Adobe Premier that enable shots to be joined together, pulled apart and reordered into infinite combinations using a virtual filmstrip on a computer. This differs from the old-fashioned linear video editing technique where the exact sequence had to be planned in advance and recorded in order on the master tape, shot by shot. If an editor wanted to trim a scene or add a reaction shot to an early sequence, they would have to start over from that point as though altering the lower storey of a house of cards. By contrast with video, film editing has always been non-linear in the sense that it is a process of physically cutting and splicing strips of negatives. Though it was always possible to make new cuts and new joins in the film strip, now that the process is computerised, it is easier to experiment with different shot arrangements. Even film and television texts shot on celluloid are now edited digitally.

> **Non-linear editing** is the contemporary mode of editing digital video footage out of order on a computer, enabling the editor to change and recombine shots at any stage.

The move towards using high-definition digital video rather than analogue video tape or celluloid makes the post-production process faster, simpler and cheaper in both film and television. It avoids the time-consuming process of capturing and digitising the rushes, which means converting the raw film or video footage into digital form. It also gives editors more choices, because cinematographers can bump up the **shooting ratio**, experimenting with different angles and more takes without blowing the budget since digital video doesn't involve film processing costs.

> **Shooting ratio** is the amount of film shot or video recorded compared with the amount used in the final cut. The shooting ratio depends on the medium (film, video or digital video), the budget, the genre, the director's style, and the cast and crew's levels of experience and competence. With a shooting ratio of 15:1, the cinematographer shoots fifteen times more footage than the editor uses, or the director gets what she or he wants in fifteen takes.

In addition to introducing key terms and techniques to spot transitions that are designed to be invisible, the remainder of this chapter contrasts associative montage editing techniques that are prevalent in 'cutting-edge' television, advertising and music video culture with the dominant continuity style of editing. We trace the history of these techniques back to early Soviet cinema and the first experiments in narrative filmmaking, tracking the reciprocal influences of film and television editing on each other's ongoing aesthetic development. In addition, we consider how multi-camera shoots that are sometimes edited and broadcast live in the television studio compare with how editing is planned and executed for single-camera shoots.

EDITING FOR MULTIPLE CAMERA SHOOTS

Film and television both use single-camera shoots and multi-camera shoots, though single-camera is the industry standard for both media, and was the basis on which editing conventions were established. Virtually all shoots require coverage of more than one scale and angle. With only one camera, multiple takes of each shot are needed. Major stunts and unrepeatable scenes like explosions are often covered by **multiple cameras** simultaneously to avoid the cost of restaging the action. In rare instances (such as the split-screen experimental digital film *Time Code*), an entire film is shot with multiple cameras, whereas in television multi-camera shoots are specific to certain genres. The visual 'looseness' arising from a multi-camera shoot has come to signify 'liveness' (Butler 2007: 222), connoting a sense of immediacy and a particular kind of realism in the film scenes or television genres in which it features. The ongoing storylines and 'real-time' formats common in television harness this feature of multi-camera shooting and editing to emulate the ongoing routines and everyday reality of the domestic environment.

> In a **multiple-camera** shoot, the action is filmed by two or more cameras from different positions simultaneously. This economical style means the shot and the reverse shot, or a long shot and a close up of the same take, can be filmed at once so the set-up doesn't have to be repeated.

Most prime-time shows like super-soaps, crime fiction and drama are single-camera, as are most commercials and music videos without live performances. Televised sports and other live events, the studio-based part of the news, game shows, sit-coms and talk shows featuring a studio audience, and programs with a lower budget or a very tight schedule such as daily soap operas are typically shot with multiple cameras (Butler 2007). Some reality television programs may have *dozens* of cameras, and may even screen different versions of the same footage. For instance, dedicated *Big Brother* fans can watch unedited video feeds streamed 24/7 online, as well as viewing the heavily edited broadcast version, and the adults-only 'Uncut' special episodes that are in fact deliberately cut to showcase the rudie-nudie bits. While the principles of cinematography remain much the same irrespective of how many cameras are on set (the trick is to get the lighting even, and ensure the cameras don't film each other), a multi-cam shoot necessitates a different process of planning and execution for editors.

Consider a sit-com like *Roseanne*, shot with multiple cameras before a studio audience and edited pretty much on the spot. Before the audience arrives, actors rehearse lines and block out movements, and the director plans where each camera should be at given points to get adequate coverage. Instead of shooting all Roseanne's lines in a scene, then shooting all her husband's lines, then editing a shot-reverse-shot dialogue sequence as in a single-camera shoot, the actors play entire scenes in one uninterrupted take. This makes the experience for the actors and the audience more like theatre than film, catering for improvisation and chance (Butler 2007: 197–220). In a soundproofed mixing booth, the editor watches monitors showing what each camera films, and puts together a rough cut on the fly by switching from one viewpoint to another, following the dialogue and action.

During this process, the editor may have to improvise if Camera B zooms in to a close-up to capture a particularly funny performance by Roseanne, while Camera A dollies out to frame the couple in a two-shot in case Rosanne suddenly moves out of the tight framing, and Camera C holds on a reaction shot. The audience, meanwhile, responds to flashing signs that cue the timing and duration of applause and laughter. This audio track is recorded with a directional microphone and mixed separately on a different audio track in case the studio audience doesn't get the jokes or laughs too long and drowns out the dialogue. Editors later augment or 'sweeten' the laugh track to provide cues for the audience watching the program at home. This is especially important because performers run through two takes of each scene before moving on to the very next scene in the script. The studio audience mightn't find the second take as funny, but the extra coverage is like an insurance policy for the editor.

In addition to the shoot being less controlled, there is seldom much time between shooting and broadcasting to fine-tune the edit. In a genre like a current affairs talk show interview, the editor may well need to switch live between different views of the speakers, or between commentators and location inserts. In such cases, there is no opportunity for a second take, much less a fine cut.

TELEVISION EDITING

In addition to the specificities of editing footage shot on multiple cameras simultaneously, and the generalities of editing that apply to both film and television, the post-production process in television includes special features that are important in maintaining attention, brand identity, ratings and flow.

Television programs are edited to incorporate advertising breaks for commercials, and to inform viewers of programs screening later the same day or week. Other than one-off special broadcasts and movies, television texts are designed to encourage repeated, ongoing viewing. Because fragmentation breaks the narrative flow in dramas, or interrupts attention between the different segments of non-narrative programs, television texts are structured to create **cliffhangers** to lure the audience back for the next segment or episode, and even the next program screened on that channel. Maintaining ongoing viewership and high ratings is an economic imperative of television, and the editor's role must support this.

> The **cliffhanger** is an editing strategy that involves cutting the narrative at a suspenseful moment or immediately after offering a teaser about what is coming up next, thereby creating an addictive hook that leaves the audience hanging with unanswered questions lingering in their minds throughout the intervening time. Cliffhangers can be used to build suspense by cutting away from the main action in a film, but the technique is most commonly used to sustain attention in the fragmented texts and interwoven, ongoing storylines of television.

To sustain viewing and prevent channel surfing (or to help viewers identify channels and programs when, inevitably, we do surf), television editors layer sounds and images over the beginnings of new scenes to enable recognition of the network and the program. These strategies are used immediately prior to and following ad breaks, since this is when viewers usually reach for the remote or leave the room. For instance, the network logo along with a banner at the bottom of the screen featuring the program's own logo, accompanied by its trademark jingle, can be superimposed to re-establish the identity of programs after ads. The station and program logos that appear in the corner of the screen, and the ads for upcoming programs that pop up or scroll along the bottom of the screen, are called bugs in the United States and **dogs** (digital onscreen graphics) in the United Kingdom and Australia (Copeland 2007: 273). These branding and advertising mechanisms are derived from developments in other screen media, such as internet advertising. The same techniques can also be used to keep viewers up to date with current information such as breaking news and lotto draws, or pop-ups and banners can be edited in to add supplemental information such as

URLs linking to blogs or extended coverage in news broadcasts.

When analysing television editing, always consider how the narrative is structured to accommodate the ad breaks and the episodic or serial format of the program. As discussed below in relation to continuity editing conventions, fade-outs and fade-ins typically cue the end of the narrative segment that leads into the ad break and the beginning of the one that resumes afterwards, and sound alone often cues a scene change within a narrative segment.

Dogs (digital onscreen graphics) or bugs often take the form of station logos or other information added at the bottom of the frame during post-production. Such graphics can brand television programs and the networks on which they are screened, prevent piracy, advertise the next program, or offer viewers extra information.

EDITING AND NARRATIVE STRUCTURE

While it is possible to make a screen narrative in a single long take (indeed, the very first films took this form), the result looks more like filmed theatre than a movie, and is inappropriate for the fragmented medium of television. What an editor does controls the entire structure of a text, and governs much of its impact through manipulating the combined effect of picture and sound, the plot, the pace, the nature of the audience's engagement with character and our comprehension of the story. Editing is used to structure the narrative in terms of the order in which it unfolds on the screen: this can be linear, retrospective, projective, elliptical, fragmented, cyclical or some combination of these styles (see Chapter 5). **Flashbacks** and **flash-forwards**, repetition, **freeze frames** and parallel plotlines presented using **crosscutting** are editing techniques that structure both the story and the spectator's response. If you notice deviation from a linear chronology, it is probably important. Always question *why* non-linear chronologies or techniques foregrounding spatial or temporal discontinuities and tensions are used. For instance, the TV series *Medium* uses a flash-forward structure to enable the audience to relate to Alison's precognitive powers. *The Butterfly Effect* and

Flashbacks, often cued by a dissolve, manipulate the temporal order of a narrative by cutting back in time to show a memory or an event that occurred at an earlier point in the story.

Flash-forwards manipulate the temporal order of a narrative by jumping forward in time to show a premonition or an event that occurs at a future point in the story's chronology.

Freeze frames are moments when the motion picture appears to freeze into a still photograph. A single frame is printed repeatedly to achieve this effect.

Crosscutting, also termed parallel editing or intercutting, shows the development of two lines of action (either simultaneously occurring in different places, or cutting between past and present or future developments) by alternating a scene from one storyline with a scene from the other.

Twelve Monkeys have cyclical structures because they are about travelling into the past to prevent a catastrophe in the future.

POINT OF VIEW

Editing governs the way a story is disclosed; thus it manipulates the relationship between the audience and the characters. For example, *Law and Order: Criminal Intent* gives the audience insight into both the criminal's and the victim's point of view early in each episode, using sustained long takes and the personalised feel of a handheld camera to deliver information to which Detective Goren and his team are not privy, then the editor withholds crucial information, creating a mystery the detectives and the viewers want to solve. For instance, the fifth shot in 'Slither' (Season 5, Episode 11) shows the victim scream in horror after opening a fridge at a party. The editor does not reveal what made her scream (a severed head) for another fifteen minutes, and does not reveal how it got there until near the end of the episode. This editing strategy of showing the victim's reaction, but using **ellipsis** and withholding a crucial point-of-view shot, makes the audience want to keep watching to find out what happened, but it also performs an ideological function by cleverly shifting viewer allegiance to the side of law and order by ensuring we don't find out what was in the fridge until the detectives do. Ultimately, it is the editor who determines whether the audience knows more or less than the characters by deciding when to reveal information and whether our experience is tightly or loosely tied to the characters' experiences via point of view editing.

Imagine watching a James Bond movie filmed entirely from Bond's perspective. You would see lots of beautiful women and high-tech gadgets, but you would never get to admire Bond's athletic physique, wry expressions, immaculate suits or daredevil escapes. The shot-reverse-shot pattern and the alternation between points of view in a narrative

Ellipsis means the omission or suppression of information, which creates a gap in the story. Events can be edited out for the sake of narrative compression, or to delay revealing information and create surprise later in the story.

facilitate character engagement. A sequence shot and edited from the first-person point of view will have a different impact if cut to show the perspective of a third party, or if an omniscient view offers the audience insight into things none of the characters could possibly see. Omniscient perspectives like aerial shots or the view of an empty room often connote objectivity and truth compared with the subjective perspective of the first-person point of view.

CONTINUITY EDITING

In addition to structuring the overall narrative, the editor makes decisions about the dramatic structure of individual scenes and transitions from shot to shot. We must question why certain techniques are chosen at this editing level too, and the answers often have to do with helping the audience navigate through the time and space of the story world, or expressing what a character is experiencing. Often the best way to do this is by making the edit point unnoticeable, so it seems as though we have naturally shifted our attention to something else in the story, as we do in daily life.

Continuity editing creates the illusion of continuous time and space in relation to a causal sequence of events. Even though the conventions of continuity editing create an illusion, it is an illusion of realistic time and space enabling the audience to concentrate on the narrative without noticing the techniques and technologies that construct the story world. Hence, somewhat paradoxically, continuity style is termed a 'realist' editing technique. Early filmmakers worried that editing long shots mixed with close-ups would be jarring for spectators used to watching theatre or actual events unfold at a stable distance from their viewing position. *The Sick Kitten* (1903) cuts into a close-up just as a little girl gives a kitten a teaspoon of medicine; however, 'magically' transporting the viewer through screen space by cutting into a close-up did not become commonplace for another decade (Cousins 2004: 31). D.W. Griffith is usually credited with being one of the founders of the continuity editing system, breaking the action into short shots with variations in scale and duration, held together by a consistent logic underpinning the direction in which action and glances played out on screen. Prior to Griffith's innovations, most filmmakers used one take to film an entire scene in long

> **Continuity editing** refers to a set of editing conventions that create the illusion of continuous time and space in a screen text. Continuity editing is the dominant style of editing in almost all screen texts worldwide.

shot. By the time he made the American Civil War story *Birth of a Nation* in 1915, Griffith had established narrative editing strategies such as 'the variation of shots for impact, including the extreme long shot, the close-up, the cutaway, and the tracking shot; parallel editing; and variations in pace' (Dancyger 2007: 5). These techniques can function almost imperceptibly to invite the audience to identify with the perspective of individual protagonists and to unquestioningly accept their world-views and goals as legitimate within the narrative context. (Often Griffith's films communicate the nationalist, patriarchal and racist ideologies of his time.)

Continuity editing involves **suturing** (stitching or connecting) together different images or shots into sequence, determining the order of screen events. In film theory, 'suture' also refers to the act of 'stitching' the audience into the story world, so we feel almost as though we're *inside* the movie. Suture is an editing technique that makes each cut scarless, seamless or invisible, as though we are watching one continuous piece of film, or a continuous flow of events, rather than pieces patchworked together into a story. In screen production, suture is a *metaphor* for what happens in digital, non-linear editing (just like the terms 'cut and paste' in your word processing program are metaphors for the old-fashioned process editors used to restructure a paper). Editors never actually cut, stitch or paste video tape or digital footage, but the term 'suture' does come close to describing the traditional process of cutting the film negative with a razor and splicing it back together in the order it would be projected. Each cut indicates the passage of time, or a transition to a new location or screen position, however small or large that shift may be. The editor can cut to show a character's reaction to something that has just occurred, like a response to dialogue, or they can cut between simultaneous lines of action in different locations, or they can cut back and forward in time. The very process of editing suggests the existence of off-screen space and **off-screen time**.

> **Suture** is an editing term that means stitch or splice together so the cutting point between two shots (seam or scar) is unnoticeable.

The audience fills in gaps in a story by imagining action occurring off screen, assuming the characters move through space and time between shots or scenes. This is especially relevant in the use of fades, dissolves and ellipses.

There are four main kinds of shot transition:

> **Off-screen time** refers to the intervals between scenes when we do not see the characters, but imagine that they continue on with their lives in the story world.

1. **Straight cuts** are the most common. A straight cut usually joins shots within the same scene, making incremental shifts in space and time in the same place.
2. **Fades** usually show the screen gradually going black. Shots can also fade in, with a dark screen becoming lighter as an image appears, or they can fade out to a white screen, as in the funeral home TV series *Six Feet Under*. It is less common to fade to colour. According to the temporal conventions of continuity editing, a fade often indicates a long gap in time between scenes. It can also indicate that a character has fallen asleep, lost consciousness or died. A fade is the visual equivalent of writing dot, dot, dot . . . so it is also commonly used to signal the ellipsis formed by advertising breaks punctuating television programs.
3. **Dissolves** show two images momentarily superimposed: the first image gets weaker as the next shot becomes clearer. Often a dissolve cues a flashback or a dream sequence, or a significant shift in time and space like a change of scene. By convention, the longer the dissolve takes, the greater amount of time has passed between one shot and the next.
4. **Wipes** are flashy shot transitions that draw attention to the constructed nature of the text because there is a visible line on the screen between one shot and the next. Because it is so noticeable, it is the least common transition in the continuity style. Wipes can cue a transition in space or time or both. If a partial wipe is used, a split-screen effect is produced, as when characters have a phone conversation. There are many types of wipe: in a horizontal wipe, the new shot descends or ascends on the screen like a garage roller door; in a vertical wipe, the new shot comes in from the left or right, creating a vertical line on the screen or sometimes opening out from the middle like curtains parting at the theatre. You may also see diagonal wipes, spiral wipes, scissor wipes or other fancy styles. The decision to use a wipe transition

Straight cuts are standard editing transitions in which one shot is joined unobtrusively to the next.

Fades are shot transitions in which the picture slowly fades in or out until the screen is entirely one colour, usually black or white.

Dissolves are transitions in which one shot replaces another through a process of superimposition.

Wipes are a form of editing transition in which one shot visibly pushes another out of the way.

may have an aesthetic motivation, or it may relate to the storyline and characterisation, or mirror movement on screen. Wipes are frequently used in *Ugly Betty* and *My Name is Earl*, television series about quirky characters whose newfound lifestyles literally push their old ideas and behaviours away. Wipes also feature in the musical *Chicago* when the old Roxie Hart's tarnished image is transformed to make way for the new, innocent Roxie, specifically using a scissor wipe as she cuts her hair.

Sometimes editors disguise cuts by hiding them within very fast camera movement such as a whip pan (a technique used to maintain the sense of a continuous subjective viewpoint in the first-person shooter sequence in the game-to-film adaptation *Doom*), or behind the motion of a figure or a vehicle crossing the screen (as in *The Usual Suspects* when we cut in to a tighter framing each time the detective walks in front of the camera while interrogating the suspects). This is called a masked edit, or sometimes a wipe-by, when the movement of the camera or an object crossing in front of the lens appears to push the old shot out of the way. Hitchcock uses this trick every time a new reel of film is loaded in *Rope* to give the illusion that it is filmed in one long continuous shot.

Cutaways involve cutting away from the main action to an image that relates to the scene being shot or screened. Cutaways provide extra information and connect together two parts of a scene that might otherwise not cut together smoothly.

Establishing shots 'set the scene' by showing the location of a new scene in a long shot that enables the audience to recognise the space and the location of figures within it.

Spatial conventions

One of the most important talents an editor can have involves helping the audience inhabit screen space comfortably and imagine off-screen space vividly. Good coveage, including a range of takes, different shot angles, sizes and camera movements, and adequate **cutaways**, will enable the editor to make creative choices and direct audience perceptions. Typically, a new scene begins with an **establishing shot** of the location to map screen space for the viewer, so that they can orient themselves. The convention of showing an establishing shot, then cutting in closer, was invented to help the audience understand the story and location. After the location is established, the bulk of most scenes is edited in a **shot-reverse-shot** pattern. A shot of a person speaking, followed by a reaction shot, is used in dialogue sequences, alternating between the speaker and listener's point of view, but it can also be used for fight scenes, or to show what a character sees in the world around them. With this editing pattern, it is important that the level and direction of the camera match the eye level and direction of the character's gaze, to create a sense of realism and continuity. Editors often cut into tight close-ups to punctuate the main action or climactic moments of dialogue and maximise emotive impact. They may also pull back to a re-establishing shot when actors move around or new characters enter the scene.

> **Shot-reverse-shot** is an editing technique that shows a pair of shots, usually alternating an image with a shot from the reverse camera angle and position, or a reaction shot showing a character's response to the first image.

Friends characteristically begins with an expensive (and reusable) aerial introduction in extreme long shot locating us in New York, then a stock long shot of the apartment block (see Figure 4.1) or Central Perk Café, followed by a wide shot of the interior situating the viewer as the seventh 'friend' seated at the table (see Figure 4.2), after which we move into a shot-reverse-shot pattern of two-shots and close-ups for the dialogue.

With continuity editing, overall lighting levels also need to be consistent in each shot, otherwise it looks like the shot and the reverse shot occur in different places or at different times of day. On a film or television shoot, a continuity person is responsible for making sure actors don't vary their movements, costumes or use of props between shots or takes to prevent continuity errors when different takes are cut together.

Crossing the line: The 180-degree rule

The 180-degree **axis of action** is an imaginary line drawn between two speakers, or between two points in space such as a stretch of road. The camera only films from one side of this line (for example, one side of the road), so it always views the action from the same perspective. This ensures screen direction and relative positions in the frame remain constant to avoid disorienting viewers. Editors avoid 'crossing the line' and using shots filmed from the other side which violate the 180-degree rule, otherwise it looks as though a character driving from left to right across the screen has done an invisible U-turn between shots. Shots containing camera movement or

Figure 4.1 *Friends* establishing shot showing the apartment exterior

Figure 4.2 The establishing shot is followed by a shot inside the apartment with the friends gathered at the table

character movement are used to get over the line if it is necessary to shoot from the other side of the axis of action.

Jump cut: The 30-degree rule

Jump cuts break the continuity of time by jerking the viewer from one moment to the next without showing the intervening movement, or indicating that time has passed. Breaking the 30-degree rule means moving the camera position

> The **axis of action** is an invisible line extending between two points on the screen, such as the start and end points of figure movement or the positions of two characters conversing. The camera can be positioned anywhere within a semi-circular 180-degree arc on one side of this line. Crossing the line, or filming from the other side of the axis of action, is called breaking the 180-degree rule because it disrupts continuity of screen direction.

less than 30 degrees between shots, resulting in a jump cut. In other words, two shots of the same subject are edited together when a continuous shot should have been used, or the second shot should have been taken from a significantly different position to motivate the shift and differentiate the two shots. You will notice jump cuts in documentary footage when the editor cuts out a boring or irrelevant bit of an interviewee's speech without inserting a cutaway or a reaction shot. Jump cuts are also used intentionally in contemporary action sequences and in footage conveying a disoriented or disorienting experience. For example, the Australian film *Kiss or Kill* opens when a young woman seducing a businessman is interrupted by her jealous boyfriend. Abruptly the tables turn, and we realise the young couple is a team working to drug and rob the lecherous older man. Their agitation and fear of being caught is conveyed using multiple jump cuts. The camera also crosses the line, mixing up the spatial relationships between characters. Here editing mirrors the rule-breaking in the storyline itself, reinforcing both the characters' experiences of law-breaking and the jolts that spectators feel when the plot twists.

> A **jump cut** is an edit that breaks continuity conventions and violates the 30 degree rule by joining two similar shots of the same subject while cutting out the interval of time or motion that would have connected them. This creates a visible jerk on the screen as the image seems to jump inexplicably to the next position.

Match edits

In addition to maintaining consistent screen direction and respecting the axis of action, another continuity editing convention is the match cut. The most common match is an **eyeline match**. This is a point-of-view editing technique that shows

> An **eyeline match** is a point-of-view editing technique that follows a shot of a character looking off screen at something, with a shot of the object at which they are looking.

someone looking off screen, thereby extending the implied story world beyond the frame, then cuts to follow the direction and level of the character's gaze to show the audience what they see.

For example, in *Some Like it Hot*, when Tony Curtis and Jack Lemmon's characters first see Sugar (Marilyn Monroe) the camera cuts to follow their gaze. This aligns spectators with a heterosexual, male viewing perspective (see Figures 4.3 and 4.4).

Most editors avoid cutting when the camera or character is in the middle of a movement unless they specifically intend to create a sense of haste, panic or disruption, or intend to match the movement with a corresponding or seemingly continuous movement in the next shot. A **match on action** carries movement across the break between two shots, giving the illusion of a continuous motion. Matches on action are quite hard to spot. There are two types to watch for, and sometimes they occur together. The first is a match on camera movement, as when a scene ends with a forward tracking shot, and the next scene begins with another tracking shot of the same speed in a different location or timeframe. The second and most common is a match on figure movement, as when a character begins to open and move through a door, then we cut to see them continuing through the other side of the door, or when we watch a character begin to swing a punch and we cut to see the punch land. For example, in *Fight Club* Edward Norton's character beats himself up to make it seem as though his boss assaulted him. When he throws a punch at himself, hits himself and lands on the floor, three shots are cut together so fast and matched on action so cleverly that it all seems to happen in one continuous motion (see Figures 4.5, 4.6 and 4.7).

> A **match on action** joins the beginning of a movement to the continuation of that movement, cutting on action to disguise the edit point and creating the illusion of continuous motion.

Matches on action in *Fight Club* seamlessly connect three shots (front view, behind, above), situating us kinetically inside the character's experience as he punches himself, falls through a glass table, and lands on the floor in what feels like a continuous shot.

In a **graphic match**, similar colours or shapes create a visual pattern or an associative relationship between shots, keeping the

Figure 4.3 In *Some Like it Hot*, an eyeline match shows Curtis and Lemon looking off screen

Figure 4.4 Then we see what their eyes are following: Monroe's sexy walk

focus of interest on the same element across the cut. For example, the diner scene of Oliver Stone's *Natural Born Killers* cuts from a canted frame of Mickey eating

Graphic matches join two shots together using similar colours or shapes to establish a visual relationship that bridges the two shots.

Figure 4.5 Match on action in *Fight Club* showing a punch viewed from the front

Figure 4.6 *Fight Club* punch seen from behind

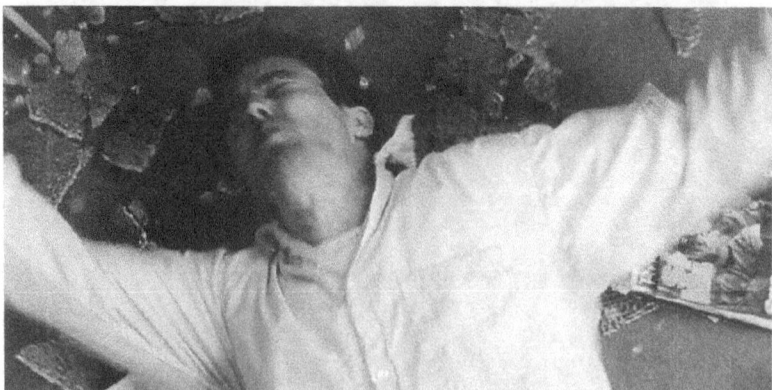

Figure 4.7 *Fight Club* punch seen from above
(*Fight Club* © Twentieth Century Fox Film Corporation, Monarchy Enterprises S.a.r.l. and Regency Entertainment (USA), Inc. All rights reserved.)

key lime pie to another canted shot that shows the same neon green colour on the jukebox, at the same angle.

In *Hero*, a Chinese film with astonishing formal symmetry and beauty, the editor frequently matches both colour and shape, such as blue lighting, circular shapes and vertical lines on a rolled bamboo mat; blue columns in a circular room; and fingers cupping a blue bowl. Sometimes one shot transition combines a number of techniques. For instance, shots of the red and black armies approaching one another in *Hero* work with the relationships between the forward rushing movement of the figures (match on action), and the visual shapes and parallel bands of colour formed by flags and shields (graphic match), as well as forming a shot-reverse-shot pattern.

Figure 4.8 *Hero*: Graphic match on the parallel lines of horsemen, and match on action as the red army rides forward in battle

Figure 4.9 *Hero*: Graphic match and match on action as the black army approaches in the reverse shot

MONTAGE-STYLE EDITING

Continuity editing is the dominant style in most screen texts, and even those that are not completely wed to a narrative logic such as television news will take care not to violate the principles of continuity too much by using unmotivated transitions or oppositional screen direction. However, continuity is not the only editing style. Since the earliest days of film and television, many texts have relied on the **montage** style of editing instead of, or as well as, continuity. The key distinction between montage and continuity is that continuity conventions are designed to suture closed the gap in space or time between shots to secure meaning, whereas montage deliberately opens up the gap between the shots, inviting the audience to fill it in. This broadens possible interpretations.

> **Montage** is a style of editing that joins together shots which are discontinuous in time and space.

The challenge of understanding montage is that the technique is at once very old and very contemporary, and the term itself is used in four different but related ways:

1. *Montage* is simply the French word for editing. You may encounter this usage in other texts, but because it collapses the distinction between different editing styles, we avoid this definition.
2. A *montage sequence* is a 'collage' of images joined together, usually by dissolves and music. It is often used in both film and television to show time passing. The film *Team America* includes a self-reflexive song explaining the function of a montage sequence, playing over images of our hero in different stages of combat training and preparation for a mission.
3. *MTV-style montage* is a contemporary editing style characterised by visual excess and a frenetic pace that intensifies the collage effect of disjointed images set to music, taking it to new extremes. Many advertisements, music videos and film trailers (which are themselves extended advertisements for CDs and movies) disregard the conventional use of montage sequences to indicate temporal compression and dispense with the logic of continuity editing in favour of a more emotive, associational, poetic style that is uniquely suited to accompany music and to heighten desires stimulated by advertising. MTV-style montage

defies the impulse to narrativise meaning. It destabilises time and place by using repeated images and jump cuts to join decontextualised close-ups, often filmed with a long lens that flattens and blurs the background and focuses on surface features like colour, texture, shape and motion (Allan 2007). A growing number of contemporary film and television texts now include innovative moments of MTV-style montage to underscore key sequences occurring within a broader narrative otherwise governed by continuity editing conventions. For instance, in the first drug deal in *Requiem for a Dream*, sound effects, music and image are edited together with extreme close-ups to make the scene play almost like a music video punctuated by the *ka-ching* sound of a cash register. In addition, many cinematic dream sequences and most title sequences for television programs are cut in MTV montage style. Sometimes, as in *Prison Break*, a rapid-fire montage of images linked by sound is even used to cue commercial breaks in a television narrative.

4. **Soviet montage** is a technique developed by Soviet filmmakers in the 1920s in explicit opposition to the continuity system's tendency to suture the audience into an ideological position without our awareness. Soviet filmmakers such as Sergei Eisenstein (famous for the rapid, rhythmic editing of the *Battleship Potemkin* mutiny 1925) wanted to see whether editing could prompt the audience to independently form ideas and meanings not determined by narrative logic. Inspired by Marxism, and by Lenin's decree in 1922 that cinema was the 'most important of all the arts' in terms of propagating Bolshevik ideals, early Soviet films therefore sought to present a world-view more concerned with the plight of a social class rather than an individual protagonist, as in the workers' strike in *Strike* (Eisenstein 1925). Surrealist filmmakers like Louis Buñuel and Salvador Dali experimented with similar disjunctive, associational techniques around the same time, for different reasons, in an effort to bypass logic, to create visceral reactions and to evoke the language of the unconscious. The Soviet montage style is more like a *collision* of images than collage or continuity, and it works on the principles of counterpoint (juxtaposition) and **dialectical synthesis**. Dialectical synthesis refers to

Dialectical synthesis means that there is a collision or tension between two opposing forces (caused by the juxtaposition of two different shots, or two opposing terms or viewpoints), which is resolved when the interpreter synthesises the two, actively thinking through the relationship between them to produce a new meaning.

negotiating between opposing forces caused by the juxtaposition of two different shots. The opposition is resolved when the viewer synthesises the two images, constructing a meaningful relationship between them. The Soviet editing experiments began when Vsevolod Pudovkin and Lev Kuleshov tried to figure out how audiences interpreted the relationship between shots by showing viewers a man's face next to three different shots: a bowl of soup, a coffin and a child playing. They found that even though the facial expression did not alter, audiences took the first pair of shots to express hunger, the second to express grief, and the third to express pleasure (Dancyger 2007: 16), suggesting that we automatically look for a narrative, causal connection between shots. As another example of dialectical synthesis, consider an image of a soldier. On its own, the image is polysemic (it has many possible meanings). Interpretations rely a great deal on personal feelings and experiences about armies, wars, authority, patriotism and soldiers. If, in the manner of Soviet montage, the image of the soldier is juxtaposed with that of a butcher hacking bloody meat with a cleaver, then you may synthesise the two shots and produce an interpretation like 'soldiers are butchers who kill people' or 'soldiers get butchered in wars'. This narrows the range of possible interpretations, but it doesn't lock it down into a narrative logic in the way that continuity editing would if it followed the image of the soldier

Metric montage involves varying shot duration to manipulate pace and rhythm, using shorter shots to build excitement or suspense.

Tonal montage uses editing to give a scene emotional atmosphere or punctuation, and involves choosing shots on the basis of expressive qualities, scale or evocative lighting, using editing to orchestrate the affective tenor of a sequence.

with a match on action showing the same soldier in long shot raising a rifle to shoot a civilian. Sergei Eisenstein's editing theory also covers a range of other terms and techniques. For our purposes, the most important are **metric montage**, **tonal montage** and **intellectual montage**. Taken together, they show the essence of the Soviet Montage style, which links shots based on rhythms, associations, discontinuities and juxtapositions.

Some editing techniques can be used within the conventions of montage *and* continuity. For instance, a graphic match is an aesthetic convention that can be used in either style of editing. Similarly, aspects of editing that govern time and timing apply to continuity and montage styles.

> **Intellectual montage**, Eisenstein's most famous contribution to editing, involves juxtaposing shots to create an idea or association that doesn't rely on spatio-temporal continuity or aesthetic harmony.

Time, pace and rhythm

Rhythmic editing can occur within continuity or montage. It involves manipulating shot duration and timing so that the image is 'edited to the beat'—that is, cut to coincide with aural rhythms such as music, or cut to the rhythms of movement on screen. **Shot duration** determines the timing, pace and rhythm in which the action unfolds. An editor decides when to cut from one shot to another, and for how long each shot is held. Such decisions depend on the nature and purpose of the shot, and the intended response. Editing decisions also determine the pace at which a scene unfolds, regulating the suspense that the audience feels by using languorous long takes, or a rapid volley of short shots. One of the primary functions of editing is temporal compression—in other words, chopping out the bits of the story that are boring or unnecessary. Such a 'gap' in time is called temporal ellipsis. Another trick that editors use to manipulate screen time is altering the frame rate to make the action run in fast forward, or slow motion, as discussed below in the case study of action sequence editing techniques. The television series *24* is unique in that the premise of action playing out in real time means that 'time cuts' such as dissolves, ellipses and fades can't be used, so the editors had to find other ways to accelerate the pace and move the action forward. The style is intentionally disorienting, full of agitated cutting with split screens and disrupted spatiality, often breaking conventions and crossing the line to create an edgy dynamism.

> **Rhythmic editing**, or 'editing to the beat', matches shot duration and the timing of each cut to the rhythm of action or sound on screen.
>
> **Shot duration** means the length of time a shot is held—that is, the seconds, minutes or frames between cuts.

SOUND TRANSITIONS

As noted previously, editing points for sound and image are often different, yet they are interrelated. It is important to consider the relationship between cutting points for the soundtrack as well as the image track. Music and other sounds (particularly voiceover narration) can unify two shots or scenes, softening an edit or disguising it by helping to maintain a continuous sound environment when the image changes. When sound anticipates image and is used to create a smooth transition to the next scene, it is termed a lead-in or **sound bridge**. For instance, in the British rom-com *Love Actually*, we hear the song 'Christmas is all Around Us', which provides an acoustic bridge to the next scene where the ageing rock star Bill Nighy is being interviewed at the radio station playing the same tune. A sound bridge can also be understood as a 'sonic match' that connects two scenes in much the same way that a 'graphic match' is used to relate two shots when editing images. In the exposition of *The Usual Suspects*, when the police are rounding up criminals they drag McMannis out of bed at gunpoint and we hear a blast of what we assume to be machine-gun fire for an instant before we cut to the next scene and see the source of the sound: a paint mixing machine rattling away in Hockney's mechanic workshop. The police never actually opened fire on McMannis. The clever sonic match between the sound of a machine-gun and the sound of a machine mixing paint creates a bridge between the two scenes and establishes a strong relationship between the two characters, while also setting up the pattern of tricking the audience that recurs throughout the film. Sound bridges differ from **sonic overlap**, where sound continues over from one shot to the next, or even to the next scene, providing continuity and hiding the cutting point for the images. The most common form of overlapping is dialogue overlap, where we see a person speaking, then continue to hear them finish their sentence off screen as we cut to the next scene or to a reaction shot of their conversation partner listening. A third kind of sound transition is called a **segue**, where one sound effect is blended into another similar sound, as in the New Zealand film *Once Were Warriors* when Beth screams upon discovering her daughter's suicide, and the sound of her scream changes or segues into the wail of the ambulance.

A **sound bridge** is an editing technique that introduces sound from the next scene or shot *before* the image appears on the screen.

Sonic overlap is a technique that provides continuity over a cut between two images by continuing sound or dialogue over to the next shot or scene *after* the speaker or source ceases to be visible on the screen.

One more aspect of sound editing that can be important in film and television is **rhythm**. The French film *Amelie* innovatively uses sound to complement the rhythms of editing, working in synergy with the actions visible on screen. As Amelie imagines the lovers throughout Paris, we cut with increasing rapidity from one carnal embrace to another as the different sounds build rhythmically to an orgasmic crescendo of pumping, moaning, panting and squeaking. The sound effects work to create a rhythmic unity that connects different images which are intercut together, establishing a build-up of narrative tension that draws the audience in towards the scene's climactic moment.

> A **segue** is a sonic transition in which one sound morphs or blends into another similar sound. Typically, as the sound segues, we cut or dissolve from an image showing the source of the first sound to one showing the source of the second.
>
> **Rhythm** refers to the pattern of sound in time: sound can have a fast or slow tempo, it can be predictable or irregular, and it can support or contradict the pace and rhythm of images and editing.

EDITING ACTION SEQUENCES

Editing styles are, to a certain extent, genre specific. For instance, soap opera relies on close-ups and shot-reverse-shot patterns to foreground facial expression and dialogue, whereas musicals use rhythmic editing cut to the beat of the music, punctuated by audience point-of-view shots. The following example details how contemporary action sequences are constructed.

Action sequences, such as the scene in *Kill Bill* when Beatrix battles the Crazy 88s, cut between opponents with clashing goals. Beatrix's goal is to kill O-Ren Ishii and the Crazy 88s' goal is to stop her. Action scenes occur at significant narrative obstacles and turning points, and are edited using a fast-paced combination of continuity editing, montage and rhythmic editing, with matches on action and exaggerated sound effects to generate energy and physicality. The sequence begins with a lengthy fifteen-second shot slowly craning up from Beatrix to a bird's eye view of her opponents encircling her. As the action builds towards its climax, the pace of editing accelerates and shot duration decreases.

'Constructive editing' breaks the action into pieces (Bordwell 2000: 212). This enables filmmakers to construct the whole sequence without a master shot or a long take so there is no need to get the whole fight right in one shot. Filming one blow at a time, joined by eyeline matches and matches on action makes anyone look like a good fighter, whereas long takes require great skill. Constructive editing gives a fast-paced, jumpy feeling of being amidst the action. Adrian Martin calls the technique of hitting the viewer with a chaotic flurry of shots so fast the spatial relations between them can't readily be distinguished '**disintegrative montage**' (2005: 182). Intense action sequences create the experience of existing 'at the edge of the cut', waiting to be 'taken over the edge' by directorial bravado and stunt fighter daring (Martin 2005: 182). The approach to each cut is a build-up of tension, so rapid-fire cutting keeps the viewer literally on edge, locked into a kinetic relation with the screen (Martin 2005: 182). Spectators lose their bearings as orientation, gravity and spatial relations are disrupted when Beatrix executes flips and cartwheels through the air, spinning about to avoid the swords and hatchets flying at her from all angles. The disorienting impact is augmented because the scene is at least partly cut to the beat of the musical soundtrack and constantly punctuated with cartoonish *woosh*, *ching*, *aaaaargh* and *crunch* sound effects.

> **Disintegrative montage** is an editing technique used predominantly in action sequences. It simulates the frenzy of a fight by breaking spatio-temporal continuity conventions in a rapid volley of brief shots taken from a crazy, 'unrealistic' mixture of camera positions.

Martial arts action is edited with a distinctive pause-burst-pause rhythm (Bordwell 2000). Pauses in the action happen when Beatrix plucks the eye of an opponent, and when she leaps on to the balustrade of the balcony, gaining advantage over the assassins charging up the stairs. The frenetic pace of disintegrative montage alternates with moments such as these when the characters shift to better footing, take stock and circle each other, or the action moves into slow motion. The editor must showcase the scale of the action by using long shots to show the agility and prowess of the fighters' bodies moving through space, or the dexterity of a stunt driver or a spectacular explosion. Close-ups are also necessary to punctuate the action with displays of effort, rage, fear or pain on performers' faces. Alternating between shot sizes within the pause-burst-pause pattern can help to reorient viewers if they lose their bearings. Often when there is a pause in the action, viewers revel in a moment of aesthetic beauty amidst extreme destruction. In John Woo action sequences, we invariably see a bird or a flight of birds scatter in slow motion or a slow motion rain of falling rubble. These editing techniques work in conjunction with fast figure movement and rapid camera movements like whip pans and crash zooms to create 'a mechanical delirium' of abstraction (Martin 2005: 185).

Slow motion, or fast motion, can be achieved at the time of shooting or during editing. In the editing process this is known as **speed ramping** 'a sudden change of speed within a movement or a shot' using digital effects to accelerate or decelerate the frame rate, or skip-framing,' which means editing out frames to give an 'unreal' quality to the action (Martin 2005: 184). In *Kill Bill*'s Crazy 88s battle, speed ramping is noticeable when hatchets are thrown. Ramping shot speed gives Beatrix's movements a superhuman agility, alternately speeding and slowing the action to create the characteristic 'pause-burst-pause' rhythm. By contrast, in the snow garden scene that follows, the characters pause amidst the fight for old-fashioned moments of absolute stillness and silence as they do in Japanese Samurai films, showing that editing techniques dating back to the earliest days of cinema, ranging through continuity and montage, to contemporary digital manipulations of frame rate and sound design, can all be deployed to great effect in a modern action sequence.

> **Speed ramping** is when the frame rate or speed at which the action unfolds suddenly slows down or speeds up, thereby making the action appear superhuman.

CONCLUSION

Editing is central to every part of a screen text, including the unification of those parts into a whole, and the style in which the text is presented. For instance, the analysis of shot scale is as much a part of cinematography as it is a part of editing; and the analysis of music pertains to both sound and editing. The overall form and style of a screen text are integrally related to the editing techniques deployed. That is, screen aesthetics are in no small part a function of the artistic choices made in the editing process. Editing is not only about structuring a story: it can also position the audience to relate to or identify with the viewpoint of a character. Additionally, editing can locate a text within a particular genre as we have seen with examples from the action genre, music videos and sit-coms. The kinds of choices made in relation to editing thus have implications for the kinds of audiences that are reached, and such aesthetic choices impact upon the branding and marketability of screen texts.

We do not want you to think of the editing styles, techniques and conventions we have described in this chapter as hard and fast rules, because all rules can be bent or broken. Instead, you should be aware that editing conventions are naturalised: audiences have learned to automatically interpret editing conventions in particular ways, accepting them as natural. Indeed, part of screen literacy involves coming to see the conventions of editing that are rarely noticed. You should now be able to see the invisible seams that join shots together, analysing the motivation and effect of particular editing decisions in both film and television in terms of the relationship between shots.

In summary, the main features and functions of editing include:

- *point of view*, which determines how relations between the viewing subject and the object of vision can be constructed using subjective or omniscient perspectives that affect who the audience identifies with;
- *structural relations* between scenes in the overall narrative architecture;
- *temporal relations*, governing shot chronology, duration, pace, and rhythm;
- *spatial relations* between shots and scenes;
- *graphic relations* between images, matching movement, colour and composition, or using juxtaposition; and
- *sonic relations*, determining how the cutting points for sound and image work together.

KEY SKILLS

Having read this chapter, you should now be able to:

- describe the role and responsibilities of an editor and discuss differences between film and television editing;
- define match cuts, montage, axis of action, dissolve, fade, wipe and sound bridge;
- apply your understanding of editing techniques by analysing the spatial, temporal and rhythmic relations in a short clip;
- evaluate how editing 'sutures' the viewer into a subject position in a film or television narrative.

5
plotting and planning:
Storytelling and reviewing techniques

Film and television texts end up in a sophisticated, technologically mediated form, but they start out requiring little but creativity and inspiration. The impact of the techniques discussed in previous chapters rests on a foundation built by screenwriters and illustrators. Having introduced the different components of screen aesthetics (*mise en scène*, cinematography, sound and editing), this chapter turns to aspects of the production process concerned with writing and visualising the story from the concept, through writing a treatment and drafting the script, to illustrating and annotating the storyboard. Laying the groundwork for narrative analysis (see Chapter 6), our aim is to offer information and techniques that enhance understanding of how the craft of storytelling informs the production process, thereby enabling you to critique screen texts more effectively, and to develop your own creative skills. Since vocational applications of knowledge about film and television form the focus of this chapter, we have also included a section about writing film reviews. Your studies might require you to undertake screenwriting, storyboarding and reviewing assignments, or you may want to apply what you learn in practical ways, working in the industry or writing for a magazine or student newspaper. In each case, understanding the writing styles and formats used in film and television is a good starting point. Narrative drama provides the model for storytelling in this chapter, but much of the information can be adapted and applied to non-fiction formats like documentary and television interviews.

SYNOPSES AND SCENE BREAKDOWNS

Two of the simplest forms in which the storylines of film or television texts can be presented are synopses and scene breakdowns. These documents offer very skeletal, stripped-down versions of a story. A **synopsis** is a brief summary of the story, usually about a paragraph in length, but sometimes just a sentence; however, it can be as detailed as one page. A one-line synopsis is usually referred to as a **logline**. A synopsis succinctly states who the story is about and what happens, giving an indication of setting and genre, and suggesting how the central conflict is staged and resolved. Preparing a synopsis can help clarify central aspects of the story during the planning process, or synthesise ideas once a script has been drafted. Like the back-cover blurb of a DVD, the synopsis serves a marketing purpose. It can be used to **pitch** the story to prospective funding bodies, producers or other interested parties. A story is rarely ready to be developed into a fully fledged script, or even pitched to others, unless the writer can distil its essence into a tight synopsis that piques the interest of anyone who hears or reads it. For superb examples of 'the pitch', see the opening sequence of Robert Altman's *The Player* in which a string of writers describe the flavour and content of script concepts, including a sequel to *The Graduate*.

> A **synopsis** is a brief summary of what happens in a story.
>
> A **logline** is a one-line story synopsis, indicating the genre, setting, protagonists and central conflict. Loglines can also be known as the 'cocktail pitch' or '30-second' version of a story. A logline differs from a cut-line, which is the kind of catchy line used for marketing purposes on a movie poster.
>
> A **pitch** means a sales pitch, usually involving the delivery of a brief verbal synopsis of what a script is about to prospective producers, broadcasters or investors.

In its industry form, a **scene breakdown** is a preliminary document used to develop scripts for television series or feature films by outlining the storyline using reported speech and descriptions of the action in each scene. As a writing tool, this kind of breakdown is a great way to see how the structure is working, and to slash or juggle scenes before they are fully written, as well as checking whether critical points of the story are timed appropriately. A scene breakdown can be an invaluable tool to tighten up the narrative structure of a script, cutting scenes that don't drive the narrative forward. Scriptwriters often fine-tune drafts or plan scripts by writing one sentence describing each scene in sequence, stating what happens and labelling the narrative function of the scene. Scene breakdowns are sometimes also called step outlines or sequence outlines. Step or sequence outlines perform much the same function as scene breakdowns, but break the action into units such as steps, acts or sequences. Conventionally, a feature film will have numerous scenes grouped into three acts, with two sequences in the first and third acts, and four in the second act. The **first act** establishes character, setting and interest in the initial quarter of the script; the **second act** develops conflict and complications; and the last quarter contains the climactic **third act** and the resolution of the story. The process of creating a step outline is described by Robert McKee as writing a sentence for each step the protagonists take towards achieving their goals, and categorising each step to create a map of the script in which inciting incidents, obstacles, turning points and climaxes are identified (1999: 412).

McKee is the screenwriting guru that Charlie Kauffman sends up

> A **scene breakdown** (sometimes termed a step outline or sequence outline) lists each scene or sequence in a script, describing what happens, and sometimes also stating why the scene is significant, or what its narrative function is.
>
> The **first act** (termed **Act One**, the **Exposition**, or the **Orientation**) sets up the story, introducing characters and locations. In the beginning there is a state of equilibrium or balance. Even if it is a state of upheaval, it is how the characters live when we are introduced to them. Then an inciting incident or catalyst occurs. This is any event that disturbs the balance and causes action, conflict, drama or change, forcing the protagonist into action. Suddenly they stand to lose something, and they have something to gain. Now the protagonist has a goal: to establish a new equilibrium. They need a plan to achieve that goal, defining their course of action.
>
> The **second act** (or the **development**) of a narrative follows the characters towards their goals. The drama hinges on the audience's emotional engagement: we hope our heroes reach their goals and we fear that they will not. This creates suspense. Obstacles such as confrontations and complications interfere with the character's plan, causing conflict. Obstacles can be caused by characters with opposing goals, environmental factors, inner conflicts like ethical dilemmas and temptations, or by chance. Such factors make protagonists change direction and form new plans to pursue their goals. These 'changes of direction' are called turning points.

> The **third act** of a narrative (the **denouement**) includes the climax of a story, which occurs just before the story ends when the protagonist has a major crisis and faces a serious obstacle preventing them from reaching their goal. The climax arises from this crisis. The third act involves revelations, reversals and significant conflict like a showdown, the outcome of which leads to the resolution. The driving tension that has sustained viewer interest is resolved, the narrative question is answered and new balance is reached, leaving the audience with a sense of unity and closure.

and to whom he grudgingly pays homage in *Adaptation*. His method of screenwriting can be described as working from the 'inside out' (McKee 1999: 417), in that it involves research, planning and character development before the writer allows the characters to speak and commences writing dialogue in script format. McKee believes that 'the premature writing of dialogue chokes creativity' (1999: 417), but not all writers feel this way. Many screenwriters follow different creative pathways that lead to good results, rather than adhering to the dictates of a 'how to' guide book. At some stage of script development, all writers benefit from thinking through aspects of the characters' lives that will never explicitly be stated in the script itself, but that will enhance understanding of the protagonists' backgrounds, flaws and motives. Knowing a character's back-story, and developing familiarity with everything from their physical attributes through their taste in food, clothing and music, to their deepest fears and strongest desires and aspirations will enable a writer to craft characters that are credible, interesting and original.

Once the characters are adequately fleshed out and the action has been plotted into a satisfactory storyline, there are a number of techniques that can be used to enhance the structure of a script by maximising audience involvement. According to Paul Joseph Gulino, author of *Screenwriting: The Sequence Approach*, which details the hidden structure of successful screenplays, the storyteller's most potent strategies include the art of telegraphing future events, delaying gratification by including a dangling cause, and creating dramatic irony and dramatic tension (2004: 9–10). An excellent example of 'telegraphing' is found in the television series *Heroes*, in which a precognitive painter called Isaac foresees a future in which New York is devastated by a cataclysmic explosion. This sets the stakes and makes the audience want to find out whether the catastrophe can be averted, and if so how and by whom.

The 'dangling cause' is another tool that writers use to cast the minds of audience members into the future, building anticipation as we wait to see the effects of the causal incident. For instance, in the comedy *There's Something About Mary*, Ted decides to masturbate prior to his date with Mary in order to release sexual tension and avoid seeming too eager to shag on their first date. When he ejaculates, he can't find where the semen landed. This is a dangling cause as the audience suspects that when the lost semen is found, it will cause problems. Later, when Mary arrives, she uses what she thinks is excess hair gel to spike her fringe. Like Ted, the audience knows the substance is not hair gel, which provides the comic payoff to the dangling cause.

Dramatic irony is like a sly wink directed towards the audience by the filmmakers, without the characters noticing. It is established by manipulating the difference between what the characters know and what the audience knows. This creates different levels of understanding within a story, establishing a certain knowing distance between the filmmakers, the characters and the audience. For instance, in the British romantic comedy *Love Actually*, Liam Neeson's character repeatedly jokes about hooking up with supermodel Claudia Schiffer. When he meets a single mum called Carol, the audience knows Carol is actually the real Schiffer doing a cameo role but the characters are clueless, which gives the scene ironic humour. The use of omniscient narration (when the camera or voiceover provides information that is not tied to the awareness of a particular character) can also create a situation where the audience has privileged insight into a situation or knows something dreadful is about to happen, while the characters obliviously go about their business.

Dramatic tension is wrought using any of the above techniques to sustain character engagement and audience interest. As discussed in more detail in the next chapter, in a conventional dramatic narrative action and conflict drive the plot and the audience's interest is maintained by a desire to find out the answer to the enigma or **narrative question** of the story. The narrative question plays on the audience's concern for the protagonist, and is closely tied to our desire to know whether particular characters will achieve their goals: Will the gifted individuals in *Heroes* use their super-powers to save or destroy New York? Will Mary

> The **narrative question**, or the dramatic question, is the central question organising the story. It keeps the audience interested, and it hinges on our fears and desires about the protagonist. The dramatic question is answered in the story's resolution.

find true love? The narrative question may change over the course of the story, but ultimately it is only answered in the resolution, drawing out dramatic tension until the end of the story. It is worth keeping these points in mind when writing and revising a story for the screen, remembering that a systematic scene breakdown provides the necessary critical distance to analyse how a story is structured and to fine-tune the mechanics of a script.

TREATMENTS

A **treatment** develops each scene in a scene breakdown, step outline or sequence outline into a descriptive paragraph. Writers developing a concept for the screen frequently begin by writing their ideas in prose form, describing the storyline and characters before including dialogue and adopting a script format. This phase of the writing process is useful for elaborating and refining ideas, and it is an ideal form to share ideas with others and interest an agent, producer or funding body in developing the project.

Confusingly, the term 'treatment' can apply to two related documents which have somewhat different purposes. One use of the term applies to a summary or synopsis of the storyline, written much like a short story. This type of treatment, which we call the 'story treatment', functions primarily to help the writer flesh out the concept and begin giving ideas structure, life and colour. The other kind of treatment, which we call the 'project treatment', is more like a project outline than a story synopsis, written for the purpose of providing a clear overview of the project in the hope of involving other people in filming the script. Project treatments explicitly discuss the intended style, including information about how to 'treat' camerawork, sound, music and editing. In both types of treatment, in order to communicate the flavour of the story, the style of writing frequently has similarities with the style of the finished production. The treatment for a quirky, fast-paced series like *Reaper* might be written in a light,

> **Treatments** summarise a storyline in prose form, as part of the script development process. A treatment is a condensed description of the central concept, storyline and character developments in a script, written like a thorough story synopsis or a detailed project outline for the purpose of developing ideas and/or conveying the intended narrative and style to prospective financiers or participants in the production.

snappy, idiosyncratic style with short sentences whereas the treatment for a story like *Crouching Tiger, Hidden Dragon* might be more lyrical and formal in tone.

Treatments are written in descriptive prose using present tense, with a paragraph break for each change of scene. A good treatment introduces characters, setting and the highlights of the dramatic action in the order that the audience will see them played out on the screen. Writers imply camera direction rather than prescribing it—for example, 'her eyes glisten with tears as she slips into a reverie' implies a close-up dissolving to a flashback.

Very little dialogue is included in a treatment, if any. Dialogue written as direct speech reads much like a play or script. For example, in the script of *Grey's Anatomy* Season 3, Episode 6:

> Meredith says, 'Derek was naked apart from a towel, and she was on his bed.'
>
> George replies, 'You caught McDreamy doing the McNasty with McHottie? What a McBastard!'

In contrast, treatments usually paraphrase what the characters talk about, rather than specifying what they say:

> George teases Meredith when she tells him about catching Derek half-naked with an attractive woman.

When dialogue is important enough to make it into a treatment, indirect speech is used to describe it, like this:

> When Meredith recounts her shock at seeing Derek half-naked with an attractive woman, George hoots at her dismay, exclaiming that she caught McDreamy doing the McNasty with McHottie.

Besides being a valuable tool for developing ideas, treatments can form part of a project proposal. Project treatments should detail how a filmmaker would treat the subject matter, as well as describing the storyline and characters and indicating the intended audience. This type of treatment talks *about* the story rather than *telling* the story. The theme and the gist of the narrative are described along with the character arcs and a sense of whether the audio-visual style will be suspenseful action, gritty realism or an edgy, experimental aesthetic.

Treatments for documentary projects introduce the subject matter and intended style, and list intended interviewees, re-enactments or archival footage, describing key locations and including a sample of voiceover commentary if appropriate.

Both forms of treatment are short, about one-tenth of the length of the finished script. Both rely on expressive prose to bring the essence of the concept to life in a succinct and engaging manner. If ever you are asked to submit a treatment to a funding body or to someone you would like to involve in your project, it is wise to clarify whether they want a project outline or a descriptive story synopsis.

SCRIPTS

Scripts are detailed written plans for shooting film or television productions, including all dialogue and all scenes, in the order they will be screened. A script is not a finished text—it is a guide to making a screen text. It goes through multiple drafts, often changing to suit available locations and talent. Like a play, a script is a plan that enables the finished text to be produced, but it also leaves room for interpretation. With the exception of writer-directors, once screenwriters have sold the rights to the script, they generally relinquish creative control over the story. The director or script editor may rewrite dialogue and cut, rearrange or alter scenes. Narrative television involves even more people in the screenwriting process. The series creator often charts the story arc for a season, plotting the main action and perhaps writing and directing climactic episodes, but a team of other writers script the dialogue and fill in the blanks for the remaining episodes. In this collaborative process, it is crucial that all writers share an understanding of characters' motives, mannerisms and speech patterns, and how interwoven storylines develop over time.

The usual guide for scriptwriters is that one page of script equates to one minute of screen time—though action sequences often play out faster and dialogue scenes can be slow. Sticking to standard script format, as detailed below, is essential to get the timing right. It may sound painful, but it also helps to read dialogue aloud and walk through your characters' movements with a stopwatch to get a sense of pacing dialogue and action and avoid over-writing. Feature film scripts are 90–120 pages long. Narrative television scripts also play out at about one page per minute of screen time, but screenwriters must bear in mind that a television hour is usually only 40–48 minutes long, with approximately 25 per cent of screen time devoted to the advertising breaks around which the story is structured. It is necessary to work these breaks into the script, building up to cliffhanger moments prior to each advertisement.

Scriptwriting style differs slightly for film and television. For film, the cardinal rule is 'show—don't tell'. Film is a visual medium, so professional screenwriters create strong images and let the pictures and the action tell the story, rather than spelling out characters' thoughts and feelings or expressing the meaning of the film in dialogue. Television, on the other hand, is dialogue driven so scripts tend to involve more wordplay. In both media, it is important to use straightforward but vivid prose in the script so the reader can visualise how the scene will look. Write economically, only describing details that advance the plot, plant cues for the cast and crew, give pointers to the audience, underscore the theme or develop character. Scripts should not be literary or poetic in style, but they should bring characters, locations, images and actions to life.

Scripts only include elements of the story that can be seen and/or heard. The test question should always be 'how do we know?' If it can't be photographed or recorded, omit it. For example, describe an actor's expression and gestures so that the audience can *infer* what they are thinking or feeling, rather than writing: 'Leila wonders whether she will ever overcome her fear of abandonment and learn to trust again.' Such aspects of a character's inner world may be appropriate for a novel, but they have no place in a script. The audience can only see or hear what a character wonders, wishes or feels if it is evident in the performance or if the writer expresses what the protagonist sees in her mind's eye as metaphoric or subjective imagery, or a flashback, or articulates what a character is thinking using voiceover narration. These techniques are not suitable for all stories and can seem heavy-handed if over-used.

Characters' names are written in block capitals when they first appear in a script and whenever they speak a line of dialogue, which brings us to matters of script format and the correct way to lay out work. Script formats are similar all over the world, but there are some regional and media-specific differences in screenwriting conventions. For instance, whereas in North America it may be acceptable for a screenwriter to include instructions such as 'zoom in to CU', in countries like Australia, New Zealand, South Africa and the United Kingdom it is considered bad form to do so. Since decisions about cinematography are the prerogative of the director, it is not customary to include film or television terms regarding shot scale or camera techniques in a script. Avoid adding camera directions prescribing angle, lens, shot scale or camera movement. Describe what the audience sees instead. If Leila arches one eyebrow and purses her lips, that's a close-up. If Blake scans the crowded bar looking for Scarlet, then lurches drunkenly towards her, it suggests a panning movement and handheld camera from his point of view. In a script, scene space is always described from the camera's point of view, which corresponds with the audience's point of view.

It is important to be scrupulous about script format, not only because it affects timing but also because industry professionals will identify work as amateur if it does not follow accepted conventions. Scripts always have 2.5-centimetre margins for the top, bottom and right side, and a wider 3.5-centimetre margin on the left. They are typed in 12 point Courier font (the one that looks like an old-fashioned typewriter script), using single line spacing with a double space inserted between scenes, and to separate descriptions of the action from dialogue. The title page should show the script's title, centred at the top of the page in bold text and capital letters, with the author's name, the date and a copyright symbol © following underneath. In the bottom left-hand corner of the title page, specify the draft stage (such as second draft) and include your contact details (see Figure 5.1).

Acknowledge the source if the script is adapted from a play or a book, name the funding body if a development grant has been received, and remember that you need to obtain an exclusive licence (known as an 'option') for the right to adapt a play script or novel for commercial purposes.

Each new scene begins with a **scene line**, otherwise known as a slug line or scene heading, typed entirely in capital letters. This includes crucial information such as the scene number, an indication of whether the scene is set indoors or outdoors (expressed as INT or EXT—meaning it is either an interior or exterior scene),

> The **scene line** is a heading typed at the start of every scene in a script. It includes the scene number, states whether the setting is interior or exterior, names the location and specifies the time of day.

followed by the name of the actual location (such as LEILA'S OFFICE). 'FLASHBACK' or 'DREAM SEQUENCE' can be indicated next to the location if necessary. It is also essential to indicate the time of day the scene takes place. There are only four terms used to indicate time in the scene line of a script: DAY, NIGHT, DAWN or DUSK.

Below the scene line, the writer describes the main action in the scene. The scene description has the same function as stage directions in a play and is sometimes termed the 'action', the 'body text' or the 'big print'. It should be concise yet descriptive, and it should be written in the present tense. Describe each 'imagined shot' or separate image in a distinct line or paragraph. As soon as a whole lot of shots are lumped into one paragraph, the timing goes way off. As a

```
                    SCRIPT TITLE

                         by
                  SCRIPTWRITER'S NAME

                  Based on a novel by
                     NOVEL AUTHOR








          THIRD DRAFT
          MAY 2007
          © SCRIPTWRITER'S NAME
          Writer's Address
          Phone number, Email
```

Figure 5.1 Script Cover Page

scriptwriter, you are writing for performance. Rather than instructing actors how to act, incorporate subtle cues about vocal tone or expression (see Figure 5.2).

Capitalise characters' names on first appearance, and every time they speak, type their name in capitals centred above the dialogue. Dialogue belongs in a central column, two tab spaces in from the left and right margins. Amateur scriptwriters often 'centre' dialogue instead of indenting it, but this is incorrect and the variable line length of centred text looks messy. Directions about how the character should speak (bemused, furiously, slyly, stuttering awkwardly) should be used sparingly, typed in lower case, bracketed under the charac-

```
                                                            7.


        3. EXT.   BONDI BEACH.   DAWN

        BLAKE jogs along the shoreline, breathing
        heavily, eyeing a woman lying on the sand
        ahead. Passing her, he notes the awkward
        sprawl of her limbs.


                       BLAKE
                      (Gently)

        You okay? Miss?

        Blake reaches out to rouse her. Alarmed
        he pulls back from the cold, unresponsive
        feel of her flesh.


                      BLAKE (CONT'D)

        Life guard! (SHOUTING)
        Help!
```

Figure 5.2 Script format with scene line and dialogue

ter's name and above their dialogue, or capitalised and inserted in parentheses within the dialogue itself. If a character's dialogue is interrupted by action, insert a paragraph break, type the description of the action in the body text, then centre and capitalise the character's name again for the rest of their dialogue and write 'cont'd' in brackets next to their name.

Try to make characters speak in unique ways, especially when they come from different backgrounds. Vocabulary and speech patterns reveal character, so write dialogue in *their* voices, not your own. Sometimes it is a good idea to write phonetically to capture accents. Read the dialogue aloud to see whether it sounds staged or natural, and keep it short and snappy. The 'rule of thumb' is that if a dialogue block is over four lines (the width of a thumb), it is almost certainly longer than it needs to be. Remember that people rarely say what they mean, and the character should never say what *you* mean. In other words, the characters should not directly express the author's intended meaning or the script's theme. In order to convey story information in dialogue, many writers contrive a situation where one character must recap, answer questions and explain plot points to another character. This exposition technique is common in detective stories, and in long-running television narratives in which there is a good chance audiences may have missed important information.

Think about the function each line of dialogue has in developing the story, rather than including padding to make a scene feel natural. Each conversation can be understood as an action. For instance, dialogue may be an act of seduction or interrogation, or it may be more like an ambush and combat sequence using words as weapons. In terms of driving the plot, dialogue can function to reveal character motivation, to cue reversals and turning points, and to set up obstacles and goals. Dialogue can also be used effectively to generate and answer narrative questions. As discussed in Chapter 3, writers can use the technique of the dialogue hook to lead the audience through the story, reinforcing important information and providing links to subsequent developments. Often, the last line of dialogue in a scene sets up what and who will be in the next location. This technique is used frequently in television scripts. To illustrate this technique, dialogue hooks are in bold print in Figure 5.3.

> **SCARLET**
>
> Don't tell me *you've* never made a **mistake**! What about that 'flirtation' with your brother's **girlfriend**?
>
> **BLAKE**
>
> *Girlfriend*? She said they was 'just good friends'. Anyway you're the one who 'made a **mistake**,' if that's what you call **cheatin'** on me with Leila.
>
> **SCARLET**
>
> It was *experimenting*, not **cheating. Go ask Leila** if you want to know what really happened.

Figure 5.3 Script format with dialogue hook.

With this technique, the scriptwriter 'hooks' the interest of the audience so we want to know what happens next, using dialogue as 'bait' that lures us towards the next plot point and sets up the subsequent scene in which Blake confronts Leila.

To reiterate, scriptwriters avoid using dialogue to spell out information that can be conveyed by other means, and they avoid writing instructions about aspects of the production process that are the responsibility of other members of the production team. If the script can show something via imagery, motion and performance, you don't need to 'say it' using dialogue or screen jargon. While camera direction is unacceptable, some abbreviations of technical terms are used in scripts when necessary to enhance understanding. For instance, writers may use POV to refer to point of view, V/O to indicate voiceover, B/G and F/G to signal background or foreground, and O/S to clarify that a certain sound can be heard off screen or out of shot. The screenwriter does not need to signal shot transitions or scene transitions in the script. It is the editor's responsibility to make decisions about the types of transitions that are appropriate. However, if editing is crucial to the story then you might leave a double space between scenes and write in capitals something like INTERCUT BETWEEN BONDI BEACH AND LEILA'S OFFICE or DISSOLVE TO FLASHBACK. In most cases, it is more appropriate to plan shot transitions and camera techniques in the shooting script or the storyboard rather than the script.

SHOOTING SCRIPTS AND STORYBOARDS

After the script has been finalised, the director groups scenes into common settings or locations that can be filmed at the same point in the shooting schedule and formulates a shot list which details the coverage required for each scene, noting the visual style and specifying the type and number of shots needed. The shot list is used to plan the look and feel of a scene in terms of camera movement, shot size, angle and focus, and it is essential in determining what equipment will be needed on each day of the shoot, such as lenses, tracks and rigging. It is also a crucial part of planning for post-production, ensuring the editor will have a sufficient range of shots to cut the scene together effectively. The screenwriter is seldom involved in shot listing since the task requires the specialised skills of the director and cinematographer. When the shot list is mapped on to the script itself, it is termed a **shooting script** or camera script. In the process of developing the shot list and shooting script, directors often prepare schematic floor plans and storyboards to show where the camera will be placed and to visualise how a scene will look on screen. For multi-camera television shoots, the shot list and shooting script detail the positions, shot size, camera angles and movements of each camera for each moment in the script.

A **storyboard** is a phase of pre-production after the script is written and before it is filmed. It consists of a series of

> The **shooting script** combines the shot list with the script, specifying how each element of the action and dialogue in each scene will be filmed.

annotated sketches of a sequence of shots, and it is as close as you can come to shooting a film without actually picking up a camera. Storyboards function to translate words into pictures, aiding realisation of the filmmaker's vision. They describe in detail what happens in a given sequence and provide instructions for the crew and actors about what each shot will look like and sound like. Storyboarding helps plan how a series of images will cut together, especially if the sequence is tricky and involves unrepeatable action or sophisticated choreography, effects or expensive equipment.

> **Storyboards** are annotated illustrations of a series of shots, made for the purpose of envisioning and planning how a sequence will be filmed and edited.

Sometimes directors sketch their own storyboards using stick figures or more elaborate drawings if they have artistic skills. A good storyboard artist, also known as a production illustrator, requires first-rate drawing skills. Although the storyboard illustrations themselves don't need to be works of art, production illustrators might also produce wardrobe sketches or sketches of sets for the art director. Like all crew members, the ability to work collaboratively and to meet deadlines under pressure is essential. Storyboards require an understanding of staging, editing, composition, cinematography (including lenses), special effects, stunt work and animation.

The storyboarding process aids creative visualisation of the script, and can be helpful in generating ideas or working out how those ideas can be implemented. As a technical tool, the storyboard is a careful shooting plan that assists the communication and realisation of complicated sequences, mapping out and experimenting with framing, composition and the connections between shots. Storyboards ensure the cast and crew are all 'on the same page', providing an inexpensive way of trying out different possible ways of shooting a sequence. Virtually every member of the cast and crew can utilise and benefit from storyboards, so when devising a storyboard consider your audience, thinking carefully about what information these different members of the filmmaking team will need to know. Also spare a thought for the spectators who will ultimately watch the film or television show. Concentrating on how the audience will experience and respond to the story will lead to the production of the most effective and interesting storyboards.

Few films or television productions have the budget or the need for storyboarding an entire script. Storyboards are most likely to be used when the director, the art director or the director of photography has fine art training and drawing skills (thereby avoiding the need to pay a dedicated storyboard illustrator), or for short productions, music videos and advertisements. In longer productions, storyboarding is usually restricted to sequences that require special effects, stunts, rigging, complex cinematography or editing, animation, or models and computer-generated graphics combined with 'real' settings and action. Such sequences require careful pre-visualisation and planning to avoid expensive mistakes.

The format of storyboards varies considerably from large, bold sketches using charcoal or pencil, through smaller sketches in ink, colour markers or paints, to digital formats using pre-visualisation tools or graphic software. For hand-drawn sketches, three or four shots per page will establish a sense of the flow of a sequence. Number each shot at the top left of each sketch, and make the boxes the shape of a television or cinema screen, using the aspect ratio appropriate to the medium in which you are working. Then draw the action from the perspective of the camera angle and distance envisioned. While drawing the key moments of action in a complex shot, you may need to draw a series of frames or an elongated frame that shows the action unfolding at different moments in time and space. Software programs such as PowerPoint or Flash can be useful for displaying storyboards if you are using computer-generated imagery, or if you are taking digital photos of locations in the process of conceptualising the shoot. Such programs enable sophisticated shot transitions to be used, and provide the opportunity to crop, reframe and annotate shots without the need to redraw sets or action.

Every shot in a storyboard should include the scene number and shot number along with visible or written information about:

- action;
- lighting;
- camera directions;
- sound and dialogue; and
- shot transition.

Remember that screen conventions have been developed for a reason: to help understand the story. The notes accompanying each shot in the storyboard are *not* an appropriate place to indicate why a particular effect has been used, or to discuss the intended impact or meaning of techniques. As is the case with scriptwriting, storyboard artists don't include details that cannot be photographed or recorded.

For shot action, the storyboard illustrations or annotations need to be detailed enough for the reader to visualise the shot clearly. It is important that figure movement is specified. There should be enough indication of the actor's expression to convey a sense of characterisation, where appropriate. Any significant props or costumes should be visible or described, but storyboards should not laboriously detail every aspect of the *mise en scène*.

For lighting, an effective storyboard will provide visual indicators of the source, intensity, colour and direction of the light, and may be annotated using technical terms such as high-key or low-key lighting, back light, top light or diffuse light if such elements are significant. Not every shot will require this level of detail, and it is acceptable to write 'as for shot 7' if the intended effect of the lighting remains the same.

Regarding cinematography, a proficient storyboard will either illustrate or specify shot scale, point of view, camera movement, camera angle, depth of field and shifts in focus, noting any filters or special lenses. Where camera movement or a zoom is used, indicate the direction and speed of the movementusing annotations and arrows on the sketch. For example, a storyboard showing a bird in flight might specify a whip pan from left to right ending when we see the bird land, or it might require a slow zoom in from a long shot (labelled shot 1a) to a tighter framing revealing the type of bird (shown as a frame within the frame, labelled shot 1b).

Sound can also be planned in the storyboarding process. Because storyboards detail what happens in each shot in a sequence, any dialogue should be written out in full alongside the shot in which it occurs. Generalisations such as 'Shamila and Dave discuss their weekend' are not helpful when planning how to shoot and cut a dialogue sequence. Storyboards can indicate when sound is off screen, and distinguish between voiceover narration and dialogue, diegetic and non-diegetic music or sound effects, and so forth.

Because storyboards are also a tool for planning how a sequence will cut together, edit points and shot transitions should be indicated. Illustrators therefore need an awareness of cinematic conventions regarding screen direction, point of view and the codes of continuity editing.

Storyboarding can be thought of as a process of adaptation, changing a script into a screen text in a form that expresses the spirit of the text and renders the characters, their situations and their goals recognisable, yet inflects them with a distinctive style. Because it is much less expensive than shooting, a storyboard is a good place to experiment with different ideas about genre, lighting, movement and mood. When devising a storyboard, it is important to begin by thinking about when to start the action, what to emphasise and what to cut. The storyboard might be the place to make decisions about whether to utilise, omit or modify the dialogue or voiceover in the script. Storyboards also provide an ideal space to consider how to manipulate spectatorial expectations and exploit generic conventions, and how to structure the narrative and sequence of shots to generate interest and suspense, and provide plot and character information. It may also be helpful to use the storyboard to plan how to evoke a sense of off-screen space or the subjective space of a character's inner realm.

For example, consider how a section of the Lemony Snicket novel *A Series of Unfortunate Events: The Bad Beginning* could be adapted into different genres using a storyboard. In the novel, the evil Count Olaf has captured Sunny, the youngest Baudelaire orphan, and suspended her atop a tall tower in order to bully Violet, the eldest child, into marrying him so he can control the Baudelaire fortune. Violet's and Sunny's brother Klaus is witness at the wedding ceremony: 'Klaus thought of poor Sunny, dangling at the top of the tower, and stood still as he watched Violet take the long quill pen from Count Olaf. Violet's eyes were wide as she looked down at the document, and her face was pale, and her left hand was trembling as she signed her name' (Snicket 1999: 144).

When adapting a novel for the screen or storyboarding a sequence from a script, the written material will suggest visual images and will indicate where the camera might be placed. The role of the storyboarder is to interpret the director's vision, which may involve enhancing or omitting elements in the written material, maximising its impact for the screen. Where Snicket's novel describes the wedding from Klaus's perspective, the director may decide that this should really be Violet's scene as she is the one under duress. To enhance the dramatic impact, a storyboard illustrator can play with point of view, experimenting with framing the action from the perspective of different characters, using a variety of camera angles or shot scales to position the audience in screen space. If the version from the novel were filmed, the spectator would be aligned with Klaus as a witness rather than a participant in the drama, whereas if the scene were focused around Violet, the spectator would be more likely to feel emotionally involved in the action.

The first storyboard (see Figure 5.4) shows how the story fragment could be adapted using a style suitable for a television soap opera shot in a studio setting. Following the conventions of the melodrama genre, the action is tightly framed and well illuminated, using high-key, three-point lighting to reveal expression and non-diegetic music to orchestrate emotional turbulence. The four shots shown are focused around Violet's subjective perception of events by zooming in to a close-up of her eyes, using dissolves to cue the transition into her imagination, and allowing the spectator to share her optical point of view.

The second storyboard (see Figure 5.5) draws on the conventions of horror films, using deep shadows and ominous off-screen sound effects to create a fearful atmosphere on location in the Count's spooky, decrepit mansion. As horror films frequently pay intertextual homage to other films in the genre, the last shot references a scene in *Nosferatu*, one of the earliest and most famous vampire movies ever shot, when the shadow of the vampire creeps towards the heroine. This framing also calls into play one of the most unsettling hallmarks of the horror genre, the predatory shot filmed from the killer's point of view.

Since still drawings cannot show optical effects or movement, these examples demonstrate a number of ways to get around the limitations of storyboards by implying mobile framing or figure movement within a shot. Storyboard artists indicate zooms by drawing a frame within the frame to indicate the intended composition as it would be seen in the camera viewfinder, with arrows indicating a zoom in or out. For example, in the soap opera storyboard shown in Figure 5.4, the camera zooms out from the close up in shot 3a to the wider shot in the frame labelled 3b. Similarly, storyboards commonly use arrows *inside* the frame to show character movement (such as an actor walking across the screen), and use arrows *outside* the frame to show camera movement (such as a tilt, track or pan). Sometimes the actual frame is extended across or down (in conjunction with arrows) to depict a track, pan or tilt. Edits can sometimes be indicated using a cross joining two frames to indicate a dissolve, but most shot transitions such as straight cuts, fades and wipes need to be written as annotations beside or beneath the drawing.

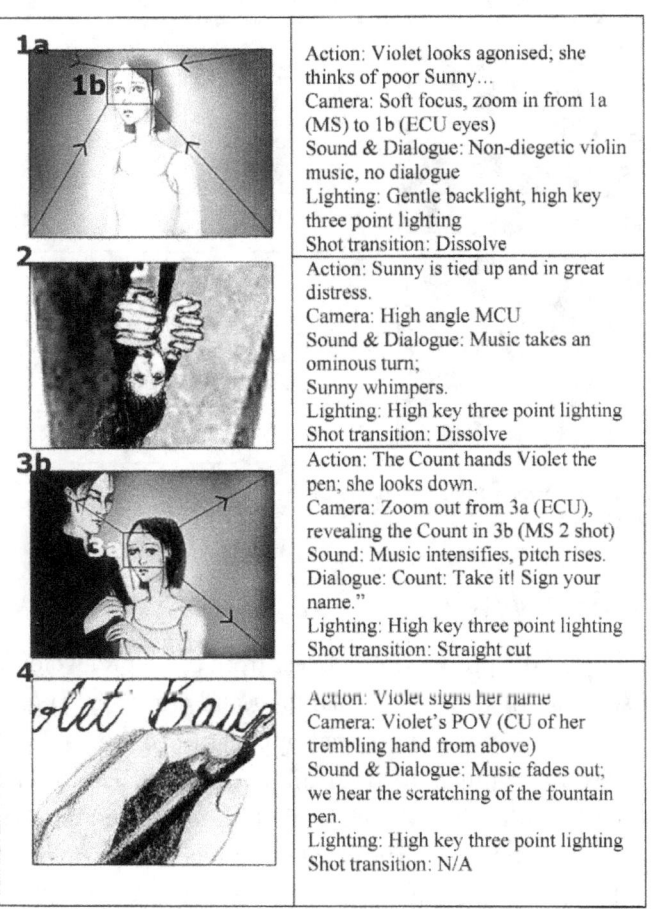

Figure 5.4 Soap opera storyboard courtesy of the Centre for Educational Technology, University of Cape Town

SCREEN MEDIA

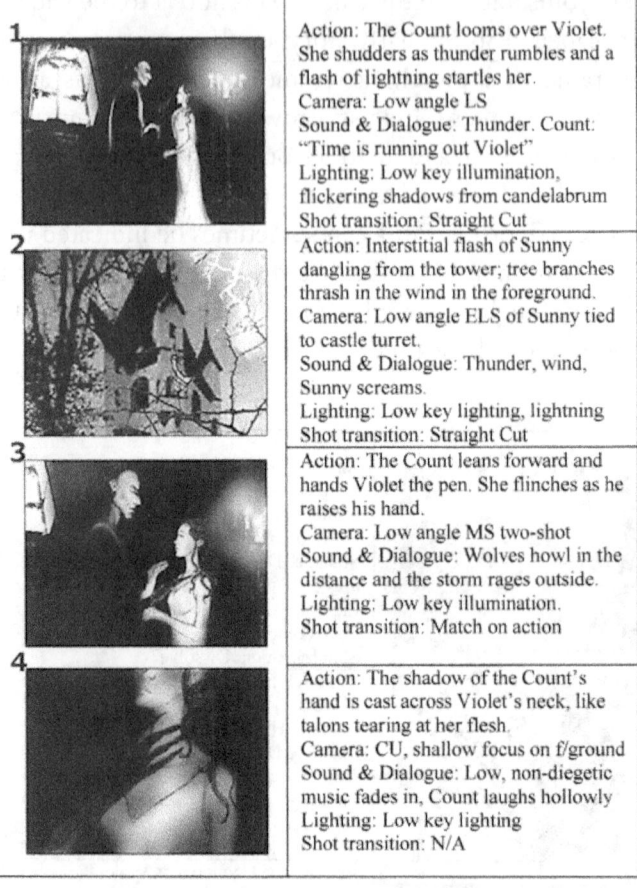

Figure 5.5 Horror storyboard courtesy of the Centre for Educational Technology, University of Cape Town

FILM REVIEWING

Having followed the production process from concept development, through scriptwriting, pitching, planning and storyboarding, let us now consider one more vocational application of the knowledge of screen texts accumulated so far: film reviewing. Film reviewing should not be confused with academic film criticism and analysis, as the style, structure and purposes of these types of writing are very different. Before writing any review, it pays to think carefully about your audience: consider who they are, what they want from a review and why they might wish to see the film. This depends largely on where the review will be published, but it also depends on the type of film, and who is paying you to write the review, or who stands to benefit from it. Some reviews are not as independent as they could be, and serve as thinly disguised publicity material for the film. Reviewing styles and strategies also vary depending on the medium in which the review is published (radio, television, specialist magazines, newspapers or websites). Here we offer general guidelines for writing a review published in the entertainment guide of a newspaper.

The tone of a review should be informal and it should express an opinion, as though describing a movie you have just seen to a friend who is considering watching it. Think critically but write casually, using a conversational tone. It is fine to write in first person, using 'I', and to write about your own interpretation, but the review should focus on the film, not the reviewer. Substantiate opinions with reasons and specific examples from the film to avoid coming across as overly familiar or opinionated.

Adrian Martin, one of Australia's leading film critics, reveals that the task of a film reviewer involves a particular kind of description:

> Who wants to read five paragraphs of plot synopsis? If I want to see the plot I'll go to see the film. I want the motor of that plot, I want something of the hook about that plot to get me interested ... a sort of sensuous description of the film, of the rhythm of the film, of the colour of the film, of the mood itself, of the changing moods of the film. Something that gives you a feeling, a really experiential feeling of the film that you try to translate into your own language. (Martin 2005: 6)

As Martin's advice suggests, a reviewer's writing style should be descriptive and informative, not weighed down with the details of the plot or clinical like a dry academic essay or a news article. Reviews are written *scenically*, without using technical film jargon. You might think about reviewing as a process of reverse adaptation—turning a screen text back into a piece of prose or 'writing a trailer' that showcases salient moments of the film and brings its style and the viewing experience to life. Avoid clichés: if you've heard a phrase used many times before, discard it. Also be aware that reviews use short, succinct sentences and paragraphs. Sentences in a print review are typically only 25–35 words long, and when writing for radio or online formats sentences will need to be as concise as 15–20 words.

A good review starts with a short, catchy title, generally seven words or less. It is advisable to use the name of the film in the title or in the first sentence of the review so that readers know what you are writing about. The first sentence, also termed the '**lead**', or the 'hook', is possibly the most important part of the review. Without an informative, interesting lead sentence that captures attention with an intriguing angle, readers are likely to turn the page. Sometimes the title of a film is unusual enough to provide an interesting starting point, and sometimes the theme, the characters or stars, the special effects or the style provide a better angle. In a short space, the lead sentence needs to pack in information about questions that readers will have regarding the film. As for other journalistic writing, the key questions a review aims to answer are often termed 'the five Ws and the H': who, what, when, where, why and how. In order to decide whether to spend money on a ticket to the film, prospective spectators want information about the following questions:

> The **lead**, also known as the hook, is the first sentence of a film review. It is designed to capture attention and entice prospective audience members to find out more about the film.

- Who is in the film?
- What type of film is it, and what is it about?
- When does the story take place?
- Where is it set?
- Why should anyone see it?
- How is it shot and scored?

It will be difficult, if not impossible, to address all of these questions in the lead sentence, so focus on those pertaining to the most noteworthy aspects of the film being reviewed. For example, *The Science of Sleep* is set in present times, which is unremarkable and does not warrant a place in the lead, but other aspects of its setting are unusual as it is a foreign film, and much of the action takes place inside the mind of the protagonist. There is little point in trying to explain what *The Science of Sleep* is about in the first sentence of a review, as it barely has a plot (a young man arrives in Paris following the death of his father, takes a dull and disappointing job, and develops a crush on his neighbour). The stand out features of *The Science of Sleep* are its magical realist style which flits whimsically between layers of dream and reality, the magnetism of its charismatic star Gael García Bernal, and its renowned art-house director Michel Gondry. The review title and lead in the example below emphasise the film's main drawcards: celebrity, character, setting and directorial style.

> **Sleep** with Gael García Bernal
> Traverse the magical landscape of director Michel Gondry's imagination in The Science of Sleep, following Bernal's adventures as Stéphane, an eccentric dreamer wandering between Mexico and Paris, memory and possibility, lucidity and fancy.

After hooking the reader's attention, the review develops information planted in the lead. For example, *The Science of Sleep* review could move on to inform readers unfamiliar with Gondry's work that he has shot music videos for Björk and the White Stripes, and brought two of Charlie Kaufman's inventive scripts to the screen (*Human Nature* and *Eternal Sunshine of the Spotless Mind*). Particularly if a film is not easy to classify within an established genre, it is helpful to relate the film to others with the same actor, director, genre, style or theme. Audiences may want to see a film if they love previous work by the star or the director. All reviews must include the names of key figures, and must distinguish consistently between actors and the characters they play (for instance, it is Stéphane, not Bernal, who is enamoured with his neighbour Stéphanie).

After the title and the hook, reviews typically include the following components, usually structured in this order: description, analysis, evaluation and recommendation. The review shouldn't read as a formulaic, methodical march through these elements, though. One of Adrian Martin's techniques as a film reviewer is to ensure that every paragraph includes something about the story, something about style and something about the acting, rather than separating the plot synopsis from the analysis of the film's aesthetic qualities (Martin 2005: 6). This strategy enables a reviewer to incorporate insights about the style of a film and to articulate an interpretation of the story, while making it difficult for an editor to cut a paragraph if a publication is squeezed for space.

Reviews should contain a brief, descriptive synopsis of the story that conveys what the film is about and who it features, *without* spoilers or a blow-by-blow summary. Avoid telling what happens.

Instead, describe characters' goals and the central conflict, theme or issue, and discuss the story in terms of structure and point of view.

In the analysis of the style, story and performance, the reviewer can address questions about the film's genre and whether it conforms to or breaks with expectations and conventions. If it is not a genre film, offer description and comparisons and consider how the story unfolds. Is it a tight script, or are there loose ends, twists or plot holes, a slow start, a satisfying ending or a circular narrative? Assess the acting, stating what makes a performance good or bad, and mention anything special you noticed about the soundtrack, score or cinematography. This is not the place to get technical: speak in a language that the 'average viewer' will understand and evoke a sense of the film's unique style and impact by giving a vivid sense of what it looks, feels and sounds like. Try incorporating memorable lines of dialogue—for instance, bring Stéphane's quirky character to life with a snippet of his stumbling French.

Evaluating the film's strengths and weaknesses forms an important part of any review. Even if the reviewer hates a film, remember that there will be people who really like it. In order to avoid alienating the audience or sounding self-important, reviewers should mention both strengths and weaknesses. For instance, the acting might be brilliant, but the story could lack resolution. A crisp example of evaluation is found in Edward Lawrenson's review for *Sight & Sound*: '*The Science of Sleep* is possibly a very shallow work, but it's also exhaustively imaginative and bustles with wit and innovation' (Lawrenson 2006: 88). Give your readers reasons to see or to avoid the film and consider whether the film meets its own objectives such as making the audience laugh, cry or ponder an issue, eliciting character engagement or pushing the boundaries of cinema with special effects or aesthetic innovation. In this respect it helps to think about what the filmmakers intended. Authorial intent is not the key to meaning, but it is worth considering what the filmmakers were trying to achieve. For instance, if a film is billed as a comedy, it is important that the review assesses whether it is funny.

Most reviews conclude with a recommendation to prospective viewers. A shorthand recommendation is to use a score out of five stars to rate a film the way hotels and restaurants are rated. It is helpful to signal who the film's target audience is, stating whether it will appeal to children, teens, aficionados of international art films, or those looking for light popcorn entertainment. As part of their recommendation, reviewers sometimes also mention how the film is rated, particularly if it contains extreme violence or other provocative material. The recommendation can be guided by an assessment of how the cinema audience responded to the film, noting whether people walked out, laughed uproariously, fidgeted restlessly or were on the edge of their seats.

Rather than attempting to cover every aspect of a film's content, style, production and reception, each review should focus on what is most relevant or interesting, using specific examples to support opinions. Reviewing may not be a substitute for academic film criticism, but it is a good way to hone writing skills and develop an appreciation of cinema.

CONCLUSION

This chapter has covered the fundamentals of film reviewing, storyboarding, script development and screenwriting structure, style and format. Those who would like to explore scriptwriting further might try script format software such as Final Draft, or read some 'how to' books for screenwriters. We recommend reading Syd Field's *The Definitive Guide to Screenwriting* (2003) or consulting Robert McKee's influential introduction to screenwriting, *Story* (1999). It is also worth investigating Ken Dancyger and Jeff Rush's guide to *Alternative Scriptwriting: Successfully Breaking the Rules* (2002) once you have mastered traditional narrative structure.

The very best way to develop as a writer is to learn from professional writers practising their craft by reading reviews written in a range of styles for different media, and reading the scripts of your favourite film and television programs. Some DVDs have special features that include storyboards, as well as scripts and interviews or commentary by screenwriters. Many feature film scripts are also available free online. The following sites may be useful:

- Daily Script: www.dailyscript.com;
- Simply Scripts: http://simplyscripts.com/full_movie.html;
- Storyboards: www.cfms.uct.ac.za/storyboard;

- Film Reviewing: http://leo.stcloudstate.edu/acadwrite/bookrevpre.html;
- Film Criticism: www.filmcritic.com.au.

The British Film Institute (BFI) and the Screen Australia websites provide many screenwriting resources, helpful examples and links that detail the types of documents required by screenwriters and filmmakers, as well as the different script formats for both film and television preferred around the world (see www.screenaustralia.gov.au and www.bfi.org.uk/filmtvinfo/gateway/categories/scripts script writing). A particularly useful document available on the Screen Australia website is called 'What is a Synopsis? An Outline? A Treatment?' This document, on which we have drawn above, overviews the phases of script development and the form in which investors like to see a production proposal presented, covering compressed and extended versions of the story that is to be filmed.

KEY SKILLS

Having read this chapter, you should now be able to:

- identify the function of each of the different stages in the development of a story for screen production;
- explain the style, layout and structure of the following forms of storytelling: synopsis, scene breakdown, treatment, script, storyboard and film review;
- apply your understanding in one of these practical and creative exercises:
    - write a logline, a one paragraph plot synopsis, and a one page review for the most recent film you have watched;
    - using correct script format, write a script for a five-minute film suitable for shooting locally with a home video camera;

- develop a shot list and a storyboard for a ten-shot sequence depicting your first kiss;
- evaluate the strengths and weaknesses of an online review and a print review for the same film, noting how review writing styles vary across media.

6

screen narratives:
Traditions and Trends

CONTEMPORARY FILM NARRATIVES

Over black we hear the crunch of metal on metal. Then silence. Unrecognisable patterns of light and texture shift across the screen, fading in and out with little focus or meaning. It takes the audience a while to figure out that we are at the scene of an accident on a wintry night in Los Angeles. With the help of a superimposed title that says 'tomorrow', we realise the accident has yet to occur. Abruptly we leave the scene and jump to an earlier point in time: 'today'. We watch an Iranian father and daughter contend with a bigoted sales clerk and purchase a hand-gun and ammunition. Then we follow two young black men whose banter about stereotypes and the racial politics of tipping a café waitress leaves us ill-prepared for the fact that they are about to hijack a fancy car and ruin the rest of the film for a spoiled, highly strung woman played by Sandra Bullock. As the convoluted narrative of *Crash* (directed by Paul Haggis) unfolds, we get tangled up in the lives of no less than fifteen characters whose different stories of racial conflict and prejudice seem to collide rather than intersect. The narrative complexity is such that audiences develop sympathy and understanding for a police officer (Matt Dillon, pictured in Figure 6.1) who molests and humiliates a woman of colour, then later shows great bravery and compassion when he resues her from the wreckage of a burning car.

Crash won three Oscars in 2006, including Best Picture, and quickly grossed over $53 million in America alone, easily recouping its meagre $6.5 million budget. The following year, Alejandro González Iñárritu's *Babel* also won an Oscar, and made back many times its estimated $25 million cost. Despite low initial box office figures in America, *Babel* earned $114 million internationally, drawing fans of Brad Pitt and Cate Blanchett to a drama of miscommunication spanning four nations and a complex snarl of disordered time, broken relationships and violently fragmented stories. While the success of these features doesn't rival earlier award-winning puzzle-plot hits like Tarantino's influential *Pulp Fiction*, which had a budget of just $8 million and cleared over $100 million at the US box office in 1994, together they form a noteworthy trend. These examples suggest that **fragmented** and **multi-strand narratives** with ensemble casts have found a viable niche in screen culture, indicating that storytelling styles are changing—becoming more complex, adventurous and experimental—and audiences are becoming more sophisticated. In order to understand these changes, however, we first need a good working knowledge of classical narrative structure. Consequently, we

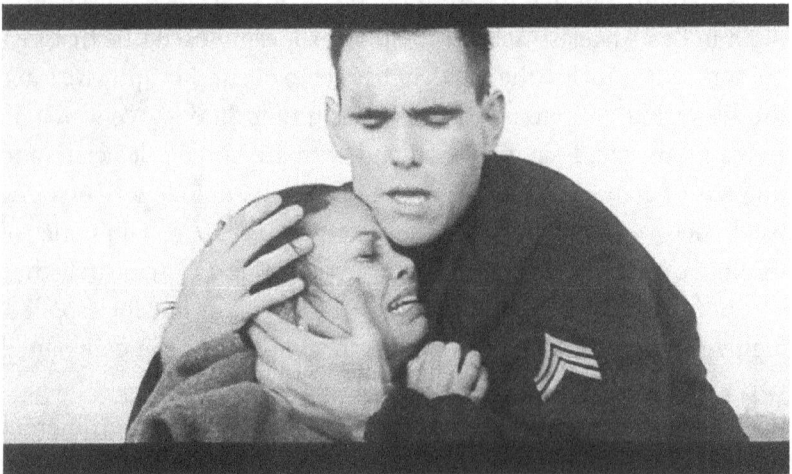

Figure 6.1 Crash

begin by introducing traditional three-act narrative structure before considering how it is modified in complex puzzle-plot films like those mentioned above, and how it relates to television's serial, segmented, episodic and character-based narratives, and to digital games.

CLASSICAL NARRATION

Classical narration relies on a stable, formulaic **'canonical' story structure** supported by a set of familiar screen conventions (Bordwell et al. 1985). Typically, narratives follow a three-act structure developing from an initial state of equilibrium, through a state of conflict (or disequilibrium), to a resolution (or a renewed equilibrium). Plots are kick-started by a catalyst that disrupts the initial equilibrium of the story world, creating an enigma or narrative question that fuels audience interest and generates goals for the protagonist. The middle of the story follows a causal chain in which individual characters play clearly defined roles motivated to solve the enigma and attain or thwart the principal protagonist's aims and desires. Conflict between the protagonist and the antagonist drives the plot forward, whatever form the forces obstructing the hero take. The tension between these opposing forces reaches a crisis point in the third act and is resolved in the climax, providing a reassuring answer to the questions posed in the narrative.

All stories are narrated and understood relative to the perspectives and

Fragmented narratives lack the unified, linear storyline of conventional narratives and undermine audience expectations. Rather than being motivated by and focused on an individual protagonist or a central narrative question, they are often decentred and broken up into jumbled segments featuring an array of characters in different places or non-sequential timeframes.

Multi-strand narratives feature several different narrative threads, either parallel to one another or interwoven in ways that often require more interpretive effort from the audience. The different stories may also unfold in a fragmented and disordered way in terms of their causal sequences or locations in time and space.

Classical narration refers to the classical style and canonic story structure of Hollywood studio filmmaking from around 1917 to 1960. It is organised around a causal sequence in which the actions of a central, individual protagonist unfurl in space and time, in response to the conflicting actions of an antagonistic force, which impedes the main character's goal. The role of the narrator is concealed in the narrative itself, and the cause–effect sequence and primacy of the individual hero are naturalised.

Canonical story structure, or canonic narrative, is a coherent, consistent format with three acts: introduction, complication and resolution.

values of those who construct and engage with them. In classical Hollywood narration, the conventions of continuity editing, unobtrusive cinematography and realist sound design frequently conceal the narrator's perspective and present it as an objective and ideologically neutral viewpoint on a story that unfolds naturally. For example, in the film *Snakes on a Plane*, we view the world through the eyes of our hero, FBI agent Neville Flynn (Samuel L. Jackson), whose adventure starts when he is tasked to protect a witness in a major criminal court case. Flynn's goal to escort the witness into protective custody on a flight to Los Angeles is stymied by his antagonist, the crime lord Eddie Kim (Bryon Lawson), and the numerous obstacles he encounters, including pursuit by armed assassins, hundreds of deadly snakes that have been smuggled aboard the plane, and the risk that the pilot will be bitten, no anti-venin will be available and the plane will crash.

There are three key features that function to make such a predictable story structure more interesting: the nature of the characters, the conflict and the questions that drive the narrative. In every story, the audience's curiosity and desire to keep watching are sustained by the central narrative question: 'Will the protagonist attain their goal?' Thinking critically about what the goal is, and what qualities and strategies are used to attain the goal, often reveals a lot about characters' priorities and values, and thus about the ideological assumptions or world-view underpinning the narrative.

Venomous airborne vipers half crazed by aggression-inducing pheromones are an unlikely villain, which indicates that the force opposing the hero can come in a range of guises. The hero might face psychological or moral conflict, or contend with external forces like traffic jams, environmental disasters or alien invaders. Any number of opposing forces can generate conflict, taking the role that the villain usually plays. In *Snakes on a Plane*, like many stories, each successive obstacle makes Flynn reappraise his path towards his goal, raising new questions in viewers' minds as to whether he will succeed, and if so how. This sustains interest through to the climactic conclusion, which shows Agent Flynn saving the day with the help of a passenger addicted to a Play Station flight simulator which enables him to land the plane, just in time for the snake-bitten passengers to receive medical attention, and for Flynn and his star witness to score dates with the most attractive women on the plane.

What such narratives encourage us to overlook are their underlying ideologies. For example, what might we make of the individualism and the violent hyper-masculinity that defines Jackson's character as heroic, or our pleasure in watching beautiful women suffer phallic snake attacks while joining the mile high club? The nature of the conflict, the characterisation and the mode of narration encourage us to take these elements for granted, just as they encourage our complicity with an industry that invests $33 million dollars in such a project when we have yet to cure cancer or overcome poverty. Classical narrative structure, by its very nature, is designed to leave us with a comforting sense of closure when the main conflict is resolved. It distracts us from thinking about the production process and many other issues that the central dramatic question masks. In such narratives, the audience's interests are mapped on to those of the hero, so we focus only on the pressing concern: will our hero vanquish the snakes on the plane?

Snakes on a Plane is a plot-driven narrative fuelled by conflict and action, but other stories such as the French comedy *Amelie* and the US prime-time TV series *House* are more character driven, and stories such as *Crash* and the Gulf War film *Jarhead* are issue based. Each involves different forms of conflict, and different questions and goals. There are so many different kinds of stories that we need a working definition of narrative that differentiates it from other modes of expression like the associative form of poetry, the argument structure of an essay, the categories of a list or the often-incomprehensible steps of an instruction manual. At the most basic level, narratives are characterised by a three-part structure: a beginning, a middle and an end forming a meaningful unit in which changing relationships between various characters, events and elements are described. Narrative events unfold in a cause and effect sequence that plays out in space and time in ways tied to the goals and interests of protagonists. This conception of narrative becomes problematic when we try to apply it to a story like *Crash* that muddles temporal order and causation. In order to refine the concept of narrative, theorists such as David Bordwell distinguish between story and plot to separate out the causal sequence of events from the order it appears on screen. This breakdown helps make sense of a film like *Crash* in which the events of 'tomorrow' happened before those of 'today' in the story world.

STORY AND PLOT

The term **plot** refers to the artistic organisation of actions and events and the order in which they are told or unfold on screen. As suggested when analysing script structure in the previous chapter, stories can be broken into narrative units like expository scenes, turning points and obstacles, and the plot can be understood as pieces of a puzzle. Some screen texts present puzzle pieces in order, so it is easy to progressively construct a linear, logical, causal sequence. Others use flashbacks, fragmentation, ellipsis and cross-cutting to mix up the puzzle pieces and make it more challenging for the audience to piece the narrative together. For example, ellipsis in *Secret Window* retards narrative understanding so the audience doesn't know what Johnny Depp's character has been up to until the protagonists themselves figure it out: the plot holes are only filled in when we retroactively construct the story.

> The **plot** refers to the elements of the narrative that appear on screen, in the order and manner that the audience sees and hears them. The time of the plot is exactly the same as the screening time.

Story can be understood as a chronological sequence of cause and effect that the audience actively infers from the raw material of the plot. The plot only provides part of the story, and the audience must fill in the gaps and (re)arrange the pieces to complete the narrative. Until the end, the story is constantly changing to incorporate new information about what happened previously, accommodating new hypotheses about what might happen next. The story can be conceptualised as the unified, finished picture made up of all the pieces of the puzzle in their right places. However, remember that because the audience plays a significant role in interpreting the story and determining its meaning, the boundaries of the story actually spill over the edges of the finished text, often encompassing territory not envisioned by the creators of the original picture.

> The **story** is the entire narrative, in order, from the earliest motivation or causal factor until the final resolution. The time of the story can far exceed the viewing time.

To summarise the distinction between story and plot, the story is *what* happens in chronological order (the narrative), whereas the plot is *how* the story is told (narration). But sometimes it is not this simple. Time-travel narratives like *Donnie Darko*, the *Terminator* series or *Twelve Monkeys* show the artificiality and limitations of the plot/story distinction. These stories, and others like the **anachrony** and **analepsis** of *Memento* or the **prolepsis** of *Medium* would lose impact and interest if they were reconfigured into a linear order. The style and structure gives such stories meaning. It is impossible to separate the story from storytelling, style or structure, and sometimes it is impossible to determine a logical causal or chronological order. Narrative structure and resolution are essential parts of the overall pattern of the story which contribute to the meaning of the text. For instance, a circular structure suggests the problems of the narrative are not solvable, but are part of an inevitable, ongoing cycle like the interplay of fears and fantasies surrounding technological advancement evident in the *Terminator* films. The manner of narration and the ways in which plot points are revealed are central components of screen style, which suggests that narrative structure warrants further examination.

> **Anachrony** is a narrative structure in which events are presented out of sequence rather than in chronological order.
>
> **Analepsis** refers to a flashback narrative structure.
>
> **Prolepsis** refers to a flashforward narrative structure where an occurrence in the future is anticipated in advance or happens earlier than it would in chronological order.

STRUCTURALISM

Structuralism is one technique for analysing screen media narratives. Developed from the linguistic branch of **semiotics** (the 'science of signs') pioneered by Ferdinand de Saussure in the 1920s, structuralism only received widespread international attention in the 1960s with the publication of Claude Levi-Strauss's (1963) *Structural Anthropology*. Levi-Strauss was less interested in the style, plot or details of stories than in the underlying tensions in narratives. He argued that the sequential beginning–middle–end organisation of stories is a surface structure and that all myths, which are stories that encode and naturalise the belief structures of a society, share a deeper logic buried in a central structure of opposing terms. He suggested that myths are organised around **binary oppositions** (drawn from de Saussure's theory that all language is organised around 'binarisms'). Of course, binary oppositions are also ideological because they place two terms in opposition to each other thus implying a value relationship.

> **Structuralism** is a type of narrative analysis originating in linguistics that attempts to disclose the deep structural architecture and patterns like binary oppositions beneath the surface features of a text.
>
> **Semiotics**, also termed semiology, is a method of studying the social meanings of signs, signification and sign systems. Originally based on linguistics, semiotics has since been applied to cultural artefacts and practices such as advertising, art, clothing, architecture and screen texts. Every aspect of a text's style, form, content and conventions can be understood as signifiers carrying meanings and connotations (signified concepts). In screen analysis, the signs we analyse are the cues and conventions that direct the audience's interpretation of the text via connotations and symbolic meanings.
>
> A **binary opposition** or dualism is where two terms are opposed to each other, so as to construct meaning from their difference. So 'bowl' has no inherent meaning except in its difference from, say, 'plate' or 'saucer'.

Typically, binary oppositions are associated with problematic and overly simplistic (gendered, raced, classed, heteronormative) oppositions, like woman/man, where 'woman' is taken to mean 'not man'. Meaning is not fixed, but arises from the differences and relationships between elements. The problem here, as feminists have pointed out, is that our understanding of 'woman' is also then influenced by popular conceptions of what 'man' is. So, as Graeme Turner has suggested, we might end up with the simple-minded dichotomy male/female, strong/weak, rational/emotional, suggesting women are weak and emotional if men are understood to be strong and rational (2006:104).

In screen narratives, the most fundamental binary opposition is usually some version of 'good versus bad', or 'hero versus villain'. This suggests that character roles and functions are central to understanding how narratives tend to be structured, and what the deeper meanings of such underlying structures might be. Vladimir Propp, whose influential work on the structure of folklore and fairytales in the 1920s was central to later developments in structuralist theory, argued that all narratives contained a limited cast of characters such as the hero, the villain, the helper, the false hero and the romantic interest (which he called the 'princess'). Propp theorised a sequential pattern of plot events and character functions common to all stories. In a fairytale, the hero usually starts out on a quest or journey, meets a helper along the way, violates a prohibition, overcomes obstacles, negotiates plot twists such as contending with the false hero and the villain, and finally attains his goal and is rewarded by marrying the princess. It is easy to see how contemporary narratives, from television's *Heroes* to the film franchise *Pirates of the Caribbean*, rework this basic formula; however, most screen narratives are considerably more complex than traditional fairytales.

It is important to go beyond identifying character functions to analyse the values and ideologies associated with each character, and figure out how screen texts manipulate us into identifying with some characters rather than others. Central to this attempt to probe how the ideological values of a story relate to the characters is an underlying question: whose story is it? Much of the information we get in a film is filtered through the experience of the characters, so narrative techniques like point of view, subjective imagery and voiceover are significant because they focus the story through the lens of a character's perception and give the audience insight into the character's experiences, priorities and feelings. The amount of dialogue, close-ups and screen time given to a character also influences audience identification, with increased screen time typically signalling increased narrative significance.

Putting binary oppositions and techniques of characterisation and narration together, we can see that most narratives tell the story of the hero and invite us to identify with the hero's world-view and ideology, thereby associating the villain with the opposite of all of the hero's characteristics and attributes. So, for instance, if the hero is law-abiding, pale-skinned and family-oriented then the villain is likely to be associated with law breaking, 'foreign' characteristics of the 'ethnic' or accented 'other', and be either a loner or someone who disrupts nuclear family groupings. M. Night Shayamalan's film *Unbreakable* is a clear, though hyperbolic, example of how this works. Bruce Willis plays the 'unbreakable' indestructible hero 'Security Man', who protects his family and his community, and Samuel L. Jackson plays his arch-nemesis, the fragile loner 'Mr Glass', whose selfish, obsessive quest for his counterpart destroys families and communities. *Unbreakable* also offers an example of structural bias in that the negative and positive elements in the film are organised into a structural pattern that is biased against certain members of the population. All the negative characteristics associated with the villain may bias the viewer against black people by aligning them with violence, insanity and destructive forces that tear apart the altruistic fabric of society. The concept of structural bias can be extended beyond discriminatory patterns in an individual text to identify patterns of marginalisation or vilification across a large number of texts.

Because binary oppositions seem to follow their own unavoidable logic, they readily distract us from things that don't fit into neat patterns or categories, or are absent from mainstream narratives. For example, we have described 'Mr Glass' as a 'loner' because he has no partner in *Unbreakable*, but this obscures the fact that he *is* part of a family—it's just not a nuclear family. His mother, a sole parent, is very much a part of the narrative. In fact, rather than vilifying single mothers, the story shows how she helped her son develop positive qualities like perseverance and an appreciation of art. The points to remember from this example are that the oppositional categories with which structuralism works tend to simplify the complexities we find in stories. It is much more difficult to train yourself to notice marginalisation and **structuring absences** than to notice patterns of binary opposition because, by their very nature, absences are invisible things that we tend to ignore. For instance, in addition to sole parents and persons of colour, homosexual or bisexual characters, elderly characters and characters with physical disabilities were almost entirely absent from the screen until the human rights movement of the 1960s and 1970s, and they still tend to be under-represented in complex or central roles.

A **structuring absence** is the systematic exclusion of particular identities or features of the world from screen media narratives.

It is important to think critically about different theories and strategies used to analyse screen texts. Structuralism is a useful technique for analysing stories, but it has been critiqued for creating reductive categories, and for creating an artificial separation between them in a way that legitimates oppositional forms of thought. For instance, a structuralist analysis might see Islam and Christianity as being diametrically opposed, instead of seeing the values and beliefs that they have in common. Binarism implicitly privileges a combative and hierarchical way of thinking and makes these structures seem natural, instead of privileging a process of negotiation, or seeing similarities and a continuum of possibilities and positions. Despite these drawbacks, binary oppositions are relevant to screen media practitioners, audiences and scholars. For practitioners, binaries function to structure texts and establish allegiances, but they may have unintended negative effects as audiences are encouraged to accept an oppositional 'us versus them' mentality. Because structuralism itself is based on the assumption that there are patterns shared by all narratives, and a pool of universal stories or myths common to all cultures, it can be used to homogenise narratives and reduce them to a fixed set of character functions and plot points. Another problem is that structuralism approaches narratives from a literary criticism perspective: as a tool designed to analyse stories in general terms, it tends to miss the unique audio-visual qualities of screen texts, and ignore the cultural context of reception. This is where **Formalist** and **Cognitivist** approaches to narrative analysis complement structuralist methods by concentrating on form, style and audience interpretation.

Binary oppositions and narrative structure in *Natural Born Killers*

As demonstrated, structural analysis is a way of approaching stories by breaking them into patterns, composite parts and underlying structures. *Natural Born Killers* begins *in media res*, meaning it starts in the middle of the action. We enter the story in the midst of a cross-country killing spree perpetrated by the two main protagonists, Mickey and Mallory Knox.

Formalist approaches to narrative analysis, as influenced by the aesthetic theories of the Russian Formalists (1915–30) and developed by David Bordwell from the 1980s on, seek to reveal how stylistic techniques such as montage or visual composition interact with plot structures such as parallelism and retardation to express cultural associations, meanings, motivations and relationships through a dynamic formal system of signs and conventions.

Cognitivist approaches to narrative analysis as developed by theorists like Edward Branigan and David Bordwell seek to explain narrative comprehension by analysing how screen texts use aesthetic techniques and formal conventions to cue audiences to construct hypotheses and inferences about the story which are tested and reassessed as the plot unfolds.

This is, for them, a state of equilibrium. It is how they function for most of the film. Fifteen minutes into the film, we flashback to the beginning of the story, when Mickey and Mallory first meet in an 'I Love Mallory' sit-com sequence. Shortly thereafter, Mickey is jailed for stealing Mallory's father's car, which is the incident that catalyses the couple's quest for liberty and romantic union in defiance of authority structures like patriarchy, convention and the law. This reinstatement of the inciting incident demonstrates that even when the linear or chronological order of the plot is disrupted by narrative devices like flashbacks or fragmentation, the structure of cause and effect often remains essentially the same, as structuralists argue.

The middle of *Natural Born Killers* develops the plot, introducing complications, obstacles and turning points that the protagonists encounter on the way towards their goal. For example, the plot points when Mickey and Mallory kill a kindly Indian and take a woman hostage are significant turning points in the second act, causing them to question their purpose, their values and their commitment to one another. The third act, or denouement, lasts from the point when they are incarcerated, through the jailbreak, until the resolution when the loose ends are tied up and a new equilibrium is reached with the final media statement and the credit sequence on the open road.

We can tease out the significance of the ending and the conflict that structures the narrative by identifying binary oppositions in the story, and analysing how those oppositions are resolved. Conflict between different characters often represents conflict between value systems. The oppositions in the story give the narrative a pattern. To find this hidden structure or pattern, the easiest place to start is to make two columns, beginning with the protagonist and the antagonist (see Figure 6.2).

Protagonists	Antagonists
Mickey and Mallory (the celebrity outlaws)	Wayne Gale (the media) and Jack Scagnetti (the law)
Freedom and nature (wild animals)	Constraint and convention (human culture)
Individualism	The social order
Criminality	Legality
Mobile	Static
Irresponsibility	Responsibility
Transgression	Conformity
Car	Home

Figure 6.2 Binary oppositions in *Natural Born Killers*

After mapping the binary oppositions, analyse the ideological implications of the film by questioning what the characteristics and values of the heroes and villains are. Binary oppositions exist in a hierarchy where one term in each pair, or one column of terms, is privileged. On the whole, the film asks us to value the traits Mickey and Mallory represent. We don't want to be associated with Wayne Gale, or Jack Scagnetti—both of whom die by the end of the film. This is how we can see most clearly that Stone's film is a critique of the mass media and the justice system.

However, *Natural Born Killers* also problematises the values of its protagonists as there is no clear-cut distinction between good and bad. Not all the terms on either side of the binary are valued positively, nor do they fit within the same value system. For instance, America sees itself as aligned with freedom and the ideology of individualism (which are both central to capitalism), but it also wants social unity and order (which means individual freedom must be both constrained and enabled by the legal system to maintain truth, justice and 'the American way'). The important point here is that narratives offer a symbolic resolution to social and ideological conflicts that are impossible to 'fix', such as these fundamental tensions in American national identity and ideology. Aesthetic style can also represent an ideological position. Through the use of mixed film stocks, montage, superimposition and jump cuts, *Natural Born Killers* deliberately resists conforming to the norms of classical narrative style, which relates directly to the critique of the media that the storyline articulates.

As discussed in Chapter 4 in relation to the juxtaposition and Soviet montage, the term 'dialectical synthesis' refers to a debate or argument between competing or opposing sides or perspectives. In a philosophical argument or an academic essay, these are the thesis (what is being argued for) and the antithesis (the alternative viewpoints that are being argued against). In a story, the thesis and antithesis correspond to the two forces that are in conflict or tension with one another and, as in an argument, each side must engage with the other and be able to understand the opposition in order to refute it or effectively counter it.

Just as the thesis and the antithesis need to be brought together into a synthesis, the protagonist and the antagonist in a film typically need to take on aspects of each other's value systems and character traits in order for the conflict to be resolved. For example, in *Natural Born Killers* detective Jack Scagnetti becomes a killer himself, strangling a prostitute. This flirtation with sex and death brings him closer to Mallory and Mickey, and helps him find the clues to locate and arrest them. Moreover, Mickey (who represents freedom) takes hostages. Both Mickey and Mallory incorporate a degree of responsibility and conformity once they have 2.5 kids to look after, though they stay on the road without ever becoming static. They have not totally rejected the social structure since the credit sequence shows they form a nuclear family. Instead of deciding between a home or a car, they opt for a mobile home, striking a symbolic—or ironic—balance between competing ideals.

Similar dialectical patterns are also present in television. For example, in *Prison Break* the binary opposition between the law and the outlaws is constantly called into question. Consider how Michael Schofield must break the law in order to find justice for his falsely accused brother, Lincoln Burrows, while prison warders and FBI agents become murderous and corrupt. However, as we argue below, the more complex the narrative structure and the larger the cast of key characters, the harder it becomes to divine the patterns structuralism seeks.

COMPLEX NARRATIVE STRUCTURES

A spate of talented directors like Christopher Nolan (*Memento*, *The Prestige*), Alejandro González Iñárritu (*Amores Perros*, *21 Grams*, *Babel*) and Darren Aronofsky (*The Fountain*) have recently released puzzle-plot films that fragment the story and rupture its cohesion and temporal order. Other alternative narrative structures work with multiple parallel or interlocking stories. For instance, Karen Moncrieff's *The Dead Girl* tells the stories of a woman who finds a corpse, the forensic worker who investigates whether the corpse is her missing sister, the mother who identifies the body, the wife of the killer, and the victim herself. *Short Cuts* director Robert Altman, a pioneer of this type of storytelling, has described his approach to narrative as similar to throwing a handful of pebbles into a still pond, each representing a single story, and watching the random intersections of their overlapping ripples. In *American Independent Cinema*, Geoff King writes that such films question the cause and effect structure of narrative and identity offered by classical narrative and present a more contingent conception of the nature of reality, one in which 'events are more open-ended and tenuously linked' (2005: 101–2). Often this different form of narration draws inspiration from art cinema movements such as German Expressionism, Surrealism and the French *avant-garde*, and playfully or cryptically disrupts audience expectations about character identity and temporal order.

Some of the different ways assumptions about identity are challenged involve twins, cyborgs, doppelgangers, ghosts or demented protagonists. In his article 'Film Futures', Bordwell suggests many science fiction and fantasy narratives that play with the dimensions of time, space and identity work to pull personal identity, responsibility and ethics into question: 'If all possibilities exist equally, then ethical action, indeed personal identity, is rendered impossible' (2002b: 88). This indicates how integral narrative form and structure are to the very foundations of human understanding.

Temporal order, which is fundamental to our everyday conception of reality, can be presented in many ways in screen narratives:

- linear, causal narrative structure (*Snakes on a Plane*);
- fragmented stories with disjunctive chronologies (*Pulp Fiction, Babel, Crash*);
- interwoven or parallel storylines (*Love Actually, The Dead Girl*);
- retrospective stories told in past tense, using flashbacks (film noir, *American Beauty*), or in reverse order (*Irreversible* and *Memento*);
- projective stories using flash-forwards and fantasy sequences (*Medium, The Boys*);
- cyclical narratives (*Terminator, Twelve Monkeys, Lost Highway, Donnie Darko*);
- repetitious stories (*Groundhog Day, Run Lola Run*);
- or a combination of any of these.

Regarding the different ways the order of events can be presented, Bordwell observes that flashbacks are easily interpreted and reconfigured into the causal framework of the unfolding narrative, whereas flash-forwards are rarer and often more difficult to decipher, 'perhaps because we assume the past to be knowable in a way that the future is not' (2002b: 90). The 1998 German film *Run Lola Run* and the mainstream US hit of the same year, *Sliding Doors*, are examples of 'forking' narrative trajectories that are increasingly common. As Bordwell explains, Lola returns to the 'switchpoint' moment of choice, the moment when the paths towards her possible futures fork, after each storyline plays out; whereas *Sliding Doors* intercuts one alternative with another, continually switching back and forth to show the parallels between the different possible lives of Helen, the protagonist (2002b: 89).

However radical the possibilities of forking narrative pathways are, a number of 'viewer-friendly' devices typically rein in such narratives. According to Bordwell, the different narrative pathways are usually linear, and 'each path, after it diverges, adheres to a strict line of cause and effect' (2002b: 91). For instance, the implications of one childhood incident in *The Butterfly Effect* are traced through the futures of each of its participants as Ashton Kucher's character Evan Treborn travels back in time to try to fix the past. The fork is 'signposted', as Bordwell would point out, in that inciting incidents or switchpoints are clearly marked either through repetition, intertitles or dialogue, as when characters repeatedly mention Evan's moments of 'lost time' which indicate points when he time travels. Bordwell also notes that forking pathways almost inevitably intersect, as do the lives of the characters within them, such as Evan's childhood friends and his college roommate. Other 'traditional cohesion devices' that Bordwell notes (2002b: 97) are appointments and deadlines, such as Evan's repeated efforts to prevent his childhood sweetheart's suicide before his own interventions into the past irrevocably wreck his own health and others' futures and reduce him to a vegetative state. Since 'what comes earlier shapes our expectations about what follows. What comes later modifies our understanding of what went before', the last narrative thread that we follow has special significance and presupposes our comprehension of the others (Bordwell 2002b: 98). For instance, there is a cumulative force to Evan's reasoning. Each time he resets the past, he learns more about his own abilities and about the consequences of interventions in the causal chain. In this sense, reality leaks from one alternative pathway into the others.

A type of narrative that is even more complex and challenging than the forking, fragmented or multi-strand stories in

The Butterfly Effect, Babel, Crash or *The Dead Girl* is called **multiform** narrative, which works with different strands of narrative woven through different levels of reality. David Lynch's films, particularly *Inland Empire* (2006), provide a good illustration of multiform narrative. *Inland Empire's* spectators might wish they were nonchalant surrealists capable of interpreting Lynch's work as audio-visual poetry mainlined from the director's unconscious, but

> **Multiform** narratives are variants of 'puzzle plots' featuring fragmented, episodic and multiple storylines. Multiform's distinguishing feature is its interweaving of multiple levels of reality into a multi-strand storyline. Multiform has parallel or alternate realities in one or more narrative strands, often featuring time travel or drawing us into the subjectivity of the protagonist via hallucinations, memories, dreams, psychotic states, movement through different dimensions, or shifts between the past, present and future.

even those willing to embrace confusion can't help but search for a story. Our minds are hard-wired to try to construct a narrative from the labyrinthine scenes and the multiple, slippery layers of fiction, reality, time and personality. Although the film lacks a conventional narrative structure overall, it includes scenes and sequences that are intelligible as stories. Each of these scenes has elements that link it to other scenes, though there are never enough links to draw the entire film together into a unified story. Lynch describes his unscripted approach to shooting *Inland Empire* as a process in which: 'I never saw any whole, W-H-O-L-E. I saw plenty of holes, H-O-L-E-S. But I didn't really worry. I would get an idea for a scene and shoot it, get another idea and shoot that. I didn't know how they would relate' (www.nytimes.com/2006/10/01/movies).

Even if audience members interpret the entire film as episodic glimpses into doppelgangers who traverse parallel worlds where the fictional storyline of a film infects the lives of its actors, or as the delusional product of a disintegrating psyche dislocated in time and space, we remain uncertain about whose story it is, what they did to whom, when and why. Throughout the film, characters and spectators are introduced to a set of strangely related people, a weird family of rabbits in a sit-com and loosely intersecting events. Because of *Inland Empire's* incomprehensibility as a complete story featuring a consistent cast of protagonists, the very denial of narrative cohesion makes it evident that narrative is instrumental in our efforts to make sense of the world.

Indeed, narrative assists interpretation by providing temporal order, describing interconnections and rendering complex causal relationships intelligible. Complex, convoluted narrative structures still rely on the spectator's quest for narrative comprehension, but their fragmented, circular, interlocking or open-ended structures suggest very different conceptions of reality and ideological meanings than those offered in the reassuring closure of classical narratives. Additionally, narratives exploring the doubling of identity and stories featuring multiple protagonists in ensemble casts undermine the ideology of individualism that underlies many conventional films. These different conceptions of reality and identity, which perhaps reflect the increasing interconnectedness of people across the globe, are also evident in the structure of television narratives.

TELEVISION AND NARRATIVE STRUCTURE

Television is one of the defining features of our time: it has had an immense impact on other media and on the way we lead our lives. After investigating the distinctiveness of television by comparison with film, we conclude by discussing how influential television has been, and continues to be, with respect to trends in screen media culture and narrative styles. To recapitulate, classical narrative film favours goal-oriented protagonists with strong psychological motivation who plough through unified narratives, following a clear chain of cause and effect to achieve the symbolic resolution of social problems. In the course of such plot-driven narratives, binary oppositions are synthesised and ideological closure is attained: good triumphs over adversity, and the hero usually gets the girl. Television narration is, by contrast, ongoing and character driven. Television storylines often lack a well-defined goal or resolution because television 'is discontinuous, interrupted and segmented. Its attempts at closure and unitary meaning... are constantly subjected to fracturing forces' (Fiske, cited in Thompson 2003: 11). Television also constantly repeats and reinforces information about characters, relationships and plotlines from previous episodes to help new viewers get up to speed. This kind of redundancy is evident in routine episode recaps, such as 'Previously in *Veronica Mars* ...'

Television theorist Nicholas Abercrombie argues that: 'Television replaces the linear form of film narrative with a serial form, whether it is a **series** or a continuing **serial**, and a major effect is the diversion of interest from events to character' (1996: 24). In other words, despite television's characteristic segmentation and lack of overall unity, a degree of continuity is provided by character and location. Because television privileges character development over plot development, and often features the familiarity of ordinary life, it is also dominated by content with a domestic nature or setting. This relates to television's concern with immediacy, liveness and reality: as a medium, television deals with more up to date information and with more 'reality genres' than cinema does. Television content also tends to be intertextual, derivative and self-referential, incorporating references to other television shows. For instance, characters from one show will often make a guest appearance on another, as in the *Crossing Jordan* cross-over with *Las Vegas*. The characteristics of television also include particular content and modes of production and reception, as detailed below.

> **Series** have self-contained episodes in which the central conflicts and problems are resolved, and the viewer is invited to return to see similar issues resolved in a similar way during the next episode.
>
> **Serials** have never-ending storylines that lack resolution in a single episode and resist ideological closure.

Fragmentation and flow

Among the key characteristics differentiating television narratives from film, its **fragmentation** and its episodic, serial, transient nature and lack of narrative closure have primacy since television features long stories that are broken into seasons and episodes, and short episodes broken by advertisements. Dangling causes and cliffhangers are techniques that suspend the narrative then bring us back to the box after the 'ad break', or for the next episode, whereas repetition and redundancy are techniques used to rejoin narrative segments. The usual format of each television show is structured around commercial breaks. Advertisements not only target the demographic of the show's audience, they often 'echo the main narrative thematically' (Thompson 2003: 15). That is, advertisements relate to the presumed interests of the target audience and to the theme of the show. For example, Panadol sponsors the medical series *Grey's Anatomy*, and Instant Scratch It

> **Fragmentation** refers to the segmentation and discontinuity that characterises television texts, and television as a media form. Each program is fragmented by commercials, and narratives tend to lack closure (they take serial or episodic form and play out over a number of nights or weeks).

lottery tickets sponsor *My Name is Earl*, which features a protagonist who wins the lottery.

Paradoxically, television narration is characterised by both fragmentation and flow; it is both segmented and ongoing. A television narrative might be as small as a 30-second advertisement, or as long as an episode, a season or multiple seasons across an entire long-running series. Because it is somewhat difficult to delineate the boundaries of a television text, **flow** is a term often used to describe the form taken by television texts. The term 'flow' indicates that the organisation of television creates a continuum via scheduling, the incorporation of ads and the serial nature of texts. This 'flow' is intended to keep the viewer tuned to a single show and a single station via **lead-ins**, **hammocking** and **tentpoling** scheduling strategies (Thompson 2003: 13). The fact that television is both continuous and fragmented produces a 'decentred' experience of viewing, which is characteristic of the postmodern condition (Abercrombie 1996: 16–17).

Mode of production

Television's mode of production differs significantly from film production. Television has smaller budgets and tighter production deadlines, and works with fewer crew members across less diverse locations. These factors sometimes limit artistic experimentation. Another related difference is the absence of an **auteur**. To an even greater extent than film, television is a collaborative medium. Often a team of writers and directors work together on a series, taking turns with different episodes or collaborating to develop content for a series of linked stories, not one unique artwork. Usually there is no author or artist

---

Flow relates to the carefully constructed schedule, a sequence of events designed to keep viewers sitting in front of the TV as they move from news through family viewing to late-night movies. The experience of viewing TV is not one of consuming discrete products (commercials, news, fiction of various genres), but rather a unified act of media consumption: watching television.

A **lead-in** is a scheduling strategy in which television producers attempt to build an audience for a series using the established popularity of one show to 'lead in' to the subsequent program. A low-rating series is advertised during a high-rating show, then screened immediately afterwards to take advantage of the established viewership already watching the channel.

Hammocking is an approach to television scheduling that brackets a show with weak ratings in between two very popular shows, in the hope that viewers will stay tuned to the same channel and form a liking for the weaker show while they wait for their favourite to come on.

individually responsible for creating a television text, and no single individual whose signature style defines the program's character. Notable exceptions include distinctive 'auteur' television creators like Joss Whedon, or television producers like Jerry Bruckheimer. The lack of focus on an individual creator in television production may be related to the way the ensemble casts of television serials and the inclusive address to the domestic audience undercut the ideology of individualism.

> **Tentpoling** is a programming strategy that attempts to retain viewers on a particular channel by propping up two weaker or newer shows with a strong-rating program in the middle. It is also a film production strategy in which profits earned from blockbusters bankroll smaller projects.
>
> The **auteur** is a screen text's creative 'author', typically a director attributed with a signature style and distinctive thematic concerns evident across a body of work. Auteur analysis emphasises screen aesthetics and individual style (as elaborated in the director's commentary and extra features of DVDs), but downplays the collaborative nature of screen production and the economic limitations constraining a director's artistic vision. Auteurism assumes a model of communication in which the director puts the meaning into a text and the audience passively accepts it, de-emphasising meaning as a context-specific act of interpretation and negotiation in which the audience participates.

Domestic context of reception

Television is often described as a domestic medium. This affects not only the narrative structure and content, but also the ways in which audiences respond to texts. Television texts are serial or episodic because they are watched *routinely*. Given its location in the home, television has a tone or mode of address that is *conversational* (it addresses or acknowledges the viewer as a participant), whereas film maintains a sense of voyeurism and generally does not acknowledge the audience explicitly. When Bernadette Casey et al. write that the domestic context of reception 'determines the form that television texts take' (2002: 86) from scheduling, through content to narrative structure, they mean that television is an 'ordinary medium' which both represents and is embedded in the domestic routines of everyday life (Casey et al. 2002: 88). Schedulers assume a multi-generational audience for television, restricting content to 'family-friendly' material such as sit-coms and family dramas devoid of sex, violence or obscene language before 9.00 p.m. This ensures advertisers can market goods to a broad demographic (Casey et al. 2002: 85). The ongoing serial or episodic nature of television narrative structure with cliffhangers and developing relationships that entice the viewer to return to the show repeatedly is devised to counter the distractions in the domestic environment. Viewers also have more autonomy and agency in their own homes than in the cinema. They have the freedom to change channels or leave the room, and they exercise their power by using the remote control and time-shifting recording technologies like Personal Video Recorders (PVRs). Technologies such as the remote control, VCR and TiVo fragment and personalise viewing behaviour, empowering audiences and undermining programming attempts to control audiences through an appeal to realness, liveness and immediacy, or programming strategies designed to secure viewer attention and loyalty.

The fragmented experience of television consumption also relates to the disruptions of the domestic context of reception. Abercrombie suggests that the social and domestic context of television consumption means that viewers often disperse their attention between the television, food, conversation and other household activities (1996). Differing contexts of reception of film and television texts mean that audience members tend to *glance* at the TV and *gaze* with sustained attention at film. These different viewing patterns also relate to the differing narrative structures and styles of the two media since the dialogue-heavy nature of television and its use of repetition makes it easy for audiences to tune in and out without missing too much.

Television and society

As a socialising agent that naturalises, negotiates or reinforces dominant ideologies, commercial television—as opposed to public service broadcasters like the ABC and SBS in Australia, the BBC in the UK and PBS in the US—is structured around consumption, driven by ideologies of capitalism, consumerism and materialism. Another important aspect of television's role in society is the relationship between the medium of communication and the type of social experiences that are implicitly privileged. This idea was introduced briefly above in relation to structuring absences in narratives, but the type of story and the intended audience also influence the narrative structure.

Situational stories (such as sit-coms) and dilemma-based dramas (such as soap operas) are character driven and, by their nature, domestic, ongoing and relational; hence it is appropriate that their narratives shouldn't require grand goals, over-arching meanings or absolute closure. Dramas like *Gossip Girl*, *Neighbours* and *Brothers and Sisters* lack definitive endings, a central hero or heroine, and happily-ever-after conclusions. The interwoven storylines and never-ending narrative structure of the serial reflect our experiences of the ongoing, open-ended nature of everyday problems. Similarly, masculine-coded stories such as *Law and Order* and *24* are often more goal oriented, following a central hero through a linear progression to a clear resolution. This reflects social assumptions about gender, often reinforcing the **dominant ideology**.

Some theorists have argued that because television is a domestic medium that focuses largely on domestic issues, concerns and relationships, it privileges female experience. This argument is reinforced by the fact that the televisual format favours intimate close-ups and conversational chat-show formats. Television personalities are literally invited into the homes of viewers, and located in the domestic, family space as a friend

> **Dominant ideology** refers to a world-view characteristic of the ruling class or dominant group in society, and entails conformity to existing value systems and social relations which naturalise and legitimate the distribution of power and wealth. The 'ruling ideas' support the interests of the most powerful group in society—that is, those who control the economic and material interests and the means of production.

would be. This means we perceive and relate to these figures differently than we would if we only had access to them through the more formal discourse of the newspaper or the public address. Other theorists go further and suggest that the medium of television is making issues that are traditionally coded as masculine (like politics and sport) be presented and received in a personalised, personality-driven, domestic manner. For example, politicians now have to take care with personal image, their personal lives are increasingly the subject of national debates, and they must appear on chat shows engaging in conversational, informal interviews if they are to be successful, whereas previously they could keep the public at a distance and limit public speaking to delivering speeches about policy decisions. Even sport has become known as a 'male soap opera' and, as such, is often shot with lots of close-ups and slow-motion inserts and interviews with sports stars about their off-screen lives and goals.

Television criticism and analysis

In analysing television, we tend to need to look at more than the particulars of individual texts. The analysis of trends running through a series or critical comparisons between audience responses to different texts and media can be more revealing than a detailed study of one particular television episode. The differences between film and television narratives identified above mean we use different criteria to analyse and interpret television. For example, television critics expect the meaning of the narrative or segment to be expressed in dialogue rather than in visual metaphor or allusive *mise en scène*, just as we would *not* expect an expensive orchestral score or soundtrack that is costly to copyright. Indeed, rather than judge television cinematography on the basis of the expressivity of fancy crane shots and complex camera movements—techniques associated with Hollywood film production—we would instead expect a lot of close-ups suitable for screening dialogue and facilitating character engagement. When analysing television, we do not perceive direct address to camera, or the sound of laughter from an audience off screen, to be mistakes because they are conventions appropriate to the types of stories television tells, and the way it addresses its audience. Similarly, an analysis of the narrative structure of a television text won't critique the fragmentation, or the lack of action or resolution, because television narration is by nature segmented, ongoing and character driven.

In addition to being intertextual, television analysis also tends to focus on audience reception and on communication technologies to a greater extent than film analysis. For instance, media and cultural studies theorist Henry Jenkins encapsulates how technological change has affected television narration:

> There has been a marked increase in the serialization of American television, the emergence of more complex appeals to program history, the development of more intricate story arcs and cliffhangers, over the past decade. To some degree, these aesthetic shifts can be linked to new reception practices enabled by the home archiving of videos, net discussion lists, and web program guides. These new technologies provide the information infrastructure necessary to sustain a richer form of television content. (2006: 145)

Such technological changes, and the changes in television narration itself, have also impacted on other screen media.

DIGITAL GAME NARRATIVES

Digital games are often spin-offs: the *Die Hard* and *Alias* games and *Buffy the Vampire Slayer: Chaos Bleeds* are based on popular films and TV series and rely on intertextual knowledge of back-story, an established fictional universe and familiar characters. Similarly, *Tomb Raider* and *Doom* are films inspired by games. Such spin-offs and tie-ins capitalise on existing audiences and attract new audiences, particularly the lucrative youth market. However, a key difference between films and games is 'the relative importance of narrative structure or narrative development', according to Geoff King and Tanya Krzywinska (2002: 21).

Games often feature narrative 'cut-scenes', which are short audio-visual sequences that 'establish the initial setting and background storyline' and occur 'at varying intervals throughout many games, to forward the storyline' (King & Krzywinska 2002: 11–12). The cut-scene narrative component often looks more 'cinematic' than the rest of the game, but lacks interactivity. Once players are immersed in the game, the story tends to unfold in real time, similar to the immediacy of live TV. Unlike films, which routinely skip over slow-moving or non-essential action, games seldom use ellipsis and they require long periods of gameplay, often using a repetitive, episodic structure. The impression of liveness and presence in the game world arises from the experience of acting as a protagonist in the narrative:

> Seeming to move 'inside' the fictional world on screen is sometimes seen as a defining characteristic of games, especially those based recognizably on individual films, franchises or film genres. The player can, at one remove, 'become' the central figure in a cinematic environment, following and extending the kinds of experiences offered in film. (King & Krzywinska 2002: 4)

Digital games require narrative intervention, not just interpretation, which shifts the emphasis away from story and character towards participation.

The narrative structure of digital games is partly based on genre, involving repetition and variation as players attempt new levels of a game. Genre furnishes game settings, characters, motives and contexts, as genres like action, fantasy and science fiction have established rules, conventions and expectations that fill in the backstory and 'offer instantly recognizable frames of reference that allow gameplay to proceed with only minimal elaboration of the specific scenario' (King & Krzywinska 2006: 55). However, while action genre conventions dictate that Bruce Willis's character John McClane will conquer the bad guys and survive to the end of the *Die Hard* films, the *Die Hard* games belonging to the same genre and modelled on the films invoke different conventions and expectations. Players expect to die many times before mastering the game, which heightens uncertainty and suspense.

Games often use the cause-and-effect structure of narrative within three acts organised around a beginning, middle and end, though they may be non-linear and often lack definitive resolution. In the first act, the cut-scenes introducing game narratives are predetermined, but games also feature an extended second act in which players control variables in the narrative and become authors of their own multiple storylines. Players can also 'author' games by creating 'skins' (customised character appearances) and 'mods' (modifications like new environments, levels and scenarios). Goal-oriented games require the resolution of binary oppositions based on a battle between protagonists and antagonists, but the ending changes each time the game is played. Other games, such as *The Sims*, are not so goal oriented or geared towards narrative resolution.

Just as games are influenced by film and television, cinematic and televisual narratives and aesthetics are influenced by game techniques and technologies. Digital game animation and films such as *Beowulf* often use the same software, like Maya, and common techniques, like motion capture. This means visual styles are converging across screen media. Despite increasing narrative and aesthetic similarities, disparities remain. Perhaps narrative theory cannot fully encompass the differences between identification with characters and active participation as a protagonist, nor can it account for the kinaesthetic, experiential and technological dimensions of gameplay.

NARRATIVE CONVERGENCE

A point of interest throughout this chapter is the increasing prevalence of puzzle-plots involving multi-strand, fragmented and multiform narrative structures. Experimental narrative forms have been present since the earliest days of cinema, but films featuring an ensemble cast and fragmented, interwoven storylines now feature quite regularly, even in mainstream cinema, television and digital games. Bordwell identifies video games as one factor influencing the rash of forking plot narratives produced since the 1990s (2002b: 102). This is explicitly signalled by the animated sequence at the beginning of *Run Lola Run*, but is implicit in the narrative structure of many other films. More complex and convoluted story structures are also leaking out of the fantastic narratives of science fiction and horror and into other genres. This is perhaps due to the ever-growing complexity of technological, social and economic interconnectedness, and cross-currents of cultural value systems experienced in the era of globalisation, as well as the unstable subjectivity that finds expression in multiform narrative (McMahan 1999). Janet Murray argues that multiform narrative is gathering momentum because living in the contemporary global mediascape means we are necessarily more aware of multiple intersecting stories and 'alternative possible selves' (1997: 38).

Television, digital games and non-linear online screen media exert a strengthening influence on contemporary cinema, as is evident in the production of narratives with multiple and interwoven storylines. Even more noticeably, it is also evident in the sequel phenomenon, and film franchises that deliver serialised episodes of a narrative like *Ocean's 11, 12, 13*; *Spiderman 1, 2, 3*; the *Pirates of the Caribbean* franchise; the *Lord of the Rings* trilogy; and the *Harry Potter* series. Such serialised narrative strategies combine the spectacle of cinema with the addictive cliffhanger narratives of television.

Sequels are bankable because they guarantee an established fan base. The ready-made audience consists of people who are loyal to the characters and stars in previous films, as well as those who are attracted to the spectacular, action-packed storylines that blockbusters typically offer. In this sense, cinema is following the lead of television in an industry characterised by media convergence. The television strategy of serialising storylines and building loyalty to characters is very effective in maintaining audience involvement and interest. As 'event cinema', blockbuster sequels are also able to offer something that television can't: the big screen experience. *Spiderman* and *Pirates* are film franchises that simply don't have the same impact on a small television set as they do on a massive screen in a sophisticated surround-sound environment. If people are going to pay for a movie ticket, rather than downloading or hiring a film, or waiting until it finally reaches commercial television, they want films offering a cinematic experience with spectacular visual effects and a sense of immersion. Story itself translates well to a small screen, but style doesn't necessarily do so. Blockbuster sequels also make money from merchandising and spin-offs in ways that narratively complex, character-driven dramas or experimental films cannot. So, with blockbuster sequels and digital game tie-ins, the industry is cleverly offering what the audience perceives to be the best of all possible worlds: converging television, cinema and game narratives.

CONCLUSION

Narrative analysis seeks to unearth patterns and structures beneath the surfaces of texts, and examines how the meanings of stories are affected by the sequencing of events and the aesthetic style in which formal elements are presented. It also considers the audience's active construction of meaning via inferences based on textual clues and evidence. This chapter has introduced classical three-act narrative structure and demonstrated how to use a structuralist approach to analyse the ideological implications of the opposing forces present in screen narratives. It has distinguished between closed-ended film narratives driven by action and conflict and the more open-ended, segmented, character-driven domestic concerns of television narratives. In addition, it has explored how storytelling styles are becoming increasingly complex in response to technological developments and the reciprocal influence of television, film and interactive digital media. By providing a foundation for understanding narrative structure across different modes of storytelling, it has established techniques for approaching other types of narratives that are introduced in the following chapters on genre, realism and cult media.

KEY SKILLS

Having read this chapter you should now be able to:

- define classical narration and describe its key characteristics;
- list key differences between film, television and digital game narratives;
- explain how television is characterised by both fragmentation and flow, and discuss how these features of television narratives influence the experience of audiences;
- give examples of the catalyst, obstacles, turning points and binary oppositions in a screen text;
- analyse the ideological significance of the ways in which conflict is narrated, negotiated or resolved in two screen narratives: one with an individual hero and a conventional linear storyline, and one with multiple protagonists and story strands;
- critically reflect on the future of screen narrative styles and structures in light of the rapidly changing technological landscape.

7
reality and realism:
Seeing is believing

On 1 February 2005, the picture shown in Figure 7.1 was posted online, along with a statement by a militant group calling itself the Mujahedeen Brigades. The group claimed credit for taking the US soldier hostage and threatened to behead him unless America released Iraqi prisoners within 72 hours. The story was picked up by two reputable news providers, the Associated Press and Reuters, who publicised it along with the dramatic image of the soldier, his hands tied behind his back, a gun pointed at his head, held captive beneath a banner with Arabic script and the rising sun insignia of an Al-Qaeda faction. In the heat of the second Gulf War and a climate of global terror, the story of terrorists holding a soldier hostage seemed frighteningly real and it immediately sparked a flurry of online activity on counter-terrorism blogs (Joyner 2005). Few people questioned whether terrorists would be dense enough to leave grenades on the hostage's flak jacket. Most were suckered by the aesthetic of authenticity, the convincingly grainy, amateur look of the photo, the signifiers of Islam, and the fact that the story was run by trusted sources like CNN. As it transpired, the hostage in the photo was actually a GI Joe doll, and the story was hastily withdrawn from the press.

Figure 7.1 US soldier held hostage

Realist screen texts have persuasive power because they present images and narratives that mimic and reflect on the 'real world'. Realist film and television ranges from texts that are supposed to be absolutely factual, such as news reports and informative documentaries, through entertaining programs that may play up the dramatic, comedic or competitive aspects of 'human nature', to feature films and television series that mock or co-opt the conventions of realism used in traditional documentaries for satirical purposes, or to explore issues of social concern.

Although realism can be entertaining (for example, reality television), it tends to be associated with a more serious educational, informative tone. Rather than distracting us from the concerns of everyday life and enabling us to escape into fantasy, a realist aesthetic often signals that a text intends us to confront or act on important issues. The romantic, uplifting films *Before Sunrise* and *Before Sunset* stand out from the crowd of naturalistic films using hand-held camera because they are *not* depressing stories about downtrodden, damaged individuals. Yet even these films address serious issues, through dialogue about environmentalism and ethics. This chapter considers how texts that use a particular set of conventions to represent real issues, events, people and stories in an authentic manner implicitly have a more direct impact on or relation to 'the real', and therefore engage both audiences and filmmakers in an ethical and political relationship with the subject matter that is screened.

We will identify the conventions of realism in film and television texts and differentiate between levels of documentation, interpretation, manipulation and falsification. After contrasting documentary-style realism with the conventions used to create an illusion of realism in mainstream cinema, this chapter provides a brief historical context for the development of 'realist' screen texts, outlining influential realist forms including reality TV, film and television documentaries, mockumentary, docu-drama and realist cinema movements. We conclude by distinguishing between realism, spectacle and narrative modes of representation, evaluating ethical and epistemological issues associated with 'truth' and 'realism'.

REALISM AND CODES OF REPRESENTATION IN FILM AND TELEVISION

One of the reasons that even seasoned journalists were taken in by the GI Joe hostage hoax is that the story was accompanied by a convincing image that apparently verified the claims of the militant group and lent weight to their demands. By comparison with more obviously stylised and artificial representations such as paintings, photographic images seem to have a privileged relationship to 'the real world' which lends them a persuasive kind of 'truth status' based on their ability to record and reproduce reality. Belief in the ability of photographic technology to reflect reality derives from the assumption that vision guarantees a certain access to 'truth' and 'reality' as observable phenomena. Indeed, 'seeing is believing' is the premise on which the concepts of 'documentary evidence' and 'eyewitness accounts' are based, and it underwrites our faith in the idea that the camera is 'candid' and does not lie. However, because fictional screen media go to such lengths to construct the illusion of authenticity, the term 'realism' can be confusing.

The illusion of reality

The codes of representation used to signal realism in news reporting and documentary forms are very different from the 'illusion of reality' maintained in fiction texts. Fictional screen media create the illusion of reality using techniques discussed in previous chapters such as continuity editing that is designed to be unnoticeable, naturalistic three-point lighting, hidden microphones and a stable camera. Together with the fact that actors don't acknowledge the camera or the audience, and because events follow a compelling narrative logic, these techniques construct the illusion that the events on screen are uncontrived. This mode of representation is known as **classical Hollywood realism**. It aims to make the technology and hard work involved in screen production as unobtrusive as possible so audiences will 'suspend disbelief' and become involved in the story as though the events on screen were really happening, despite the fact that everyone knows narrative drama is actually shot in a studio, that the characters are actors, and that the events are scripted, assembled and displayed for our viewing pleasure. The conventions of classical realism are not restricted to Hollywood. Despite the misleading name, they are the dominant conventions in narrative film and television worldwide.

Classical Hollywood realism uses a cohesive cause and effect narrative structure and naturalistic acting along with unobtrusive cinematography, studio lighting, continuity editing and sound conventions to conceal traces of the technical production process in order to make the story world depicted on screen seem like a natural environment in which time and space extend seamlessly beyond the borders of the frame.

Essentially, when the terms 'realism' or 'realist' are used to refer to mainstream fictional narratives, they actually refer to the *illusion of realism* that is created by concealing the signs of production. In response to these 'deceptions' of classical cinema, realist movements privilege real footage and reportage in an attempt to give audiences more 'faithful' and less 'illusionist' or 'manipulative' images of the world.

The naturalistic aesthetic

Realism is a broad term that operates on a variety of levels and can relate to:

- ***content*** (showing things that actually happen in the world);
- ***form*** (reporting or screening things 'live' as they happen,

using a direct, unscripted or personal form of address within a format that foregrounds facts and authenticity);

> **Realism** refers to the nature and degree of a text's relationship with reality in terms of its subject matter, audience response, and formal and stylistic conventions.

- *style* (using techniques and conventions that conceal or reveal screen technology, the production process, and the 'raw' qualities of light, sound and action in order to convey a sense of veracity);
- *reception* (encouraging audiences to actively participate or respond to the footage. 'Real' action demands a 'real' reaction such as cheering at a live sports match, voting on a reality TV contestant, or changing beliefs and behaviours in reaction to documentary or news stories).

The following characteristics comprise the naturalistic aesthetic of realist film and television formats that attempt to capture a sense of authenticity:

- Available light is often used instead of three-point lighting.
- Dialogue is unscripted, or loosely scripted and improvised.
- The action that is represented may be unstaged or based on real events, or it contains elements of spontaneity, immediacy and improvisation.
- 'Real people' or non-professional actors often feature.
- People on screen may directly address the camera, looking straight into the lens and acknowledging the audience.
- The off-screen voice of an interviewer, subtitles or voiceover narration may be used to compensate for muffled diegetic sound or to provide authority.
- Screen media technologies such as microphones are often visible.
- Conversely, hidden cameras or surveillance-style footage from 'night vision' cameras may capture events and behaviour that isn't modified by or performed for an audience.
- Unstable handheld camera, grainy imagery, poor focus or exposure, and haphazard composition give the footage an accidental, amateur feel.
- Shots are often edited together roughly, using jump-cuts rather than seamless continuity conventions.

- Narratives are often episodic, lacking closure and featuring ensemble casts.

No single screen text is likely to include *all* these features, but you will recognise many of them clustered in texts ranging from 'gritty' social realist drama, through documentary, to reality television. Each of the elements listed above carries connotations of authenticity that help to construct the realism of screen texts according to conventions that have become associated with truthfulness and reality over decades of documentary-style filmmaking and news reports. In short, the less contrived something appears to be, the more likely we are to believe that it is true. Paradoxically, this means that the signs once associated with amateur filmmaking are now the most convincing, and those that bear the mark of carefully constructed high-tech professionalism are coded as fiction.

DOCUMENTARY

Epistemological issues

Documentaries are non-fiction film or television texts that aim to document or record subject matter based on factual or actual people and events. When considering different styles, genres or modes of documentary, two important questions to ask are:

- What types of evidence are being used, and how reliable are they?
- To what extent are the representational techniques deployed documenting, interpreting, modifying, manipulating or fictionalising the subject matter, and for what purpose?

These questions are **epistemological**, meaning that they consider how we know what we think we know. A key point to remember is that *every* mode of representation relies on certain truth claims, involves an element of persuasion, and entails a degree of intervention in reality—even if it is as simple as choices about what to include in or exclude from the frame and the final edit, or the fact that the camera's presence affects how people behave.

Epistemology is a branch of philosophical inquiry relevant to the study of realist screen texts in that it examines knowledge, explores conceptions of reality and truth, and questions how we know what we know.

Approaches vary from John Grierson's opinion that documentary entails 'the creative treatment of actuality' to Richard Leacock's belief that any intervention by the filmmaker is a form of falsification of the events taking place before the camera. These two renowned documentary filmmakers have different understandings of the capacity of photography and cinematography to document or mirror reality, and different opinions about whether filmmakers who alter the aesthetic or the context are being 'creative' or 'manipulative'— revealing or distorting the 'truth' of the image by staging the action, using filters, adding mood music or commentary, or altering chronology or context during editing. Grierson and other British documentarians of the 1930s sought to construct a picture of working-class social issues based on enactments, commentary and interviews with people who faced problems like poverty and unemployment. These films were like a form of investigative journalism geared to inform and educate the public, and they unashamedly focused on selective elements of the story that served their rhetorical purpose. Following Leacock's **'direct cinema'** approach to filming J.F. Kennedy running for president in *Primary* (1960), Fred Wiseman observes his subjects in a 'natural' context without interfering; he recorded subjects going about their business as though the camera wasn't present (as exemplified in *Titicut Follies, High School I & II,* and *Hospital*). Such filmmakers never interview or stage action, believing that manipulating events in any way is a form of fictionalisation.

Depending on the subject, documentaries might employ everything from stunt work to CGI to creatively represent aspects of the real. Hybrid and experimental texts such as *American Splendor* (a 2003 biopic about cartoonist Harvey Pekar) incorporate mood music, actors, scripted segments and cartoons. Indeed, some documentary subject matter *requires* the use of artistic licence: *Walking with Dinosaurs* is a documentary that involves speculation (scientists can't be sure what happened in prehistoric times) and fictionalisation (mixing real locations and CGI dinosaurs, simulating

> **Direct cinema** is a mode of documentary that was prevalent in America in the 1950s and 1960s. It capitalised on the ability of lightweight audio-visual equipment to follow and observe everyday people and events with as little participation or intervention by the filmmakers as possible. Direct cinema used a slow paced fly-on-the-wall approach without voiceover, interviews, music, special lighting or staged action.

life and death scenarios). The sheer diversity of styles and genres emerging from the documentary tradition is possible because documentary itself has always encompassed a wide range of techniques and topics from the African story of Namibian tribes in *Ochre and Water*, through the BBC documentary series on Auschwitz, to Werner Herzog's *Grizzly Man*. Documentaries can include interviews and the use of archival footage, commentary, dramatic re-enactment, nature studies, educational formats and propaganda techniques.

Types of documentary: Six degrees of manipulation

Documentary theorist Bill Nichols divides documentaries into six sub-genres: poetic, expository, participatory, observational, reflexive and performative (2001: 99). Each uses different strategies and types of evidence to represent and make claims about reality. Such categories are not watertight, and any non-fiction film or television text may incorporate one or more of these modes of representation:

1. The ***poetic mode*** of documentary interprets reality creatively and experimentally, linking images associatively. This unusual type of documentary is based on the assumption that it is not possible to document reality objectively so the filmmaker aims to honestly express an aspect of subjective perception. *Baraka: A World Without Words*, for example, is a feature-length montage of images and impressions of different cultures juxtaposed together and rhythmically edited to music without any plot, dialogue, commentary or text.
2. In ***expository documentaries***, a discourse of authority tells the viewer about the meaning and importance of the footage, with the implication that there is one objective true account of the subject matter and it is the job of the documentary to communicate or expose the facts. The expository mode, as used in David Attenborough and Jacques Cousteau's natural history television documentaries, 'addresses the viewer directly, with titles or voices that propose a perspective, advance an argument, or recount history' (Nichols 2001: 105). *March of the Penguins*, with its authoritative 'voice of God' narration by Morgan Freeman, is an expository documentary that uses voiceover commentary to frame the Emperor Penguins' 100-kilometre journey to and

from their Arctic breeding grounds in sub-zero temperatures as a heroic quest for love and family. As is typical of many nature documentaries, this rhetorical strategy anthropomorphises and personifies the subject.

3. In the **observational mode** the filmmaker records events much like a surveillance camera, without apparent intervention or interpretation of material for viewers. As in the direct cinema movement: 'Honoring this spirit of observation in post-production editing as well as during shooting resulted in films with no voice-over commentary, no supplementary music or sound effects, no intertitles, no historical reenactments, no behaviour repeated for the camera, and not even any interviews' (Nichols 2001: 110). While there are few recent examples of this form, Albert and David Maysles' *Salesman* (1968) is a classic that shows door-to-door bible salesmen and their clients who seem unaware of the camera's presence. Documentaries using 'masked interviews' (where the interviewer is neither heard nor seen) are variants of the observational mode. *Jesus Camp*, made nearly 40 years after *Salesman*, unobtrusively observes participants of an evangelical youth camp, using masked interviews and diegetic music without voiceover commentary.

4. **Participatory documentaries** derive from the participant observation methods of anthropology, resting on the belief that the filmmaker is best able to create an authentic representation of events if they are personally involved and have intimate knowledge of the subject. Participatory filmmakers are those who 'seek to represent their own direct encounter with their surrounding world and those who seek to represent broad social issues and historical perspectives through interviews and compilation footage' (Nichols 2001: 123). Michael Moore's work, Al Gore's *An Inconvenient Truth* and Morgan Spurlock's *Supersize Me* are participatory documentaries. *Supersize Me* features the filmmaker participating in an experiment to determine the health consequences of eating only McDonald's food for a month. As his liver deteriorates and he turns to flab, Spurlock himself interviews fast food consumers and various stakeholders in the fast food industry, the health professions and schools to determine where the responsibility for obesity lies.

5. ***Reflexive documentaries*** call the process of representation and the techniques of realism into question: 'Instead of *seeing through* documentary to the world beyond them, reflexive documentaries ask us to *see documentary* for what it is: a constructed representation' (Nichols 2001: 125). The Australian documentary *Forbidden Lie$* is about Norma Khouri, a con-woman who wrote a hoax novel *Forbidden Love,* purporting to document the honour killing of a Muslim for dating a Christian. The filmmaker Anna Broinowski, who was nearly seduced by Khouri's lies, uses dramatisation and **self-reflexive** techniques to problematise the construction of truth. In the end, the backdrop depicting the environment in which Khouri is being interviewed is abruptly revealed to be a studio set and the actress playing the woman who was allegedly killed opens her eyes and looks directly at the camera, shattering the illusion of the re-enactment.

> **Self-reflexivity** is a mode of representation that consciously reveals the artifice of the text in order to deconstruct our perceptions of screen realities, revealing screen realism as a carefully constructed representational strategy.

6. ***Performative documentaries*** address the audience emotionally and expressively, seeking to communicate different *experiences* of reality from a subjective position, as discussed in relation to *Touching the Void* below. This type of documentary 'freely mixes the expressive techniques that give texture and density to fiction (point of view shots, musical scores, renderings of subjective states of mind, flashbacks and freeze frames etc.) with oratorical techniques for addressing the social issues' (Nichols 2001: 134).

Experiential realism

The idea that screen media can describe experience so audiences share the embodied, emotional or subjective perceptions of protagonists has been taken up by filmmakers who reframe realism and authenticity as a subjective, visceral, experiential matter rather than as an objective record. This mode of representation, experiential realism, is a style that can be used in fictional texts as readily as in nonfiction. *Touching the Void* is a hybrid film that combines elements of the performative documentary style with the expository mode and mainstream action cinema techniques to create a gripping, experiential docu-drama. The film tells the story of Simon Yates and Joe Simpson who had a disastrous accident scaling the Peruvian Andes. The story is recounted by Simpson and Yates using interviews direct to camera inter-cut with re-enactments of the climb featuring the protagonists themselves, and actors, in the Andes and the Swiss Alps. What makes the film exceptional and experiential is that documentary techniques are mixed with aesthetic strategies from action films (rapid cutting, aerial photography, daring angles and vertiginous point-of-view shots plunging into icy crevasses, special lenses, CGI climbing figures digitally inserted into mountain shots, and makeup to show frostbite). There are also techniques from experimental film (expressionist lighting, hallucinatory sound and image sequences) that vividly communicate what Simpson *really felt like* when he lost one third of his body weight, suffered hypothermia and dehydration, was out of his mind with pain, and feared dying alone to the sound of a Boney M song looping in his mind (see Figure 7.2). Although Simpson was frustrated by the artificiality of repeated takes, during which he relived painful memories while the film crew fussed with jibs, framing and focus, he felt the finished documentary called his reality into being and accurately represented his gruelling experience.

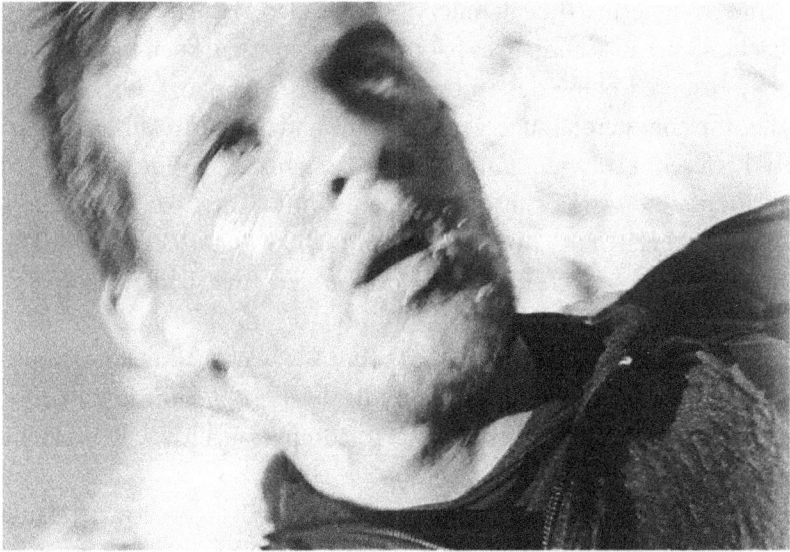

Figure 7.2 *Touching the Void* hallucinatory experience

MOCKUMENTARY FILM AND TELEVISION

A mockumentary is a documentary style film or television program in which:

> contrived events and individuals are depicted as though they are real, employing the conventions of documentary... The mockumentary draws attention to the fabricated nature of all films, documentaries included, and the fallibility of the spectator, wishing to believe in the veracity of films in general and documentaries in particular. (Armstrong 2005: 89)

Mockumentaries usually 'mock' the pretensions of their own subjects or mock documentary techniques. *The Blair Witch Project*, which captured the misadventures of three film students making a documentary about a legendary witch in the woods near the town of Blair, is an unusual and infamous mockumentary for several reasons. *Blair Witch* used documentary conventions to subvert generic expectations about horror films in innovative and frightening ways; it nauseated movie audiences with relentless, unstable mobile framing; and the phenomenal array of archival material, interviews and court transcripts on the promotional website constructed a convincing illusion that the film was a *real* documentary. In illustrating what Armstrong terms 'the fallibility of the spectator', the film generated a backlash because audiences felt their gullibility had been mocked and they resented being duped by the faux documentary style. Despite this, the commercial success of the film validated the realist aesthetic, and offered 'a coherent anti-Hollywood stance, a European edge and technique' to American independent filmmakers like Larry Clark (*Kids*) and Harmony Korine (*Gummo*) who were disenchanted with the rules and conventions of mainstream cinema (Badley 2006: 82). The popularity of mockumentary amongst independent filmmakers in America, and even more so in countries like Australia and South Africa, is in large part financial. Making a virtue out of the low-budget, low-tech aesthetic is seen as a way to compete against well-financed Hollywood productions.

The increasing use of mockumentary in TV comedy is related to the rise of reality television and the focus on self-development prevalent in talk shows like *Oprah* and the public confessional of

Big Brother's diary room. Comedy often arises from the disparity between a character's self-perception and the perceptions of viewers. We laugh when characters take themselves seriously, knowing others find them ludicrous. The gap between these different perceptions (and therefore the humour) is augmented in mockumentary when characters lacking in self-reflexivity expose their 'real self' to the camera with apparent sincerity. This gap and the opportunities we have to judge the behaviour and self-image of contestants is one of the smug pleasures of reality television. It is exploited in the 'Australian of the Year' mockumentary television series *We Can Be Heroes*, and features in *Kath and Kim*, which uses a realist aesthetic and mockumentary framing devices.

In *Faking It: Documentary and the Subversion of Factuality* (2001), Roscoe and Hight argue that a certain distrust of special effects and cinematic illusions has arisen from computer-generated imagery (CGI), chroma-key and other technology capable of producing convincing fakes and even manipulating news reportage. Such techniques threaten the truth status of screen texts that would previously have been taken for 'documentary evidence', hence technological developments have led us to question the concepts of truth and reality. Perhaps the popularity of the spate of successful mockumentaries such as the Australian 'port-a-loo' film *Kenny*, the UK and US TV series *The Office*, and reality television programs that followed *Blair Witch* can be interpreted as both a symptom and a cause of this escalating distrust of the media and the uncertainty about what we can count on, what we know, and what counts as knowledge.

REALIST FILM MOVEMENTS

Alongside the development of documentary styles, a realist tradition spanning many nations and eras emerged in narrative cinema, beginning with the Lumiere brothers' 'actuality footage' of workers leaving a factory and a train arriving at Ciotat station in the 1890s. Although we cannot cover the history of realism comprehensively, we will introduce precedents for and precursors to reality television and contemporary realist film to demonstrate the influence of realist traditions on contemporary screen media.

Soviet Montage (1924–1938)

After the Russian revolution of 1917, there was a shift away from film that functioned as an 'elite' narrative art form telling the stories of individuals, towards the use of film to document and comment on social and political conditions of the proletariat. The movement and its key figures, Sergei Eisenstein and Dziga Vertov, were renowned for innovative editing techniques, using montage, rhythm and juxtaposition to break continuity conventions. Vertov was fascinated by the technological tricks and illusions of fiction film, but also wanted to use film to expose social reality. Bringing these two impulses together, his most famous film, *Man with a Movie Camera* (1929), includes superimposition and animation along with actuality newsreel footage of everyday life and work in Moscow, Kiev and Odessa, and even images of the film's own cinematographer, editor and audience. While some sequences are staged, he did not use professional actors. Vertov wanted the audience to be aware of the actual process by which filmmakers construct a selective representation of reality. His ideas about the role of film, technology and the honesty of the filmmaker influence poetic and reflexive documentaries, fiction film and experimental *avant garde* film to this day. Eisenstein's emblematic work often depicted real events like military and industrial action. *Alexander Nevsky* (Eisenstein 1938) was a pinnacle of Soviet cinema, and the montage style ultimately influenced editing in film trailers, commercials and music videos.

French Poetic Realism (1936–1939)

As typified by the work of director Jean Renoir, French Poetic Realism was influenced by impressionist painters such as Renoir's famous father, Peirre Auguste-Renoir. The film movement itself became a formative influence on Italian Neorealism, and affected the naturalistic style and poetry of everyday life in contemporary Iranian **paradocumentary** cinema. Prominent films include Renoir's *The Grand Illusion* (1937), which features French officers taken prisoner in World War I, and *Rules of the Game* (1939), which investigates the lives of wealthy chateau owners, their guests and their servants at the onset of World War II. These films are known for their 'poetic' use of settings, staging the action in long takes with a sense of depth and space that allows the viewer's eye to wander undirected across the screen. They feature ensemble casts without clear heroes or villains. The depressed economy of the 1930s, and the preoccupation with war and class tensions in these films, often result in downbeat endings.

> **Paradocumentary** is a realist form alongside or beyond documentary itself that incorporates fact and fiction in fascinating ways. Iranian filmmakers like Kiaostami and Makhmalbaf and Licinio Azevedo's Mozambique films jump the fence between fiction and documentary, using real people to re-enact their own life stories.

Italian Neorealism (1945–1953)

A film movement in post-Fascist Italy that utilised real locations and non-professional actors to depict 'slice of life' working-class stories, Italian Neorealism was an alternative to the Hollywood 'realist' aesthetic following World War II. It is significant because of its moral and political dimension and its honesty in attempting to reveal reality rather than creating an illusion of reality. The experience of war and the demise of Mussolini's dictatorship, which had lasted from 1922 until 1943, allowed filmmakers to pursue themes that were not tolerated under Fascism, and to use cinema to critique social problems afflicting ordinary people (Bondanella 2006: 31).

The period from 1942 until the early 1950s was a time of unemployment, poverty and defeat in Italy, so it is no wonder that Neorealist films are melodramatic and depressing. Instead of showing a unique protagonist overcoming personal problems, Neorealist films often feature protagonists who represent a social class, struggling with problems that are widely shared and cannot be 'solved' by one person. A defining feature is that the stories lack closure and do not have 'happily ever after' Hollywood endings. The films have a grainy newsreel appearance and are a hybrid of documentary, narrative and experimental techniques. Shot using black and white film, naturalistic dialogue (often with sound dubbed in post-production to cut costs), natural light and mobile framing, the films convey the sense of unscripted everyday events in a melodramatic combination of 'pathos and verisimilitude' (Armstrong 2005: 71).

Featuring enduring classics such as *Obsessione* (Visconti 1942), *Rome Open City* (Rossellini 1945) and *The Bicycle Thief* (De Sica 1948), the Neorealist movement ended once Italy recovered from the war. Neorealism influenced French New Wave directors because of the creativity and the independence from industry conventions and studio control. Subsequently, Italian Neorealism influenced Danish, British and Brazilian filmmakers to shoot films about ordinary people without trying to emulate Hollywood. It became known as a 'benchmark for authenticity' and an 'alternative to lavishly financed productions', escapist illusions and the star system (Bondanella 2006: 39).

Cinéma Vérité (1940s–1960s)

Cinéma vérité translates as 'film truth' and it is characterised by a participatory documentary mode involving hand-held authenticity and self-reflexivity blended with an observational mode similar to direct cinema (but with more overt involvement of the filmmakers). In films like *Chronicle of Summer* (Rouch 1960), *cinéma vérité* makes its construction apparent and features unscripted, intimate, everyday stories and ordinary people, an ethnographic approach, chronological 'in camera' editing, the use of sync sound without 'voice of God' narration, and the avoidance of invasive zooms. Jean Rouch 'invented' *cinéma vérité* when he was on location filming in Nigeria in 1945 and accidentally knocked his camera tripod into the river (Cousins and Macdonald 2006: 265). From that point on, he had to hold the camera, creating the unsteady footage and mobile framing now associated with 'documentary realism'. This resulted in less staged or controlled footage because the camera could be amidst the action, responding dynamically to changes. Rouch believed the presence of the camera alters reality, describing *cinéma vérité* as 'cinema-provocation'—that is, life as it is provoked by the act of filming (Rouch 1995). This acknowledgment of the filmmaker's impact on the events and people filmed is one of the main features distinguishing *cinéma vérité* from direct cinema, though the terms are sometimes used loosely and interchangeably.

Nouvelle Vague: French New Wave (1958–1964)

The French New Wave was a counter-cinema movement that opposed genre films, formulaic plots and accepted filmic conventions. Like Soviet Montage and poetic documentaries, it featured innovative, experimental techniques, often breaking the rules of continuity editing and shooting on location using natural light. This *avant garde* movement also saw the emergence of auteurs (directors regarded as artists with distinctive signature styles, rather than as a cog in the factory-like production process of a film). New Wave auteurs such as Godard (*Breathless* 1959) and François Truffaut (*Jules and Jim* 1961; *Fahrenheit 451*, 1966) had a love–hate relationship with Hollywood, enamoured by its product but critical of the commercial industry and the formulaic process. New Wave films were influential partly because of their challenge to conventions that maintain the classical 'illusion of realism' in mainstream fiction films. For instance, they include jump cuts, deliberate continuity errors, freeze frames and disjunctive sound and image.

British New Wave (1960s) and 'Brit Grit' Kitchen Sink Social Realism (1980s–)

The British New Wave films of the 1960s were influenced by documentary and by the French New Wave. The subject matter showed a preoccupation with social change, 'the decline of British working-class culture and the traditional model of masculinity that went with it' (Armstrong 2005: 93). By the 1980s, Thatcherism, the floundering welfare state and rising unemployment had made their mark on British cinema. British social realist cinema does not use stars or special effects in the manner of Hollywood films (Lay 2002: 102). Instead, it features ensemble casts including non-professional actors, a 'loose' narrative structure, bleak urban locations and naturalistic light, sound and dialogue (Lay 2002: 111). Ken Loach (*Ae Fond Kiss* 2005), a director well known for addressing working-class, socialist issues, and using wide shots, long takes and a quasi-documentary style, is one of the best-known pioneers of the 'Brit Grit' tradition that emerged after the New Wave. He is rivalled only by Mike Leigh (*Secrets and Lies* 1996), whose films focus on family dramas, using improvised acting and open-ended scripts that are finalised during rehearsals to achieve emotive authenticity. These directors have influenced the use of realism to address social issues within the United Kingdom (in the films of Michael Winterbottom, Gary Oldman and Tim Roth) and abroad, influencing Harmony Korine, Larry Clark and Richard Linklater in the United States, Meirelles and Lund in South America (*City of God* 2002), and Rowan Woods (*The Boys* and *Little Fish*) in Australia.

Dogma (1995–)

At a 1995 film conference, Lars Von Trier proclaimed cinema to be in need of a makeover, and challenged filmmakers to take his Vow of Chastity (available at www.dogme95.dk). After throwing the Dogma manifesto at the audience, he left abruptly. The manifesto and its launch were deliberately provocative because they were partly intended as a means of promoting Danish cinema. In the television documentary *The Name of this Film is Dogme95*, co-writer of the manifesto Thomas Vinterberg explains:

> The reason for hitting the table so hard is because of course when you're a small country you have to yell to get heard. It's the same thing as a person with a small penis wanting a huge motorbike. I think part of the arrogance behind *Dogme95* is that we represent a very small country with very small penises.

Dogma's influences include documentary, Italian Neorealism, the French New Wave, and *cinéma vérité* (Hjort & MacKenzie 2003). Like the French New Wave, Dogma is a reaction against Hollywood excess and the strictures of stylistic conventions. Unlike the French New Wave, Dogma also critiques *auteurism* for its individualism and bourgeois concepts of art. Dogma mobilises *cinéma vérité's* understanding of cinema as provocation, and shares Italian Neorealism's concern with picturing the struggles of everyday life. In the case of von Trier's *The Idiots*, mockumentary is also influential. Interview footage frames *The Idiots* as a mock-documentary, augmenting its claim to realism as the protagonists discuss why they fake mental disabilities.

The Dogma manifesto contains ten rules called 'The Vow of Chastity', stipulating the method for 'purifying' film and expunging the corrupting aesthetic and ideology of commercial cinema. In this respect, Dogma echoes the critique of classical cinema enacted by earlier forms of realism. The commandments decree that filmmakers shalt not:

1. use sets or props that aren't present on location;
2. use voiceover, post-production sound effects or non-diegetic music;
3. use tripods: hand-held camera follows the performers without blocking or staging;

4. use arty black and white film or artificial lighting;
5. use optical works, special effects, filters or post-production effects;
6. use superficial action such as murders, weapons or fake blood;
7. use temporal or geographical alienation, futuristic or historical settings—the film takes place in the here and now;
8. use genre formulae;
9. use anamorphic widescreen—the finished product must be standard TV aspect Academy 35mm;
10. credit the director.

Despite the fact that the manifesto was written under the influence of alcohol, Dogma is a serious film movement that mounts an ideological critique of the film industry and its generic entertainment products. Claiming 'the financial structures of contemporary filmmaking ensure the dominance of a certain kind of often thrilling but easily digestible product whose aesthetic and intellectual quality is subservient to all-important commercial concerns', Dogma attempts a genuine, provocative challenge to mainstream films (Walters 2004: 41).

The emphasis on characters and performance rather than technology, artistry or special effects lends Dogma films psychological intensity and authenticity, and the tight framing and handheld footage invite intimacy with characters. Furthermore: 'The moving camera and the use of very long takes privileged an acting style that is much closer to real life and that allows for far greater freedom to use the human body, for non-verbal communication and emotional expression' (Bondebjerg 2003: 84).

Julien Donkey-Boy is an American Dogma film about a mentally impaired teenager's dysfunctional, incestuous family. It self-consciously uses documentary strategies such as actual bystanders, handheld footage and concealed cameras when Julien carries his sister's stillborn baby home. Additionally, like Neorealist films, it lacks a happy ending. Rather than turning Julien's life into entertainment using conventional dramatic structure, *Julien Donkey-Boy* has the episodic 'slice of life' quality to which *cinéma vérité* aspired. It also features the experimental aesthetic characteristic of French New Wave films, using freeze frames and degraded video footage that is unfocused, jerky, pixellated and over-exposed. It is debatable whether *Julien Donkey-Boy* undermines Dogma's own rules, reveals ethical issues about realism or creates an unwatchable movie.

The politics of form

Given that Dogma is politically motivated, it is worth considering how a film like *The Idiots* can offer social critique or challenge the film industry and its practices. *The Idiots* critiques both cinema and bourgeois culture through its counter-hegemonic form and content. In terms of form (filmmakers breaking cinematic conventions), as well as content (characters breaking social conventions), *The Idiots* throws what is considered normal 'under critical scrutiny by (re)presenting its opposite' (Walters 2004: 45). The open-ended narrative form and realist aesthetic thus reveals mainstream film and middle-class culture to be 'fake' and 'cosmeticised to death' through commonly accepted cinematic 'illusions' and insincere social etiquette. Unlike the comforting resolution of problems and ideological closure offered by Hollywood endings, the problems of conformity, inclusion and exclusion in *The Idiots* cannot be resolved in two hours of screen time. By breaching conventions, Dogma seeks to reveal the ideological underpinnings of screen conventions.

'Economical' style and democratic filmmaking

While the market-driven Hollywood film industry can be considered 'democratic' in that the public 'votes' on which films are most popular (the box office is our ballot box and genre films are the candidates running for office), the low-budget, inclusive, non-elitist style of filmmaking touted in the Dogma manifesto is a very different form of democratisation. Just as the *cinéma vérité* style was made possible by lightweight, portable camera and sound equipment, the emergence of Dogma (and the popularity of mockumentary) coincided with the development of inexpensive home-video cameras and digital editing software. As von Trier and Vinterberg write in the manifesto, 'a technological storm is raging, the result of which will be the ultimate democratisation of cinema. For the first time, anyone can make movies' (www.dogme95.dk). In a new film movement, **CCTV filmmaking**, the politics of form and the democratisation of screen media are being taken to extremes, advocating 'opportunistic infections of the surveillance apparatus' in the manifesto (www.ambienttv.net). Films such as *The Duellists* and *Faceless* don't even use their own cameras; they construct fictional narratives entirely from footage appropriated from security cameras. This problematises the boundary between public and private and challenges assumptions about realism and surveillance culture. As discussed below,

> **CCTV filmmaking** appropriates closed circuit surveillance camera footage to create screen narratives. Techniques include **'video sniffing'** which uses inexpensive receivers to scan or 'sniff' wireless transmissions and record the live feed from CCTV cameras, or performing before CCTV cameras then requesting copies of the footage under freedom of information legislation.

reality television has taken the 'economics of style' and the 'democratisation' of screen media in a different direction. Extending the use of working-class subjects as anchors of authenticity, therapeutic talk shows with experts, confessional video diaries, social experiment programs and webcams have all contributed to a new realism in the digital age, revealing the everyday lives of ordinary individuals.

REALITY TELEVISION

The proliferation of reality television programming since the 1990s is due in part to the low costs of shows that do not bankroll elaborate sets, fancy cinematography or professional actors. Furthermore, the fascination with unattainable, impossibly glamorous movie stars is matched by a desire to see something of ourselves represented on screen. The domestic nature of television and its sense of immediacy, intimacy and 'liveness' means it is a medium ideally suited to representing ordinary, 'everyday' people and routine, banal events.

Because the field is so broad, it is difficult to define reality television or to establish where it came from or where it is heading. The general premise is that reality-based programs portray people who are not actors saying lines that are not scripted in situations drawn from real life and filmed in a manner designed to capture a sense of authenticity, immediacy and realism. Extending the metaphor of cross-breeding and genetic engineering implicit in theories of genre hybridity, we can think of reality television as 'engineered reality'.

Categories of reality television

Reality television evolved from observational documentary, newsreel images of actual events (which fed into 'candid camera' capers and amateur style footage of disasters and crime) and news reportage that discussed the impact and import of actual events (spawning talk-show formats). In addition, 'soap opera's structure (multiple storylines and characters, open endedness and patterns of time that echo real life) and its emphasis on the personal and quotidian make it an important precursor to reality TV' (Biressi & Nunn 2005: 102). Given such diverse influences, reality television has developed along several trajectories: one blends documentary with comedy; another merges documentary and drama; and the third focuses on competitions and makeovers and extends to lifestyle programming.

Comedy

The blend of comedy and documentary strategies has a long history, culminating in mockumentaries like *The Office*. It was originally called *comedy vérité*, which developed out of candid moments caught on experimental film and funny responses in vox pop surveys, and included programs such as *Funniest Home Videos*. The hugely popular Australian series *The Chaser's War on Everything*, with its disruptive interventions in the lives of real politicians and its CNNNN satire, shows the roots of *comedy vérité* in news media.

Docudrama

Drama has also been harnessed to documentary in generic hybrids such as docusoaps which, like the UK series *The Living Soap*, often focus on personality clashes and interwoven stories within workplaces and home environments and 'are light entertainment docos which value everyday experience over "expert" opinion and in doing so make celebrities out of ordinary people' (Thomas cited in Cousins & Macdonald 2006: 419). Other shows document danger and crime (such as *Rescue 911*, and the re-enactments in *Crimewatch*), and docudramas aim to enlighten viewers about historical events (for example, *The Path to 9/11* starring Harvey Keitel and directed by David Cunningham in 2006 and the World War II series *Band of Brothers*, co-produced for television by Steven Spielberg and Tom Hanks in 2001). This variant of reality television capitalises on the successful formula of the soap opera by focusing on relationships and emotional dramas playing out between a range of characters. It draws on the cliffhanger format of ongoing storylines and a kind of voyeuristic fascination with other people's crisis situations to hook the audience, and it spices it up with the special relevance that realism provides.

Competitions and makeovers

Game shows like *The Apprentice*, talent quests like *Dancing with the Stars*, makeovers like *X-treme Makeover*, and Britain's *Trinny and Susannah Undress*, as well as lifestyle shows that focus on garden makeovers and renovation, and competitions like *The Biggest Loser* and *Survivor*, represent another major development in reality television.

Of the many reality television competitions, the international franchise *Big Brother* is perhaps the most famous. While *Big Brother* claims to film the housemates' 'real' reactions and interactions without scripting or staging interactions, it includes many 'unrealistic' aspects. These range from the manner of selecting the housemates based on their psychological profiles and propensity to create interesting drama and conflict, through the artificial living environment, to the fact that competition stakes and constant surveillance via hidden cameras change behaviour and alter everyday routines. In addition, even in the streamed video footage online which augments the immediacy of the 'live' broadcast version, the images made available to the public are heavily edited.

In terms of the aesthetic style of reality TV and the ways it cues audience responses, Mowena Crago notes:

> *Big Brother's* unself-reflexive unveiling of the 'workings' of the documentary process is specifically designed to produce authenticity, just as the proponents of *cinema vérité* thought it would be possible to display the 'truth' of their own observation, guaranteed in some way because we, the audience, could observe them apparently in the act of observing. (2002: 113)

However 'authentic' *Big Brother* seems, our overview of the varied conventions of realism has demonstrated that an objective view of reality is impossible, even when we are able to see the way a representation has been constructed. Like many reality television programs, *Big Brother* is more provocative and less sincere than news reportage or documentary film, and its objectives differ significantly, even though the filmmaking techniques and the overall aesthetic may be quite similar. News and documentaries are generally intended to further understanding. Reality television programs may inadvertently be informative, but they are primarily commercial ventures designed to exchange entertainment for profit.

Ideology, democracy and audience participation

Reality programming often invokes audience participation via voting for or against contestants. Combined with the fact that the means of production in many reality formats is so inclusive and inexpensive that virtually anyone can become a participant or can produce their own content and post it on YouTube, the degree of audience participation in reality television has led to the genre being labelled 'democratainment'. Reality TV has even been touted as a platform to stage public debates about important issues. For instance, the alleged racism experienced by Bollywood actress Shilpa Shetty on UK *Celebrity Big Brother* (2007) generated widespread controversy and news coverage in the United Kingdom, India and abroad about class, culture and prejudice. Fictional characters frequently express racist views in screen texts, but contestant Jade Goody's words caused public outrage precisely because her views were authentic and unscripted, reflecting the attitudes of some viewers and bruising the sensitivities of others who identified with the painfully real impact on an actual person, Shilpa Shetty.

Reality television is not merely entertaining, informative and capable of generating 'democratic' debate: it is also ideological in that it **interpellates** audience members as social subjects and as consumers. Reality TV serves both a surveillance and a therapeutic function, both of which are involved in the construction of social subjects as good citizens:

> The apparent omnipresence of media observation is internalised as a sort of self-scrutiny. But also the self becomes dependent on the consumption of media images. So paradoxically the media image becomes both the de-realisation of reality and—through reality TV, game shows, talk shows, social experiments, CCTV footage and so on—the source for unhindered observation and detailed monitoring of real people. (Biressi & Nunn 2005: 100)

Regarding consumption, advertising often reinforces the concerns of reality shows, and product placement during episodes also addresses the audience at home as consumers. For example, in *How to Look Good Naked* Carson Kressley teaches viewers to 'shop for your shape', activating the desire to purchase the hair and skincare products and clothing used to rescue insecure, style-challenged women from themselves. Commercials and promos shown during advertising breaks often use the program's celebrities or rework the program's themes in order to sell products. This is evident when *Jamie's Kitchen Australia* provides a platform to advertise kitchen cleaning products and Leggo's tomato paste, and uses the show's

> **Interpellation** is a term coined by Marxist theorist Louis Althusser, describing the way texts 'hail' or address their intended audiences as though they occupy a certain subject position. Interpellation thus implicitly invites us to occupy the position of, for instance, the role of a consumer, the role of a citizen of a nation, or traditional gender roles.

focus on helping disadvantaged youngsters achieve success to advertise the aspirations, possibilities, respectability, security and affluence associated with National Australia Bank and its slogan 'What is it you want?'

Because of its investment in actuality, reality television often works to maintain the social order. In reality crime TV especially, 'the programs work hard to provide a cultural prop for the law's authority and much of the footage is provided by law enforcement agencies' (Biressi & Nunn 2005: 122). Shows like *Crimewatch* ask audiences to identify with authorities or ordinary citizens, which contrasts sharply with the approach taken in many crime fiction genres like *The Sopranos* and gangster films, which facilitate identification with criminals. To give another example, through 2006 to 2008 *Border Security*, a docusoap about coast guards and customs officials busting suspected smugglers, terrorists and illegal immigrants, was regularly the top-rating program on Australian television, watched by over ten per cent of the nation. This indicates that it is not just gripping television, but that it successfully engages with widespread concerns about the permeability of national borders in an era of globalisation and that it simultaneously 'feeds on' and 'feeds' xenophobia (fear of foreigners).

By comparison, other reality television series are related to the impulses of the 'cinema of social concern' that dominate documentary film. For example, in the internationally roving series *Jamie's Kitchen*, celebrity chef Jamie Oliver gives underprivileged youths the opportunity to train as chefs in top restaurants. This kind of 'makeover' show focuses attention on problems like poverty and domestic dysfunction that disadvantage the participants. In the process, Oliver and his staff try to improve the prospects of participants in the series by teaching them how to cook and run a restaurant.

Each of these examples of reality television, from programs that reinforce the dominant ideology to those that engage with social concerns and seek to change reality or inspire the participants and the audience to do so, foreground the importance of thinking critically about the ethics of realist screen media.

THE ETHICS OF STYLE AND THE SPECTACLE OF THE REAL

The remainder of the chapter considers how the form or style in which a story is told creates a particular relationship between the filmmaker, the viewer and the screen, arguing that style is intrinsically connected to the narrative or issues a text conveys.

Films and television programs motivated by entertainment and profit often showcase glamorous stars, and flashy cinematography, cut to a marketable soundtrack and accompanied by spectacular special effects. Special effects and action sequences may eclipse intimacy and emotional engagement with character and overshadow important issues in the narrative, as is the case in blockbusters like *The Day After Tomorrow*, a film that confronts climate change in a style radically different from Al Gore's documentary on the same subject, *An Inconvenient Truth*. Scott McQuire argues that special effects driven narratives 'eschew traditional narrative values such as character, plot development and even star power, for the sheer visceral thrills of spectacle' (1999: 135). The 'illusion of realism' that such screen texts offer derives from classical screen conventions and special effects that aestheticise and dramatise interactions and events, giving audiences a sense of voyeurism or vicarious participation. Indeed, newer screen media such as digital games and simulation technologies aspire to replicate the perceptual experience of the 'real' world, augmenting this experiential participation with immersion in spectacular adrenaline charged action.

The distinction between spectacle and narrative suggests Hollywood's most spectacular techniques are suited to creating flashy entertainment media, while the examples in this chapter show that a gritty realist aesthetic is well suited to representing more serious stories. This gives rise to ethical issues concerning the relationship between style, content and audience response. Is it, for instance, problematic to use a spectacular style to represent actual tragic events? Can this be resolved by using a realist aesthetic, or does that just create another conceit to disguise the fact that someone is profiting from real suffering? These questions about the significance of style are central to *United 93*, directed by Paul Greengrass in 2006.

Rather than capitalising on the suffering of those involved in and affected by the tragedy of 9/11 by trivialising and sensationalising it as a genre film, *United 93* negotiates the difficulties of making a spectacle of the real in a different manner. By reportedly donating over a million dollars of its box-office takings to the Flight 93 memorial in Pennsylvania, the producers deflected criticisms that the film was profiting from the suffering of real people. The tagline for *United 93* reads: 'September 11, 2001. Four planes were hijacked. Three of them reached their target. This is the story of the fourth.' Although the Internet Movie Database listing for the film says 'if you like this title, we also recommend *Die Hard 2*', *United 93* uses markedly different representational strategies from a typical action movie about a plane hijacked by terrorists. For a start, a well-known star such as Bruce Willis wasn't cast in the lead role, and audiences knew there wouldn't be a Hollywood ending.

The film offers a real-time account of the hijacking, including dialogue from actual phone conversations passengers had with their loved ones during the event. It combines a disturbing non-diegetic musical score with CNN footage of hijacked planes crashing into the World Trade Center, and uses realist strategies including hand-held cameras to avoid the appearance of trivialising the event. Little-known actors and actual flight controllers were cast in the film and encouraged to improvise. Although the plane crashed at over 900 kilometres per hour, making an impact crater 35 metres deep, the film ends with a black screen rather than a massive explosion or footage of the crash site.

While the film commemorates those on the flight for their heroic attempt to thwart the hijacking, the way it is framed as a 'realist' eyewitness account resists what Elizabeth Anker identifies as a tendency in media coverage of 9/11 to construct a melodramatic plotline. Anker argues that in 9/11 reportage, 'comprehension of the attack was generated through the news footage that situated the United States as a morally powerful victim in a position that required it to transform victimization into heroic retributive action for crisis resolution' (2005: 23). On one level *United 93* did reinforce the binary opposition between victims and villains in an effort to elicit authentic performances: 'The actors who played the terrorist hijackers and the actors who played the passengers and crew on the flight were kept in separate hotels during filming... so that the director could capture the separation, fear and hostility between the two groups' (www.imdb.com). Although the hijackers were represented in fairly stereotypical ways (the brainwashed youth, the crazy extremist, the conflicted pilot), the refusal to cast a corn-fed, blue-eyed hero embodying American ideals against a swarthy, accented arch villain representing Al Qaeda undercuts the media's usual melodramatic style.

The audience is not left admiring a hero, hating a villain and desiring retribution, nor are we given an authoritative account of the causes or consequences of the crisis. Instead, we feel as though we too experienced the fear, confusion, desperation, dread and adrenaline of those involved. This personalises events, augmenting understanding and empathy. The style of the film, from its low-profile ensemble cast through the use of dialogue from real phone calls, to the real-time, shaky-cam aesthetic, is carefully designed to signal authenticity and respect for what really happened, instead of attempting to dramatise or glamorise the tragedy.

Ethics of the gaze

Screen theorist Vivian Sobchack suggests that different representational strategies used in documentaries (and increasingly prevalent in other screen texts) correspond to a particular ethical stance to the subject being filmed: 'Any intentional camera angle or camera movement or editorial juxtaposition will comment on what is [perceived] and will inscribe it in an act of human vision that makes visible an ethical insight' (Sobchack 2004: 257). The mode of representation signifies how the filmmaker is physically situated in relation to the filmed subject 'and thus his or her capacity to affect the events before the camera lens' (Sobchack 2004: 249). This possibility of intervention distinguishes realism from fictional texts. Documentary gazes range from the steady, technically proficient gaze of professional cinematographers through the 'accidental gaze' of those who unintentionally capture a significant event on film, to footage that encodes the helplessness or danger experienced by the filmmaker (Sobchack 2004: 249). Due in part to the fact that mobile phones with video chips enable eyewitness accounts of newsworthy events to be publicised, many of these modes of representation are now incorporated into news footage like the unsteady, frightened clips of the London Underground bombings. While the accidental gaze is coded as unprepared and therefore incapable of intervention, another style that Sobchack terms the 'interventional gaze' occurs if the filmmaker tries to step in and alter the events being filmed. Documentary realism draws the ethics of style, intervention and the type of gaze a filmmaker directs at the subject matter to the foreground.

CONCLUSION

Even though audiences cannot participate in filmed events in the same way that filmmakers and their subjects can, the ethical imperative and the impulse to intervene characterise many of the realist movements introduced above. While audiences grasp that screen texts merely provide a representation of some version of reality, we perceive in these texts a reflection of the substance and experience of 'real life'. Further, we may respond in real ways, from feeling voyeuristic, moralistic or materialistic when we watch *Oprah*, through voting on *Big Brother*, to joining an environmental group after watching *The Eleventh Hour*. As argued in this chapter, realist screen texts call into question a variety of epistemological and ethical issues related to form, content, style, context, and the responses and responsibilities of filmmakers and audiences.

KEY SKILLS

Having read this chapter you should now be able to:

- identify codes and conventions associated with realism;
- discuss the influences, intentions and impacts of realism, outlining the historical trajectory informing contemporary texts;

- apply your understanding of realism in an analysis of a particular text;
- analyse the ethical issues arising from the style, content and structure of a realist screen text;
- evaluate epistemological and ideological considerations associated with the use of aesthetic strategies, forms of 'evidence' and appeals to 'reality', and levels of documentation, manipulation and fictionalisation in realist screen media.

8

genre:

'Something new based on something familiar'

Why is it that so many of us see films like *Spider-Man 3* or watch TV series like *Alias* when we already know, well before we enter the cinema or sit down in front of the television, how these texts are likely to end? We know that at some point, for example, Spiderman's secret identity will be threatened, that he'll have an argument with girlfriend MJ, that he'll have doubts about his ability to be a superhero, and that, probably near the end of the film, he'll have to save the world (or at least the city) by fighting the super-villain. We also know that Sydney Bristow will be given a life-threatening assignment, be given reason to distrust her superior's motives, and that, near the end of the episode, she'll likely have to fight the bad guy/girl to complete the mission. Yet what we can be most certain about is that both Spiderman and Sydney will ultimately prevail by overcoming their respective obstacles. But if the outcomes of these and other screen media texts are so easy to predict, then why do we like watching them so much? And what can the popularity of genres tell us about these screen media and the media industries from which they emerge, not to mention ourselves and our culture? The answers lie in understanding the pleasures and prevalence of *genre*.

To explore these and other questions, this chapter is divided into two main sections: the first overviews what genre is, how it operates (in theory and in practice), and the roles of the different stakeholders throughout the life-cycle of a genre text; the second overviews six key approaches to studying genre: the structuralist, aesthetic, political economy, socio-cultural, family resemblances and discursive approaches.

WHAT IS 'GENRE'?

Genre, a French word meaning 'type' or 'kind', is one way that films and television programs are classified into recognisable groups and sub-groups by privileging particular similarities to (and dissimilarities from) other films and television programs. To think about genre with any clarity, however, we first need to distinguish between *genre texts* (for example, *Spider-Man 3* is a genre text in the action-blockbuster genre) and *the category of genre* (the action-blockbuster is a genre category, itself part of larger generic processes). While genre texts and genres apply across the arts, we will focus on screen media examples. Jason Mittell advocates this distinction because 'there are texts that are categorized by genres, but their textual sum does not equal the whole of the genre . . . Analyses of generic texts are certainly worthwhile, but they do not explain how genres themselves operate as categories' (2001: 8). In this chapter, we follow Mittell and distinguish between genre texts and the category of genre.

A *genre text* is a text that conforms to the established codes and conventions of a genre (or genres). It is most commonly associated with fictional screen media (action blockbusters, sitcoms, etc.), but it is also applied (and applies) to non-fictional screen media (the evening news, nature documentaries, etc.).

The content or subject of a story seems to be the most obvious way to classify genre, but Robert Stam argues that 'subject matter is the weakest criterion for generic groupings because it fails to take into account how the subject is treated' (2000: 14). For example, *Scrubs*, *House* and *Grey's Anatomy* take hospitals as their subject, but are treated as comedy, detective story and soap opera respectively.

Further, Chris Marker's experimental French film *La Jetée* could be classified as a mock-documentary shot with still 'archival' images and voiceover narration, but the story—a man travelling back in time—is the same as the science fiction action film it inspired: *Twelve Monkeys*, starring Brad Pitt and Bruce Willis. This suggests that we need to consider a combination of elements when using a term like 'genre'. Five of the most common conventions around which genre texts are classified are:

- a formulaic plot;
- setting;
- characters;
- style and structure; and
- **iconography**.

So, while most genre texts draw on all of these conventions (and more) in distinctive ways, we might begin to recognise: a romantic comedy because of its formulaic 'boy meets girl' plot, the evening news because it is set in a news studio, a gangster film because it is primarily populated by gangster characters, film noir because of its low-key lighting, or a Western because of its frontier iconography (including six-shooter pistols, Stetson hats and horses). Most people recognise these codes intuitively, which is the 'I know it when I see it' mode of genre definition (Mittell 2004: 1).

> **Iconography** refers to visual conventions that function symbolically, such as costume or setting. The science fiction genre, for instance, has distinctive iconography, which includes being set in the future (often in space), spaceships, high-tech weaponry and non-human characters.

In theory, a genre text is classified into a particular genre depending on the degree to which it conforms to that genre's conventions (which also emphasises the inherently derivative nature of genres). This process is both contextual and **intertextual**, because it is an articulation of one text's relation to other texts, in terms of their shared features. For example, when Shrek says 'that'll do Donkey, that'll do' in *Shrek*, it intertextually references a scene in *Babe*, in which Farmer Hoggett says to Babe, 'that'll do pig, that'll do'. And indeed, the most common conception of genre is as a textual cataloging or taxonomy that is loosely akin to biological taxonomies used to categorise different species (Feuer 1992; Bordwell & Thompson 2008: 318). In practice, however, genres are far easier to recognise than they are to define (Bordwell & Thompson 2008: 318), so creating or classifying a genre text is, as we will discuss shortly, a highly fraught process. In fact, unlike the biological sciences, where taxonomies were traditionally based on the cataloguing of immutable physical characteristics, the classification of genre texts is not based on inherent textual qualities that reside in each text; rather, it is a culturally negotiated process that privileges particular aspects of a text over others. As a result, it is much easier to find texts that do not easily conform to a genre than it is to find texts that do.

> **Intertextual** or **intertextuality** refers to instances where one text references one (or more) other text/s, thus setting up a reading relation between the texts.

Inevitably, then, there is frequently disagreement over how to classify any given genre text. For while formulaic plots, setting, characters, style and iconography are certainly among the most common textual aspects around which genre texts are classified, they are by no means the only ones. Consider the following conventions and the examples provided (Bordwell 1989: 149; Stam 2000: 14), thinking carefully about whether you would use these to classify a genre text:

- preferred audience response (comedy, horror, sit-com);
- race (blaxploitation films, J-horror for Japanese horror, and K-drama for Korean TV drama series);
- budget (blockbuster, community television);
- artistic status (the art film);
- nationality (foreign films, national cinemas);
- politics (feminist cinema);
- audience (children's film, 'chick flick', family film);
- sexuality (queer cinema, queer television channels);
- auteur (a body of work by a director or star—say, 'Woody Allen films').

These categories are often used to either classify genre texts or to organise texts in ways that parallel genre classification. But before you decide on whether you would use these categories in a genre analysis, let's complicate matters further by considering what happens when a text draws on the conventions, however they are understood, of *more* than one genre. For example, is *Harry Potter and the Order of the Phoenix* a fantasy film, an adventure film, a children's film or a thriller? It contains elements of each of these categories, but is it more consistent with one of these genres than the others, or is it a combination of generic conventions such that it represents a mixed or hybrid genre text (a 'fantasy-adventure' perhaps)? While few of us are likely to agree on precisely where 'fantasy' ends and 'adventure' begins, mixed- or **hybrid**-genre texts are not only common, but also much more common than single-genre texts. In fact, hybridity—perhaps paradoxically—is increasingly recognised as one of the *characteristics* of genre film and television in the 1990s and 2000s (see Dixon 2000; Abercrombie 1996).

However, this isn't necessarily new. Janet Staiger suggests that genre texts have never been 'pure' or based on a single genre; instead, she argues, genre texts have always been caught up in a perpetual process of transformation and recombination. For instance, melodrama, comedy and romance are properly understood as narrative elements that can be identified in many genres, while even Westerns or martial arts films can include characteristics of, say, the musical or the horror genre. Consider *Kung Fu Hustle*, a Hong Kong martial arts-action film that draws on the genre conventions of musicals and Westerns. In reality, we can only understand a textual category in contextual relation to a different category, so genre texts always implicitly reference more than one genre (Staiger 1997: 3). Further, this hybridity may be inherent in both film and television, because of their multimedia histories—for instance, film genres emerged by 'borrowing from other media. The melodrama has clear antecedents in stage plays and novels,' while some versions of 'comedy can be traced back to stage farces or comic novels' (Bordwell & Thompson 2008: 321). Similarly, early television drew on radio and live theatre for inspiration, with Vaudeville the basis for one of the earliest television genres: the 'variety show'. Thus genre texts are 'something new based on something familiar' (Bordwell & Thompson 2008: 326).

> The term **hybrid** is drawn from genetics and refers to interbreeding between two separate species that generally results in a sterile offspring (just as a liger results from breeding lions with tigers, or mules are the sterile offspring of horses and donkeys). **Genre hybridity** refers to texts that exhibit the recognisable style, storyline, structure and/or characterisation of two or more established genres.

There are also very good economic reasons for the pervasiveness of genre hybridity, including the industrial imperatives associated with the production of genre texts. Genres 'exist within the context of a set of economic relations and practices' (Neale 1980: 51–2), functioning as both a marketing strategy and an economic strategy. That is to say, genre acts like an insurance policy for production studios, because they are investing in a proven formula—which is no small thing when the average cost of making and releasing a Hollywood film is well over a hundred million dollars. Genre is equally crucial in television: without genre, television producers 'could not assure the delivery of the weekly audience, as do the episode series and continuing serial' (Feuer 1992: 144). Nicholas Abercrombie continues by noting that, for television producers, the goal is to produce as many texts in the same genre as possible, because it allows considerable cost-saving, not least by being able to use the same sets, properties and costumes 'over and over again' (1996: 43). For media industries, then, genre is about reaping the largest reward for the least amount of risk, though even genre is no guarantee of a text's success.

Mixed- or hybrid-genre texts, like *Harry Potter and the Order of the Phoenix*, reflect these industry imperatives. As Todd Gitlin says, 'the logic of maximising the quick payoff has produced that very Hollywood hybrid, the recombinant form, which assumes that selected features of recent hits can be spliced together to make a eugenic success' (Custen 1992: 64). For instance, while *Shrek the Third* is an animated film marketed to children (and their parents), it also contains elements of comedy, fantasy, the Western and the musical. And on television, the outrageous irony and scandalous mega-drama of *Desperate Housewives* capitalises on the success of *Sex and the City* by incorporating the romantic comedy exploits of several very different women, yet it also draws in viewers who like the melodramatic intrigue, cliffhangers, and interwoven storylines of soap operas like *The Bold and the Beautiful*.

Genre hybridity is usually understood primarily from a production standpoint as a marketing strategy. The inclusion of several different genres broadens the appeal of a film or television series, potentially increasing its market share by drawing diverse audience segments to the same text. So how does a media professional go about creating a successful genre text, when there are no guarantees for a text's success, and no consensus on how to classify genre texts or even define genres in the first place? Bordwell notes that there is ultimately 'no set of necessary and sufficient conditions' to classify a genre text, and thus to define a genre, which 'all experts or ordinary film-goers would find acceptable' (1989: 147). Rather, genre is a broad and sometimes fuzzy grouping of texts intuitively recognised by audiences and industry alike (see Bordwell & Thompson 2008; Mittell 2004: 1).

So on what basis are genre texts created? In film and television, producers try to replicate success. Consequently, producers might try to replicate the actor, director, character, theme, issues or setting of a popular genre text, depending on what they perceive to have been the drawcard that made that text popular. Hence the 'spin-off' may even be in a different genre. So when *Dreamgirls* followed soon after the successful releases of *Walk the Line* and *Ray*, was it because producers surmised that the musical genre, or the 1950s setting, was popular with audiences? Or perhaps it was the 'talent and ambition overcomes childhood trauma' storyline? In reality, few genre texts are successful for only one reason; most are successful because of their distinctive *combination* of genre conventions, which highlights how difficult it is to try to isolate the aspects of a particular genre text that make it popular with audiences.

Even so, Rick Altman suggests that the process of creating genre texts can effectively be boiled down to what he calls the 'Producer's Game'. Altman's 'Producer's Game' begins by looking at recent box-office hits and trying to identify what it is that made those films a hit, before applying that 'formula' to the process of creating a new film, tracking that film's success at the box office, and beginning the whole process again:

1. From box-office information, identify a successful film.
2. Analyse the film in order to discover what made it successful.
3. Make another film stressing the assumed formula for success.
4. Check box-office information on the new film and reassess the success formula accordingly.
5. Use revised formula as a basis for another film.
6. Continue the process indefinitely. (Altman 1999: 38)
   'The Producer's Game' extract produced courtesy of Rick Altman, *Film/Genre* (1999) and BFI publishing.

What Altman's formula, and all of our discussions thus far, suggest is not simply that there is no 'correct' or foolproof way to classify or create a genre text—although this is certainly true—but that there are also a large number of people, institutions and industries which have a stake in those processes (from media professionals and investors to scholars and everyday audiences). As Altman says, genre is a 'multivalent term multiply and variously valorized by diverse user groups' (1999: 214). Consequently, genre is much more than any one genre text; it exists **extra-textually** as a cultural category.

> **Extra-textual** refers to something that is 'outside' the text, such as a film's publicity or an actor's celebrity, but that nevertheless plays a part in how we read that text. So we might watch *Mr and Mrs Smith* closely, not for its action-packed storyline, but to try to look for evidence—as gossip magazines asserted at the time—that co-stars Brad Pitt and Angelina Jolie began their relationship during the making of this film.

Genre is a cultural category because it 'surpass[es] the boundaries of media texts and operate[s] within industry, audience, and cultural practices as well' (Mittell 2001: 3). In fact, we might argue that genre does not so much operate 'within' industry, audience and culture, but at the *intersection* of industry, audience and culture (Krutnik 1990: 57). Thus genre is simultaneously negotiated at the levels of text, industry and audience, which can be delineated as follows:

1. **Genre text**
   A type or category of text with:
   - a formulaic plot;
   - familiar setting;
   - characters;
   - style and structure;
   - and iconography.
2. **Industry**
   A marketing device and an economic strategy.
3. **Audience**
   Audience preferences, expectations and responses ('audience' includes viewers, critics, and scholars).

Each of these categories represents cultural sites where genre is negotiated, but while we have previously discussed both genre texts and the media industries that create them, we have yet to discuss the audiences of genre texts. Genre is, of course, one of the main ways that media is organised for audiences' consumption—from the video store, where most aisles are organised by genre, to pay television, where select channels are devoted to genres, to film reviews on the internet that are categorised according to genre. Genre is equally one of the main ways that audiences choose to organise their own viewing practices. We might, for example, have a preference for 'chick flicks' (just as we might have a friend who refuses to see 'chick flicks' with us). Audiences love, or at least respond emphatically to, genres. But what do audiences like about genre texts and what role do audiences have in the definition and/or formation of genres?

Though little empirical research has been conducted on the topic, most scholars argue that audiences enjoy genre texts because of the familiarity associated with genre conventions. There are two different (but related) lines of opinion here. The first is that audiences find pleasure in being so familiar with a genre that it becomes possible to predict the outcomes of a particular genre text (Chandler 1997). When we watch a romantic comedy, for example, we can predict that the majority of the film will focus on the re/formation of a couple and that, by the film's end, that couple will probably end up together, perhaps even married. The pleasures of predictability are equally true in television, where it is again about 'knowing what the genre rules are, knowing that the programme has to solve problems in the genre framework, and wondering how it is going to do so' (Abercrombie 1996: 43). In both film and television, audiences also experience pleasure when their expectations are met, so we might breathily sigh as Alex (Hugh Grant) ends up with Sophie (Drew Barrymore) in Hollywood romantic comedy *Music and Lyrics* or feel avenged when Agent Jack Bauer (Keifer Sutherland) stops an assassination attempt in US TV series *24*.

The second line is that it is not simply the familiarity with a genre that is pleasurable, but being surprised by the particular differences or moments of unpredictability of a genre text. To this end, Neale argues that genres are characterised both by their 'repetition and difference' (1980: 48–9), and that it is only the combination that maintains audiences' interests. Consider, for instance, the Hollywood romantic comedy *My Best Friend's Wedding*, directed by PJ Hogan in 1997. Like most romantic comedies, *My Best Friend's Wedding* begins by identifying a probable couple: Julianne (Julia Roberts) and Michael (Dermot Mulroney). Julianne realises she loves Michael after finding out about his engagement to another woman. She then sets out to win Michael back. However, Julianne does not succeed with her initial goal. Instead, Michael stays with his fiancée and Julianne is left, in the final scene of the film, dancing with her gay best friend, George (Rupert Everett). This represented a major alteration to the generic conventions of the romantic comedy and caught a lot of audiences by surprise. But in fact audiences demanded that surprise: after test audiences responded poorly to the film's original ending, a new ending was filmed, after which the film went on to enormous success. *My Best Friend's Wedding* is now one of the top 20 most successful romantic comedies of all time (Rubinfeld 2001: 157). This scenario evidences the pleasures of the (albeit infrequent) *unpredictability* of genre, but also the explicit negotiation of generic boundaries that occurs between audiences and industry.

What is true in both instances, of course, is that audiences' opinions *matter*. In fact, audiences play a crucial role in genre definition, to the extent that the main way a genre text fails, or 'bombs', is by disappointing or otherwise not fulfilling audiences' expectations of that genre. Over time, a lack of audience interest can even wipe out entire genres, at least for a time. The Western, for instance, was a popular genre for many years, before audiences gradually lost interest in it. By the early 1990s, studios were forced to stop producing them because they had stopped being financially viable. Trends change, however, and the release of Westerns like *The Assassination of Jesse James by the Coward Robert Ford* and *3.10 to Yuma* may suggest something of a revival. Some critics believe that science fiction feature films are struggling in the early 2000s, as opposed to science fiction television programs, which continue to be popular. So audiences influence genres first and foremost by their mass: the greater the number of people who watch a television program or see a film, the more likely it is that a producer will try to replicate that success (thus maintaining or growing a genre). And, of course, the converse is also true. Moreover, the longer a genre exists, the more variation we are likely to see, as the pressure for variation increases for producers to maintain audience interest.

Less dramatically, audiences also influence genres by their engagement in public and private discourses about genre texts. Here the term 'audiences' includes not only everyday or non-specialist audiences, but also specialist audiences like critics and scholars.

Collectively, audiences' discursive engagement with genre texts can range from, but is by no means limited to, talking about a film with friends (word of mouth) or writing about a television program on a blog, through attending a fan convention or buying a celebrity magazine, to writing a film review or academic paper. All of these are examples of audiences functioning as part of a discursive community, organised around particular genre texts or genres. Some of these engagements are more influential than others. Reviews are particularly important, because they are designed to influence whether or not the reader then chooses to see the reviewed film or television program. They construct 'horizons of expectations' (Jauss 1982: 22), and are part of the 'intertextual relay', or the 'systems and forms of publicity, marketing and reviewing that each media institution possesses', both of which generate expectations around a genre text and/or genre (Neale 2001: 1). These expectations are also developed by critics' use of genre as a succinct descriptive frame. For example, Australian film critic, David Stratton frequently categorises the films he reviews in *The Australian* newspaper according to genre, in order to provide audiences with a set of expectations about that film in relatively few words. This is significant: 'Genres do not consist only of films: they consist also, and equally, of specific systems of expectation and hypothesis which spectators bring with them to the cinema, and which interact with films themselves during the viewing process' (Neale 1990: 46).

The role of the audience is an important part of the overall economy of genre. Genre pervades every aspect of a genre text's life-cycle, from the moment it is pitched to an investor, throughout its production and marketing, to its reception and consumption by audiences. In fact, we know from political economy approaches to genre (which we overview in the following section) that the media industries are profit-oriented industries and have been since their inception. So genres actually circulate textually, culturally (extra-textually, discursively, etc.) and economically. If we were to try to align all of the approaches that we've discussed thus far, we would end up with an approach to thinking about genre as an intersection between audience, industry and text, with one that recognised each of these sites as a particular stage of a genre text's circulation (see Figure 8.1).

Text A type or category of text with: • formulaic plot • familiar setting • stock characters • trademark style and structure • distinctive iconography	**Production** Pitch, script, filming, editing, post-production
Industry A marketing device An economic strategy	**Marketing** Publicity, distribution, exhibition and, for TV, scheduling
Audience Audience preferences, expectations and responses	**Consumption** Absence/presence of audience, fan practices, word of mouth, film reviews, academic scholarship

Figure 8.1 An overview of 'genre'

This approach details the cultural construction and circulation, as well as the economic construction and circulation, of genre. But before we consider what this means for how we study genre, it is useful to first think about how genre operates differently in film and television.

DIFFERENCES IN MEDIUM: GENRE IN FILM AND TELEVISION

Film and television developed out of different media: film from live theatre and photography; television from film, live theatre and radio. But how do those histories affect what kinds of genres tend to be associated with each medium? One difference that we might connect to these histories is narrative resolution: film genres tend to be closed narratives (meaning that a narrative is set up and resolved by the end of the film), whereas television genres tend to be open narratives (meaning that a narrative is developed in ongoing instalments, whether nightly, weekly, or using some other timeframe). Obviously, this is because films are consumed on an individual basis, whereas television programs tend to be consumed in an ongoing fashion, usually as part of our domestic lifestyles (we might, for example, habitually watch the evening news after work or our favourite evening drama series after dinner). This is the difference between, say, the 'closed' narrative of a Hollywood drama like *American Gangster* and the 'ongoing' narrative, with its weekly instalments, of a US television drama series like *The Sopranos*. Live theatre, like film genre, often developed around one-off productions that are consumed individually; while radio, like television, began to specialise in genres with ongoing narratives (the 'radio serial' is the best example). Perhaps the closest example of an ongoing narrative in genre film is the Hollywood sequel (like the *Charlie's Angels* franchise, where later films can reference the events in earlier films, not to mention its television history) or multi-part film series (like *The Lord of the Rings* three-part series, or the intratextuality of, say, Steve Irwin documentaries).

There are also differences between the film and television industries, and corollary technologies and practices. In television, for example, genre is inseparable from scheduling (when a text is broadcast). Certain times of the day and week are associated with particular genres. To demonstrate, weekday afternoons are associated with 'children's television.' Scheduling boundaries, at least on free-to-air commercial television, are enforced through classification. In Australia, commercial television is regulated by the Commercial Television Industry Code of Practice, which covers, among other things, program classification. So, while you probably already associated afternoon television with children's television—and perhaps were once a fan of the Australian children's TV programs *The Shak* or *Totally Wild*—you may not have known that 4.00–7.00 p.m. timeslot is actually bound by a 'general audience' G-rating. It is a 'G Classification period', so that while content—and thus genres—do not necessarily have to target children, they must be so 'mild' that children can watch without supervision (Free TV Australia, 2004: 23). Similarly, in the United Kingdom, television is regulated by the Office of Communications (OFCOM), which does not permit television broadcasters to show material 'unsuitable' for children, including the positive depiction of drug-taking, violence or offensive language, between 5.30 a.m. and 9.00 p.m. (OFCOM, 2005). Scheduling and classification clearly impact what television genres can be shown and when.

There are equally issues of viewing practices and technology which also separate genre on film and television. Feuer (1992: 157–8) considers the emergence of the remote control, for instance, as resulting in a different approach to consuming genre. She argues that viewers now need to recognise genre much more quickly as they rapidly 'zap' between channels. Neale describes this as the 'rapid deployment of genre-recognition skills' (2001: 4). Of course, this also means television professionals have the much more difficult task of making any given text identifiable within a genre in the split second an audience member might flick past it—just generically identifiable enough to try to grab their fleeting attention. This is quite unlike film exhibition, where audiences have chosen to come and watch a particular film without any possibility of changing the channel. This is one of the reasons, according to Feuer, that television genres are characterised by hybridity rather than purity (if there ever was such a thing). At the same time, of course, we have also seen the emergence of genre-specific channels on cable television, like the Sci-Fi Channel or the Comedy Channel. Even as genre evolves in particular ways, then, television, and certainly film, are both still centrally organised around genre.

How, then, to study it?

KEY APPROACHES TO STUDYING GENRE

Genre has been used to categorise texts since Aristotle used the concept to divide texts into 'tragedy' and 'comedy' some 300 years before the birth of Christ. Our interests are more recent, of course: genre has been a central concept in the analysis of film and television almost since the emergence of their respective disciplines in the academy (the late 1960s and 1970s for film studies and the mid- to late 1970s for television studies). Applied to Hollywood cinema from the very beginning, genre study initially took the place on film scholars' mantles which had been held by auteur theory, one of two analytical models popular in the 1950s (the other being the largely descriptive 'journalistic' mode). In television, genre study emerged through Horace Newcombe, whose *TV: The Most Popular Art* (1974) and *Television: The Critical View* (1976) were the first to study television genre and among the first publications of television studies. Since then, there have been a number of trends—some more successful than others—in the analysis of genre in film and television. Six of the most significant are the structuralist, socio-cultural, political economy, aesthetic, family resemblances and discursive approaches. Inevitably, there is a lot of crossover between most of these approaches because, by and large, they all draw on each other's strengths and try to address each other's weaknesses. In the following pages, we overview each of these approaches to studying screen media, but pay particular attention to the major differences between them.

The structuralist approach

As discussed in Chapter 6, the structuralist approach aims to distil genres down to a generic narrative and relationship structure, where character types (hero, villain, victim, etc.) interact in structurally predictable (and delimited) ways. For example, Jim Kitses (1969) argues in his landmark structuralist account of the Western genre, *Horizons West*, that the Western is organised around a civilisation/wilderness binary. This might seem benign, but implicit in this binary are a host of other binaries:

- civilisation/wilderness;
- community/individual;
- culture/nature;
- corruption/purity;
- humanity/savagery (Kitses 1969: 11).

So, quite quickly, one binary opposition reveals a much larger (and highly problematic) set of associations, which results in the racist 'humanity/savagery' (binary oppositions tend to be heavily ideological).

The adoption of structuralism in film studies in the 1960s and 1970s was one of the earliest examples of film studies adopting the methodologies of other disciplines to bolster the new discipline's credibility through disciplinary association. Two of the first structuralist analyses of film genre—in this case, the Western—are Kitses' *Horizons West*, mentioned above, and Will Wright's *Six Guns and Society* (1975). A more recent example is Mark Rubinfeld's *Bound to Bond* (2001), which incorporates a structuralist account of the Hollywood romantic comedy genre. Rubinfeld surveys 155 of the most popular Hollywood romantic comedies, released between 1970 and 1999. He argues that there are four generic plots in the Hollywood romantic comedy, and five generic 'types' (or five ways that the four plots unfold). Because the structuralist approach peaked in popularity in the 1970s, it was nowhere near as popular in television studies (which only emerged in the mid- to late 1970s). Even so, there are a handful of examples: one of the most recent is Michael Real's (2003) structural analysis of *The Cosby Show*.

One of the strengths of this approach is that it produces a quantifiable analysis that arguably remains quite useful to large surveys of texts. However, it has also been heavily criticised. Because structuralism is focused on 'uncovering' an underlying narrative structure, it rarely sheds light on the visual or contextual aspects of a genre text, which limits the kinds of conclusions it is possible to draw from such an analysis. Structuralism's focus on binary oppositions has also tended to be far too simplistic because it fails to account for the nuances surrounding the employment of binaries and/or reduces more complicated representations to binaries. Binaries are also frequently (some say always) associated with racist, sexist and/or heteronormative ideologies. So use with care.

The socio-cultural approach

There are two opposing strands of the socio-cultural approach: the ritual approach and the ideological approach. The ritual approach understands genre as a popular social ritual. It privileges audience agency over industry agency and sees genre texts as a collective cultural expression of socially prevalent ideas and dilemmas (Neale 2000: 220). From this perspective, it is not the variation, difference and innovation, but the repetitive nature of key elements that imbues a genre with social significance; here, genre conventions demonstrate the importance or popularity of particular identities, issues and ideas. The ritual approach, in its simplest form, is sometimes (and derogatively) described as 'reflectionist' because it positions genre as though a 'reflection' of what mainstream audiences think and/or desire. In this understanding, the formulaic nature of genre, demonstrated by the similarities between genre texts, is what enables shared fantasies to be articulated and negotiated. Consequently, a genre text's conclusion symbolises the restoration of harmony by (textually) resolving social tensions. In other words, a genre text's 'happy ending' is understood as having social meaning. In reality, of course, the 'happy endings' of genre texts always privilege one perspective over others (usually the dominant culture's perspective over marginal cultures).

Critics of the ritual approach, and there are many, point out that the box office success and popularity of genre texts do not necessarily mean that the majority of audience members agree with the way the representation of culture is negotiated in that text, let alone how conflict is resolved or different identities are represented (Neale 2000: 225). Generalising about individual responses to genre texts on the basis of box office success can, quite obviously, be significantly misleading, just as privileging audience control over the content and reception of genre texts can also under-play the contentious aspects of the media industries and the genre texts they produce.

The ideological approach emphasises industry agency and control over audience agency. However, the relationship is anything but equal: this approach casts the audience as being manipulated by the media industries in ways that validate and reinforce dominant economic, social and ideological positions (Neale 2000: 227). This approach, one development of the pessimism of mass culture theorists, argues that the 'happy ending' narrative resolution of genre texts is actually an ideological deflection away from the problems the genre texts depict. Here, then, genre texts lure audiences through the pleasures of genre, distracting them from action or revolt through such pleasures, all the while normalising the hegemonic values they depict (Neale 2000: 227). In a similar (but more productive) vein, John Fiske argues that genre conventions 'embody the crucial ideological concerns of the time in which they are popular' (1987: 110). Neale adds that genres do not simply 'embody', but also actively *negotiate,* such 'crucial ideological concerns' (1980: 16). One of the major criticisms of this approach is that it vastly simplifies reception: it attributes conscious agency to the industry, yet neglects to look at either the conscious agency of audiences or the policies and financial constraints that might govern industry choices and mechanisms (Neale 2000: 228). The political economy approach, however, focuses exclusively on the industry and its mechanisms, for better and worse.

The political economy approach

The political economy approach to genre analysis developed from the work of mass culture theorists like Theodor Adorno who, among others, analysed mass or popular culture as the product of 'the culture industry', 'characterized by standardized production and consumption' and 'based on processes of mass reproduction and mass distribution' (Hollows 1995: 20). Adorno thought that this was highly problematic: he argued that standardised products—and he considered Hollywood genre cinema a prime example—were not only simple-minded and identical, but also socially pernicious because they embodied capitalist ideologies that were then uncritically consumed by a lazy and passive audience. These ideas were later developed by other scholars into a more complicated analysis which, among other developments, recognised that audiences are rarely duped by culture but instead engage with it in a range of sophisticated ways.

For screen media, the political economy approach focuses on how the industrial mechanisms and imperatives surrounding production, distribution and exhibition affect not only the kinds of texts created but the kinds of audiences they reach. While Janet Wasko (1999) and Altman (1987) are among the best-known proponents of the political economy approach—we discussed Altman's 'Producer's Game' earlier—Jim Hiller also adopts the political economy approach to understand the late 1980s/1990s emergence of genre texts focused on African American central characters. He uses a political economy approach to argue that the best way to understand this emergence is as being 'built on' the industry's increasing 'recognition of the size and the purchasing power of the black audience' (1992: 148). Similarly, we might understand the explosion of reality television in the 1990s as being about the television industry's ongoing desire for popular television that is relatively cheap to produce, rather than a genuine sociological interest in the recorded interactions of ordinary people.

One of the strengths of the political economy approach is that, while film and television scholars often exaggerate the independence of genre texts by focusing exclusively on the textual (thus implying an inaccurate separation between genres and their economic foundations), the political economy approach forces us to examine the implications of these foundations. However, this approach is also frequently criticised, not only because it tends to simplify this very relationship (between text and industry), but also because it fails to consider the ways audiences consume genre texts. Moreover, while the earliest examples of this approach analysed genre texts as vehicles of dominant culture, the reality is that genre texts have always addressed select diverse audiences, if only to capture the widest possible market (Hollows 1995: 33).

The aesthetic approach

The aesthetic approach stresses patterns of repetition and variation, similarity and difference. In each genre, we can identify familiar, typical characters, settings and storylines that vary slightly from film to film. Traits of repetition and similarity between films of the same genre lead to assumptions that the films are formulaic, clichéd and stereotyped. Consequently, while the socio-cultural approach focuses on similarities between genre texts, the aesthetic approach focuses on the creative variations and differences that distinguish films in a genre, as evidence of their artistic worth and innovation. This is based on the earliest approaches to studying film, which saw it as 'art'; it is equally a reaction against the mass culture theorists' conception of genre as 'art-less'.

Due to the emphasis on art, aesthetic approaches to genre attend to screen style, noting the camera and editing techniques and use of sound and *mise en scène* common in a genre. For example, romantic comedies and sit-coms feature a predominance of close-ups to capture emotive expressivity; they are edited in an unobtrusive, linear manner; the storylines are dialogue-heavy with a soundtrack that underscores the characters' emotional journey; and the *mise en scène* involves high-key lighting, naturalistic performances and, frequently, domestic interior settings. Westerns, by contrast, have sparse dialogue and wide-angle extreme long shots to showcase the untamed landscapes and action as the cowboys and Indians gallop into the sunset. In relation to the notion that genre texts contain stereotyped stock characters, one of the thematic functions of a protagonist in a standard three-act narrative is their mediation of conflicting forces (masculinity and femininity in romantic comedy; civilisation and wilderness in a Western). Because of this mediating function, even genre characters are necessarily multi-dimensional (Neale 2000: 208).

Familiar settings are also important because they frame the action and, to an extent, define the characters: 'setting inflects the ways in which the cultural milieu is represented' (Neale 2000: 211). Consider, for example, how the fact that Joss Whedon's defunct

US TV series *Firefly* and Hollywood science fiction film *Serenity* are Westerns set in space inflects the outlaw characters and storylines with the discourses of globalisation and technology. Everyone speaks Chinese, while the settlers on far-flung planets are threatened not by an intergalactic railroad but by additives the government puts into the air and water to make them 'better' people. Although the endings of genre texts may be largely predictable (boy gets girl, etc.), the pathway to that resolution is always varied. As Neale reminds us, 'predictability is not an absolute quality but a matter of degree' (2000: 210). Other genre theorists, like Altman (1987), vary this approach by focusing on the semantic characteristics (or common traits, styles and characters) and syntactic structures of particular genres (of which the latter might involve an analysis of narrative structure and relationships, drawing on the tradition of the structuralist approach).

The family resemblances approach

The family resemblances approach is based on philosopher Ludwig Wittgenstein's categorisation of games. He asks, in his posthumously published *Philosophical Investigations* (1953), what the shared characteristics are of 'games', from sporting games to card games (and we could probably add 'computer games' as a contemporary addition to the category). They are all described as 'games' but what, Wittgenstein asks, is 'common to them all?' (1978: 31). In fact, Wittgenstein found no conventions that occurred across all games; instead, he identified a network of intertextual relationships between games. Based on this observation, he proposed using the family as a critical analogy to discuss the kinds of similarities he found: 'I can think of no better expression to characterize these similarities than "family resemblance"; for the various resemblances between members of a family: build, features, color of eyes, gait, temperament, etc. etc. overlap and criss-cross in the same way—And I shall say: "games" form a family' (1978: 32).

Scholars like John Cawelti (1985) have applied this idea to film and television genre analysis, where the approach exceeds aesthetic analyses by focusing on loose intertextual similarities, rather than on strict textual definitions. Using this approach, then, a genre text could be classified into a genre not because genres are consistent categories that are identified by a 'common defining trait, but because, like families, they share a group of traits and because, like family members, some [genre texts] possess traits which others do not' (Neale 1980: 229). For example, we have already classified *My Best Friend's Wedding* in the same genre, the romantic comedy, as *Music and Lyrics*, because while the central couple do not end up together—one of the central conventions of the genre—the film is nevertheless a comedy focused on the formation of a couple. In television, to offer a less obvious example, we might categorise the series *Buffy the Vampire Slayer* alongside *I Love Lucy* or, say, *Roseanne*, as all drawing on certain conventions of the 'unruly woman' sit-com. *Buffy*, for example, focuses on a comedic but (selectively) un-stereotypical female lead, is (partially) received as a comedy, and chronicles the on-again, off-again relationships between characters. (These are all features of the sit-com, and the 'unruly woman' sit-com in particular.) (Rowe 2003).

One of the strengths of this approach is that it acknowledges genre texts rarely conform to all of the conventions of a genre and allows generic evolution to be mapped across a range of texts. Yet one of the criticisms of the family resemblance approach is that such a loose, intertextual 'family resemblance' can potentially be asserted between any two texts, especially as genres are increasingly dispersed across contemporary media. This approach is nevertheless valuable, as long as we remember that it is ultimately reception-centric, unlike the preceding approaches that tend to be either text-centric or industry-centric.

The discursive approach

One of the more recent approaches to genre study, and one that seems to be gaining in popularity, is the discursive approach proffered by Mittell (2001). While Mittell over-emphasises the 'newness' of this approach—not least because scholars like Neale (1995), Altman (1999) and Robert Allen (1989) have all engaged in discursive genre analyses up to a decade before Mittell—Mittell's approach is nevertheless a useful development. His approach, developed in television studies but equally applicable to film studies, draws on the discursive tradition of Michel Foucault. He argues that because genres are inherently intertextual—a point on which we elaborated at the beginning of this chapter—text-based approaches (such as structuralist or aesthetic approaches) are necessarily inadequate ways of considering genre as a whole. Instead, genres should be understood and studied as 'sites of discursive practice' (Mittell 2001: 9). Such discursive formation takes place in three different ways:

1. *definition* (for instance, 'this show is a sit-com because it has a laugh track');
2. *interpretation* ('sit-coms reflect and reinforce the status quo'); and
3. *evaluation* ('sit-coms are better entertainment than soap operas') (Mittell 2001: 9).

These discourses do not 'reflect' any existing generic category; rather, they *constitute* genre through the processes of discursive repetition. While we have already emphasised the benefits of the discursive approach through our partial engagement with it in this chapter, Mittell's approach is not unproblematic. There is, for instance, a chicken-and-egg counter-argument implicit here. To begin with, Mittell over-invests in the extra-textual and significantly under-invests in the textual. By locating genre as a category that is formed entirely outside of genre texts, the discursive approach fails to account for the fact that genre is materially negotiated *at the level of the text*. Consider the following: obviously, we all have a broad and intuitive sense of what any given genre 'is', which is based on how we've previously experienced that genre, what other people say about that genre, how that genre has evolved in relation to our own taste, and a host of other elements. These ideas are consistent with Mittel's idea that genre is a cultural category. However, it is equally true that genre is defined on a text-by-text basis, at the level of the text. Genre is, for example, the device used to frame a text when an idea is first pitched to investors: 'Imagine a comedy, with spice'.

In fact, genre is central throughout the life-cycle of a genre text. So genre is negotiated first at the pitch (in a room populated by, say, producers and a handful of potential investors), then during production (in the relationship between studio/investors, producers, director and key staff), and then as studios begin to market texts before and during their exhibition (or scheduling and broadcast, in the case of television). The last stage is the first time audiences are directly addressed. All of the above decisions about what genre should be are in relation to a particular genre text (and, indeed, result in a finished genre text). Whether their decisions about and/or negotiations of genre are successful, of course, will finally become evident when that text begins to be consumed by audiences (and where success will be measured in audience metrics and profit). At this moment, the genre of that particular text does begin to be seriously negotiated by audiences, but again it will occur at the level of the text—albeit in the context of generic and cultural contexts. Even so, while genre is obviously a category of collective cultural knowledge that is more than any one text, genre is *also negotiated* on a *text-by-text basis* that occurs *at the level of the text*.

The discursive approach also downplays visual aspects of genre, and is notoriously incomplete. Not all discourses are readily available—particularly historical discourses—and even when they are, they are likely to reveal broader trends, but little else. There are also cultural issues. Scholars like Bordwell and Thompson have noted that most filmmaking countries tend to have their own genre that is popular with domestic audiences. In the Hindi cinema of India, it's the 'devotional'; in Mexico, it's the *'cabaretera'* (Bordwell & Thompson 2008: 318). But what about, say, China? In China, public discourse is heavily regulated, to the extent that a discursive analysis of genre in China, particularly Chinese underground filmmaking—which is where most filmmaking occurs—would be seriously inadequate. In other words, it is simply not true that genre exists and/or is negotiated *only* at an intertextual or extra-textual level. Nevertheless, the discursive approach is a useful one that, for best results, is best wielded alongside a text-based approach.

Collectively, the above approaches offer us a productive way to start thinking about the intricacies of genre in screen media; which approach you adopt, of course, will ultimately depend on what it is you particularly wish to examine. Perhaps the most practical way to start thinking critically about genre is to begin thinking about the genre texts you watch, including why you watch them and what you think of them when you do watch them.

APPLYING GENRE ANALYSIS: *GREY'S ANATOMY*

American fictional television has long been the domain of 'lawyers, cops and doctors' (Anderson 2005: 65, 78), or of legal, cop and hospital dramas. In fact, the ensemble hospital drama, focusing on a group of hospital-based characters (usually doctors or nurses), has been particularly successful in recent years. After experiencing a decline in popularity in the United States in the 1980s, hospital dramas burst back into mainstream popularity in the early to mid-1990s with the premiere of successful US hospital dramas *E.R.* and *Chicago Hope*, although UK hospital dramas like *Casualty* had been successful since the mid-1980s. *E.R.* has, quite extraordinarily, reached its fourteenth season by 2008, but *Grey's Anatomy* has taken its place as the most popular hospital drama.

As a genre text, *Grey's Anatomy* tries to repeat the successful formula of hospital dramas like *E.R.* by conforming to genre conventions like formulaic setting, characters and iconography. For instance, *Grey's Anatomy* is set in the fictional 'Seattle Grace Hospital' and features medical iconography (including scrubs, white lab coats, stethoscopes, and the like, see Figure 8.2). Hospitals are an ideal setting for television drama because they allow shows to introduce new characters each week with dramatic life-and-death storylines. This is equally a genre convention: in hospital dramas like *Grey's Anatomy*, 'patients (and their illnesses)' are used as 'vehicles for the exploration of particular issues and topics' (Jacobs 2001: 25), from AIDS and international travel to urban violence and poverty, and to bring in stars or celebrities to do single-episode cameos.

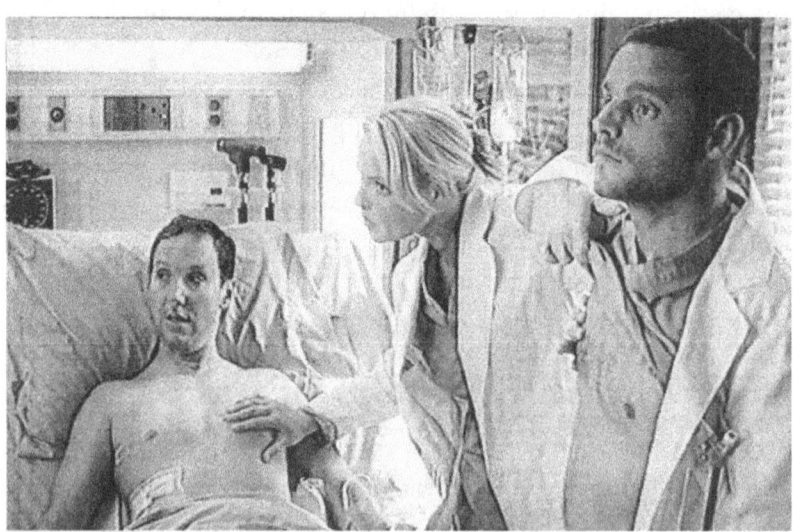

Figure 8.2 *Grey's Anatomy* iconography

Grey's Anatomy, named after a widely used medical textbook, focuses on a group of interns—including the eponymous Meredith Grey—and the attending physicians who supervise them. Like its predecessors, *Grey's Anatomy* combines the tense drama of medical emergencies with a soap opera structure, including ongoing interwoven storylines that follow the interns' relationship dramas. The social function of such a hospital drama includes working through gender and power relations as well as informing audiences about health issues by incorporating factual information regarding, for example, sexually transmitted diseases like syphilis.

Hospital dramas like *Grey's Anatomy* feature:

> a rapid alternation between scenes of action—emergency medical treatment—and those of reflection and introspection. The 'action mode' foregrounds the radical contingency of accidents and the 'sudden turn for the worse' that can befall patients ... These scenes alternate with moments of reflection, where characters assess the consequences of a medical procedure, for the patients and, more importantly, for themselves. (Jacobs 2001: 26)

The combination of single-episode narratives of basically realist medical drama and ongoing interwoven narratives of individual introspection and personal relationships demonstrates *Grey's Anatomy*'s hybridity as a combination of the television series (self-contained episodes) and serial (continuing storylines). While there may have been a clear distinction between series and serials in 1980s television, contemporary prime-time sitcoms and dramas—typically considered 'series'—increasingly incorporate serialised elements.

The addition of ongoing narratives to hospital dramas like *Grey's Anatomy* is crucial for the industry. Not only do viewers have significant choice in what dramas they choose to follow, making it harder for studios to compete for their attention, but most television dramas also fail to make it to a second series, putting increased pressure on producers to try to ensure their series warrants a green light. Television dramas are also the 'most costly type of program to produce', costing an estimated US$2 to $2.5 million per episode (Anderson 2005: 66). The comparatively small number of successful television series combined with their extraordinary cost highlights why 'networks and studios both depend financially on those few series that remain on the air for several years, like *Grey's Anatomy* (Anderson 2005: 62). The emphasis on an ongoing narrative is one of the key strategies studios use to hook viewers' interest and keep audiences tuning in each week.

CONCLUSION

Genre pervades every aspect of the life-cycle of a text, from the moment it is pitched to an investor all the way through its production and marketing to its eventual consumption by audiences. It does not exist outside of the media industries, nor does it exist outside of audiences; instead, it is an intuitive category shared between industry and audiences, but one which is nevertheless negotiated at the level of the text and on a text-by-text basis. As a result, it is enormously challenging to define genre and/or to classify a genre text, but it is also enormously rewarding to be engaged in a process that is so central to the conception of media in our societies. Genre has the potential to reveal much about the evolutionary nuances of media production, distribution and reception or the relationship between genre and the media industries that rely on it; however, it also has the potential to reveal a lot about our culture, organised as it is around genre and other processes of classification. It might also reveal something about who you are, because people's preferences in film and television genres provide insight into their attitudes and interests. Of course, there is already a range of approaches that offer us useful ways of studying genre—including, but not limited to, structuralist, socio-cultural, political economy, aesthetic, family resemblances and discursive approaches—each with particular strengths and weaknesses. These are the same strengths and weaknesses of which you, as newly minted genre analysts, need to be aware.

KEY SKILLS

Having read this chapter you should now be able to:

- identify the textual codes and conventions of a genre text, based on at least a formulaic plot and familiar setting, characters, style and structure, and iconography;
- describe the difference between 'genre text' and 'genre as a cultural category';
- explain the operation of genre at the intersection of text, industry and audience, and the alignment of each of these sites with the economic circulation of a genre text (production, marketing and consumption);
- distinguish between the structuralist, socio-cultural, political economy, aesthetic, family resemblances and discursive approaches to genre analysis;
- apply your knowledge of these approaches to studying genre in an analysis of a genre text;
- critically reflect on the differences between genre in film and television.

9

star struck:

Fandom and the discourse of celebrity

Journalist and cultural theorist Julianne Schultz thinks that contemporary culture is 'addicted to celebrity', describing celebrity as the 'new *lingua franca* of a media age' (2004: 7). We're all, she thinks, a little starstruck. And there's evidence to support her claim. Outside of the films and television programs in which stars or celebrities appear, their fame is developed and sustained by an 'enormous industry stoked and maintained by an army of publicists, stylists, agents, managers and media producers' (Lumby 2004: 113). The most visible examples of celebrity are the staged interviews and red carpet attendances that both film and television promotion demands. Yet, beyond these events, there is also a parallel industry that caters to our desire to consume images of and gossip about celebrities. Television programs like *Entertainment Tonight* or *Access Hollywood* are dedicated to reporting on celebrity culture, as are, to some extent, most teen, gossip, women's and men's magazines, from *Who Weekly* and *New Idea* to *Dolly* and *Alpha*. There are numerous websites devoted to particular stars or shows, whether run by fans ('unofficial' sites) or publicists ('official' sites), just as there are increasing numbers of websites committed to counter-celebrity discourse (perezhilton.com is the best known). Fan communities are equally expanding on sites like YouTube, where fans post and comment on clips created by other fans (such as edited clips of their favourite star) or simply have greater mobility in their fandom by accessing the millions of ripped clips uploaded to the site. At the same time, we've also witnessed the growth of everyday celebrities, epitomised by US reality TV shows like *American Idol*, and what Catharine Lumby talks about as 'DIY celebrity', or the 'camgirl' phenomenon where girls 'set up cameras in their bedrooms and invite virtual voyeurs to visit them online via a website' to target a certain level of fame (2004: 116). For instance, Sandi Thom's singing career, and her internationally successful pop single 'I Wish I Was a Punk Rocker', is attributed to this phenomenon. After working as a back-up and studio singer for a number of years, Thom finally gained celebrity by giving a series of webcasts of her performances from the basement of her London flat, which she promoted on her website and on MySpace. Over the course of a fortnight, her audience grew from 70 people to 70 000, culminating in her signing a record deal with a major label a month later, a moment she also caught on web cam (SandiThom.com 2007).

Clearly, celebrity—a discursive construction generated by the production, distribution, and reception of information about certain individuals in the media—is *everywhere*. In fact, it would be difficult to 'exaggerate the pervasiveness of celebrity in contemporary media' (Turner et al. 2000: 2). It's no wonder, then, that 'real' news has also been 'celebritised': sections of newspapers and news programs—supposedly the exclusive forum for politics and world events—are now also partially devoted to celebrity culture. Broadsheets have entertainment liftouts; *60 Minutes* regularly features celebrity interviews. As Schultz laments: 'Whole sections of newspapers have become a profitable part of the back office of the celebrity business' (2004: 8). But what does all this mean? Is it really a case, as Schultz goes on to argue, that celebrity culture is so culturally 'corrosive' that *politics* has become the 'media shadow' of *celebrity*? (2004: 9, 12) What does it mean, for instance, when ex-Hollywood star Arnold Schwarzenegger can be elected the governor of the state of California (popularly known as the 'Governator', in one of the best examples of the intersection of political and celebrity discourse)? Similarly, what does it mean when the United Nations, the peak body dedicated to preserving international peace, needs Angelina Jolie's support to help refugees?

To consider Schultz's concerns, we first need to understand the phenomenon we're dealing with by addressing a series of questions: What *are* stars and celebrities? What role do they play for the media industries? What do they reveal about our culture? And what is *our* relationship to *them*?

HISTORY

Celebrity culture developed alongside the growth of the mass media and consumer culture, and as an extension of the existing star system around stage performers in the nineteenth century (Hampton 1970). To some extent, the existence of the stage star system, in terms of both the public's demand for stars and the industry's organisation around stars, made the emergence of a star system in film, and later television, something of an inevitability, if only because film initially drew its first audiences, and much of its content and artistic cues, from popular theatre (Dyer 1998). However, the screen media star system did not materialise immediately. In the earliest films, actors were not typically named; instead, they were anonymous performers (akin to today's television extras). This is obviously quite different from contemporary film culture where stars' names are an important part of film publicity and feature prominently on film posters. There are at least three reasons why early actors were not named (though there are exceptions, of course). For one thing, films were initially marketed on the basis of their technology: the moving image was still scientifically special, so the performances within them were, at best, of secondary importance (DeCordova 1991). Second, film acting was still widely considered to be an amateur occupation, largely because the industry itself was not yet large enough to financially sustain actors with enough work to make acting their sole profession. And third, there was industry concern that if actors were named and began to receive individual attention, they might demand, among other things, higher salaries (Jacobs 1968). However in the early 1900s these three things changed: film production increased, acting became professionalised and actors began to be named with greater regularity. The latter is particularly important: because stardom requires an emphasis on the individual—it is, among other things, an 'elaborate discourse on individuality' (Marshall 2006)—the industry shift towards naming actors was a crucial step in the emergence of the screen media star system.

The increased attention on individual actors and their expertise are best, or at least most entertainingly, highlighted by the infamous story of Florence Lawrence's death. Specifically, less than five years after the first feature film was released in 1906, the first publicity stunt was also staged: in 1910, Carl Laemmle, then head of IMP (Independent Motion Picture Company), is said to have circulated a series of rumours that Lawrence, a young actor then working for the dominant Biograph studios, had been killed in a car accident. Laemmle then 'bought huge ads in all the leading newspapers' announcing that not only was Lawrence alive, but that she was 'now working' for his company, IMP (American Mutoscope 2006). Laemmle staged the event not only to bring Lawrence's name to widespread public attention, for perhaps the first time in history, but also to publicise the now famous actor's move from Biograph to IMP, giving both Lawrence and IMP unprecedented publicity (Dyer 1998). Lawrence became a huge star, 'earning $80,000 in 1912' (Cousins 2004: 42). In fact, some scholars argue that she was the *first* film star (Brown 2007).

As actors became celebritised in greater numbers in the 1910s, institutions of stardom also grew, including the Hollywood star system. The Hollywood star system, where stars were contracted to studios rather than to individual films, was dominant for the first half of the twentieth century. During this period, each studio had a stable of stars and most stars were associated with particular genres: John Wayne, for example, was a star of the Western genre. Stars' images were managed by their studio and were constructed through their best-known characters or, at the very least, as a complementary parallel to their characters. Consequently, studios worked very hard to shelter stars' private lives from public interest, through a 'voluminous stream of official and unofficial publicity' (Gallagher 1997). However, these character-based star images soon began to fracture after a number of high-profile star scandals—from Fatty Arbuckle's murder trial to Wallace Reid's drug addiction—drew attention to the considerable differences between a star's constructed celebrity and their personal life. Some stars, like Mary Pickford, also actively resisted the studio's 'celebritisation' of them, as Richard Dyer has shown (1986). The result was an increasing schism between character and actor. By the 1920s, stars' private lives were of real public interest and were one of the focuses of the emerging entertainment media, an 'entire industry' that 'openly celebrated movie stars and their lives' (Marshall 1997: 8). To demonstrate, in a survey of popular magazines between 1901 and 1914, Daniel Boorstin notes that more than 70 per cent of newsworthy individuals came from 'politics, business and the professions,' but that after 1922, when advertising films through film stars had become the industry norm, 'well over half of them came from the world of entertainment' (2006: 80). In other words, the emergence of film stars was also part of a larger cultural shift in what counted as 'newsworthy' in public culture. But by the mid-twentieth century, the rise of television and the results of a landmark legal case, the Hollywood Antitrust Case of 1948—which ruled *against* the practice of **vertical integration**—had begun to cause the collapse of the classical Hollywood studio era and its star system. In the vertical integration business model, a film studio would not only 'own' the film and its cast and crew—'owned' because at that stage they were contracted to studios, not to individual films—but also owned film theatres, in which the studio would only exhibit their own films. Vertical integration was ruled against because it was considered an anti-competitive or monopolising practice, though it does still occur in different forms today. From then on, previously contracted stars increasingly acted as free agents, negotiating contracts on a film-by-film basis and becoming, in the process, even more powerful. While there were numerous precedents, this represented a major industrial shift that still characterises the way most stars and celebrities operate today.

But what of today's stars and celebrities?

> **Vertical integration** describes a concentration of power in the media industry when a company owns various parts of the production chain—for example, printing press, magazine company, content providers such as photographic databases, the disribution vehicles and retail outlets. For example, the media giant News Corporation owns the website MySpace, the Fox broadcast network and the Twentieth Century Fox movie and television studios, as well as News Limited, which publishes many newspapers.

WHAT ARE 'STARS' AND 'CELEBRITIES'?

A **star** is a famous individual in a highly publicised leading role—usually, but not always, in film—whose personal and professional

A **star** is a person who plays a prominent leading role, eclipsing others with their excellence in some widely recognised way. In film, the star is the actor who plays the main protagonist; in sport, the star may be a champion or the captain of a winning team; and in music, a 'pop star' or a 'rock star' is usually the lead singer or performer in a band. However, playing a leading role and excelling in a professional capacity does not guarantee fame and stardom.

A **celebrity** is a celebrated, widely known individual whose private life and public appearances frequently attract media attention.

life attracts extensive media attention (Gledhill 1991: xiii). A **celebrity** is also a highly publicised individual, but where a star typically achieves stardom through an initial public interest in their work, celebrity is a 'mode of stardom relatively unconnected to the sphere of professional work. In other words, celebrity is sustained not by someone's excellence or ability in their chosen profession' (Watson 2003: 173). Thus, while both stars and celebrities are produced through the very same 'publicity regimes and fame making apparatuses' (Langer 1999: 53), there are some reasonably consistent differences between them. The first difference is, as Christine Gledhill argues, that celebrities are usually associated with television rather than the cinema (1991: xiii), as in the case of particular television presenters or soap stars. A celebrity can also come from other spheres, like sport, music, journalism or politics, or even be 'famous for being famous'. To adopt Boorstin's description, a celebrity 'is a person who is well-known for their well-knownness' (2006: 79). However, it is not always clear precisely where the distinction lies between stars, celebrities and famous people, the latter of which can be famous (or infamous) without necessarily being a star or celebrity (as in the case of Paris Hilton). How would you classify Kelly Slater, Kevin Federline or Timothy McVeigh (the Oklahoma bomber), for example?

Despite these definitional differences, fame is never solely about professional merit: there are people who excel in all professional spheres, but few become stars or celebrities. In the case of film actors, playing a leading role and excelling in a professional capacity does not guarantee fame or stardom. Consider, for example, an actor like Aaron Eckhart, who has been nominated for a Golden Globe and has played leading roles in major films, a notable example being his role as Nick opposite Kate (Catherine Zeta-Jones) in the romantic comedy *No Reservations*. Despite his expertise and acclaim, you'd be hard-pressed to call Eckhart a star. Instead, Gledhill argues that actors 'become stars when their off-screen life-styles and personalities equal or surpass acting ability in importance' (1991: xiv). So, while Brad Pitt and Angelina Jolie have also been recognised as skilled actors—Pitt won a Golden Globe for his performance in *Twelve Monkeys* and has been nominated for others, while Jolie has won several Golden Globes and an Oscar, the latter for her performance in *Girl, Interrupted*—their acting does not, on its own, explain their stardom. They are stars, individually and as the power couple 'Brangelina', because their personal life sells vast amounts of copy. In August 2007 alone, for instance, Brangelina were on the front cover of Australian magazines *Who*, the *Weekend Australian Magazine*, *Famous* and Australian *OK!*, to name just a few. It's noteworthy that the power couple can attract so much headline coverage outside of the United States, demonstrating their global pull. As journalist Susan Chenery, introducing an interview with Jolie, notes: 'Every day, all over the world, photographs of her [Jolie] are published accompanied by a script for her life that is written by someone sitting at a desk far, far away' (2007: 17). In fact, given the enormous media coverage of Brangelina, we might argue that they have an exemplary celebrity that demonstrates better than most that a star's fame is related to the successful uptake and reach of their branded identity (see Figure 9.1).

Figure 9.1 The ubiquity of celebrity: Jolie 'Tomb Raider' cocktail on the menu at The Red Piano in Siem Reap, Cambodia. Image courtesy of Dr Chris Tiffin, photograph by Deborah Turnbull.

Indeed, stars and celebrities are not only 'product[s] of mass culture' (Gledhill 1991: xiii); they are equally marketing devices used to target a mass audience. Stars and celebrities are hired on to projects specifically to bring wider attention, and thus larger audiences, to those projects, and it is their significant marketing power that allows them to command such enormous salaries: actors like Brad Pitt and Johnny Depp, for example, are reported to earn more than $25 million per film, while television counterparts Felicity Huffman, Eva Longoria, Teri Hatcher and Marcia Cross, the popular leads of witty US TV drama *Desperate Housewives*, are reported to earn more than $400,000 per episode. However, the highest-paid television celebrity, Oprah Winfrey, eclipses them all: she is estimated to earn more than $200 million per year. Like genre, then, stars are a kind of insurance policy for producers because they are investing in a proven formula. A star or celebrity is employed, first and foremost, to sell the screen media they appear in or create through a range of publicity and promotional strategies, from posters and trailers, to interviews and merchandise. A media text thus also becomes part of a star's brand, either building on or detracting from that brand, depending on its critical and/or financial success. For example, *Mission Impossible* is just as much a part of its star's, Tom Cruise's, oeuvre of blockbusters, as it is a specific story about an American spy, just as the success of *Dr Phil* is equally part of Oprah Winfrey's global television celebrity. But stars also use their celebrity to sell or promote innumerable other things, from watches (Brad Pitt and Tag Heuer), credit cards (Robert DeNiro and American Express) and skin care products (Cate Blanchett and SK-II) to environmental sustainability (Leonardo DiCaprio), children's education (Oprah Winfrey) and the plight of international refugees (Angelina Jolie). The biggest stars have global media reach, just as their global media reach continues to build their star profile. Like Coca-Cola or Nike, major stars operate as branded commodities in a global marketplace.

Celebrities tend to have a more local or national reach, and are more likely to advertise less prestigious products or issues. This difference not only points to the different export power of Hollywood versus other media and professional spheres, but also to another difference in the discursive construction of stars and celebrities. Where stars are constructed around *aspirational* discourses of individualism—we might, for instance, aspire to be able to afford the Tag Heuer watch Pitt models, whether as part of a desire to be like him, be with him, or simply have a lifestyle like his—television celebrities are constructed around discourses of *familiarity*. So film stars are more likely to promote products associated with high-end lifestyles, while television celebrities are more likely to endorse products associated with everyday lives and, for major celebrities, special occasions. Examples include George Foreman's grill, which plays on the ex-boxer's health-conscious past, or Sarah Jessica Parker's perfume, Covet, and clothing line, Bitten, which to different extents play on her most famous role as fashionable New York writer Carrie Bradshaw, from the hit television series *Sex and the City* (indeed, both products were launched in Parker's/Bradshaw's home-town, New York City).

That Parker's endorsements draw on the television character with which she achieved international prominence flags a final difference between film stars and television celebrities. That is, where a television actor's celebrity is likely to be largely *limited* to their on-screen character (the actor will be 'celebritised' through their character and the two conflated), a film actor's stardom is likely to *exceed* their on-screen characters (the character will be celebritised through the actor). This is epitomised by recent examples where television *characters* are used to sell everyday products: for instance, a cartoon version of harried wife and working mother of four Lynette Scavo, Felicity Huffman's character on *Desperate Housewives*, advertises Kit-Kat chocolate bars. Graeme Turner suggests that, while stars 'develop their reputation by playing someone else' (2004: 15) and then shoot to stardom because of a (however constructed) public fascination with their personal lives, television celebrities 'simply perform themselves'—at least they perform what the audience perceives as their authentic identity. (This is obviously quite different from the earliest film stars who, like today's television celebrities, were initially promoted as being like their characters.) Today, however, we might go to see a film because it is, for example, the latest by Adam Sandler, rather than because we have a specific interest in the narrative development of Chuck and Larry's faux-gay romance in *I Now Pronounce You Chuck and Larry*. Occasionally, a star's fame can even be a hindrance to their acting. Consider the recent example where Tom Cruise was criticised by the German defence ministry for playing Claus von Stauffenberg in *Valkyrie*. The reason? Because Cruise is a Scientologist, and Scientology is classified as an anti-democratic cult in Germany, the government has objected to the actor playing an historical German figure and initially rejected applications for Cruise to film in German military sites (BBC News 2007). In an interview with the BBC, co-producer Paula Wagner emphatically stated that Cruise's 'personal beliefs have absolutely no bearing on the movie's plot, themes, or content' (BBC News 2007). Whether or not that's true, it certainly demonstrates how Cruise's stardom, as the extra-textual circulation of information about his personal life, has not only exceeded the character he's playing, but has also become a fascinating obstacle.

Numerous scholars have offered ways to understand different kinds of celebrity. One of the most recent and, for Turner at least, the most interesting, is Rojek's discussion of three paths to celebrity: ascribed, achieved, and attributed celebrity (Rojek 2001: 17–19).

1. *Ascribed celebrity*, or hereditary celebrity, describes those who become celebrities because of their lineage. The most obvious examples are royal families (Queen Elizabeth, Prince Charles), but this also holds true for those born or adopted into major political or entertainment families as well. Paris Hilton, heiress to the Hilton fortune, Nicole Ritchie, daughter of Lionel Ritchie, and Brangelina's children are all examples of ascribed celebrities.
2. *Achieved celebrity* describes an individual who, through a particular skill or talent, becomes a celebrity on the basis of professional achievement. Achieved celebrity describes the celebrity of film stars, sporting celebrities and others, such as UK television host Michael Parkinson or golf champion Tiger Woods. Sports stars are the key exemplars of achieved celebrity as proven prowess is essential to success in sport. Here, Rojek combines our distinction between 'stars' and 'celebrities,' and in this broader taxonomy it is a useful conflation. There is also crossover between these categories: Jolie, for example, was initially an ascribed celebrity, as the daughter of actor Jon Voight. However, since becoming a recognised actor and star in her own right, Jolie's stardom now translates to a global achieved celebrity.
3. *Attributed celebrity* describes a celebrity that is largely thrust upon an individual—often an ordinary person—by intense, often

temporary, media interest. This can be a variation of achieved celebrity, but it is a media-led rather than achievement-led or public-led celebrity. Indeed, where achieved celebrity is constructed by publicists and managers, attributed celebrity is usually outside of the individual's control and is often based on their participation in or association with an unusual event or occurrence. For example, Brant Webb and Todd Russell, the Australian miners who were trapped underground in a collapsed mine and were the subject of a dramatic rescue, have an attributed celebrity. Since their rescue, they have been guests on countless talk shows, the subjects of numerous magazine articles, and have even co-authored a book about their experience. Another example, this time from Europe, is the case of Madeleine McCann, the (then) three-year-old who went missing in Portugal while her British parents were having dinner nearby. The tragic case has been the site of enormous international interest, to the extent that Madeleine and her parents, Kate and Gerry McCann, all have an attributed celebrity. Rojek (2001: 17–19) suggests, and Webb and Russell's and the McCann's experiences demonstrate, that attributed celebrity is a direct reflection of the mass media's organisation around 'sensationalism'.

In each of his categorisations, Rojek usefully emphasises the 'constructedness' of celebrity: an individual is celebritised, irrespective of on what basis, *through the media*. Unlike earlier work that positioned celebrity as the exclusive terrain of uniquely gifted individuals, whose celebrity simply reflected their talents, Rojek demonstrates that celebrity is, as we noted earlier, a discursive construction formed at the intersection of industry and audience, and mobilised around an individual. Obviously, certain individuals are more likely candidates for celebrity status than others. Being a high achiever in the entertainment industry or in sports, for example, probably gives you greater celebrity potential than, say, being a bored administrator in a local office. But who knows? There are lots of bored administrators on reality TV show *Big Brother*. While a handful of you may very well become celebrities, there's one thing we all have in common: we're audience members.

AUDIENCES, IDENTIFICATION AND FANDOM

If the role of the star or celebrity is, through their presence on a project, to draw a mass audience to it, then clearly celebrity is dependent upon audience engagement and, specifically, on audience consumption. However, until recently the audience–celebrity relationship has largely been derided. And maybe this is unsurprising: while the word 'fan' refers to an individual who demonstrates a particular interest in or attachment for a famous person or profession, the term originated as a nineteenth century abbreviation of *fanatic*, or someone who demonstrates that interest or attachment in extreme or irrational ways. Perhaps it is to be expected, then, that scholarship in the mid- to late twentieth century frequently characterised fandom as a 'chronic attempt to compensate for a perceived lack of autonomy, absence of community, incomplete identity' or, in other words, as revealing some kind of personal problem (Jenson 1992: 17). This conception of audiences' one-sided fascination with stars is generally (and pejoratively) referred to as '**para-social**.' Inherent in this line of thinking is that stars and celebrities are an industry construction, an inauthentic media mirage at best, designed to con a passive and unsophisticated audience out of their money and time. And while there's truth to the industry's goal of increased sales, recent scholarship has come to recognise that not only are audiences much more sophisticated in their consumption of celebrity than previously thought, but that their engagement with stars and celebrities—who, for most of us, are distant media constructions—is nonetheless important and genuinely intimate. Celebrity is, as Gilbert Rodman has noted, not a 'purely mercantile phenomenon imposed "from above" by profit-hungry media conglomerates as much as it is a socially based phenomenon generated 'from below' at the level of real people who make affective investments in particular media figures' (1996: 12).

> **Para-social interaction** refers to mediated or imaginary interactions and relations with people we do not personally know, such as stars or celebrities.

Audiences engage with celebrities, for the most part, through a star's or celebrity's occupation (for a film star, through their films; for a television celebrity, through their role on a particular program) and the entertainment media (gossip magazines, television interviews, red carpet appearances). Audiences can also engage in more active fan practices, such as emulating stars' mannerisms or style, buying products they endorse, collecting DVDs, posters, articles and memorabilia, hosting a fan website, writing slash fiction, creating artwork or posting clips on YouTube. To different extents, all of these engagements can be understood as participating in a larger discursive community around the relevant star or celebrity, as well as being part of a broader negotiation of the audience's identity and relationship to the world: our consumption of stars and celebrities is part of the way we position ourselves in relation to different communities, styles, ideologies and value systems. This is also the reason we might have guilty celebrity pleasure: we might, for example, enjoy listening to Britney Spears' latest CD, but be embarrassed to tell our friends that we are a fan of Spears precisely because Spears' celebrity is inconsistent with our own construction of self. While we discuss some of the most common approaches to studying stars and celebrity in the following section, it is worth pointing out here that audience engagement with stars and celebrities has generally been thought to occur either through our *identification with* them (or anything they represent) or our *desire for* them (or anything they represent), both of which can take a range of (often overlapping) forms.

Identification refers to the process of constructing our identity through our consumption of stars and celebrities (Turner 2004: 102). It is not as simple as 'finding oneself a role model to emulate (or the reverse)' (Turner 2004: 102). Still, being a 'good role model' is certainly one of the dominant discourses around celebrities in sports and in girl media, who are expected to provide a model of ethical and heroic sportsmanship and a model of appropriate gender comportment respectively (evidence of the different circulations of gender). Being a good role model is less prominent in discourses around television celebrities and, until recently, was virtually non-existent around film stars. However, film stars and rock stars are increasingly using their celebrity to support particular issues and/or causes, as part of an emerging discourse of ethical celebrity, where stars seemingly use their

> **Identification** refers to constructing our identity in relation to a star and/or celebrity. For film stars, Jackie Stacey argues that identification involves the 'negotiation between self and other' via 'the recognition of similarities and differences' (2006: 253). It is also a negotiation 'between the self and an imaginary self' (2006: 254).

celebrity to 'make a difference'. Pink's campaigning against animal cruelty and Leonardo DiCaprio's promotion of environmental sustainability, including his arrival at the 2007 Oscars in a hybrid car, are useful examples of this. Even so, some scholars have argued that identification with celebrities is little more than naïvely taking on the values of dominant culture and its stereotypes. The most famous proponents of this line of thinking are mass culture theorists like Max Horkheimer and Theodor Adorno who, in their *Dialectic of Enlightenment* (1972), argued that stars offer little more than a 'pseudo individuality' which dominant culture uses to deceive audiences into a conformist passivity.

However, as scholars like Lawrence Grossberg note, while the screen media industries certainly wield celebrity culture as an inviting frame for us to consume the 'popular images, pleasures, fantasies and desire' on offer, it does not follow that we necessarily submit to dominant commercial and cultural interests (2006: 589). Rather, audiences have agency or control over how they consume media texts: they can pick and choose what aspects of a celebrity's image they enjoy or support, and what aspects they do not like and resist. Thus audiences 'interpret the meaning of the celebrity in a grand narrative on the dimensions of individuality and identity in contemporary culture where comparisons between the self and the celebrity are continuously made and cultural norms are supported, altered, or dismantled' (Marshall 2006: 3–4). 'Comparisons between the self and the celebrity' are central to a more specific form of audience-celebrity identification, too. **Narcissism**, meaning 'self-love', refers to the Greek myth in which Narcissus falls in love with his own reflection in a pool of water. Narcissistic identification, then, describes when we identify with a star or celebrity because we perceive them to be an ideal version (whether real or imagined) of aspects of ourselves. In this form of identification, we might enjoy identifying apparently shared experiences, attributes, mannerisms or appearances between a celebrity and ourselves. For example, we might identify with Justin Timberlake's experience of

> **Narcissism**, or 'self-love', is from the Greek myth of Narcissus, a boy so beautiful that everyone fell in love with him. When Narcissus rejected Echo's advances, however, he was doomed to fall in love with his own image, and spent the rest of his life captivated by his own reflection. In screen media, narcissistic identification refers to when audiences view stars or celebrities as an idealisation of themselves.

being bullied at school or have an uncanny resemblance to ex-*Xena* celebrity Lucy Lawless.

We might also *desire* them. Desire is another common means of engaging with stars and celebrities: audiences might be attracted to certain stars or celebrities, particular roles they have played, or particular products or issues they have represented ('attracted' whether acquisitively, sexually, emotionally or intellectually). Audiences might also be attracted to the glamour of the celebrity lifestyle or enjoy the process of celebrity consumption, because we like seeing or hearing about the *faux pas* or quotidian problems of the rich and famous, thus allowing us to consume the 'ordinariness' of the 'extraordinary'. In addition to these desiring engagements, audiences often 'take their cues as to what is significant and what is at the very least in fashion' through celebrity culture (Marshall 2006: 12). Getting 'the Rachel', for example, was a major hairstyle trend in the 1990s, as consumers tried to emulate Jennifer Aniston's enormously popular hairstyle(s) as Rachel in *Friends*. To a large extent, stars and celebrities represent the 'in your wildest dream' potential of consumer culture, the peak of individual potential (if only we had their bank accounts). And it's no wonder that one response to celebrity culture is often through the lens of desire. As Su Holmes and Sean Redmond suggest, the '*desire* for fame, stardom, or celebrification stems from a *need* to be wanted in a society where being famous appears to offer enormous material, economic, social and psychic rewards' (2006: 2). Thus the desire for celebrity is equally bound up with ideologies of affluence and individualism—a desire for social mobility, for material success and for greater appreciation of our uniqueness.

Often implicit in both identification and desire is an interest in knowing the star's or celebrity's real identity. Who are they when there are no cameras to document their every move? Richard Dyer, in his influential study *Stars*, has suggested that a search for the real or 'authentic' person behind or away from a star's fame is always implicit in audiences' engagement with celebrity culture. Dyer's claim sets up a distinction between real (unmediated) personhood and unreal (mediated) celebrity. And indeed, the idea of revealing the real person behind the celebrity is precisely the premise of the paparazzi, who literally stalk stars and celebrities for a lucrative photo opportunity. As Linda Mizejewski writes:

> Fans are incited to peel away public and textual images in order to discover the 'real' or private person underneath ... While star appeal depends on connection and identification, for example, it also depends on adulation and glamour; fans simultaneously need to imagine the star is fully human and ordinary, but also larger than life and extraordinary. (2001: 166)

Like Dyer's earlier work, an emphasis on the 'real person' behind the fame continues to be a focus for recent scholarship (Kasson 2000). However, for some audience members, reality is the least interesting aspect of celebrity. For John Ellis, for instance, celebrity identification 'involves two different tendencies': the first is narcissistic identification, which we have already mentioned; the second is fantasy (1982: 43). Fantasy refers to our identification with stars or celebrities within the diegetic world of the screen media texts we consume, where we fantasise about being a part of the story 'seemingly [from] within the scene' (McDonald 1995: 90). But, unlike earlier conceptions of audience–celebrity identification thought audience members could only really identify with stars of the same sex, fantasy acknowledges that 'any narrative provides the spectator with multiple and shifting points of identification' (McDonald 1995: 90). So, to continue with the example of *Friends*, we might simultaneously find ourselves fantasising about looking like Rachel, being best friends with Monica and/or being in a relationship with Chandler (as Monica was in Seasons 5–10), thus engaging in spectator relationships with more than one character. Significantly, in the fantasy conception of the audience–celebrity relationship, stars and celebrities can either become more important to our engagement with screen media texts, because we can establish an identification 'with more than one star' in any scene, or less important to it, because the 'individual star is no longer seen as the defining point of' our viewing pleasure (McDonald 1995: 90). In either case, fantasy is about the flexible and diverse nature of desire: it describes 'the multiple and contradictory tendencies within the construction of the individual' (Ellis 1982: 43).

If identification and desire are both common ways of understanding the audience–celebrity relationship, then what other approaches are available for thinking critically about celebrity?

KEY APPROACHES TO STUDYING STARS AND CELEBRITY

Film stars emerged as an occupation in film studies in the 1970s, partly as a response to the then disciplinary infatuation with auteur theory. In television studies, the response was less enthusiastic: it took time for the new medium to establish its own celebrities, to the extent that celebrity studies eventually emerged in the 1980s through scholars like John Langer. In 1981 (republished in 2006), Langer proposed the now standard distinction between film stars and television personalities (though, with media convergence and globalisation, the distinction is becoming less pronounced). Since its emergence in the academy, there have been a number of trends—some more successful than others—in the analysis of celebrity in film and television. Three of the most significant approaches are the semiotic, ideological and political economy approaches, which we overview below.

Semiotic

The semiotic approach emerged in film studies through Richard Dyer. Dyer's *Stars* (1979) and his subsequent *Heavenly Bodies* (1986) marked a significant shift in film studies away from the biographical analyses of charismatic stars which were prevalent at the time and which sought to understand stardom as a logical outcome of innately gifted individuality. Instead, Dyer proposed a number of ideas that are now central to celebrity studies in a range of disciplines: first, he proposed investigating stars as texts, which recognised that stars (and celebrities) are constructed by elaborate media systems. Second, he argued that stars were one of the primary points of engagement for audiences in viewing screen media. Third, he argued that audiences consumed stars not only through the films in which they appeared, but also through the wealth of extra-textual information circulating about them (in magazines and film advertisements, for example). Fourth, he argued that stars were also mobilised as part of larger, often contradictory, mythologies and ideological discourses about the individual. For example, Dyer looked at Marilyn Monroe's celebrity by examining the films she appeared in, the interviews she gave, the pictures taken of her and the way the media discussed her. He observed an apparent contradiction: Monroe signified both an active sexuality, as arguably the most famous sex symbol in the world, and a childlike innocence that seemed very much at odds with her adult sexiness and with prevailing constructions of the ideal woman (think of 1950s sit-coms and their cheery, but homebound, mothers). Instead, Monroe was frequently described as a sex symbol—and, indeed, this was a conscious construction of her celebrity by the Hollywood studios: Monroe was, for instance, advised to cut her hair short and dye it platinum blonde, practise a different smile (to 'hide a high gum line'), and develop a breathier mode of speaking. At the same time, she was also publicised as an ingénue: the studios widely circulated extra-textual stories about her teenage marriage and divorce, and played up (as did Monroe herself) her frequent naïve comments to the media (called 'Monroeisms'). As Dyer says, Monroe's 'parted lips' could signal both a 'yielding sexuality' and a 'vulnerability' (1998: 139). Read together, however, Dyer argues that these characterisations were not contradictory so much as revealing the nuances of larger discourses around 1950s femininity. Namely, Monroe's sexual image was articulated through her construction as an innocent but sexual young woman, thus rendering her sexuality ideologically unproblematic because of her apparent need to be 'protected' by a man. In other words, Monroe's apparent difference from prevailing norms was quite the opposite: she was very much a part of the stereotyping of women as objects for the hetero-patriarchal gaze. In making the connection between text and context, however, Dyer paved the way for understanding how stars reveal dominant discourses about gender, sexuality and race. In this sense, stars and celebrities are not only ideological markers of cultural periods, but are also part of an individual's negotiation of those ideologies.

Aside from its strength in bringing a culturally contextualised textual and discourse analysis to 'star studies', as the field was then known, Dyer's work also provides detailed case studies of classic stars like Monroe, Judy Garland and Paul Robeson, which emphasise how different stars are constructed in particular rather than homogenous ways, the latter a problematic assumption of the mass cultural theorists. Scholars like Robert Kapsis (1992) and Barbara Klinger (1994), among many others, have adopted the semiotic approach in their studies of stars. Weaknesses of this approach include that, because it focuses on the textual and extra-textual construction of a star's image, it can only ever be a partial account of historical stars (because some texts will cease to be available and first-hand accounts are notoriously difficult to access). Another weakness is that the approach tends to privilege the star as text, without paying adequate attention to either the industrial imperatives involved in constructing that text or the ways audiences actually consume those texts. The latter is the focus of scholars like Jackie Stacey who, in her *Star Gazing* (1994), conducted extensive empirical work on how women responded to specific star images (empirical methodologies still vastly underrepresented in scholarship on stars and celebrities). Nevertheless, the semiotic approach remains a methodological touchstone for contemporary analyses of stars and celebrities.

Ideological

According to Gledhill, 'stars personalise social meanings and ideologies' (1991: xiv). In other words, stars and celebrities are also social signs, inscribed in, by and with ideologies—which Stephen Heath (1981: 4) defines as the 'imaginary relation of individuals to the real relations under which they live'—of race, class, gender, age, sexuality, and so forth. Consider, for example, ex-*Baywatch* celebrity Pamela Anderson. According to a *New Weekly (NW)* magazine cover story, at the height of Anderson's *Baywatch* fame, a woman who the press described as a fanatical 'obsessed stalker' entered Anderson's home, searched it and donned her red *Baywatch* swimsuit. The *NW* magazine cover (see Figure 9.2) juxtaposes an image of the woman, Christine Roth, wearing Anderson's swimsuit beside an image of Anderson in the famous outfit. The cover shows how identification with a celebrity and the aspiration to emulate the ideal that they represent can cross the boundary of acceptable fandom and slide into fanaticism. The media actively encourages a sense of familiarity with celebrities, as is evident in the use of first names and pet names (Pammy). Unsurprisingly, Roth, the 'stalker', said that she only wanted to be Anderson's friend: 'I'd bought her a beautiful box of chocolates from France. All I wanted to do was eat them with her and explain how much I admired her work' (*New Weekly* April 2001: 13).

The representation of Pamela Anderson and Christine Roth is one example of how the discourse of celebrity reinforces norms associated with the dominant ideology in more than one way. In this

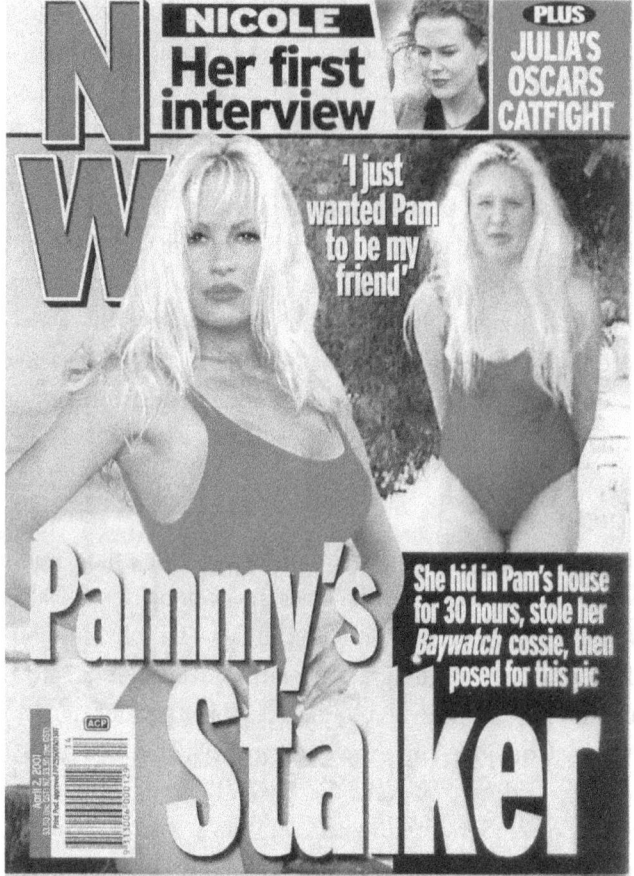

Figure 9.2 Pamela Anderson and her fan, Christine Roth on the cover of *NW* magazine

instance, it functions to cement the appeal of the star by offering proof of her desirability as an ideal, and simultaneously constructs the identity of the magazine's reader as 'normal': 'the obsessive fan appears to have been "taken over" by the text in a way that "we" have not, or has willfully submitted to a zealousness that, in the extreme, can manifest itself in the pathological behaviour of a stalker' (Casey et al. 2002: 93). We, the readers, have our own fascination with the star and our consumption of the products with which she is associated legitimated and normalised by the extremity of the obsessive fan's behaviour. We also have our 'normality' constructed in relation to stars' extraordinary bodies and professions, and their ordinary personal lives.

The *New Weekly* cover of Anderson and Roth contains many of the same signifiers: both women are young, slender blondes, and both are photographed in the same red swimsuit. Yet those signifiers are coded and interpreted very differently. These differences emerge through readings of the quality and style of the photographs (Roth's is an amateur photograph, Anderson's a slick professional photograph), body type and posture, the codes of representation that each photo employs, and also through inter-textual references to the reader's prior knowledge of Anderson's character in *Baywatch*, signalled by the beach in the background.

The fact that Pamela Anderson's image is professionally lit and composed, and her hair and makeup are immaculate, signal her socio-economic status and class. It is expensive and time-consuming to maintain such a look, and when the cost of a personal trainer and plastic surgery are factored into the equation, it becomes evident that Anderson embodies the ideology of affluence. The kind of inexpensive, unpolished, un-posed look in Christine Roth's photo is not common in representations of female stardom and is rarely celebrated in the media. Roth stands with her arms held awkwardly behind her body and her long blonde hair covering her breasts as though she is uncomfortable about being exposed to the camera and being compared with Pamela Anderson. The real star knows that she has a heavenly body, and she exudes sexual confidence as she displays herself to the public and invites their desire. In Anderson, we may celebrate an active female sexuality, at the same time as critiquing the objectification and commodification of the female body.

Ideologically speaking, Pamela Anderson embodies a heterosexual ideal: her body is displayed primarily for the (hetero-)male gaze. The ideologies that are celebrated or valued in Anderson as a celebrity text are able-bodied youthfulness, wealth, heterosexual desirability, and patriarchal ideologies of gender in which women are objectified. We might also suggest that the image of a fair-skinned, blonde woman is assumed to be universally desirable to all ethnic and cultural groups, thus implying a Eurocentric ideology of race. While these are not the only values that stars embody, many major stars and celebrities represent a similar set of values. Moreover, the woman-to-woman bonding or 'friendship' that Roth seeks, while not articulated as lesbian desire, is nevertheless coded as socially transgressive and culturally marginalised. While transgressive and marginal identities feature in cult media texts that are designed to appeal to a niche audience and a rebellious youth market, they are less frequently celebrated in mainstream images of celebrity aimed at a mass audience. This is because stars and celebrities, by definition, have widespread popular appeal and target the desires of the majority. As such, they are a barometer of mainstream ideals and values. Stars embody and individuate social types subscribed to by the dominant groups in society. As Dyer puts it: 'If you are not white, middle-class, heterosexual and male you are not going to fit "the cultural world" too well—women only fit uneasily, whilst blacks, gays and even the working-class hardly fit at all' (2006: 162).

Marxist theorists also address the ways in which stars embody ideologies; however, rather than analysing individual stars, **Marxism** critiques the ways in which the star system as a whole functions to reinforce the values of the ruling class. In doing so, a Marxist approach foregrounds the economic and class-based aspects of stardom. For Dyer, public fascination with stardom is facilitated by the myth of 'bootstrapping' which offers possibilities of success and social mobility, and the transcendence of class: 'Consumption and success, with their intimations of attendant values such as democracy, the open society, the value of the common/ordinary person, are the key notes of the image of stardom' (Dyer 2006: 159). As Alberoni phrases it, stars are 'a living testimony to the possibility of achieving a rise in personal status' (2006: 122). Even though 'their wealth, the manner of life they lead, constitute evident affronts to egalitarian ideals' (Alberoni 2006: 119), stars do not inspire class resentment and are not perceived as reminders of social inequity because the process of identification and the discourse of celebrity work together to overcome the gap between the star and the audience. As Langer writes: 'By appearing to reduce

> **Marxism**, a theoretical approach originating in the 1940s, is the name commonly given to the influential ideas and writings of Karl Marx, Friedrich Engels and their followers. Classical Marxism is founded on the idea that economic relations between workers and employers, sellers and buyers, and the upper and lower classes form the 'base' or foundation of social life, and that culture (along with education, religion, law, communication and politics) forms the 'superstructure' which builds on and reinforces the economic structure. Marx argued that those who control the material wealth and the means of production in society also tend to have control over the belief systems that hold together the social order.

the distance through intimacy, the personality system operates to mask the gap between the powerful and the powerless, ensuring that the real unities of power, class, prestige, and interest can continue relatively intact and unexamined' (Langer 2006: 194). Indeed, Alberoni argues that the star system supplies media consumers with 'an escape into fantasy and the illusion of mobility, in such a way as to prevent their taking stock of their real condition as exploited masses' (Alberoni 2006: 120). While these insights are significant, the disadvantage with an ideological approach to celebrity is that it de-emphasises the agency of the audience.

Political economy

As noted in our discussion of genre in Chapter 8, the political economy approach in film and television scholarship is based on the work of scholars like Adorno, who saw Hollywood cinema as an institution that encouraged a passive audience to consume unoriginal and politically pernicious products. Adorno, together with Horkheimer (1972), argued that film stars are particularly problematic, because they represent a 'pseudo individuality' which deceives audiences into engaging with screen media only as a means of conning them out of their money. Leaving aside Adorno and Horkheimer's distaste for popular culture, stars and celebrities do play a crucial role for the screen media industries: to put it crudely, they exist to court a mass audience. However, while political economy approaches have been challenged in other realms of film and television scholarship, it is only in the last decade that scholars have really begun to offer alternatives to this work in relation to celebrity culture. Work like Turner's *Understanding Celebrity* (2004), Turner, Marshall and Bonner's *Fame Games* (2000) and Marshall's *Celebrity and Power* (1997) have all adopted the political economy approach to examine celebrity as an industrial system, rather than to produce textual readings of individual stars, as in the semiotic approach. The political economy approach is a useful one because, in light of the current over-representation of text-based approaches, this approach insists on examining the industry machinations of stardom and celebrity. After all, as Turner et al. argue, the 'publicity and promotions industries have been comprehensively incorporated into all aspects of media production' (2000: 1). Indeed, audiences' desire for stars and celebrities is rarely unsolicited. It is created through specific communication strategies to boost sales of cinema tickets, merchandise and other products. Persuasion strategies that manipulate desire and identification also work to create appetites for other non-essential items. Gledhill describes stars as 'cogs in the mass entertainment industry selling desires and ideologies' (1991: Prologue). Attaching the name of a major star to a project is often the basis on which media texts get financed. Stars also provide the labour that helps produce the texts, and they function as a selling point for the texts and associated merchandise. Stars can therefore be understood as a product of capitalism and a sophisticated industrial marketing device. Understanding this industrial back-end to the production, circulation and reception of celebrity is central to the political economy approach.

Further, sponsorship and endorsements are two ways that stars, particularly sports stars, function as commodities in the media industry. For instance, professional golfer Tiger Woods earned US$100 million in 2007, and most of his income came from endorsements according to *Forbes Magazine*'s 'Celebrity 100' issue (June 2007). The practice of celebrity endorsement has been referred to by Jesse Bier (1995) as a kind of prostitution, as it involves selling one's body (or the image associated with one's body). By this Bier means that, unlike other professional people who sell their expertise and labour, advertisers pay to use celebrities' bodies—not for sex, but certainly to seduce consumers and to give them pleasure. The phrase 'sex sells' is not used accidentally: advertisers often deliberately trade on the star's sex appeal to sell products. Hence the star is using their sexuality to make money.

CONCLUSION

This chapter has employed a range of approaches to explore stars and celebrities, not only as discursive constructions but also as embodiments of identities, desires and ideologies that are commodified and communicated to us through the mass media. As we've discussed, celebrity is based upon on a public fascination with prominent individuals, and it is through those individuals that the screen media industries link public fantasies and desires to ideological and economic interests. Consequently, stars are only as powerful as the size of audience they can court. To conclude, let's examine this chapter's assertions in a final case study: Leonardo DiCaprio on the cover of *Vanity Fair*'s 'Green Issue' in May 2007 (see Figure 9.3).

DiCaprio stands in the middle of an ice field in black snow gear with his hands on his hips, hair wind-swept, and trademark intense stare directed into the camera. At DiCaprio's feet is a polar bear cub, gazing up at him. The image connotes affluent style, in his expensive sports gear; the rugged masculinity of an arctic adventurer; sophisticated spectacle, with his commanding black outfit amid an entirely white background; kind-hearted protectiveness, with his shielding stance over the vulnerable cub; economic power, given extra-textual information about DiCaprio's wealth; and 'wildlife warrior', standing equally protectively between an untouched landscape and the lens of the camera (signalling the threatening 'modern world'). In other words, there are numerous meanings embedded in this image.

Figure 9.3 Leonardo DiCaprio featured on the cover of *Vanity Fair*'s 'Green Issue'

These meanings reference the kind-hearted tough guy established in DiCaprio's recent films *The Departed* and *Blood Diamond*, and reinforce dominant ideologies of masculinity as 'protector' and 'explorer'. This intertextual network of associations might activate narcissistic fantasies of being protected and cared for by DiCaprio, or being protective and caring like him. Interestingly, while DiCaprio's association with environmentalism may indeed represent his personal values, the entire image is constructed to *sell*. DiCaprio is not on an iceberg; he was photographed in a studio and photoshopped on to a melting glacier (photographed in Iceland) with a polar bear cub (photographed in Germany). The image is being used to sell a magazine issue as well as DiCaprio's celebrity, by reinforcing his reputation as an environmentalist and actor. Indeed, frequent mention is made of his films and website (www.leonardodicaprio.com). The image is also being used to advertise the expensive designer label clothes DiCaprio wears and grooming products he has supposedly used. This doesn't mean DiCaprio isn't genuine in his 'green' intentions; it highlights the complicated industry machinations of his celebrity.

Of course, an effect of the conflation of celebrity and political, social or environmental discourses, as in DiCaprio's stardom, is that worthy issues and well-intentioned celebrities share the limelight. The benefit is that important causes gain access to the global media visibility that stars command, even as such publicity potentially commodifies and trivialises important issues, deflecting attention from the melting glacier to the star's love life. Perhaps Schultz (2004) is right to worry that 'real' news has become 'celebritised'. But is she right that celebrity culture is so 'corrosive' that it has become more important than politics? Catharine Lumby doesn't think so. She argues that celebrity culture is 'highly diverse and inclusive', and is a site where 'important social issues once deemed apolitical, trivial or personal are now being aired' (1999: xiii). Lumby argues that celebrity culture is actually part of a broader democratisation of the mass media. But does this democratisation make us, to return to our examples, more or less able to discuss environmental sustainability because of DiCaprio's involvement?

Celebrity is not a one-sided phenomenon. The voyeuristic pleasures of unauthorised photos of the beautiful, rich and famous stars in gossip magazines are situated on a continuum that bleeds into the stalking of celebrities, and the problematic impact on body image and self-esteem created by the impossibly glamorous creatures that our culture celebrates. But perhaps the biggest lesson from the political economy approach is that we must always keep in mind the financial dimension of celebrity, as our analysis of DiCaprio demonstrated. Each time we consume media involved in the discourse of celebrity, we support a system that values entertainment and attractiveness over almost everything else. Ever wonder what the top scientists researching renewable energy earn, or why our culture doesn't value them as highly and ravenously seek to discover the intimate details of their personal lives?

KEY SKILLS

Having read this chapter you should now be able to:

- identify some of the main ways 'celebrity' is circulated;
- explain the role and significance of stars and celebrities within and to the screen media industries;
- distinguish between the semiotic, ideological and political economy approaches to celebrity analysis;
- consider how stars contribute to discourses and ideologies, revealing the values celebrated in Western media culture;
- define the term 'identification', giving examples of three different ways in which fans identify with stars and celebrities, explaining what the impact of such identification might be;
- explain how stars and celebrities are used as a marketing device and how image management strategies are used to appeal to a mass audience;
- apply your knowledge of these approaches to studying a particular star or celebrity;
- critically reflect on the differences between stars, celebrities and other famous figures (including cult figures).

10

skating the edge:
Cult media and the (inter)active audience

'You're skating the edge,' Trevor Goodchild warns his lover, nemesis and would-be assassin. 'I *am* the edge' Æon Flux retorts in the cult media classic that bears her name. 'What you truly want, only I can give,' he insists. Æon's reply, delivered with characteristic certainty, could just as well apply to the transgressive pleasures of cult fandom itself: 'Can't give it, can't even buy it, and you just don't get it.' Cult media texts often feature pleasures and narratives that mainstream audiences just don't get. Indeed, J.P. Telotte argues that a transgressive, oppositional stance in relation to mainstream culture is central to understanding cult texts and their audiences, citing Michel Foucault's quip: 'It is likely that transgression has its entire space in the line it crosses' (Telotte 1991: 5). This chapter questions just how transgressive cult media and cult fandom really are, considering screen texts that walk the line, audience desires to cross the line, industry imperatives to toe the line, and academic research that seeks to measure the line dividing 'fanatics' from 'ordinary' audiences and mainstream hits from cult classics. In the process of addressing these questions, we will work through a variety of ways of researching and theorising film spectators and television audiences.

Cult media theorists Sara Gwenllian-Jones and Roberta Pearson begin from the loose, common usage of 'cult media' as a term that applies to any text 'that is considered off-beat or edgy, that draws a niche audience, that has a nostalgic appeal, that is considered emblematic of a particular subculture, or that is considered hip' (Gwenllian-Jones & Pearson 2004: ix). Most cult media texts will have several of these characteristics, but since *Æon Flux* (a television series created by the Korean-American animator Peter Chung, and later remade as a feature film) incorporates every element of this definition, it will be the principal example in this chapter. *Æon Flux* is as definitively edgy as its heroine proclaims. It first aired as animated shorts for Liquid Television in 1991, which developed into a season of half-hour episodes for MTV and, in today's fast-moving media landscape, it is already acquiring 'nostalgic appeal'. Through the obvious influence of Japanese animation styles, it also hooks into *anime* subculture. The show was born from a desire to break the conventions of screen language, and to push creative boundaries with an enigmatic and aggressively anti-narrative style. It seduced its niche target audience, the late-night young adult market, with an anarchic heroine styled as a leather-clad 'bitch fatale'. and it offered viewers more aesthetically and intellectually challenging material than standard MTV fare.

The label 'cult media' covers such a broad territory that it cannot be distinguished as a clear category or genre. Even if we could describe cult media as a genre with 'characteristic markings or "family resemblances," those markings will never quite produce the sort of relationships that genre usually implies' because cult media 'simply transgresses even the boundaries we usually associate with the very notion of genre' (Telotte 1991: 6). For instance, cult texts cannot be categorised by stars, storylines, character types, style, setting or themes as genre texts can. Nor can cult texts be categorised or explained by auteur theory, which considers the appeal of a text to be generated by the distinctive style and authorship of the director. Although some auteur directors can be said to have a 'cult following' (for example, Joss Whedon, Tim Burton, Wes Craven and John Waters), the cult phenomenon is not restricted to texts generated by such individuals. Telotte suggests that it is the audience and its fanatical devotion to the texts that defines 'cult' as a category or phenomenon, and that the nature of the cult 'transgresses' the ability of academics to define and analyse it, or industry to produce and reproduce it (1991: 6).

Etymologically, both 'cult' and 'culture' come from the same root. The Latin term *cultus* signifies both 'worship' and 'cultivation' (Telotte 1991: 14). These two meanings come together in the worship of the text by cult communities, and the cultivation of specialised knowledge and a personal identity based around the text. Telotte's anthology *Beyond All Reason: The Cult Film Experience* was published in 1991. We expand on Telotte's work to address more recent discussions of cult media, including cult television and questioning earlier assumptions about the relationships between audience, industry and text. Preceding chapters in this book have focused on textual analysis and examined how screen conventions and narratives tend to reinforce dominant ideologies. This chapter is devoted to reception practices and texts that define themselves in opposition to the mainstream, as a counter-culture.

APPROACHES TO CULT MEDIA: TEXTS, AUDIENCES, INDUSTRY

As the mass audience for films declined when television was introduced in the 1950s, cinemas began courting cinephiles and devoted fans by organising special midnight screenings of long-standing favourites and exhibiting quirky, arty films. Mark Jancovich and Nathan Hunt write: 'Cult movie fandom developed out of the art cinema and repertory theatre movements of the postwar period. These cinemas developed as cinema audiences declined, and certain cinemas began to service a small, highly educated, economically exclusive audience' (Jancovich & Hunt 2004: 36). So while cult film isn't a category that fits neatly underneath one umbrella, as an eclectic group of texts it does have certain marketing and exhibition tendencies, and non conformist narratives and aesthetics. These characteristics overlap with those of exploitation cinema and the European 'New Wave' films of the 1960s, and with excessive, esoteric texts in the genres of fantasy, horror and science fiction.

Cult television developed later but targeted a similar lucrative demographic to cult film. *Star Trek* and *Doctor Who* had amassed cult followings and grass-roots fan clubs by the early 1970s, spreading information about the series and organising conventions via newsletter and word of mouth. However, cult television proliferated and shifted away from this spontaneous, fan-led phenomenon as a result of developments in the media industry which threatened television's established audience base. Network television's grip on its formerly captive audience weakened following the introduction of domestic technologies like the remote control and video cassette recorders (VCRs), and the explosion of cable and satellite television channels in the 1980s and 1990s. Each of these technological innovations gave audiences more choices, and more power, and made it much more difficult for media producers to secure their market share and ensure that advertising messages reached their targets. Like the university film societies and art cinemas that began screening classic and *avant garde* films to enthusiasts, changes in the television industry led to nostalgia-fuelled reruns of old television shows, and the emergence of arty and risqué shows which were able to evade the censors by airing on subscription television.

The historical context sketched above suggests that cult media can be recognised, defined and understood in three main ways, each of which is dealt with in turn in the course of this chapter:

1. **Text:** As a text-based phenomenonon, cult media can be understood through textual analysis of the shared properties of a group of narratives with similar forms, content, structures and aesthetic characteristics.
2. **Audience:** As a nexus of fan activities and practices, cult media attracts a particular kind of devotional investment and fetishisation which can be understood by studying fan behaviour (Hills 2004: 511). In this audience-based definition, cult media can be identified as such because they evolve a substantial fan culture and develop a cult following.
3. **Industry and technology:** As a phenomenon facilitated by technological and economic factors in the media industry, cult media can be studied by focusing on the ways in which the industry strategically responds to technological changes by designing content likely to attract a cult following, and by enabling a cult discourse to circulate through merchandising and secondary texts like fanzines, magazines, reviews and online forums. Interactive and digital technologies and

technologies of exhibition and distribution enable certain texts to be differentiated from mainstream fare, thereby generating inter-textual and meta-textual material that distinguishes texts as 'cult'.

CULT FILM

Cultists love certain movies 'beyond all reason', exhibiting a 'quasi-religious' reverence, as Telotte points out. The unusual texts and the impassioned response of audiences suggest something distinctive not just about the films, but about the fans' identity too (Telotte 1991: 5). As the conversation at the beginning of this chapter between Æon and Trevor suggests, fan identity is based on a distinction between those who do, and those who 'just don't get it'. That is, cult fandom expresses an exclusive mode of appreciation for the fact that a text is rare, deviant, difficult or somehow distinct from the mainstream. Cultists accrue subcultural capital from the very fact that only a relatively small group of people 'get it'. A person's taste in film and television, along with the style of music and clothing that they like, is a significant part of what constructs their sense of identity. In this sense, taste and style reflect value systems and express how we position ourselves in relation to dominant ideologies and social norms. For this reason, it has been suggested that cult film is unified by a '"subcultural ideology" that draws together films, filmmakers and fans that exist in opposition to the cultural mainstream' (Jancovich et al. 2003: 1). The category of 'mainstream mass culture' provides a touchstone against which cultists define their own oppositional, marginal identities and fan(atical) practices.

Telotte identifies two types of cult films: nostalgic classics and midnight movies (1991: 9–10). Classics are conventionally successful films from a bygone era that draw a cult following over time. As rarity and exclusivity are often central to cult status, so texts that have long ceased to feature in the mainstream media can eventually develop a following (Jancovich & Hunt 2004: 31). The second type of cult film, 'midnight movies', is more interesting in relation to this chapter's focus. 'Midnight movies' attract a smaller and more homogenous audience with alternative viewing practices. For example, fans of *The Rocky Horror Picture Show* often dress in costume and participate in the narrative. Like the exploitation films and art films included in their canon, many cult films are independent, low-budget productions featuring themes of sex, drugs and alienation that reflect the experiences and desires of the audience (Telotte 1991:10). Telotte's discussion of cult audiences attending midnight screenings was applicable to 1980s and 1990s audiences, but is less relevant in the digital age. What remains consistent are alternative viewing practices and a fixation on texts with non-mainstream conditions of production, and an appeal based on their marginal or taboo status (Telotte 1991: 10).

Rather than addressing viewers as though we are a homogenous mass, cable and satellite stations enable a type of niche marketing that parallels the way cult film speaks to a special interest group. This is changing how the industry addresses its audience. While cult was formerly defined by difference from the mainstream, normal and transgressive texts and viewing practices are now converging, following patterns of technological convergence. The industry has adopted deliberate marketing strategies to harness this trend. For example, the off-beat teenpic *The Chumscrubber* was billed as '*Desperate Housewives* meets *Donnie Darko*', a mainstream television hit blended with a cult film, targeting a crossover audience. (As it happens, *Weeds* meets *The Virgin Suicides* may have been an equally apt and more accurate description.) Cult texts have a long shelf life and tap into the DVD, merchandising and collectors' markets and, as the *Chumscrubber* example suggests, this strategy provides a cunning way for film to ride the popularity of television and compete with the pull of the internet and modes of alternative content distribution. Cult film can therefore be understood as a form of audience segmentation, addressing a market with 'special tastes' (Telotte 1991: 8).

Gaylyn Studlar develops the idea that cult audiences with a taste for excess and perversion express dissatisfaction with the status quo by identifying with transgressive characters and 'ritualiz[ing] perversion into a subcultural icon of rebellion against bourgeoisie norms by celebrating the possibilities of sex as ironic play and playacting' (Studlar 1991: 141). The social function of many cult films is linked to redefining social norms by representing sexual 'deviance' and gender performativity (Studlar 1991: 138). Certainly, in Æon Flux, Æon's persona is built around a dominatrix aesthetic (see Figure 10.1), secret messages exchanged via tangled tongues engaged in an illicit kiss, and a recurring lesbian subtext. As a cult text, Æon Flux can therefore be seen to show characters challenging the status quo. Through identification with screen characters, cultists may also vicariously participate in this transgressive challenge.

CULT TELEVISION

Cult television often features 'campy humour, insider gags, a coherent and well-populated fictional world, deep backstory, offbeat and charismatic major characters, metatextuality, "mythic" themes and plots and the extension of the cult fiction across a full range of media and merchandise products' (Gwenllian-Jones 2003: 174). Like cult film, cult television includes texts that have nostalgic appeal (such as *Bewitched, Lost in Space, Astro Boy* or *Monkey*), those that feature a defiant, quirky or risqué tone (*Nip/Tuck, South Park* or the animated reality television spoof *Drawn Together*), and those that challenge accepted aesthetic norms via innovation, experimentation or outlandishly poor taste. However, cult television's most common form is fantasy and science fiction series characterised by complex narrative worlds and an 'endlessly deferred narrative based on narrative enigmas that are central to each programme's

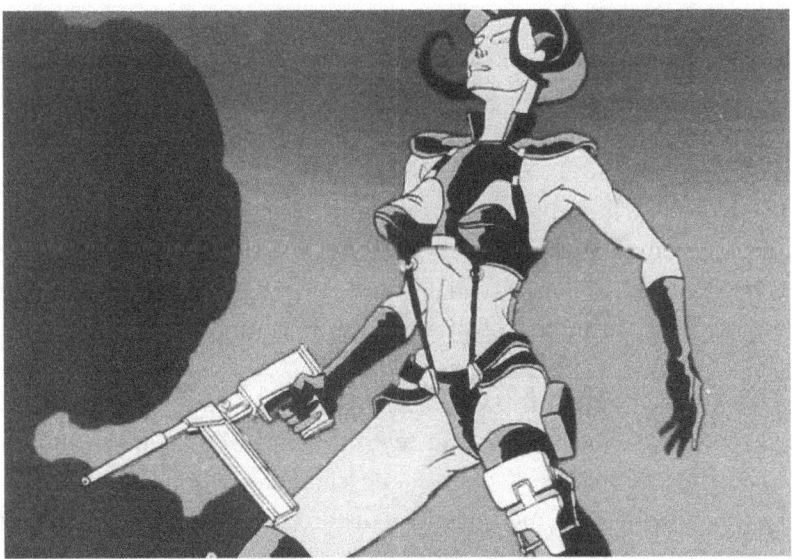

Figure 10.1 *Æeon Flux*–a bitch fatale in a dominatrix costume

character-based and fantasy-based format' (Hills 2004: 513). Such programs 'formulate complex internal logics, combine realistic and archetypal characters, and construct fantastical worlds where philosophical and ethical issues can be explored and grand gestures enacted free from the obscuring trivia and mundane concerns of everyday reality' (Gwenllian-Jones & Pearson 2004: xvi).

Gwenllian-Jones points out that, while cult film frequently caters to the tastes and interest of a minority, differences in distribution and reception practices and the serial nature of television texts mean that cult television often includes mainstream quality series. For television, as distinct from film, cult status can be especially lucrative because cult television attracts 'a significant following of fans so devoted that they will not only watch every episode but also tape and archive it and buy official video releases as well, who will purchase a range of spinoff products, and who will participate in loyal fan cultures that promote and "support" the series in a variety of ways' (Gwenllian-Jones 2003: 164–5).

Because prime-time broadcast television must cater to 'family viewing' and a 'general audience', television series often focus more on ideas and characters rather than subversive themes, taboo content or special effects, providing another distinction between the types of texts that acquire cult status in film and television (see Jancovich & Hunt 2004: 35). Despite the tendency towards cross-over mainstream appeal, there is still a sense in which cult television is marginal, as 'perverse' texts that break taboos or are banned frequently acquire cult status. For instance, *Æon Flux*'s incorporation of a sexualised, violent anime aesthetic, and *Nip/Tuck*'s late night adult content mark these texts as 'forbidden fruit'. This enhances their desirability, especially in a context where network television is subject to conservative constraints on language, sexuality and violence, by contrast with the more liberal parameters of cinema or subscription television.

The cult of Æon Flux

Æeon Flux is a science fiction text influenced by Japanese animation styles, film noir's femme fatale characterisation and German Expressionism's extreme angles and distorted perspectives, alienating cityscapes and stylised intertitles at the beginning of each episode. Recognising that the series tapped into the established fan base for *anime* and harnessed nostalgia to the purchasing power of Generation Y who now have a disposable income and access to a wide range of screen technologies, the show has been rerun on MTV and on television channels targeting specialist audiences. By 2005 it was also digitally remastered and released on DVD, distributed in instalments on the screens of mobile phones, and downloaded from the internet by a whole new generation of techno-savvy teens. This cemented its reputation as hip by conflating its exhibition and reception context with the early adoption and incorporation of mobile and digital technology into everyday life. In these ways, *Æeon Flux* garnered enough of an underground cult fan base to spawn a feature-length live-action film (directed by Karyn Kusama and starring Charlize Theron), which in turn reinvigorated interest in the original series and generated lucrative DVD sales for the television series and the film.

While delighting in the fact that *Æeon Flux* was finally receiving critical and popular acclaim, many fans of the original series resented the mainstreaming of their passion, and the appropriation of Æon's identity by a blonde actress and a mass audience. The very act of 'mainstreaming' undercuts some of the primary pleasures of cult fandom associated with identity and identification. When the adored text becomes something that is widely appreciated, the true fan's identity is no longer experienced as elite or discerning and the knowledge community to which they belong is no longer that of a specialised interest group that defines itself as distinct from the cultural mainstream. The aura of exclusivity surrounding fans' relationships with cult texts is evident in the kinds of online material they generate, such as 'The Purity Test' (www.sadgeezer.com/aeon/aeontest.htm) which one fan website uses to test knowledge of *Æeon Flux* and implicitly determine whether visitors to the site are 'pure' fans or casual drop-ins from mainstream culture. In addition, the expansion of the fictional world of *Æeon Flux* beyond what is shown on screen is evident in a fan-produced graphic novel and comic book mini-series, the Monican Spies online community, and the DVD menus of both the television series and the film, which reference the virtual world of the *Æeon Flux* video game, produced as a movie tie-in.

As the adaptation from television to film demonstrates, any attempt to expand the market for a text often compromises the specific features that made it unusual or created its unique appeal.

When *Æon* was expanded to fill a half-hour timeslot, the creative team was under instructions from MTV to cut down the amount of violence in order to avoid Federal Communications Commission (FCC) restrictions and make the 30-minute episodes appealing to a broader audience. They had to find more subtle ways to 'maintain the edge' and 'push the boundaries', including double entendres in the dialogue, suggestive sound and evocative music, and oblique sexual references in the imagery. This conservative impulse, which was geared to attract (or at least avoid offending) a broader audience, was amplified in the feature film.

A residue of the original series remains in the remake: in the television episode entitled 'Utopia or Deuteranopia', Trevor has usurped the ruler of Bregna; this theme carries over into the feature film, where Trevor's own position as ruler is threatened. Other aspects of the original that were incorporated into the film are the opening shot of Æon trapping a fly in her eyelashes like a Venus Fly Trap, the character Scafandra with feet that grip like hands, and the covert transfer of information via a French kiss. As a whole, the film retains superficial elements of the original series, but offers a simplified narrative which blunts Æon's edge.

The television episode most closely related to the film's storyline is 'A Last Time for Everything', in which Trevor copies Æon using a process similar to cloning, and she and her exact duplicate surreptitiously swap places (see Figure 10.2). The original Æon lets down her guard and embarks on a steamy affair with Trevor, while the copy completes her mission. The duplication of identity relates to fears about duplicity since Æon is a double agent, but also reflects the desire and need for a partner and an ally. At the end of the television episode, despite her feelings for Trevor, Æon remains loyal only to herself and works in partnership with her copy, drawing lethal fire from the border guards to enable the second Æon to return safely to Monica. Death is no stranger to the series: Æon died with the methodical regularity of Kenny in *South Park*, meeting her demise in each and every one of the original shorts. The certainty of death meant that she was completely unrestrained.

In the television series, Æon is an independent agent with her own agenda, exhibiting strong traits of feminism and individualism. These characteristics are taken up in the film in Æon's defiance of the matriarchal power of the Monican ruler (played in the film by Frances McDormand, even though in the television series Monica had no head of state and was therefore ungovernable) and in her quest to derail the Bregnan patriarchal reproductive fantasies and messiah complexes of Trevor's bureaucracy, which strives to propagate the human race in the face of infertility. Unlike the television series, however, the film ends by taming Æon—not quite domesticating her, but resolving the tension between masculinity (Bregnan technology) and femininity (Monican spirituality) by binding Trevor and Æon in a romantic union that sends them forth into the brave new world beyond the walls of the city, like Adam and Eve in Eden. Needless to say, fans of the original series were unimpressed with this ending, which seemed to shackle their deviant, free-spirited heroine to the heterosexual, monogamous conventions she had always usurped. For example, the Æon that fans loved in the original series tartly replied to Trevor's offer to take care of her in 'Chronophasia' with the retort: 'Naturally, I'd rather be dead'. Such negative fan responses to filmic remakes of cult television series are often based on a sense of allegiance and ownership, an investment of fan identity in the original series, or a sense that the remake has not been true to fans' detailed knowledge of the vast mythology that surrounds the characters and fictional worlds of cult texts.

Figure 10.2 Æon and her copy

Fantastic narratives

Matt Hills notes that many cult television programmes construct a fantastic **hyperdiegetic** fictional world which extends beyond the borders of the screen into other media, and ultimately into fan culture through fan fiction and merchandising. The broad genre of 'the **fantastic**' encompasses science fiction, fantasy and horror, often incorporating supernatural powers, alien landscapes and alternate dimensions into the fabric of everyday life. Cult television 'works serially, by reiteration and by accumulation of detail, to make fantastic worlds appear normal within a format and narrative structure' (Hills 2004: 511). Cult television also repeatedly represents character relationships that often feature a form of exclusivity, allegiance and secrecy amongst those 'bound together through shared knowledge of the fantastic' (Hills 2004: 512). For example, 'special powers' unite the characters in the TV series *Heroes*, encouraging the fans who identify with them to construct their own identities as different from the mainstream.

The meta-genre of the fantastic is founded on ambiguity and enigma, so it is perhaps not surprising that a narrative structure lacking closure and driven by a central enigma is one of the most distinctive characteristics of cult television, and is closely linked to the formation of a dedicated fan culture (Hills 2004: 513). Hence cult television series tend to be based in science fiction, horror or other 'fantastical' genres, because those genres can more easily incorporate 'non-linear narratives that can go backward and sideways as well as forward, encompassing multiple time frames and settings', which allows the creation of a 'potentially infinitely large metatext and sometimes the seemingly infinite delay of the resolution' (Gwenllian-Jones & Pearson, 2004: xii). For example, *Donnie Darko* involves fans in attempts to

> **Hyperdiegesis** refers to the representation of an expansive narrative world (a diegesis) that extends beyond what is shown in the text itself at any one time to include rules that govern narrative events, the accumulation of history and detail over multiple episodes in the series, and even the extension of this story world and its characters into fan fiction, artefacts and other media like films, books and video games.
>
> **Fantastic** narratives are characterised by a departure from the rules governing everyday reality, and the uncertainty of familiar boundaries and categories. They often feature elliptical, cyclical, fragmented narrative structures that lack resolution and open spaces for the imagination, shaping the way spectators inhabit the story. Common themes include doppelgangers, the transformation of time and space, and moments when reality is called into question.

decipher the time loop paradox, and in *Heroes* Hiro teleports through time and space, and Isaac paints the future.

Cult media can be characterised by fantastical, unbounded, non-linear narrative structures that capitalise on television's capacity for inter-textuality, indefinitely deferred resolution and diegetic expansion. The combination of series and serial narrative structures is enormously successful, following the popularity of *The X-Files*' adoption of an ongoing conspiracy enigma and unconsummated attraction between its protagonists Mulder and Scully, teamed with the short-term satisfaction of solving the riddle of the episode or vanquishing the monster of the week. This format of self-contained episodes embedded within an ongoing story arc and developing relationships has become typical of the cult television format.

Transgression, alienation and marginality

Cult texts are positioned as marginal in relation to some aspect of mainstream media culture, whether that be the relation between nostalgic texts of the past and contemporary texts; risqué, kitsch or offbeat texts in relation to dominant tastes and aesthetics; fanatical, immersive audience activity in relation to 'normal viewing behaviour'; or fictional worlds that deviate from everyday norms. Fantasy and science fiction texts are often set in the distant past, in the future, on other planets or in alternative dimensions, but they typically confront problems that contemporary audiences face. For instance, *Children of Men* features concerns with terrorist activity and refugees (termed 'fugees' in the film); Buffy and Angel both battled demons entering California through the 'Hellmouth', reflecting the anxieties of contemporary Americans concerning immigrants (termed 'illegal aliens') infiltrating America via the Mexican border; and *Heroes* confronts the threat of terrorism in a world changed forever by a massive explosion in New York City, causing a group of individuals designated as different or 'other' to be regarded with suspicion, fear and distrust. Clearly these fictional texts express contemporary, everyday concerns about foreigners and national boundaries.

In 'Flexing Those Anthropological Muscles: *X-Files*, Cult TV and the Representation of Race and Ethnicity', Karen Backstein argues that the 'otherworldly' fantastical storyline, generic hybridity and innovation of *The X-Files* and many other cult media texts make them ideal 'for dealing metaphorically with real life concerns' because 'it has always been easier to deal with troublesome social issues when they're applied to some other universe or level of reality' (2004: 116). Many cult texts displace ethnic conflict on to 'alien' races, and engage on a metaphorical level with contemporary social issues and fears of cultural change in an age of multiculturalism and globalisation. For instance, it is no accident that Frankenfurter from *The Rocky Horror Picture Show* is both a 'sweet transsexual' and literally an alien from the planet Transylvania: on an allegorical level, the film confronts issues of alienation associated with sexual and racial difference.

In *Æeon Flux,* the impulse to tackle social issues on a metaphorical level is evident in typical science fiction themes such as the fear of dehumanisation arising from technological advancement (consider Scafandra's prosthetic hands and Trevor's genetic duplication experiments), and also in the *mise en scène* itself. The world Æeon inhabits is a fractured space characterised by extreme separatism and social stratification. The heavily armed border separating the nations of Bregna and Monica is based on the series creator Peter Chung's experience of the division between North and South Korea as he was growing up, and his desire to critique the arbitrariness of national boundaries. One episode in particular, 'Thanatophobia', also explores the politicised military surveillance technologies that police citizens' personal responses to such boundaries, showing Æeon's voyeuristic relationship with her neighbour Sybil who lives in the apartment across the border in Bregna. 'Thanatophobia' reveals how political boundaries infiltrate the private spaces of personal life, resulting in self-surveillance and interpersonal suspicion that compounds the physical, military and legal boundaries that protect the state and can literally cripple individual agency. *Æeon Flux* has a thematic affinity with films like *Children of Men* in terms of expressing fears of infertility, and of a massive border patrol problem developing from the tension arising from policing national boundaries in an era of globalisation.

THEORIES OF SPECTATORSHIP

While the themes and characteristics of cult media are fascinating in their own right, the way fans respond to texts is of central importance to understanding the cult phenomenon. There are two main traditions of studying the reception of screen texts: audience studies and spectatorship theory. The first is typically used to study television, and the second predominates in film studies. Below we contrast understandings of film spectatorship and text-based analysis with more contextual, ethnographic approaches to audience research and with empirical research methods, bearing in mind that cultists form a niche fan subculture and are not representative of the general audience.

Questions about the relationship between the audience and the text are not just academic; they are questions about power and meaning. Implicit in the different ways of analysing and researching screen texts and their audiences are assumptions about where the balance of power rests in the production and consumption of media. This, in turn, rests on questions about who decides what meanings a text might hold: the producers who create the text or the audiences who interpret it? When we watch screen texts, we often view film and television as entertaining and informative commodities that we choose to consume. However, every time we watch a screen text there is someone out there in the industry who sees *us* as commodities. The media industry not only conceptualises its audience as a target market, but also as a commodity whose value can be measured via television ratings and box office figures. The audience is a commodity in the sense that it can be exchanged for revenue from advertisers and financers. Audiences have also been conceptualised as passive couch potatoes, active meaning-makers, consumers, publics, knowledge communities, homogenous masses and heterogeneous taste communities. The way media producers imagine their target audience has a significant bearing on how texts are constructed to address the audience.

For example, compare *Æon* the television series and its address to a loyal late-night youth audience, with *Æon* the film and its address to mainstream cinemagoers used to a dual plot structure with an action storyline and a romantic sub-plot, with little challenging material in between. These two very different texts emerged from what the producers imagined different audiences wanted, but the vast budget for a feature film as compared with a short format television series meant that fewer risks could be taken when there was more money at stake:

> Feature films are generally targeted at and marketed for the broadest possible audience, as production companies, distributors and theatre owners all try to capture as great a share of the viewing dollar as possible. As a result, most films still take the most conservative path, following a classical narrative pattern that reiterates far from disturbing truisms about the movie-goers' culture. Controversial topics tend to disappear. (Telotte 1991: 7)

The type of analysis featured in the first part of this book can be termed aesthetic analysis or formalist semiotic analysis because it analyses how form and style communicate meaning. While piecing plot events together into a narrative, the spectator is simultaneously interpreting the significance of aesthetic techniques and contextualising the meaning of things like camera angles and music within our understanding of the story and its characters. For example, a stealthy tracking shot, dark shadows and ominous music might be signs that we should fear for the safety of a character in a thriller. The chapters on storyboarding, narrative, realism and genre involve narrative analysis as well as aesthetic analysis. Screen aesthetics and narrative analysis both focus on the text, yet assumptions about the audience are implicit in such textual analysis. Semiotics implicitly suggests that the power to make meaning is located in the style and structure of the text itself, though it also considers the encoding and decoding practices involved in authorship and audience interpretation. Broadly speaking, text-based forms of analysis assume that the spectator engages with film and television on a cognitive level, responding to the narrative form and style in much the same way a police investigator would respond to clues while trying to solve a case, or drivers respond to road signs and traffic signals that direct us through town.

Cognitive theories of spectatorship analyse the role of the film audience in constructing meaning like a detective, figuring out what the visual and aural cues or clues in the film text mean. Though usually applied to film, cognitive analysis can also be used to analyse television. The objective of cognitive analysis is to explain what is going on in the spectator's mind as they view. Using cognitive analysis to understand the relationship between the spectator and the screen entails addressing the following questions:

- How does the spectator acquire knowledge in the narrative?
- What cues prompt the spectator to make meaning?

This approach sees the spectator as a detective who makes inferences and forms hypotheses about what will happen next in the story, based on clues and cues in the text.

In order for the audience to understand the story, narrative **cues** and **conventions** enable us to put events into a coherent order comprising causal factors and their consequences. Tracing these clues through the text enables researchers to analyse how the spectator is positioned, manipulated or lured through the narrative. Gaps are a particular kind of cue whereby story information is withheld to generate questions and hypotheses, curiosity and suspense. For instance, gaps can involve temporal ellipsis (gaps in time created when jumping forward to the next plot point), or they can entail deliberate delays in revealing information spectators need to piece the story together, as when the TV series *Lost* withholds information about the characters' lives before the crash, about the nature of the island itself, and about the significance of certain numbers and coincidences. Most films eventually provide all of the information required for the spectator to fill in the gaps and tie up any loose ends in the plot, whereas most television series contain ongoing enigmas and, like *Lost*, indefinitely play on and flaunt gaps in our understanding so that we continue to seek further pieces of the puzzle week after week.

Like cognitive theory, psychoanalysis has been used to try to understand how audiences make sense of film. Where cognitive theory is particularly useful for figuring out how spectators make sense of complex, enigmatic texts, psychoanalysis is often used to analyse films in the horror genre and perverse texts that draw a cult following. As spectators, we believe our responses to

> **Cues:** The screen text gives the spectator clues that cue or prompt us to develop questions and form expectations. For instance, ominous music cues suspense and indicates that a screen character is facing imminent danger.
>
> **Conventions** are the ways cues or clues are communicated through the screen text's stylistic system, which uses a language or formula for creating spectatorial expectations and providing interpretive cues using *mise en scène*, cinematography, editing and sound. For example, continuity editing is based on conventions that help the spectator to follow the logic of movement through space and time in the story world.

film and television are related to what we see, hear and think, just as cognitivists argue. Psychoanalysts claim our responses to cinematic texts are affected by long-forgotten things that happened during early psychological development. According to psychoanalytic theory, screen texts express and disguise repressed wishes and anxieties. As a way to understand spectatorship, the aim of psychoanalysis is to decode the language of the unconscious in order to figure out the hidden desires, fantasies and ideas that influence behaviour. For example, monsters, villains and aliens in cult media texts can be interpreted as embodying repressed fears and desires: 'Images of the monstrous help define the boundaries of community . . . the monster dramatises all that our civilisation represses and oppresses' (Donald 1989: 106). In such texts, the shadow side of self or society is projected on to screen villains, letting *them* take punishment for enacting *our* forbidden wishes. In addition, images of monstrosity, impurity and perversion can enable spectators to vicariously live out infantile or adolescent urges to rebel against oppressive norms, as the transgressive figure of Æon Flux does when she defies all efforts to constrain her freedom or sexuality.

AUDIENCE RESEARCH

By contrast with film, television is often studied using a social science approach. Audience reception studies can be divided into qualitative and quantitative methods. As Toby Miller explains, **quantitative** audience research 'is primarily concerned with the number and conduct of people seated before screen texts: where they come from, how many there were, and what they did as a consequence of being present. The audience is understood as an empirical concept that can be known via research instruments derived from sociology, demography, social psychology and marketing' (2004: 189). Quantitative surveys, box office figures and television **ratings** are often used by the industry as 'market research' to measure, predict

Quantitative research uses empirical methods to measure and analyse data about screen texts and their audiences. It works with figures like audience demographics, budgets and box office profits, ratings and results of polls and surveys, and statistics about the frequency with which particular types of media content or audience reactions occur. This mode of research is useful for analysing broad patterns, predicting trends or generalising about averages.

and exploit audience behaviour. This approach conceptualises the audience as a target market and uses research to sharpen the industry's aim: fans literally have a price on their heads. Other quantitative studies like empirical media effects research (for instance, research into the correlation between screen violence and viewer aggression) can be used to inform media policy regulating what types of content can be screened. Media effects research often conceptualises the audience as relatively passive and impressionable, and sometimes even as victims of powerful media messages that influence our attitudes and behaviour. Such research, which indicates that sustained exposure to screen violence perpetrated by an attractive character may cause viewer aggression, prompted MTV executives to muzzle *Æon*'s animators and decrease the amount of violence in the half-hour episodes. The drawback of quantitative research is that there are so many variables affecting the viewing experience that it is extremely difficult to isolate the influence of screen texts from other factors like socialisation, personal background, education and the cumulative effect of previous viewing experiences, all of which can affect immediate and long-term responses to texts. Even the reception context can make a difference to audience responses so, although empirical research undertaken in artificial viewing environments like laboratories may serve to limit variables and external distractions, it also alters how audiences would normally react. For example, if kids roughhouse after watching a violent cartoon at home, they usually get into trouble, which inhibits more rough activity. In a laboratory, without household rules and parental intervention, further aggressive behaviour is likely so researchers may over-estimate how much TV violence incites aggression.

> **Ratings** is a quantitative research method that can measure whose television set is tuned to which program, but it can't reveal who is actually paying attention or how viewers make sense of the programs they watch.

Qualitative research uses methods that aim to develop holistic, contextual accounts of the nature of people's media experiences. **Ethnography** is a qualitative research method derived from anthropology. Often it involves 'participant observation', in which the researcher joins people for an extended period in their normal environment and participates in their activities, while observing them. In screen studies, ethnographic research can be used to develop

> **Qualitative research** evaluates the meaning and value of texts and audience responses, rather than assuming that we can understand them by quantification and measurement. This mode of research is useful for case studies and in-depth analysis of small groups of texts or viewers.
>
> **Ethnographic** approaches to audience research offer a qualitative, detailed study of actual personal viewing behaviour via participant observation and interviews.
>
> A **cultural studies** approach investigates how texts communicate ideological messages about class, gender and consumerism through advertising strategies, modes of address, narrative resolution and reception practices, considering how media technologies and media industries and institutions inflect meaning and interpretation. Cultural studies makes sense of texts in the context of their production and consumption.

insight into how media consumption integrates with everyday life through subcultural lifestyles and community practices. Studying how fans incorporate screen media in banal, everyday routines or exalt special screenings of cult favourites to significant events, and observing how they gossip about their favourite texts or spend time in online fan activities, can reveal a great deal about the social structure of fan communities and the ways in which the media are integral to identity formation. Open-ended interviews and focus groups are other qualitative research methods that can be used to deepen understandings of how audiences make sense of texts, and how the media is embedded in lifestyles and value systems. The drawback of qualitative research is that findings are difficult to prove or generalise beyond specific case studies. **Cultural studies** uses qualitative approaches to investigate how screen texts fit into larger socio-political contexts, encompassing texts, ideological meanings, technologies, institutions and practices of production and consumption.

Cultural studies approaches to fandom

In the early 1990s, Henry Jenkins, a cultural studies researcher, self-confessed television fan and early adopter of interactive internet technologies, looked at 'textual poachers'—fans who actively integrate screen media into their lives, identities and creative practices, and create new communities around a chosen text. As Jenkins puts it, stories generated by the media 'need to be reworked so that they more fully satisfy our needs and fantasies. We "appropriate" them, or to use another term, we "poach" them' (Jenkins 2000: 175). The metaphor of poaching is based on the idea that the media industry claims intellectual property rights over the texts it produces, in much the same way that farmers protect their property from those who might sneak in and 'appropriate' or steal their produce, taking it for themselves and making it their own. To illustrate appropriation, Jenkins gives the example of Trekkies who write their own scripts for *Star Trek* characters and use DVD images on fansites: 'Kirk and Spock belong to Viacom. In that sense, fans are, indeed, "poachers," who assert their own roles in the creation of contemporary culture, refusing to bow before pressures exerted upon them by copyright holders' (Jenkins 2000: 175). In this way, Jenkins locates cult fandom as a resistant, alternative, participatory cultural phenomenon comprising active audience members who deliberately appropriate, manipulate and subvert media texts for their own ends.

Jenkins' cultural studies approach is used to develop a contextual understanding of the relationship between text and audience and what it reveals about the culture-producing and consuming media. Jenkins essentially advances a version of the **uses and gratifications** approach to reception theory, showing how fans 'poach' or appropriate aspects of the text to provide personal meaning and gratification, while discarding or rejecting other aspects. This involves studying how the context of reception and audience engagement shapes textual uses and interpretations. The uses and gratifications model sees the audience as both active and empowered, and able to appropriate, resist or subvert the ideologies and preferred readings promoted by producers. This indicates that films and television programs become cult objects, 'not so much because of their intrinsic properties, as through the process of interpretation and appropriation' (Jenkins 2000: 167).

Despite the interest of cultural studies academics in cult fandom as a mode of resistance to dominant ideology, fandom rarely translates to political action (Miller 2004: 193). Fans themselves are more likely to regard their own activity as a matter of entertainment and social connection, and to be unaware of the implications of their complicity with or resistance to media commercialisation. There are some instances of politicised engagements within fan culture, such as online debates about 'issues of identity and otherness'; however, researchers like Jenkins may have overstated the power and politicisation of fans and their oppositional relation to the media industry (Gwenllian-Jones 2003: 163–5).

> **Uses and gratifications** research uses qualitative methods to study how audiences actively engage with media texts, using them to satisfy personal needs or desires. Unlike empirical forms of media effects research, it focuses attention on the practices and powers of the audience in constructing meaning, rather than the power of the industry, artists or texts.

Fan cultures, fansites and fantasies

The fan activity surrounding cult media is characterised by intense identification and interpretation, as discussed above, and by immersion and interactivity. In 'Virtual Reality and Cult Television', Sara Gwenllian-Jones develops the concept of 'immersive engagement' in fictional worlds that extend beyond the borders of the screen. Cult media texts extend themselves beyond their textual or narrative boundaries, bleeding into other media, other narratives, other lives and realities, fostering active, imaginative interaction with the text that releases the fiction from its container, the screen. Gwenllian-Jones sees fan activities like creating and collecting artefacts and merchandise as ways of extending the fictional world into the real world, enhancing the immersive engagement with the text, and eroding the boundaries between fans and texts. Fans produce archives, galleries, fan fiction like **slash** narratives and **scratch videos**, and they consume spin-off texts, posters, t-shirts, DVDs and soundtracks. These texts and products (along with the open-ended seriality of the texts themselves, and the extra-textual and inter-textual information circulated in secondary texts such as episode guides and novels), function as conduits for imaginative engagement with the texts and convey a powerful sense of presence within the fictional world of the cult text (Gwenllian-Jones 2004: 87).

Fan activity is socially interactive, as well as relying on interactive media technologies. Rather than being the idiosyncratic activities of individuals, cults are communal and fan activity is organised via conventions, online communities and appreciation societies. Fandom involves the formation of taste cultures and knowledge communities because fan networks are united by shared preferences, and 'are held together through the mutual production and reciprocal exchange of knowledge' (Jenkins 2006: 137). Online fan communities define themselves in terms of mutual interests and affinities, rather than shared localities. As such, 'cyberspace is fandom writ large' (Jenkins 2006: 138), given that

> **Slash** stories are a genre of fan fiction that reworks conventional representations of gender and sexuality by inventing 'homo-erotic relations between fictional characters, most often the male partners commonly found in science fiction or action-adventure stories' (Jenkins 2000).
>
> **Scratch videos** are compiled from fragments of film or television texts, cut to a soundtrack, sometimes embellished with inter-titles or voice-over narration to change the meaning of the original text.

discussion forums, file-sharing and chatrooms facilitate fan communication and exponentially increase the number of people actively involved in producing, consuming, sharing and communicating about media texts. Jenkins terms the knowledge of cult media that fans pool online 'collective intelligence'. Collective intelligence includes but also exceeds shared knowledge (information known to all fans). It produces new knowledge by freeing 'individual members from the limitations of their memory and enabl[ing] the group to act upon a broader range of expertise' (Jenkins 2006: 139).

TECHNOLOGICAL DEVELOPMENTS

Just as technologies like the VCR did in the 1980s, digital media have delocalised fan practices and enabled the formation of a larger, but more dispersed, cult community. This larger cult community is a cohesive and significant market force; however, perhaps ironically, 'this also threatens the sense of distinction and exclusivity' on which cult fandom relies (Jancovich et al. 2003: 4). In a way the internet has enabled fans to claim a greater degree of 'ownership' of cult texts by facilitating the ease of appropriation via screen grabs, digital downloads and so forth. Yet it has also enabled fans to be 'owned' as industry firmly fixes the target market (fans) in its sights and co-opts cult fandom back into the mainstream, controlling it using copyright law and exploiting it via merchandising. Many fan sites simultaneously contain links to 'official' websites and merchandise sales portals, as well as receiving 'cease and desist' letters from production studios ordering them to take down material infringing copyrights over registered trademarks, images and texts.

Technological developments such as high-speed broadband and sophisticated file-compression formats facilitating downloads and digital piracy have increased the accessibility of previously rare texts, and enabled the production and dissemination of high-quality fan materials derived directly from source texts (Gwenllian-Jones 2003: 168). Gwenllian-Jones describes the relationship between cult fans and the media industry as one of 'profitable symbiosis', arguing that, 'far from threatening the capitalist machinery of the culture industry, online fan culture encourages and participates in its commercial operations' (2003: 172). Fan sites not only provide free publicity for cult films and cult television series, they also locate the target audience in the crosshairs of the industry's sights, enabling the producers to measure and track audience responses to a series by monitoring traffic on websites and tracking topics on discussion forums. Ultimately, Gwenllian-Jones argues that fandom fuels consumption and that it is in the financial interests of the industry to 'nurture rather than to eradicate a thriving fan culture' because 'fans buy official products *as well as*, rather than instead of, accessing and creating unofficial ones' (2003: 175).

INDUSTRY AND INSTITUTIONS

From the 1990s on, as subscription television channels proliferated, audiences fragmented and the demand for diverse programming content rose, the profile of the media industry and the legislation that governed it changed. Broadcast networks had to contend with restrictions that subscription television stations avoided, and conglomerates began syndicating content and airing reruns of nostalgic series. Demographically lucrative international niche audiences superseded the national public as the new target market, and syndication and franchising began to outstrip the importance of domestic profits based on the first run of television series.

The television industry is currently characterised by synergy, convergence, conglomeration, vertical integration, deregulation and the collapse of boundaries between production, consumption, distribution and reception. Ownership is concentrated in the hands of a small number of powerful companies such as Disney, AOL Time-Warner, Viacom and Fox, which own wide-ranging enterprises spanning production, distribution and merchandising. As Jennifer Holt points out in 'Vertical Vision: Deregulation, Industrial Economy and Primetime Design' (2003), subscription television content and scheduling aren't bound by the same regulations as free-to-air television, so it is difficult for networks to compete with racy cable content. Major media companies buy websites, gaming companies, book publishers and toy manufacturers which effectively means that their business interests are integrated across a range of production and distribution platforms. This allows **multi-platforming**, which ties into fan activity and extends the fictional world of the text in more complex ways than the themed and branded t-shirts and hats that fans wear to signal their love of a text.

Ted Turner, vice chairman of AOL Time Warner and the visionary behind Turner Classic Movies, worked on the principle of multi-platforming. He bought Hanna-Barbera's cartoon library and MGM's massive movie archives and made a fortune out of nostalgia reruns, then bought the Atlanta Braves and Atlanta Hawks sports teams and made a virtue out of ongoing broadcasts of 'the world's worst two sports franchises' (Turner cited in Holt 2003: 17). As Turner told *Forbes* magazine when discussing his 'reduce, re-use, recycle' programming philosophy:

> **Multi-platforming**, which is possible because of digital media convergence and the conglomeration of ownership, involves the recycling of content across a variety of distribution channels and media forms or 'platforms', such as movies, digital games and music. Multi-platforming functions to maximise financial returns on the content development investment by releasing DVDs, soundtrack CDs, books, games and toys, along with the primary text.

> Television is like chicken farming. Modern chicken farmers, they grind up the intestines to make dog food. The feathers go into pillows. Even the chicken manure they make into fertilizer. They use every bit of the chicken. Well, that's what we try to do over here with television products, is use everything to its fullest extent. (Turner cited in Holt 2003: 17)

It is easy to see how well cult audiences fit into the bigger picture of Turner's approach to programming: cult fans are inclined to watch their favourite texts repeatedly; they avidly participate in popularising marginal nostalgic texts like reruns of old television series and classic films; and they benefit from dedicated special-interest channels that enable the formation of communities founded on shared tastes.

Market segmentation is evident in dedicated channels such as the Sci-Fi Channel, Turner Classic Movies, or The Cartoon Network that produce content targeting subcultures and special-interest groups rather than a mass audience, thereby both constituting and targeting cult audiences. Despite catering to smaller audience numbers, this is financially viable because cultists are such loyal fans and avid consumers of licensed merchandise. This makes it possible for producers to build syndications and 'franchise empires' that reap profits far beyond any advertising revenue or gain from first-run broadcasts (Gwenllian-Jones & Pearson 2004: xiii). The best example of a franchise empire is *Star Trek*, which had 79 episodes of the original series, followed by ten feature films and four subsequent television series. Increasingly, the film industry also banks on established, loyal audiences and the capacity for serialisation that cult television programs have. Even if they do not expect to make a profit from initial box office takings (as was the case with *Serenity*, the film based on Joss Whedon's short-lived *Firefly* series), films based on cult television represent a strategic investment in future economic returns since fans collect DVDs and audiences build over time as the original television series are rerun, attracting new viewers to the films like a well-designed long-running advertising campaign.

Given the significant financial value of cult fandom, there has been something of a shift from cults emerging spontaneously in response to texts, through cults being fostered and facilitated by technological developments such as digital media and the internet, to the strategic design of cult television by an industry keen to take advantage of the visibility of cults online, and the segmentation of the market due to cable, satellite and high-definition digital television. Unlike programs like *Doctor Who* and *Star Trek*, which spontaneously developed organised followings of Whovians and Trekkies as early as the 1960s and 1970s, shows like *Roswell* and *Buffy the Vampire Slayer* can be understood as attempts to target a fan audience that was already known to exist for cult television.

Producers hope to attract avid and loyal viewers with a programming strategy known as 'appointment television' or 'must see TV', which offers the kind of compulsive viewing that anchors programming schedules and audience routines to a particular series, mooring audiences to their television sets on certain nights in a way that is intended to 'bring people to the network and extend the duration of their viewing loyalty' (Jancovich & Lyons 2003: 4). Cult television is a form of 'must see TV' that courts the audience demographic most attractive and valuable to advertisers: loyal, affluent, educated, middle-class and between eighteen and 35 years of age (Jancovich & Lyons 2003: 3). Such programming tactics mean that the boundaries between cult fandom and mainstream audiences are increasingly indistinct. Since the 1990s a growing number of texts have established 'crossover' appeal to both casual viewers and avid fans. For instance, following the success of *The X-Files*, both *Lost* and *Heroes* were developed as calculated attempts to generate significant online fan activity, and television texts such as *Æon Flux* and *Ali G* which once catered to marginal audiences, have now spawned feature films and made the transition to the mainstream.

CONCLUSION

In summary, cult media mobilises a fan base that is not dependent on stars, auteurs, genre, or short-term financial success. Traditionally, cult media texts have often been those that take risks rather than appealing to the broadest possible market because aiming for widespread popularity often generates conservative, and blandly pleasurable, texts. Unlike mainstream genre texts, which are formulaic and share strong intertextual resemblances, cult texts are enigmatic and transgress boundaries. Cult media can only be understood as a unified category in terms of the 'excessive' nature of the relationship between spectators and the text, and the fact that the fictional worlds of cult film and television constantly spill off the screen to infiltrate other media platforms and the everyday lives of fans. Cult fandoms tend to emerge when a text is prescient and its content touches on issues of central social concern for a generation or an era. The impassioned response to cult texts indicates their narratives contain powerful ideological messages, hence studying cult media has the potential to reveal important insights into the concerns and values of the culture in which the texts originate and circulate.

Concepts of cult texts and audience are changing as technological developments segment the market and foster interactive audiences. Despite programming deliberately geared to capitalise on these trends and to attract a cult following with crossover mainstream appeal, the short lifespan of series like James Cameron's *Dark Angel* (banking on the creator's own cult status with science fiction fans), and *Tru Calling* (which counted on drawing fans of *Buffy* to watch Eliza Dushku—who played Faith, the dark slayer—in her own fantasy series) shows that, even with all the right ingredients, there is no certain formula for creating cult status or predicting audience preferences.

KEY SKILLS

Having read this chapter you should now be able to:

- become aware of the assumptions about audiences, texts, producers and meanings underlying different ways of approaching screen texts;
- describe the role of the audience in actively interpreting and constructing the meaning and significance of screen texts within a socio-cultural context;
- compare and contrast the characteristics of cult film with cult television, and distinguish cult media from mainstream media;
- explain differences between qualitative and quantitative approaches to audience analysis;
- analyse how technological developments and changes in the media industry have begun to blur the boundaries between cult and mainstream texts and audiences;
- critically evaluate whether online fan activity associated with a particular cult text expands the fictional world and gives evidence of immersion, interactivity and interpretive activity.

11
the crowded screen:
Transcultural influences and new directions in visual culture

Quentin Tarantino's *Kill Bill: Volume One* (2003) and *Kill Bill: Volume Two* (2004), hereafter referred to simply as *Kill Bill*, has been described as everything from innovative to derivative and inbred. This chapter takes the analogy of inbreeding and runs with it, exploring what it means in terms of the combination and transformation of different genres and screen media forms and arguing that *Kill Bill* is best understood as a transcultural generic hybrid, marked by the discourses of globalisation, postmodernism and postfeminism. Using *Kill Bill* as an example, this chapter demonstrates how to perform a **critical analysis** of a screen text by 'thinking on both sides of the screen', considering the text itself, its contexts and influences, production and reception. In the process, it investigates new directions in and influences on screen culture, such as the gradual erosion of clear demarcations between film and television styles and structures; developments in digital media technologies and techniques; and the impact of video games, *anime* and Asian cinema. We show how understandings of genre hybridity, globalisation, postmodernism and postfeminism

> **Critical analysis:** Film and TV essays include evidence of reading and research as well as analysis of screen texts. Essays should have a clear **introduction**, a **thesis statement** and a conclusion, and they should argue for your interpretation of the subject and its significance, as well as reviewing and critically evaluating published research in the field to broaden understanding of the subject and substantiate your ideas. Incorporate references to texts and terminology from your course, define key concepts and list works cited including screen texts, journals, websites or books to which you directly refer, or which you quote or paraphrase.

are central to theorising contemporary screen culture and are relevant to the analysis of screen texts.

HYBRIDITY: THEORISING GENERIC COMBINATION AND TRANSFORMATION

Genre hybridity is an interesting starting point for a critical analysis of a film as richly intertextual as *Kill Bill*, so we will consider how it has been understood by screen theorists and how different approaches can be applied. There are a number of ways of conceptualising generic hybridity. *Kill Bill* can be thought of as a Western haunted by the ghost of Bruce Lee and the kung-fu film tradition he embodies, but because of its eclectic blend of styles and influences it exceeds everyday understandings of generic hybridity as the combination of characteristics from two or more genres. Nor does it fit understandings of genre blending as **genre mutation**, or of genre transformation as an evolutionary process. Through mutation, new characteristics dramatically alter the relationship with the parent genre, instead of growing from it in an incremental process of repetition and variation. Lars von Trier's 'anti-musical' *Dancer in the Dark* might be considered a generic mutation in which melodrama and social realism deform what Dyer calls the 'utopian' qualities of musicals (2000: 20). The problem with the mutation metaphor is that genres have never been pure-bred categories, and it would be hard to say which one of the many genres it contains was the 'origin' from which *Kill Bill* mutated. **Genre evolution** suggests that new genres emerge as a response to changing social and industrial conditions, gradually taking the place of older genres by out-competing them in the market. For instance, science fiction films and road movies can be understood as genres evolving from Westerns when the historical setting, social concerns

> **Genre mutation** is a metaphor that implies radical change as new variants of genres spontaneously supersede an original, pure genre.

and models of race and gender typifying Westerns became outmoded. In road movies, cars replace horses but the protagonists are still outsiders with few possessions or ties to a job or home, travelling beyond civilised society, law and order. Science fiction evolved from different aspects of Westerns: the fascination with new frontiers and unknown cultures, and the dangerous appeal of technological progress and colonisation. Although *Kill Bill* may be a product of changing times, as we discuss below in relation to postfeminism, postmodernism and globalisation, evolution isn't the best way to describe how Tarantino's film has transformed genre categories.

> **Genre evolution** is a way of understanding how genres combine and transform over time in response to social change, new technologies and shifting market forces that enable new genres to out-compete older genres.

Janet Staiger suggests that what we usually refer to as generic hybridity (such as the science fiction horror film *Sunshine*) can often best be described as **genre 'inbreeding'** because it involves the union of genres from the same Hollywood family or film culture (1997: 1). True hybridity in screen texts, she argues, must be cross-cultural, just as biological hybridity refers to interbreeding between two *different* species. In Staiger's terms, a film like *Moulin Rouge* is a hybrid because it combines a melodramatic storyline of star-crossed lovers with the backstage musical genre, once a staple of Hollywood, and the cross-cultural influence of popular Indian cinema evident in the Bollywood-style stage play *Spectacular Spectacular*.

> **Genre inbreeding** refers to the combination of two or more genres that share family resemblances or are from related film cultures.

Kill Bill's genetic lineage as an inbred genre film

Although *Kill Bill* exhibits elements of true cross-cultural generic hybridity, the metaphor of inbreeding is a particularly apt way to describe the incestuous relationships between the auteurs and genres that gave birth to it. The first half is crowded with material from action blockbusters, Japanese samurai swordplay movies (**chanbara**) and miscellaneous genres, including *anime* and Westerns. In *Volume Two*, the Western elements are accentuated, subsequently following a road movie trajectory that takes the heroine Beatrix Kiddo (a.k.a. the Bride) across desert wastelands, through California and over the border into Mexico on a roaring rampage of revenge. In addition, a flashback shot with discernibly different film stock in the style of a Hong Kong kick-flick depicts extended, brutal training sessions showing 'the cruel tutelage of Pai Mei' as he instructs Beatrix in kung-fu animal-style fighting techniques. Kung-fu films typically involve vengeance, the defence of honour, tournaments and training sequences, initiation rituals and rites of passage, battles between rival fighting styles, and episodic fights loosely linked by a thin story with weak psychological motivation. Spectacle invariably outweighs narrative, culminating climactically in a lengthy duel with hand-to-hand combat. In traditional kung-fu films, which *Kill Bill* emulates, firepower (gun-fu) is eschewed in favour of demonstrating 'the art' of martial arts. In contemporary films, authentic fight scenes are rare and most actors power up with CGI, much as Neo did in *The Matrix* when he said 'I know kung-fu!' after uploading a computerised training module.

Chanbara refers to Japanese samurai films involving swordplay, loyalty and honour.

In terms of *Kill Bill's* inbreeding, we can trace the genre genealogy as follows: John Ford's classic Hollywood Westerns inspired Terrence Malick's influential road movie *Badlands* (1973) and Akira Kurosawa's dark and dusty *chanbara* samurai films, the latter were in turn remade as spaghetti Westerns by Sergio Leone and incorporated into various Hong Kong martial arts movies, Japanese *judo* and *anime* films and the fantastical, historical Chinese genre **shenguai wuxia pian**, all of which spawned *Kill Bill*.

Shenguai wuxia pian refers to 'sword and sorcery' martial arts cinema with the theme of chivalry, first popularised in Shanghai films from 1928–31 and originating from *tanci* oral narrative traditions with musical accompaniment, *guzhuang baishi pian* historical period costume dramas and *shenguai pian* fantasy films including magic powers, gods and demons (Teo 2005: 191–2).

Beatrix's vengeance narrative has twisted connections to several genres and directors. Ingmar Bergman, director of the influential rape-revenge film *The Virgin Spring* (1960), referred to his film as a 'lousy imitation of Kurosawa' and stated at the time he made the film that his admiration for Japanese cinema was so great that he was 'almost a samurai' himself (Björkman et al. 1993: 120). Indeed, many directors have conducted love affairs with Akira Kurosawa's movies: *Seven Samurai* (1954) was remade as *The Magnificent Seven* (Sturges 1960); *Yojimbo* (1961) was reworked as

A Fistful of Dollars by Leone in 1964; and *Rashômon* (1950) inspired *Hero* (a *wuxia* film directed by Zhang Yimou in 2002, promoted and 'presented by' Tarantino). Malick, it would seem, has been almost as promiscuous. *Badlands* was a version of the actual Charlie Starkweather and Caril Fugate killings of 1958, and Tarantino based two of his own road movie scripts loosely on Malick's film: *Natural Born Killers* (Stone 1994) and *True Romance* (Scott 1993). In addition to the directors with whom Tarantino flirts in *Kill Bill*, he also used the film to pursue relationships with stars that he loves. Tarantino states that Sonny Chiba represents Japan, reprising his role as Hattori Hanzo from the *Shadow Warriors* series; Gordon Liu re-enacts his role of Pai Mei from *Executioners of Shaolin* and represents Hong Kong; and Bill is David Carradine who, as the star of the TV series *Kung Fu*, represents America (Rance 2005: 185).

CHARACTERISATION, IDEOLOGY, AND SOCIAL CHANGE

As distinct from nostalgic, sincere evolutions of genre, **ironic hybridisation** is a form of hybridity that refers to a television series or a film in self-referential dialogue with its influences, in an 'attempt to master the media-saturated landscape of contemporary culture' (Collins 1993: 243). *Scream*, *Kung Fu Hustle* and, of course, *Kill Bill* are examples of this type of generic hybridity in that they cleverly and self-consciously reference a wide variety of iconic screen texts in a manner that seems to simultaneously mock and pay homage to those influences.

The process of ironic hybridisation tends to involve appropriation of superficial characteristics of a genre, rather than harnessing its social import or core concerns. Characterisation, distinctive iconography and trademark shots are replicated, whereas the structural and thematic components of the narrative and the ideological conflicts it negotiates may be glossed over. For example, as Jim Kitses' structuralist analysis shows, the narrative formula of Westerns hinges on a dialectical struggle between civilisation and savagery in which ideologies

> **Ironic hybridisation** is a postmodern form of genre hybridity in which texts incorporate the influences of several genres, boldly and self-consciously juxtaposing generic elements and signalling eclectic intertextual references.

of law and social order confront lawlessness (Kitses 1969). An ironic hybrid like *Back to the Future III* uses Western iconography but neglects these deeper concerns. *Kill Bill* certainly incorporates the trappings of Westerns; however, its relationship to core components of the genre, like dialectical structure, ideology and characterisation, requires analysis.

The Western hero negotiates between lawlessness and social order in a manner epitomised by *The Searchers*, which is an intertext of *Kill Bill*. Characteristically, the Western hero is an individual who protects civilisation but does not comfortably belong to it. Like road movie anti-heroes, he exists outside the law and is more at home in the untamed wilderness than in urban, civilised spaces. *The Searchers* begins when Ethan Edwards (played by the inimitable John Wayne) leaves behind the life of a soldier and considers working with his brother on the family ranch. When the ranch is raided by Indians led by the Comanche chief Scar, his family is massacred and his nieces are abducted. Ethan's goal to find his surviving niece, Debbie, is initially shared by a band of fellow 'searchers' who are representatives of the law, the state, the family and the church. Much is made of Ethan's bloodthirsty quest to avenge the honour of his violated nieces and murdered kin. In the morally redemptive ending, Ethan reclaims Debbie, perceives some humanity in the 'savage' Indians and partially overcomes his own savage impulses. However, the resolution of *The Searchers* leaves Ethan poised in the homestead doorway and framed against the wild, uncultivated desert landscape just as we see him in Figure 11.1. Rather than being recuperated into the social order, he remains caught between two worlds as he looks—perhaps with longing—into the domestic realm to which he clearly does not belong.

Kill Bill deliberately references this tough and masculine breed of hero with a shot virtually identical to that of *The Searchers* by placing Beatrix 'on the threshold'. In *Kill Bill*, however, the protagonist is a woman and the defining shot is located at the beginning of the narrative as Beatrix gazes out towards the freedom of the unpopulated landscape. Bill shoots 'the Bride', Beatrix, in the temple as she is about to leave the savage life of an assassin to become a wife and mother, an upstanding citizen with an honest job in a music store (see Figure 11.2). In doing so, he aborts her attempt to conform to social norms, just as Scar's attack prevented Ethan from settling down.

While Ethan spends the duration of *The Searchers* trying to rescue his niece from savagery, striving to reunite the family and return her to the homestead, Beatrix's journey is a bloodthirsty quest in which she destroys families and homes.

Figure 11.1 John Wayne as Ethan, caught between domesticity and the desert in *The Searchers*

Figure 11.2 Uma Thurman as 'the Bride' on the threshold of motherhood and marriage in *Kill Bill Volume Two*

It is striking that, in *Kill Bill*, the frameworks of law and order are almost entirely absent, as is convincing evidence that Beatrix is motivated by a desire to either escape or protect the social order. Like Ethan, Beatrix initially flirts with the idea of settling down and ultimately rescues a young girl from a life of 'savagery'; however, she is unaware that her daughter has survived until the final act of *Kill Bill, Volume 2*. This means Beatrix's motives and values differ substantially from Ethan's—though, as Lisa Coulthard notes, *audiences* know BB is alive and this affects narrative interpretation (2007: 167). The film leaves us with the impression that the social order has only partially, precariously been restored when mother and child are reunited and the father is slain. Beatrix and her daughter BB end the film in the indeterminate space of the road rather than ensconced in a town with a home, secure employment or a community. Indeed, the structuring absence of the discourses of law and social order suggests that *Kill Bill* defines itself *against* the ideological frameworks that govern the genres of the Western and the road movie. If westerns and road movies are structured around binary oppositions of the law versus the outlaw, and if *Kill Bill* is explicitly referencing these texts and presenting itself in a 'disorderly' way in terms of form and content, then how are we to make sense of it? What is Beatrix opposing, and what might her victory and vengeance signify?

POSTFEMINISM AND ACTION CINEMA HEROINES

The title itself, '*Kill Bill*', and further intertextual references—this time to the *Charlie's Angels* TV series and films—indicate that 'the Bride' is struggling with gender roles and railing against patriarchy. Like Charlie, the anonymous boss in *Charlie's Angels*, Bill represents an authority figure encompassing the roles of teacher, employer, father figure and love interest for the women he employs. *Volume One* establishes a direct link to *Charlie's Angels* as the actor Lucy Liu (playing O-Ren Ishii) is a former Angel and Bill is introduced as a voice on the other end of the phone giving orders to Elle Driver (Darryl Hannah's character) in much the same way that Charlie communicates his instructions to the action women he employs. Bill's face is never revealed in *Volume One*. Additionally, Bill literally replaces

O-Ren's father after her parents are slaughtered in Tokyo on the orders of Boss Matsumoto. Indeed O-Ren's father is slain by a long-haired, ring-wearing *anime* assassin with sinister similarities to Bill himself, as shown in Figures 11.3 and 11.4.

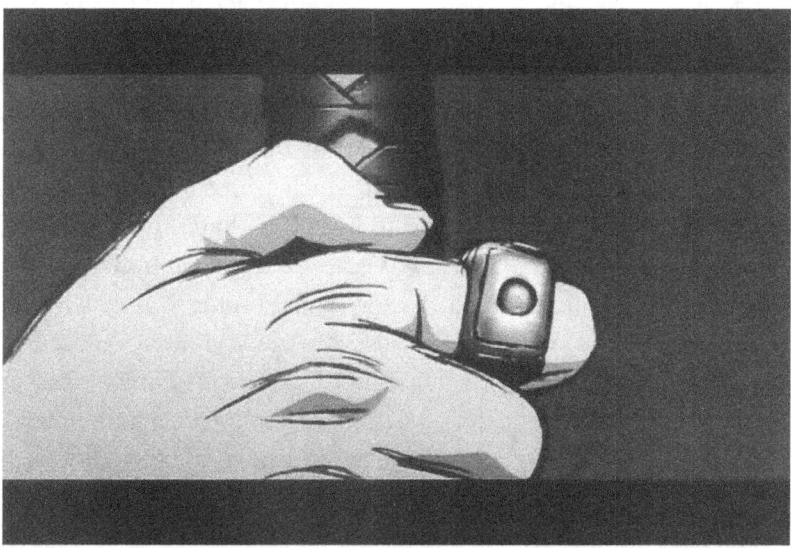

Figure 11.3 The assassin's hand gripping a samurai sword after killing O-Ren Ishii's father in the *anime* sequence of *Kill Bill, Volume One*

Figure 11.4 Bill's hand gripping a samurai sword as he speaks to Elle Driver on the phone in *Kill Bill, Volume Two*

In terms of the power and control the 'snake charmer' Bill wields over Beatrix and other members of the Deadly Viper Assassination Squad, he could be interpreted as a representation of patriarchy, and the film could be read as a complex postfeminist text. **Postfeminism** is a popular cultural expression of contemporary feminist attitudes and contemporary attitudes to feminism dating from the mid-1980s or 1990s on—a period that involved a **backlash** against feminism. It challenges assumptions underpinning **first-wave feminism** and **second-wave feminism**, and it critiques the way feminism manifested in cultural representations in which women were perceived as trying to be the same as men (think of the butch roles of Demi Moore in *GI Jane* and Sigourney Weaver in the *Alien* films, and the slogan 'anything a man can do a woman can do better'). In such media images of 'musculinity' (muscular, masculine women), Yvonne Tasker argues, 'the female action hero poses a challenge to gendered binaries through her very existence' (1998: 69). Since equality does not mean 'sameness,' but rather equity of opportunity, postfeminism acknowledges the *differences* between men and women and the diversity amongst women. Those who take the gains of earlier feminism for granted and accept contemporary gender relations tend to reject any conception of women as victims, and consequently avoid political activism around issues like sexual objectification, rape, pornography and sexual harassment in favour of emphasising individual autonomy and empowerment, seeing postfeminism more as individual choices about lifestyle and personal appearance than a political commitment (Gamble 2001: 44).

While postfeminist culture is characterised by the commodification

> **Postfeminism** is individualistic rather than a unified movement. Postfeminism can be associated with apolitical, anti-feminist discourse branding earlier feminist activism as essentialist or outmoded; with an era 'after' feminism; or with taking women's empowerment for granted and accepting contemporary gender relations. If deemed part of third-wave feminism, postfeminism indicates a postmodernist, post-colonialist or post-structuralist critique of earlier feminist thought. Postfeminism manifests in screen texts with strong heroines who typically combine a feminine appearance with power, choice, agency and consumerism.
>
> **Backlash:** In addition to naturalising and incorporating aspects of feminism in popular culture, postfeminism contains elements of what Susan Faludi (1992) terms a 'backlash' against feminism. Anti-feminist backlash media represents feminism and feminists as angry, extremist, difficult, hard, man-hating women who are greedy to 'have it all' (to be professionally and personally successful). This backlash allegedly turned young men and women away from feminism in the 1990s.

of difference (for example, the inclusion of streetwise black women to add 'colour' and 'attitude' to screen texts, and 'lipstick lesbians' to titillate heterosexual men and bi-curious women), postfeminism is also sometimes understood as one aspect of **third-wave feminism**. Third-wave feminism articulates theoretical and political aspects of contemporary life, including postfeminist culture itself, and 'facilitates a broad-based, pluralistic conception of the application of feminism, and addresses the demands of marginalised, diasporic and colonised cultures for a non-hegemonic feminism capable of giving voice to local, indigenous and postcolonial feminisms' (Brooks 1997: 4). In this more academic sense, 'postfeminism expresses the intersection of feminism with postmodernism, poststructuralism and post-colonialism' (Brooks 1997: 4). As an aspect of third-wave feminism, postfeminism features an 'innate acceptance of hybridity, its understanding that no account of oppression is true for all women in all situations all of the time' (Gamble 2001: 43).

Uma Thurman presents as a powerful, resourceful and above all independent female role model, equalling (and often eclipsing) the skill of the men who oppose and oppress her. However, the fact that much of the violence in the film is perpetrated by women, against women, throws the film's power dynamics off balance. This undermines a feminist interpretation and muddies the opposition between masculinity and femininity.

First-wave feminism: the first organised feminist movement emerged in the 1850s. Early feminists were concerned with legal equity and women's role as citizens in the public sphere, including suffrage (voting rights), education, employment and property ownership.

Second-wave feminism emerged in the late 1960s and 1970s with identity politics and the civil rights movement. The catch-cry 'the personal is political' expressed a focus on gender inequity in private sphere personal relationships, and the politicisation of childcare, domestic labour, sexuality and media representations. Second-wave feminist film theory focuses on the power relations of the gaze and the representation of women as passive, as victims, as objectified erotic spectacles and as the romantic interest in narratives.

Third-wave feminism uses postmodernist, post-structuralist and post-colonialist theory to critique the universalism and dualism of earlier feminist thought and reflect on contemporary manifestations of patriarchy and feminism. For instance, drawing on post-structuralism's deconstruction of essentialist concepts of race and gender, it critiques the ideological processes by which 'black' and 'white', or 'man' and 'woman', are placed in oppositional categories. Like postmodernism, postfeminism emerges from late capitalist consumer culture and focuses on the performance of identity, superficial images and consumption, as evident in the popularity of makeover films and shows like *Sex and the City*. Incorporating post-colonial critiques of the effects of colonial oppression, postfeminism celebrates pluralism and difference, acknowledging that patriarchy does not have the same effects on all women.

Typically, action films legitimate a particular form of masculinity embodied by physical size and aggression, strength and charisma. Action heroes, according to Mark Gallagher, require formidable villains 'against which to test the hero's mettle; the plot must continually place the hero in danger to prove his courage and fortitude; perhaps most importantly, other characters must appear to take the hero seriously lest his fabricated, ritualized maleness be revealed' (1997: 23). *Kill Bill* undermines this norm by placing women at the centre of the narrative and populating the film with flawed male figures that hold positions of power yet are difficult to take seriously either as heroes or villains, as they seem past their prime and ill-equipped to deal with the righteous wrath of a vengeful woman.

The choice of a kick-ass female protagonist has its origins not in action cinema, road movies or Westerns, but in another genre from which *Kill Bill* borrows. The woman warrior is a favourite in martial arts legends and kung-fu films, and in one instance has led to a fighting style being named after the woman who developed it. Wing Chun is the fighting style that Bruce Lee mastered before initiating his own 'Jeet Kune Do' style ('the way of the intercepting fist'), which is an amalgam of Wing Chun and other martial arts forms adapted for street fighting. The story of how the Wing Chun technique came into being is an interesting one. A nun who escaped the destruction of the Shaolin temple in ancient China taught fighting skills to a young woman called Yim Wing-Chun so that she 'could defend herself against unwanted suitors. Yim then used her skills to help the people against the oppression of the Manchurian government. Wing Chun, the basis of the film by the same name starring Michele Yeoh and Donnie Yen, is an effective street-fighting style' (Rance 2005: 15). The woman warrior prominent in traditional Chinese stories virtually vanished in the late 1980s and early 1990s and, even in her heyday, was distinct from Western heroines in that she was 'very rarely an object of desire for the male protagonist' (Dai 2005: 88). As Dai points out, the role of martial arts action hero carries a social cost for women: 'In most films in which a woman warrior is the main character, she can be the action hero, saviour, and a person of power, but she cannot gain social acceptance in her world' (2005: 88). Usually, the woman warrior is exiled at the end of such narratives, transcending gender identity to become an otherworldly figure within martial arts mythologies. It is this tradition, as much as postfeminist culture and the Western action heroines documented in Yvonne Tasker's book *Spectacular Bodies* (1993), which informs the character of the Bride.

According to Yvonne Tasker and Diane Negra, postfeminist culture 'perpetuates woman as pinup, the enduring linchpin of commercial beauty culture. In fact, it has offered new rationales for guilt-free consumerism' (2007: 3). In this light, glam female-centred action hits like *Alias*, *Mr and Mrs Smith* and *Charlie's Angels* are specious attempts to enlarge the predominantly male market for the action genre and attract female consumers (Coulthard 2007: 154). As Coulthard writes, action heroines 'articulate a postfeminist discourse of individualistic "have it all" feminism that yokes violence to individual, personal, erotic, and financial success' (2007: 172). This may be the case in *Lara Croft: Tomb Raider* and its sisters, but in *Kill Bill*, the excess of referentiality, irony and genre hybridity raise deeper issues involving cultural appropriation, race and gender.

Unlike action women such as Jane Smith, Lara Croft or Charlie's Angels, Beatrix is not overtly objectified or represented as a sexualised fantasy, nor is she filmed so as to encourage consumption and conformity to the glamorous ideals of femininity that many postfeminist texts playfully and strategically deploy. The character that Uma Thurman plays and helped to script in *Kill Bill* is not a creature from a fairytale version of femininity, as her names, Beatrix Kiddo and 'the Bride'—with their connotations of childhood and romance—misleadingly suggest. Yet, as a lethal assassin codenamed Black Mamba, nor is she intended to represent a 'real' woman. Despite this, and perhaps because Thurman herself had such an investment in the development of the character, Beatrix does confront and overcome problems specific to her gender.

After emerging from her coma, Beatrix's objective may be to eliminate those who wronged her, but her problems actually began in a situation any woman could face: she had an affair with her boss, Bill, which resulted in an unplanned pregnancy. When she attempted to leave this inequitable relationship in order to bring up her child in a healthy environment (assumed at that point to mean a nuclear family), her jealous and controlling ex would rather see her dead than married to another man. Bill's attack on Beatrix during the massacre at Two Pines may present as a spectacular cinematic hyperbole, but it is unfortunately representative of situations in which women are beaten into submission after attempting to leave abusive relationships with controlling men. When Beatrix lies vulnerable and comatose, she is pimped out and raped, and her ex takes custody of their child. The climactic showdown at the end of the film is, ultimately, a lethal custody battle in which Bill manipulates Beatrix's emotions, using their daughter BB as a pawn and assaulting Beatrix with recriminations about their past relationship. The story ends with Beatrix attaining her original goal: eliminating Bill from her life in order to raise her child in a healthy environment. As it turns out, this means she literally breaks Bill's heart and parents BB as a single mother.

Significantly, Beatrix overcomes problems frequently faced by women by using a conflict resolution strategy typically associated with men: violence and cunning rather than negotiation or conciliation. Early in the film, in conversation with Vernita Green (Vivica A. Fox), she explicitly undermines the expectation that she will operate according to traditional norms of femininity (in which women are assumed to be passive and emotional, whereas men are active and rational) when she says: 'It is mercy, compassion and forgiveness I lack, not rationality.'

Like the mythical martial arts action heroines who also champion justice at great personal cost using qualities considered to be 'masculine', Beatrix triumphs over all opponents and obstacles in a fair fight, but she cannot find social acceptance in a patriarchal world and must, in the end, face exile. In *Kill Bill* this exile takes the form of driving off into the distance with her daughter, but otherwise alone, independent and without a partner, a support network, a home or a job.

POSTMODERN CHARACTERISTICS OF SCREEN CULTURE

First used in literary criticism in ways that resisted notions of fixed narrative meanings and rejected elitist distinctions between high culture and popular culture, postmodernism expresses a loss of faith in the ideals and the cultural and industrial practices of modernism, an aesthetic movement prevalent in the first half of the twentieth century (Waugh 1992: 1–3). Postmodernism describes a way of structuring and representing social experience in an era of globalised capitalism and technological development. As a theory of socio-economic change associated with the destabilisation of aesthetic and textual conventions of representation since the 1960s, **postmodernism** is ideally suited to an analysis of genre hybridity, but it is not appropriate for divining a text's deep themes and meanings. Postmodern texts 'invite attention to their own superficiality and, in turn, to their own engagement with codes of excess and transgression' (Coulthard 2007: 169), and *Kill Bill* has been described as having a surplus of style over substance. Tarantino himself speaks of it as: 'The ultimate movie-movie: A movie where characters have garden hoses for veins... It's not about being realistic, it's about being theatrical, operatic. You know it's not real. It couldn't more obviously be a movie' (Tarantino cited in Olson 2003).

The tendency to privilege spectacle over realism, and to play with ironic and intertextual references within a fragmented plot rather than focusing on the meaning of the narrative or the moral of the story, is typical of postmodern media texts. Todd Gitlin writes that postmodernism is 'not just a style but a general orientation, a way of apprehending and experiencing the world and our place, or placelessness, in it' (1998: 60). As such, postmodernism is also closely associated with the global or transnational quality identified above as an important aspect of contemporary screen culture.

> **Postmodernism** refers to an ambiguous contemporary attitude and the style of cultural texts produced in the era of postmodernity—that is, the socio-historical period after modernism dating from around the 1960s onwards and described as an advanced stage of multinational capitalism. Postmodernism is characterised by fragmentation, style and surface, intertextuality and hybridity, the parodic or ironic subversion of categories and hierarchies, and the nihilistic erosion of assumed truths, meanings and unifying narratives. Postmodern theory critiques or destabilises modernist ideals of reason, progress, science, reality and subjectivity.

Six characteristics of postmodernism that are relevant to the analysis of screen texts are identified below, and their applicability to *Kill Bill* is illustrated:

1. ***Spectacle, simulation, superficiality and image-saturation:***
   The society of spectacle is 'a society (modern capitalism) in which direct experiences are replaced with represented experiences' (Elsaesser & Buckland 2002: 167). Knowledge is increasingly based on representations rather than direct experience. This means that matters of central cultural value tend to be those that can be

captured and conveyed in a succinct sound-byte or represented in images. Contemporary media therefore privilege vivid images and the transmission of information in a simplistic and spectacular manner over the articulation of complex, abstract values and ideas. This leads to an over-investment of value in image, surface and superficiality. Significantly, the fetishisation of image supports consumerism and capitalism as media texts convince us that we can purchase a style or image that will make us happier.

2. ***Dissolution of traditional boundaries:*** The breach of boundaries includes gender-bending, generic hybridity, consumer and producer interactivity, the lack of distinction between elite and popular culture, and various ways of making fun of conventions. According to Simerka and Weimer, 'the "contamination of genres," including juxtapositions of elite and popular filmic genres, is a common aspect of postmodern film' (2005: 6). This is evident in *Kill Bill*, along with a blurring of distinctions between the narrative structures associated with video games, television and cinema.

3. ***Intertextual referentiality,*** **pastiche,** *parody and irony:* Postmodern texts constantly and self-consciously reference and appropriate other aspects of pop-culture. *Kill Bill* is rife with intertextual references. One of the most prominent is Beatrix's costume, which is based on the iconic yellow tracksuit worn by Bruce Lee in *Game of Death*, the movie he was filming when he died in 1973 (see Figures 11.5 and 11.6). This costume is central to establishing her character as a great warrior in the martial arts tradition, by association with Lee. Further, the Kato mask worn by Lee in the 1960s TV series *The Green Hornet* is the same mask worn by the Crazy 88s (the theme song of the TV series also features on the soundtrack and plays when Beatrix arrives in Tokyo). Even the Pussy Wagon is inspired by the lyrics of a song in another film: the musical *Grease*.

> **Pastiche**, like parody, is a form of mimicry and appropriation, but it lacks parody's satirical meaning or political purpose.

4. ***Celebration of artificiality:*** Postmodern media texts expose the cinematic and televisual apparatus, questioning the status of truth and reality. The animation sequence in *Kill Bill* foregrounds the postmodern premise that reality is a construct. *Kill*

Bill's characters live in a 'virtual' world based on the movies they would have watched if they were real people. In other words, the film is not referencing a real world. The cultural theorist Jean Baudrillard might describe *Kill Bill* as a representation with 'no relation to any reality whatsoever; it is its own pure simulacrum' (Baudrillard 1994: 6).

5. ***Amorality and the waning of affect:*** According to Maja Mikula, 'the rejection of moral responsibility goes hand in hand with the overall abandonment of faith in a "universal truth" motivating moral choices, characteristic of postmodernism'

Figure 11.5 Bruce Lee's yellow tracksuit in *Game of Death* (1973)

Figure 11.6 Uma Thurman as the Bride, wearing Bruce Lee's yellow tracksuit in *Kill Bill*

(Maja 2003: 83). Frederick Jameson writes that the 'waning of affect' is also typical of postmodern culture (Jameson 2001: 557). This occurs through media desensitisation to violence; compassion fatigue from being bombarded with images of suffering; and images that are visually arresting in a superficial or gratuitous way that fails to elicit an emotional response because they are strangely flat, aimless and empty of affect. The criticism that *Kill Bill* is 'all surface no feeling' has certainly been made by reviewers.

6. ***Fragmentation and the lack of a meaningful, unifying narrative:*** Instead of a master narrative, postmodern texts and technologies such as television, digital games and the internet feature disjointed narrative structures that refuse closure, non-linear plot development, fragmentation and open endings. For instance, *Kill Bill* is open to a sequel in which Sofie Fatale (played by Julie Dreyfus) is to raise Vernita Green's daughter Nikki, who is slated to star in the sequel, fighting it out with BB to avenge her mother's death. *Kill Bill's* narrative, like an increasing number of popular films, is also organised into achronological chapters, fragmenting the causal sequence, employing interwoven storylines and utilising an episodic, cliffhanger structure typical of TV serials. The cliffhanger technique is evident when the Bride is about to receive a bullet to her brain. She gasps: 'Bill, it's your baby...' whereas the closing line of *Volume One* is 'Does she know her daughter is alive?' Later we leave Beatrix trapped in a coffin and move into a flashback training sequence with Pai Mei. In this sense, *Kill Bill* is formally similar to a TV serial because it is episodic and fragmented into chapters with multiple storylines and characters rather than a single hero and villain. *Kill Bill's* postmodern fragmentation and televisual quality are further enhanced by the impression of 'channel hopping' that arises from abrupt shifts between chapters and genres, the heavy reliance on dialogue in *Volume Two*, and by references to television programs such as *Kung Fu*, *The Green Hornet* and *Charlie's Angels*. As elaborated below, the narrative structure of *Kill Bill* can also be understood to follow what Thomas Elsaesser and Warren Buckland call 'video game logic' (2002). This is particularly evident in the way the disordered chapter structure is arranged, moving from the easiest task or level to the most difficult challenge.

Video game logic

A critical understanding of a new type of text or medium requires 'an evaluation of the type of subject it encourages, while a viable articulation of postmodernity must include an elaboration of its relation to new technologies of communication' (Poster 2001: 609). As such, an evaluation of a text such as *Kill Bill* requires some analysis of the new media texts and technologies which have made a mark on the film and which have, therefore, influenced how audiences engage with the film.

The term 'video game' can be used to refer to arcade games, digital games played on console platforms, or computer games played online or offline via personal computers. In the world of video games, 'play occupies a zone known to be one of make-believe or unreality' (King & Krzywinska 2006: 19); however, video games have given rise to considerable moral panic due to their interactive, participatory nature and subsequent fears about the nature of their interface with reality. Unlike a film, where the spectator witnesses a character enacting violence, in a game the player *participates* in the violence. This distinction between identification and participation is a significant difference between the consumption of these two types of media text. Here, we are not interested in the audience's participation in *Kill Bill* (all texts involve a degree of interactivity in the form of interpretation, but unlike game players audience members can not alter the course of the narrative). Instead, we focus on the ways in which the narrative structure and content of *Kill Bill* has similarities with the structure and content of action oriented video games, several of which are also films or television programs featuring postfeminist heroines (*Lara Croft: Tomb Raider*, *Alias* and *Buffy the Vampire Slayer*).

According to Elsaesser and Buckland, video games are characterised by the following: serialised repetition of actions; multiple levels of adventure accessed at an accelerating pace; space–time warps that function like hyperlinks transporting characters to another level of gameplay; immediate rewards and punishment whereby unsuccessful characters are eliminated; magical transformations and disguises; and last but not least, interactivity (2002: 162). In addition, violence is frequently used as a problem-solving device and is therefore a key skill or action to be performed or mastered by players. While *Kill Bill* does not require the interactive gameplay, and while the use of 'magic' and disguise is limited to the five-point palm exploding heart technique and the duplicitous Elle Driver's brief masquerade as a nurse, *Kill Bill* does exhibit many characteristics typical of violent action genre video games. As prefigured above, the film is organised according to 'video game logic' in that the easiest targets on Beatrix's hit list are taken out first. Beatrix progresses from Vernita Green, who she kills with relative ease, to Bill himself, the master assassin.

Many action games emphasise developing fighting skills, and contrast the different fighting styles of avatars (game characters). New weapons become available when the player develops new skills or 'powers up' (King & Krzywinska 2006: 12–14). *Kill Bill* follows a similar pattern of narrative interruption geared to enhance combat. For instance, Beatrix acquires her Hanzo sword which enables her to kill O-Ren, then develops the necessary kung-fu techniques with Pai Mei in order to kill Bud (Michael Madsen), and eventually Bill.

Kill Bill has been criticised for lacking narrative and character development, and in this sense it also exhibits a similarity to action video games. Games have less need for character development or back-story because 'the central character tends to become 'our complete surrogate ego', David Joiner suggests, with little or no intrinsic personality of its own' (in King & Krzywinska 2006: 41). *Kill Bill* literally unfolds more like a disordered list than a narrative causal sequence, which is similar to the tendency for video games to establish the main character's motivation, goals, back-story and tasks at the outset by means of cut-scenes that offer a thin framing narrative, and then plunge into a series of action-tasks with increasing levels of difficulty.

Of course, there are many other types of games besides violent action games, but this genre is most applicable to an analysis of *Kill Bill*. However stereotypical it may be, games that address women and girls as the target market tend to involve more role-playing, narrative, character development and emphasis on appearance (King & Krzywinska 2006: 209). For instance, in contrast with a first-person shooter like *Doom* that simulates military training, engaging players in hand-to-hand combat and free-for-all slaughter with weapons like the BFG9000 (an acronym for 'Big Fucking Gun' in the words of The Rock), a game like *The Sims* interpellates the player into consumer capitalist ideology by immersing them in the activity of developing families of avatars and nurturing their relationships and careers, while building and furnishing their homes.

Animation

Anime, with its close relation to the video game aesthetic and a shared preoccupation with hyper-sexualised violence and technology, is another component of *Kill Bill*'s generic hybridity and a significant influence on contemporary screen culture more generally. American cartoons originate from comic strips, whereas Japanese animation (widely called *anime*, although the term actually refers to all animation) originates in graphic novels called *manga*, which means 'irresponsible pictures'. The iconography of *anime* texts includes the informationalised cityscape: urban, industrialised settings with a bleak feeling of alienation, and the dominance of technology. Common themes in *anime* film and television texts, video games and *manga* include sex and violence, and a preoccupation with technology, identity and subjectivity evident in the ubiquitous android and cyborg characters. Animation is often concerned with filming the unfilmable and speaking the unspeakable: breaking taboos, exploring identity, and doubting aspects of reality that are taken for granted in many live action genres. The apocalyptic themes recurrent in *anime* reflect the trauma of Japan's past, anxiety about the future, and 'disenchantment with the values and goals that much of postwar Japan has been built on' (Napier 2005: 29). Typical animation techniques and motifs include 'squash and stretch' sequences, metamorphosis and dismemberment, paired with improbable sound effects that enhance the impossible contortions.

Many *anime* features such as *Ghost in the Shell* explore the themes of gender, age and power that are clearly evident in the animated sequence detailing O-Ren Ishii's back-story in *Kill Bill*. Frequently in *anime*, animals or child protagonists represent the hope for the future. The term *shōjo* refers to a young girl, often the protagonist of *anime* texts. As illustrated in Figure 11.7, O-Ren Ishii embodies the *shōjo* poised on the cusp of womanhood and empowerment as the *anime* sequence depicts her at a time in her life when she takes control of her destiny, kills Boss Matsumoto for having her parents murdered, and later proves herself in the criminal underworld of Tokyo. *Kawaii* is a

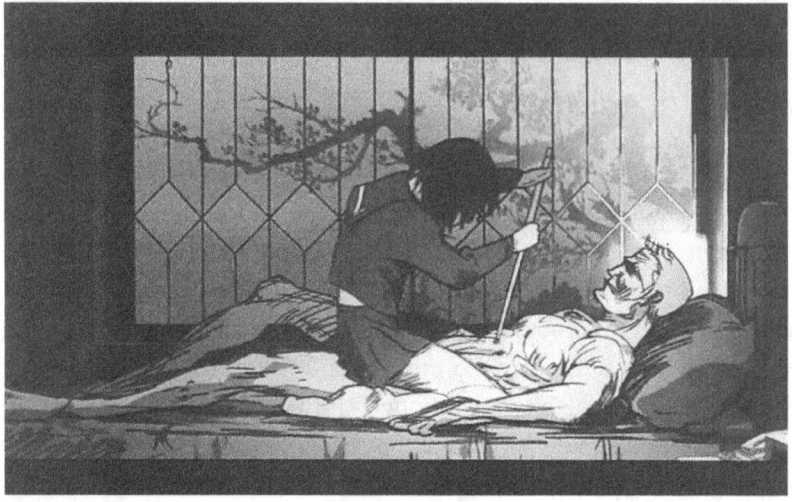

Figure 11.7 Dressed as a schoolgirl, O-Ren seduces and kills the pedophile, Boss Matsumoto

term for the cult of cuteness, epitomised in the *anime* image of the big-eyed Japanese schoolgirl with her hair in pigtails and a Hello Kitty bag slung over her shoulder. Gogo (played by Chiaki Kuriyama) in *Kill Bill* is an ironic reworking of this popular cultural type, which is in itself a parodic exaggeration of gender norms in a patriarchal society. Many contemporary Japanese films, from *anime* through horror, explore gender tensions as men gradually lose patriarchal dominance: 'In the animated space female characters seem to glory in manifestations of power still denied them in the real world' (Napier 2005: 31).

Anime style is sometimes termed 'limited animation', as it involves the use of pans and zooms to simulate motion, rather than drawing motion in each frame. Limited animation is also characterised by static poses, an emotional focus, economy and suggestion. For instance in *Kill Bill*'s *anime* sequence the characters often appear to float through space or remain poised for action while the camera itself zooms, pans or tilts to suggest movement—as when the assassin holds his pose while we tilt slowly up the sword blade embedded in O-Ren's father until, finally, we are able to see the perpetrator gripping the sword (see Figure 11.3 above).

Susan Napier describes *anime*'s ideological work as follows:

> Much of the best anime resists any attempt at 'ideological containment' and, given the dark tone of many of its most

memorable texts, could well be considered a cinema of 'de-assurance' rather than 'reassurance', which film scholar Robin Wood asserts is the dominant tone of most Hollywood films. Even in its less overtly apocalyptic mode, anime tends toward open ended, often tragic story lines, which sometimes include the death of the hero(es), and they are often told within a narrative framework that is deeply critical of contemporary technology and society. (2005: 33)

One of the most important aspects of *anime* as an art form with global appeal is that it 'celebrates difference and transcends it, creating a new kind of artistic space that remains informed and enriched by modes of representation that are both culturally traditional and representative of the universal power of the human imagination' (Napier 2005: 34).

GLOBALISATION AND SCREEN CULTURE

In the Hollywood blockbuster *Kill Bill*, the adoption of the *anime* aesthetic along with other influences from Asian cinema, and characters like the multi-ethnic Chinese-Japanese-American O-Ren and the homeless American Bride who uses Asian martial arts to vanquish her far-flung opponents, is symptomatic of how globalisation is affecting both personal identity and screen culture. Historically, globalisation has been shaped by economic, political and military interests and technological innovation since the beginnings of international trade in the fifteenth and sixteenth centuries, through colonisation and industrialisation in the seventeenth and eighteenth centuries, to the formation of global communication networks in the nineteenth century. The twentieth century was a time of explosive technological development in the media and communication industries, and each development has led to increasing levels of global interrelatedness. Media globalisation is broadly characterised by the following features:

- *Instantaneity:* A sense of immediacy is produced by communication and transport technologies that collapse time and space.
- *Interactivity:* Interactive digital technology diminishes the distinction between media producers and consumers,

empowering consumers to participate in textual manipulation and production.
- ***Interconnectedness and interdependence:*** Communication technologies render 'co-presence' unnecessary, enabling new communities to form independently of geographic proximity. In economic and political terms, different regions of the globe are increasingly interrelated and interdependent.
- ***Convergence and conglomeration:*** Media industries are characterised by mergers, acquisitions and the concentration of control in the hands of a few powerful transnational companies. At the same time, new media technologies are developing and distribution platforms are converging as texts proliferate via satellite, cable, video and digital transmission.
- ***Asymmetric flow of media products:*** The United States remains the main exporter of media products, raising fears about **cultural imperialism**.
- ***Inequalities of access:*** The term '**digital divide**' is used to express the idea that globalisation benefits those with technology, education and money, and that a lack of access to digital technologies widens the gap between the wealthy and the impoverished.

Cultural imperialism is a form of transnational corporate cultural domination in which values and ideas are disseminated culturally, through media and commodities rather than through military invasion or economic trading. The concern is that the globalisation of communication will result in cultural homogenisation and the destruction of traditional cultures through the intrusion of Western values.

Digital divide is a term referring to a form of 'information poverty', describing the economic division between people who have access to new media texts, technologies and skills, and those who do not. There is a digital divide between developed and developing nations, but the gap also exists within nations based on age, gender, race, ability and urban or rural locations.

These features of globalisation affect the ways in which screen media texts are produced and consumed, and raise important questions about who benefits from the patterns of globalisation that contemporary screen texts embody.

As the preceding analysis indicates, *Kill Bill* incorporates—or, more problematically, appropriates—Eastern and Western cinematic traditions, character types and settings. The film draws on screen conventions from Asian cinema and is ostensibly set in Japan, China, Mexico and North America. In her travels, Beatrix encounters a whole range of wittily deployed cultural stereotypes: her wise but cranky *sifu* Pai Mei who hates Americans; O-Ren Ishii who kills people for disrespecting her mixed heritage; Hattori Hanzo, who enthusiastically congratulates her on her amateur Japanese; and Esteban Vihaio (Michael Parks), the Mexican pimp who indiscriminately deploys his Latin *suavé* in the disfigurement of prostitutes who displease him whilst attempting to charm Bill's vengeful ex. The 'inbreeding' and cross-referencing of different martial arts films also contributes to the complex discourse of globalisation that pervades *Kill Bill*. Even Tarantino's use of a Moriccone spaghetti Western score during the showdown between O-Ren and Beatrix in the Japanese snow garden delocalises the space, creating a scene that is neither Eastern nor Western.

While it may seem that *Kill Bill* is a product of the globalisation of communication that characterises the new millennium, the Chinese and Japanese swordplay films and the Hong Kong martial arts movies from which Tarantino drew inspiration are, and always have been, transnational generic hybrids. Indeed, as Steven Teo writes:

> In the 1920s *wuxia* imbibed influences from the medieval European romance, the Hollywood swashbuckler, the western, and the European detective mystery à la the Méliès serials; in the 1960s, there were obvious influences from the sword-and-sandal epic, James Bond spy thriller, Italian spaghetti westerns, and Japanese *chanbara*. The absorption of all these influences is a sign of the transnationalism of the Chinese cinema; but it is just as important to note that the Chinese cinema had digested and remade foreign influences into a veritable indigenous form that accommodated the tastes and demands of a disasporic audience. (2005: 192)

Like other martial arts movies, the *wuxia* film has truly become a global genre, even though it has a distinctively Chinese flavour. This is in part due to the fact that such films address a diasporic audience, given that globalisation has produced highly mobile populations and widespread immigration, guaranteeing that millions of individuals reside outside of their nation of origin. Globalised postmodernism represents deracialised, denationalised identities, and economic production processes and imperatives in which 'narrative conventions of film genres are reconstructed to take account of a new global entertainment economy. This tendency allows for instant commodification of a foreign culture, where foreknowledge of such culture is not taken for granted' (Teo 2005: 198). In this process, the 'indigenous' qualities of screen media texts are translated and made 'more presentable' to a global audience (Teo 2005: 200).

The Japanese term *mukokuseki*, which means to be stateless or without a national or distinctively ethnic identity (Napier 2005: 24), can increasingly be used to describe both Asian cinema and transnational audiences. Discussing the international popularity of Asian cinema, which includes but is not restricted to *anime*, Susan Napier writes of a new mode of hybridity appealing to a global youth culture that is increasingly familiar with international popular culture:

> Contrary to Homi Bhabha's vision of 'hybridity' in terms of a colonial (or postcolonial) exercise of power and discrimination, this vision of hybridity is an equalizing one. Safe within the stateless fantasy space that *anime* provides, both Japanese and non-Japanese can participate in trying on a variety of what might be called 'postethnic' identities ... an appeal that goes beyond the constraints of any particular culture. (2005: 26)

Like Japanese *anime*, kick-flicks do have significant cross-cultural appeal, and have developed a fanatical fan base throughout Asia and beyond, largely catalysed by martial arts film stars. In a manner emblematic of postmodernism, Hong Kong films are marked by what Bordwell (2000) calls a 'scavenger aesthetic' that borrows from many different sources, incorporating elements from Hollywood and other film cultures as avidly as Hollywood appropriates Asian and European cinema. The enduring celebrity currency of both Bruce Lee and Jackie Chan has been central to popularising Hong Kong cinema and martial arts film in much the same way that Gordon Liu, Sonny Chiba and David Caradine's status as established martial arts movie masters functioned as a drawcard for *Kill Bill*. In each instance, the stars and the characters they play are texts that articulate the tensions and potential of globalisation. Perhaps the best example of this is to be found in television advertising, where both Lee and Chan's star personae and cultural identities as Hong Kong action heroes have been commodified and used to sell products as diverse as candy bars and Visa cards. Unlike Lee's fierce nationalism, typically exhibited in his conflicts with villainous 'white devils' and evil Japanese imperialists, Chan is emblematic of multiculturalism (Yuan Shu 2003). In Chan's Visa ad, he deploys his trademark martial arts acrobatics to comically catapult around the world, giving viewers the message that Visa is accepted everywhere, and so is Jackie Chan.

The Hong Kong film industry has been profoundly influential, producing a distinctive action aesthetic along with world-renowned directors and international stars. Hong Kong cinema's first generation of directors and stars came, of course, from mainland China; Hong Kong films have therefore retained strong links to other parts of Asia and have always been created by and marketed to a diasporic audience. The 1960s saw the establishment of the Shaw Brothers Studio (the logo with which Tarantino brands *Kill Bill* as an ironic marker of authenticity). The Shaws achieved record breaking production and attendance, rivalling that of Hollywood. In the 1970s, a competing studio, Golden Harvest, began to make low-budget kung-fu action films (many of Jackie Chan's early films are Golden Harvest productions). In the 1980s and 1990s, 'New Wave' directors with a unique aesthetic and higher production values entered the industry, notably John Woo and Wong Kar-Wai. In 1997, Britain ceded the colony to China, following close on the heels of the Asian economic crisis, and the Hong Kong film industry nosedived. Major stars and directors like Jackie Chan and John Woo began courting Hollywood, and Korea began to overtake the Asian film market. Hong Kong cinema's importance cannot be under-estimated, although the industry peaked in the 1960s and 1970s and has been in decline since the Asian economic crash of the 1990s and the transfer of custodianship from Britain to China in 1997. Even so, as Meaghan Morris notes: 'Hong Kong cinema is now a benchmark of achievement, a site of inspiration and cross-cultural borrowing, a model for emulation and a target of rivalry' (2005: 2).

NEW DIRECTIONS IN SCREEN CULTURE

Contemporary screen culture is now characterised by the cross-cultural hybridity and borrowing that made Hong Kong cinema so distinctive. While kick-flicks and *wuxia pian* are good illustrations of the fact that hybridity is not a one-way street, other Asian cinemas and Latin American and Indian film movements and genres also hybridise with American film and borrow from European art cinema. For example, Korea is often described as 'the new Hong Kong', as it is one of the fastest growing film industries and is becoming the dominant source of Asian cinema production, rivalled only by the productivity of Indian popular cinema, particularly the 'Bollywood' industry in Mumbai which is famous for combining Hollywood musicals with melodrama and other genres and giving the resultant hybrid a distinctively local flavour. New directions in screen culture are characterised by two-way global media flows, and Korean film and television exemplify the mutual exchange of genre conventions and influences.

The Korean film and television industry was initially dominated and governed by Japan, and subject to strict state censorship and media regulations. Subsequently, national division and civil war retarded the film industry. Only since the 1990s has Korean cinema finally come into its own due to increased economic stability and more liberal, supportive media policies. A local style of 'new wave' action cinema known as *hwalkuk* has emerged, which bears the traces of the struggle between imperial Japan and colonised Korea in its narrative threads and in the effects of repressive media policy (Soyoung 2005: 100). Korea has also produced distinctive 'K-drama' (Korean drama television series) that are popular amongst Asian audiences, Hong Kong-style kung-fu films such as *Arahan* and *Volcano High*, as well as *The Host*, a creature feature with anti-American sentiment. Korean media frequently capitalises on the popularity of other established Asian styles and genres like J-Horror (Japanese horror cinema) by making spoofs, sequels and spin-offs. For instance, *The Ring Virus* is a Korean companion to Hideo Nakata's *Ringu*, which also spawned a video game (*The Ring: Terror's Realm*), a prequel (*Ring 0*), two sequels (*Rasen* and *Ringu 2*), and American remakes (*The Ring* and *The Ring 2*). These texts engage with the postmodern, transcultural theme of the electronic mediation of culture that has its heritage in the work of Western directors such as David Cronenberg (*Videodrome* and *eXistenZ*). Together with the J-Horror *Kairo* (a.k.a. *Pulse*, originally directed by Kiyoshi Kurosawa and remade in Hollywood on the basis of a Wes Craven screenplay) and the Thai horror film *Shutter*, these films constitute a global genre cycle of media horror, reflecting fears of the swift technological change that marks our times. Given the increasing technological proficiency coupled with innovative young filmmakers, expanding transcultural screen culture and a profitable genre production base, Korean national cinema is an emerging force to contend with in the global film market. Korean filmmakers are increasingly likely to set trends rather than follow them, drawing on multiple genres, influential Asian cinemas and game culture, and creating narratives that problematise and negotiate transnational global identities, thereby challenging accepted norms regarding gender, ethnicity and nationality.

CONCLUSION

We have argued that, while *Kill Bill* can broadly be termed action cinema with a revenge plot, it doesn't fit neatly into any particular film genre or style. Instead, it borrows from many sources and is indebted to a number of influences. As a hybrid text, *Kill Bill* exemplifies the characteristics of postmodernism and signposts the changing norms of representation and characterisation in narrative cinema, while also revealing emerging relationships between cinema, television and video games. We have demonstrated that full appreciation of *Kill Bill*'s significance in terms of the directions in which contemporary screen culture is moving therefore requires an understanding of its rich intertextuality and its identity as a transcultural hybrid.

This chapter has contextualised developments in contemporary film and television in relation to film styles and genres, diasporic audiences, global media flows and the development of Asian film influences. It has outlined the importance of concepts such as postmodernism, postfeminism, globalisation and generic hybridisation in understanding contemporary visual culture, and it has shown how the convergence of television, video games and cinema is leading to new directions in screen media.

KEY SKILLS

Having read this chapter you should now be able to:

- explain the difference between generic hybridisation and other ways of theorising the combination and transformation of genres;
- list key characteristics of postmodernism and discuss how they relate to a contemporary television series;
- discuss the impact of globalisation and postfeminism on contemporary screen culture;
- give examples of the key features and characteristic styles of Japanese *anime*, and Hong Kong martial arts movies;
- compare and contrast the video game aesthetic and narrative structure with those of contemporary action film and television texts;
- apply your understanding by analysing the postmodern characteristics, intertextual references and stylistic influences in a fight sequence from an action film or television series;
- critically evaluate how screen media technologies and techniques such as television and video games are converging under the influence of globalisation in ways that impact on the style and structure of film and television texts.

glossary

Aerial shots mount the camera on a device that can fly or move through the air in any direction.

Ambient sound or atmos (atmospheric sound) is also known as the 'buzz track'. It consists of sound that naturally occurs in the environment of a scene or the location in which the scene is meant to be set.

Anachrony is a narrative structure in which events are presented out of sequence rather than in chronological order.

Analepsis refers to a flashback narrative structure.

Aperture is the size of the adjustable iris opening that allows light into a camera. Aperture is measured in f-stops (the smaller the number, the bigger the opening, and the shallower the focal range or depth of field).

Aspect ratio is the width-to-height ratio of a screen which affects image framing, size and scope. Television and video is typically 1.33:1, which is modelled on the 'academy ratio' of 1.37:1 that was standard in feature films when television was introduced. The contemporary widescreen standard is 1.85:1 for cinema and 1.77:1 for HDTV. Cinerama format and CinemaScope's anamorphic widescreen format has an ultra-wide aspect ratio of 2.35:1.

The **auteur** is a screen text's creative 'author', typically a director attributed with a signature style and distinctive thematic concerns evident across a body of work. Auteur analysis emphasises screen aesthetics and individual style (as elaborated in the director's commentary and extra features of DVDs), but downplays the collaborative nature of screen production and the economic limitations constraining a director's artistic vision. Auteurism assumes a model of communication in which the director puts the meaning into a text and the audience passively accepts it, de-emphasising meaning as a context-specific act of interpretation and negotiation in which the audience participates.

The **axis of action** is an invisible line extending between two points on the screen, such as the start and end points of figure movement or the positions of two characters conversing. The camera can be positioned anywhere within a semi-circular 180 degree arc on *one* side of this line. Crossing the line, or filming from the other side of the axis of action, is called breaking the 180 degree rule because it disrupts continuity of screen direction.

Backlash: In addition to naturalising and incorporating aspects of feminism in popular culture, postfeminism contains elements of what Susan Faludi (1992) terms a 'backlash' against feminism. Anti-feminist backlash media represents feminism and feminists as angry, extremist, difficult, hard, man-hating women who are greedy to 'have it all' (to be professionally and personally successful). This backlash allegedly turned young men and women away from feminism in the 1990s.

The **best boy** is an assistant electrician who helps with film and television lighting.

A **binary opposition** or dualism is where two terms are opposed to each other, so as to construct meaning from their difference. So 'bowl' has no inherent meaning except in its difference from, say, 'plate' or 'saucer'.

Bird's eye refers to an elevated camera position, situated high above a subject, usually looking straight down.

The **boom** is a long pole to which a microphone can be attached. It is used like an extended arm to reach into the action and hold the microphone close enough to record clear sound, while ensuring the crew and equipment remain out of shot.

Canonical story structure, or canonic narrative, is a coherent, consistent format with three acts: introduction, complication and resolution.

CCTV filmmaking appropriates closed circuit surveillance camera footage to create screen narratives. Techniques include '**video sniffing**' which uses inexpensive receivers to scan or 'sniff' wireless transmissions and record the live feed from CCTV cameras, or performing before CCTV cameras then requesting copies of the footage under freedom of information legislation.

A **celebrity** is a celebrated, widely known individual whose private life and public appearances frequently attract media attention.

Chanbara refers to Japanese samurai films involving swordplay, loyalty and honour.

Chromakey is a visual effects technique that involves photographing actors in front of a blue or green screen which can later be substituted for a different background or setting.

Cinematography involves the use of a motion picture camera to record images on celluloid, video tape or a digital format that can subsequently be edited and viewed on a screen.

Classical Hollywood realism uses a cohesive cause and effect narrative structure and naturalistic acting along with unobtrusive cinematography, studio lighting, continuity editing and sound conventions to conceal traces of the technical production process in order to make the story

GLOSSARY

world depicted on screen seem like a natural environment in which time and space extend seamlessly beyond the borders of the frame.

Classical narration refers to the classical style and canonic story structure of Hollywood studio filmmaking from around 1917 to 1960. It is organised around a causal sequence in which the actions of a central, individual protagonist unfurl in space and time, in response to the conflicting actions of an antagonistic force, which impedes the main character's goal. The role of the narrator is concealed in the narrative itself, and the cause–effect sequence and primacy of the individual hero are naturalised.

The **cliffhanger** is an editing strategy that involves cutting the narrative at a suspenseful moment or immediately after offering a teaser about what is coming up next, thereby creating an addictive hook that leaves the audience hanging with unanswered questions lingering in their minds throughout the intervening time. Cliffhangers can be used to build suspense by cutting away from the main action in a film, but the technique is most commonly used to sustain attention in the fragmented texts and interwoven, ongoing storylines of television.

Close-up: a shot in which a person's head and shoulders, or an object or detail of equivalent size, takes up the whole screen. A shot of the human face alone is sometimes called a 'big close-up' or a 'choker close-up', whereas a shot of the head, neck and shoulders is a standard close-up.

Cognitivist approaches to narrative analysis as developed by theorists like Edward Branigan and David Bordwell seek to explain narrative comprehension by analysing how screen texts use aesthetic techniques and formal conventions to cue audiences to construct hypotheses and inferences about the story which are tested and reassessed as the plot unfolds.

The **colour palette** of a screen text is a colour scheme for lighting, décor and costume devised by the production manager to express and chart the shifting moods of characters and scenes over the course of the story.

The **compiled score** is a compilation of popular music that features on a movie soundtrack. Such music can consist of diegetic and non-diegetic songs that have usually had quite a bit of radio exposure independently of the film.

Composite shots use techniques like mattes, superimposition and double exposure to create special effects, usually by masking or blocking out areas of the frame, or filming two aspects of the image (such as the actors and the background) separately, then combining the images in post-production.

Continuity editing refers to a set of editing conventions that create the illusion of continuous time and space in a screen text. Continuity editing is the dominant style of editing in almost all screen texts worldwide.

Contrast refers to the degree of difference between the darkest and lightest areas of an image. High-contrast lighting always shows a distinct difference between light and dark areas, whereas low-contrast images are characterised by mid-tones of light and shade.

Conventions are the ways cues or clues are communicated through the screen text's stylistic system, which uses a language or formula for creating spectatorial expectations and providing interpretive cues using *mise en scène*, cinematography, editing and sound. For example, continuity editing is based on conventions that help the spectator to follow the logic of movement through space and time in the story world.

Convergence can refer to economic integration (business conglomerates and mergers) in the media industries, as well technical developments (like digital photography and editing, and broadband internet) that enable the provision of shared media content across different media formats and transmission systems.

Coverage refers to the number of set-ups (various takes of each shot from different angles and distances, with static or moving camera) that are needed to cut the scene together effectively. Virtually all shoots require coverage of more than one shot scale and angle, and more than one take so the editor has adequate footage from which to choose.

Crane shots enable a wide and sophisticated range of camera movement by mounting the camera on a vehicle with wheels as well as an elevated mechanical arm that can move the camera, up, down or sideways.

Critical analysis: Film and TV essays include evidence of reading and research as well as analysis of screen texts. Essays should have a clear **introduction**, a **thesis statement** and a **conclusion**, and they should argue for your interpretation of the subject and its significance, as well as reviewing and critically evaluating published research in the field to broaden understanding of the subject and substantiate your ideas. Incorporate references to texts and terminology from your course, define key concepts and list works cited, including screen texts, journals, websites or books to which you directly refer, or which you quote or paraphrase.

Crosscutting, also termed parallel editing or intercutting, shows the development of two lines of action (either simultaneously occurring in different places, or cutting between past and present or future developments) by alternating a scene from one storyline with a scene from the other.

Cues: The screen text gives the spectator clues that cue or prompt us to develop questions and form expectations. For instance, ominous music cues suspense and indicates that a screen character is facing imminent danger.

Cultural imperialism is a form of transnational corporate cultural domination in which values and ideas are disseminated culturally, through media and commodities rather than through military invasion or economic trading. The concern is that the globalisation of communication will result in cultural homogenisation and the destruction of traditional cultures through the intrusion of Western values.

GLOSSARY

A **cultural studies** approach investigates how texts communicate ideological messages about class, gender and consumerism through advertising strategies, modes of address, narrative resolution and reception practices, considering how media technologies and media industries and institutions inflect meaning and interpretation. Cultural studies makes sense of texts in the context of their production and consumption.

The term **cut** is used in filmmaking to signify the end of a shot or a take (on set) or the edit point (in post-production), and it can also refer metonymically to a complete edited sequence or story (as in the 'director's cut'). Note that one shot or one take on set may actually be cut up into several different shots in the editing process.

Cutaways involve cutting away from the main action to an image that relates to the scene being shot or screened. Cutaways provide extra information and connect together two parts of a scene that might otherwise not cut together smoothly.

Depth of field refers to the range of distances in front of the camera lens in which an image is in focus. If a lens has a limited depth of field (e.g. a telephoto lens), objects in the foreground and background may be blurred when a narrow area of the middle ground is in focus.

Dialectical synthesis means that there is a collision or tension between two opposing forces (caused by the juxtaposition of two different shots, or two opposing terms or viewpoints), which is resolved when the interpreter synthesises the two, actively thinking through the relationship between them to produce a new meaning.

The **diegesis** is the fictional reality of the story world, including places, sights, sounds and events that occur within it which are accessible to the characters.

Diegetic sound emanates from the diegesis, which means that its source is in the story world and it is audible to screen characters.

Digital divide is a term referring to a form of 'information poverty', describing the economic division between people who have access to new media texts, technologies and skills, and those who do not. There is a digital divide between developed and developing nations, but the gap also exists within nations based on age, gender, race, ability and urban or rural locations.

Direct address is where a person looks straight into the lens of the camera.

Direct cinema is a mode of documentary that was prevalent in America in the 1950s and 1960s. It capitalised on the ability of lightweight audio-visual equipment to follow and observe everyday people and events with as little participation or intervention by the filmmakers as possible. Direct cinema used a slow paced fly-on-the-wall approach without voiceover, interviews, music, special lighting or staged action.

The **director of photography** (also called the DP or the cinematographer) is the head of the photography department, responsible for designing and organising camerawork and lighting, as per the director's vision.

Disintegrative montage is an editing technique used predominantly in action sequences. It simulates the frenzy of a fight by breaking spatio-temporal continuity conventions in a rapid volley of brief shots taken from a crazy, 'unrealistic' mixture of camera positions.

Dissolves are transitions in which one shot replaces another through a process of superimposition.

Dogs (digital onscreen graphics) or bugs often take the form of station logos or other information added at the bottom of the frame during post-production. Such graphics can brand television programs and the networks on which they are screened, prevent piracy, advertise the next program, or offer viewers extra information.

Dog's eye level shots are filmed with the camera positioned at a low level, near the floor, showing the action unfold from an eye level similar to that of a dog.

A **dolly** is a camera mount with a wheeled base, enabling smooth, quiet camera movement.

Dominant ideology refers to a world-view characteristic of the ruling class or dominant group in society, and entails conformity to existing value systems and social relations which naturalise and legitimate the distribution of power and wealth. The 'ruling ideas' support the interests of the most powerful group in society—that is, those who control the economic and material interests and the means of production.

Editing is the final process of determining the order in which events unfold on the screen and what information is revealed to the audience. It involves decisions about what to include, what to discard, and how to join individual shots to create sequences, scenes, stories, affect and associations. It is also a process of structuring the text, usually using continuity conventions to enable the audience to navigate through the space of the story world and follow the temporal and causal sequence of events.

Ellipsis means the omission or suppression of information, which creates a gap in the story. Events can be edited out for the sake of narrative compression, or to delay revealing information and create surprise later in the story.

Epistemology is a branch of philosophical inquiry relevant to the study of realist screen texts in that it examines knowledge, explores conceptions of reality and truth, and questions how we know what we know.

Establishing shots 'set the scene' by showing the location of a new scene in a long shot that enables the audience to recognise the space and the location of figures within it.

Ethnographic approaches to audience research offer a qualitative, detailed study of actual personal viewing behaviour via participant observation and interviews.

Exposure is the amount of light entering the camera through the aperture. **Over-exposed** images are too bright and light, while **under-exposed** images are dim and dark.

The **extra-diegetic** world refers to actions, spaces and events outside the story world and includes the reception context in which the audience is located and information like subtitles, credits and the musical score of which only the audience is aware (see also diegetic and non-diegetic sound).

Extras are members of the cast who do not have a speaking part or a prominent individual role and whose presence on screen serves to give the story world an authentic 'lived-in' feel.

Extra-textual refers to something that is 'outside' the text, such as a film's publicity or an actor's celebrity, but that nevertheless plays a part in how we read that text. So we might watch *Mr and Mrs Smith* closely not for its action-packed storyline, but to try to look for evidence—as gossip magazines asserted at the time—that co-stars Brad Pitt and Angelina Jolie began their relationship during the making of this film.

Extreme close-up: a shot scale that shows a very small detail, like a person's eyes filling the frame.

Extreme long shot: a shot scale using very distant, wide framing to display setting and landscape, rather than figure expression or movement.

Eye level refers to a camera position that matches the eye level of the cinematographer with the eye level of the character being filmed.

An **eyeline match** is a point-of-view editing technique that follows a shot of a character looking off screen at something, with a shot of the object at which they are looking.

Fades are shot transitions in which the picture slowly fades in or out until the screen is entirely one colour, usually black or white.

Fantastic narratives are characterised by a departure from the rules governing everyday reality, and the uncertainty of familiar boundaries and categories. They often feature elliptical, cyclical, fragmented narrative structures that lack resolution and open spaces for the imagination, shaping the way spectators inhabit the story. Common themes include doppelgangers, the transformation of time and space, and moments when reality is called into question.

Fidelity is to sound what verisimilitude is to image: the term refers to the degree of realism or similarity that a recorded sound has when compared with its source.

Film stock refers to the physical properties of a strip of celluloid, including whether it is colour or black and white, its dimensions, and how sensitive to light it is.

The **fine cut**, also termed the final cut, is the finished product of the last phase of editing when the text takes the form that audiences see and hear on screen.

The **first act** of a narrative (termed **Act One,** the **Exposition,** or the **Orientation**) sets up the story, introducing characters and locations. In the beginning there is a state of equilibrium or balance. Even if it is a state of upheaval, it is how the characters live when we are introduced to them. Then an inciting incident or catalyst occurs. This is any event that disturbs the balance and causes action, conflict, drama or change, forcing the protagonist into action. Suddenly they stand to lose something, and they have something to gain. Now the protagonist has a goal: to establish a new equilibrium. They need a plan to achieve that goal, defining their course of action.

First-wave feminism: the first organised feminist movement emerged in the 1850s. Early feminists were concerned with legal equity and women's role as citizens in the public sphere, including suffrage (voting rights), education, employment and property ownership.

Fish eye lenses are extreme wide angle lenses (with a focal length of 8 mm and below), creating a warped fishbowl effect that bulges the image.

Flashbacks, often cued by a dissolve, manipulate the temporal order of a narrative by cutting back in time to show a memory or an event that occurred at an earlier point in the story.

Flash-forwards manipulate the temporal order of a narrative by jumping forward in time to show a premonition or an event that occurs at a future point in the story's chronology.

Flow relates to the carefully constructed schedule, a sequence of events designed to keep viewers sitting in front of the TV as they move from news through family viewing to late-night movies. The experience of viewing TV is not one of consuming discrete products (commercials, news, fiction of various genres), but rather a unified act of media consumption: watching television.

Focal length is the distance from the centre of a lens to the point where the light rays converge to focus the image on the film stock, video tape or digital light sensor.

Forced perspective is a technique used in set design to manipulate the size of elements in the foreground and background of the set in order to create an illusion of depth, distance or distorted spatial relations.

Formalist approaches to narrative analysis, as influenced by the aesthetic theories of the Russian Formalists (1915–30) and developed by David Bordwell from the 1980s on, seek to reveal how stylistic techniques such as montage or visual composition interact with plot structures such as parallelism and retardation to express cultural associations, meanings, motivations and relationships through a dynamic formal system of signs and conventions.

Fragmentation refers to the segmentation and discontinuity that characterise television texts, and television as a media form. Each program is fragmented by commercials, and narratives tend to lack closure (they take serial or episodic form and play out over a number of nights or weeks).

Fragmented narratives lack the unified, linear storyline of conventional narratives and undermine audience expectations. Rather than being motivated by and focused on an individual protagonist or a central narrative question, they are often decentred and broken up into jumbled segments featuring an array of characters in different places or non-sequential timeframes.

GLOSSARY

A **frame** is a single complete photograph, one still image out of a series projected in sequence to give the illusion of motion.

The **frame line** (also called the 'edge of frame') is the line defining the borders of the frame in the camera viewfinder that corresponds to the borders of the image on the cinema or television screen, separating what is visible from what is out of shot or off screen.

Frame rate refers to the number of frames screened per second to create the illusion of fluid motion. Frame rates differ for different media: film has a normal rate of 24 frames per second (fps), the Australian industry standard PAL video is 25 fps and the North American standard NTSC is 30 fps, whereas HDTV can range from 25–60 fps.

Freeze frames are moments when the motion picture appears to freeze into a still photograph. A single frame is printed repeatedly to achieve this effect.

The **gaffer** is the head electrician for a film or television production who is responsible for lighting. The term 'gaffer' means electrician and derives from the use of electrical tape called gaffer tape or duct tape for gaffing down electrical cables and cords so nobody trips over them when moving about a set or location.

The **gauge** of film stock refers to the width of the film strip in millimetres, which affects the definition and quality of the image. Video tape also comes in different gauges, but in addition the video image itself is made up of hundreds of horizontal lines of picture information which also affects the perceived quality of the image when it is screened.

Genre inbreeding refers to the combination of two or more genres that share family resemblances or are from related film cultures.

Genre evolution is a way of understanding how genres combine and transform over time in response to social change, new technologies and shifting market forces that enable new genres to out-compete older genres.

Genre mutation is a metaphor that implies radical change as new variants of genres spontaneously supersede an original, pure genre.

Graphic matches join two shots together using similar colours or shapes to establish a visual relationship that bridges the two shots.

Grips are production crew members who work with the photography unit, helping to move and set up equipment.

Hammocking is an approach to television scheduling that brackets a show with weak ratings in between two very popular shows, in the hope that viewers will stay tuned to the same channel and form a liking for the weaker show while they wait for their favourite to come on.

Handheld camera is a mobile framing technique in which the cinematographer carries the camera instead of using a tripod, producing a wide range of movements with a jerky look.

Hard light originates from an intense source and casts dark, sharp-edged shadows.

High-angle shots are those in which the camera is positioned at a higher level than the subject on screen, tilted downwards to view the subject.

High-key illumination employs the three-point lighting system to create a naturalistic effect with graduated shadows and gentle illumination that reveals expression and detail, even in scenes set at night.

The term **hybrid** is drawn from genetics and refers to interbreeding between two separate species that generally results in a sterile offspring (just as a liger results from breeding lions with tigers, or mules are the sterile offspring of horses and donkeys). **Genre hybridity** refers to texts that exhibit the recognisable style, storyline, structure and/or characterisation of two or more established genres.

Hyperdiegesis refers to the representation of an expansive narrative world (a diegesis) that extends beyond what is shown in the text itself at any one time to include rules that govern narrative events, the accumulation of history and detail over multiple episodes in the series, and even the extension of this story world and its characters into fan fiction, artefacts and other media like films, books and video games.

Iconography refers to visual conventions that function symbolically, such as costume or setting. The science fiction genre, for instance, has distinctive iconography, which includes being set in the future (often in space), spaceships, high-tech weaponry and non-human characters.

Identification refers to constructing our identity in relation to a star or celebrity. For film stars, Jackie Stacey argues that identification involves the 'negotiation between self and other' via 'the recognition of similarities and differences' (2006: 253). It is also a negotiation 'between the self and an imaginary self' (Stacey 2006: 254).

Ideology refers to a system of assumptions, beliefs, attitudes, values, practices and images that form a naturalised or 'commonsense' worldview. This belief system can be illusory (as in false consciousness) or characteristic of a particular class or group (as in bourgeois ideology, capitalist ideology or feminist ideology).

Intellectual montage, Eisenstein's most famous contribution to editing, involves juxtaposing shots to create an idea or association that doesn't rely on spatio-temporal continuity or aesthetic harmony.

Interpellation is a term coined by Marxist theorist Louis Althusser, describing the way texts 'hail' or address their intended audiences as though they occupy a certain subject position. Interpellation thus implicitly invites us to occupy the position of, for instance, the role of a consumer, the role of a citizen of a nation, or traditional gender roles.

Intertextual or **intertextuality** refers to instances where one text references one (or more) other text/s, thus setting up a reading relation between the texts.

Ironic hybridisation is a postmodern form of genre hybridity in which texts incorporate the influences of several genres, boldly and self-consciously juxtaposing generic elements and signalling eclectic intertextual references.

GLOSSARY

A **jump cut** is an edit that breaks continuity conventions and violates the 30 degree rule by joining two similar shots of the same subject, cutting out the interval of time or motion that would have connected them and thereby creating a visible jerk on the screen as the image seems to jump inexplicably to the next position.

The **lead**, also known as the hook, is the first sentence of a film review. It is designed to capture attention and entice prospective audience members to find out more about the film.

A **lead-in** is a scheduling strategy in which television producers attempt to build an audience for a series using the established popularity of one show to 'lead in' to the subsequent program. A low-rating series is advertised during a high-rating show, then screened immediately afterwards to take advantage of the established viewership already watching the channel.

A **logline** is a one-line story synopsis, indicating the genre, setting, protagonists and central conflict. Loglines can also be known as the 'cocktail pitch' or '30-second' version of a story. A logline differs from a cut-line, which is the kind of catchy line used for marketing purposes on a movie poster.

Long shot: a shot scale framing the whole human body in the context of their environment.

Low-angle shots film the subject from a position below eye level, tilting the camera upwards.

Low-key illumination relies on a single light source with little or no fill light, producing sharply contrasting areas of hard light and dark shadows.

Marxism, a theoretical approach originating in the 1940s, is the name commonly given to the influential ideas and writings of Karl Marx, Friedrich Engels and their followers. Classical Marxism is founded on the idea that economic relations between workers and employers, sellers and buyers, and the upper and lower classes form the 'base' or foundation of social life, and that culture (along with education, religion, law, communication and politics) forms the 'superstructure' which builds on and reinforces the economic structure. Marx argued that those who control the material wealth and the means of production in society also tend to have control over the belief systems that hold together the social order.

A **masked edit** is a straight cut that is disguised because the view of what we are cutting to is temporarily blocked by an object passing in front of the lens.

A **match on action** joins the beginning of a movement to the continuation of that movement, cutting on action to disguise the edit point and creating the illusion of continuous motion.

Medium close-up: a shot scale framing a person's chest and head.

Medium long shot: a shot scale framing a person from the knees up.

Medium shot: a shot scale framing a person from the middle half of their body, such as from the waist upwards.

Metric montage involves varying shot duration to manipulate pace and rhythm, using shorter shots to build excitement or suspense.

Mise en scène refers to everything that can be seen on the screen, including four key elements: costume, performance, setting and lighting.

Montage is a style of editing that joins together shots which are discontinuous in time and space.

Multiform narratives are variants of 'puzzle plots' featuring fragmented, episodic and multiple storylines. Multiform's distinguishing feature is its interweaving of multiple levels of reality into a multi-strand storyline. Multiform has parallel or alternate realities in one or more narrative strands, often featuring time travel or drawing us into the subjectivity of the protagonist via hallucinations, memories, dreams, psychotic states, movement through different dimensions, or shifts between the past, present and future.

Multi-platforming, which is possible because of digital media convergence and the conglomeration of ownership, involves the recycling of content across a variety of distribution channels and media forms or 'platforms', such as movies, digital games and music. Multi-platforming functions to maximise financial returns on the content development investment by releasing DVDs, soundtrack CDs, books, games and toys, along with the primary text.

In a **multiple camera** shoot, the action is filmed by two or more cameras from different positions simultaneously. This economical style means the shot and the reverse shot, or a long shot and a close up of the same take, can be filmed at once so the set-up doesn't have to be repeated.

Multi-strand narratives feature several different narrative threads, either parallel to one another or interwoven in ways that often require more interpretive effort from the audience. The different stories may also unfold in a fragmented and disordered way in terms of their causal sequences or locations in time and space.

Narcissism, or 'self-love', is from the Greek myth of Narcissus, a boy so beautiful that everyone fell in love with him. When Narcissus rejected Echo's advances, however, he was doomed to fall in love with his own image, and spent the rest of his life captivated by his own reflection. In screen media, narcissistic identification refers to when audiences view stars or celebrities as an idealisation of themselves.

The **narrative question**, or the dramatic question, is the central question organising the story. It keeps the audience interested, and it hinges on fears and desires about the protagonist. The dramatic question is answered in the story's resolution.

Neutral-angle shots position the camera at eye level, without tilting.

Non-diegetic sound such as the musical score emanates from an unspecified source external to the world of the screen narrative and cannot be heard by screen characters.

Non-linear editing is the contemporary mode of editing digital video footage out of order on a computer, enabling the editor to change and recombine shots at any stage.

GLOSSARY

A **normal lens** has a medium focal length (from 35 mm to 50 mm) which corresponds to normal perception without distorting depth or perspective.

Oblique-angle shots tilt the camera to one side so that the horizon line is not level and the world is represented from a skewed perspective.

Off-screen space is the space of the story world that the audience imagines to extend beyond the four sides of the screen, as well as into the background behind the screen and into the foreground, where the camera is located and beyond.

Off-screen time refers to the intervals between scenes when we do not see the characters, but imagine that they continue on with their lives in the story world.

Omniscient shots are filmed from the viewing perspective of an invisible observer, not a character in the narrative.

Pan and scan is a means of copying footage shot in wide screen format and reframing it to fit on a squarer screen, by scanning the image for the most significant information and panning to the left or right to keep it in shot when the edges of the wide image are cropped. The process is much like using a scanner to copy a photograph, but with the added facility of being able to pan over the moving image and position the new frame line over the important part of the action.

Panning is a camera movement that scans screen space along the horizontal plane, moving right or left to give the impression of a head turning, often to follow a moving figure.

Paradocumentary is a realist form alongside or beyond documentary itself that incorporates fact and fiction in fascinating ways. Iranian filmmakers like Kiaostami and Makhmalbaf and Licinio Azevedo's Mozambique films jump the fence between fiction and documentary, using real people to re-enact their own life stories.

Para-social interaction refers to mediated or imaginary interactions and relations with people we do not personally know, such as stars or celebrities.

Pastiche, like parody, is a form of mimicry and appropriation, but it lacks parody's satirical meaning or political purpose.

Pitch refers to whether a sound is high or low.

A **pitch** means a sales pitch, usually involving the delivery of a brief verbal synopsis of what a script is about to prospective producers, broadcasters or investors.

Pixels are picture elements or the points of light that make up a photographic image. The pixel is a measure of the quality or resolution of an image, calculated in terms of the density of pixels in an area.

The **plot** refers to the elements of the narrative that appear on screen, in the order and manner that the audience sees and hears them. The time of the plot is exactly the same as the screening time.

Point of view (POV) refers to the perspective from which the camera is positioned to view the action in a shot. In a POV shot, the camera position is aligned with the viewing position of a character on the screen.

Postfeminism is individualistic rather than a unified movement. Postfeminism can be associated with apolitical, anti-feminist discourse branding earlier feminist activism as essentialist or outmoded; with an era 'after' feminism; or with taking women's empowerment for granted and accepting contemporary gender relations. If deemed part of third-wave feminism, postfeminism indicates a postmodernist, post-colonial or post-structuralist critique of earlier feminist thought. Postfeminism manifests in screen texts with strong heroines who typically combine a feminine appearance with power, choice, agency and consumerism.

Postmodernism refers to an ambiguous contemporary attitude and the style of cultural texts produced in the era of postmodernity—that is, the socio-historical period after modernism dating from around the 1960s onwards and described as an advanced stage of multinational capitalism. Postmodernism is characterised by fragmentation, style and surface, intertextuality and hybridity, the parodic or ironic subversion of categories and hierarchies, and the nihilistic erosion of assumed truths, meanings and unifying narratives. Postmodern theory critiques or destabilises modernist ideals of reason, progress, science, reality and subjectivity.

Prolepsis refers to a flash-forward narrative structure where an occurrence in the future is anticipated in advance or happens earlier than it would in chronological order.

Qualitative research evaluates the meaning and value of texts and audience responses, rather than assuming that we can understand them by quantification and measurement. This mode of research is useful for case studies and in-depth analysis of small groups of texts or viewers.

Quantitative research uses empirical methods to measure and analyse data about screen texts and their audiences. It works with figures like audience demographics, budgets and box office profits, ratings and results of polls and surveys, and statistics about the frequency with which particular types of media content or audience reactions occur. This mode of research is useful for analysing broad patterns, predicting trends or generalising about averages.

Racking focus, pulling focus or shifting focus redirects the audience's attention from an object in the foreground of a shot to an object in the background (or vice versa) by changing what part of the image is clear and what part is out of focus.

Ratings is a quantitative research method that can measure whose television set is tuned to which program, but it can't reveal who is actually paying attention or how viewers make sense of the programs they watch.

Realism refers to the nature and degree of a text's relationship with reality in terms of its subject matter, audience response, and formal and stylistic conventions.

Rhythm refers to the pattern of sound in time: sound can have a fast or slow tempo, it can be predictable or irregular, and it can support or contradict the pace and rhythm of images and editing.

GLOSSARY

Rhythmic editing, or 'editing to the beat', matches shot duration and the timing of each cut to the rhythm of action or sound on screen.

The **rough cut**, also termed the assembly edit, is like a first draft. It is an early phase of the editing process in which the scenes and narrative structure are roughly blocked out in the manner indicated in the script and shot list.

Rushes, also known as 'dailies', refer to the raw footage shot on set each day, before certain takes are discarded or selected and edited into scenes. For film, the rushes are the first prints made from the processed negatives. Video and digital video does not require processing, so the rushes can be viewed immediately.

A **scene** is a section of a film or television text set in one time and shot in one location, edited to form a self-contained dramatic or informative unit.

A **scene breakdown** (sometimes termed a step outline or sequence outline) lists each scene or sequence in a script, describing what happens, and sometimes also stating why the scene is significant, or what its narrative function is.

The **scene line** is a heading typed at the start of every scene in a script. It includes the scene number, states whether the setting is interior or exterior, names the location and specifies the time of day.

Scratch videos are compiled from fragments of film or television texts, cut to a soundtrack, sometimes embellished with inter-titles or voiceover narration to change the meaning of the original text.

The **second act** (or the **development**) of a narrative follows the characters towards their goals. The drama hinges on the audience's emotional engagement: we hope our heroes reach their goals and we fear that they will not. This creates suspense. Obstacles such as confrontations and complications interfere with the character's plan, causing conflict. Obstacles can be caused by characters with opposing goals, environmental factors, inner conflicts like ethical dilemmas and temptations, or by chance. Such factors make protagonists change direction and form new plans to pursue their goals. These 'changes of direction' are called turning points.

Second-wave feminism emerged in the late 1960s and 1970s with identity politics and the civil rights movement. The catch-cry 'the personal is political' expressed a focus on gender inequity in private sphere personal relationships, and the politicisation of childcare, domestic labour, sexuality and media representations. Second-wave feminist film theory focuses on the power relations of the gaze and the representation of women as passive, as victims, as objectified erotic spectacles and as the romantic interest in narratives.

A **segue** is a sonic transition in which one sound morphs or blends into another similar sound. Typically, as the sound segues, we cut or dissolve from an image showing the source of the first sound to one showing the source of the second.

Selective diegetic drop-out is a technique whereby one element of the diegetic soundtrack, such as background noise, is faded out after the scene is set in order to direct attention to dialogue or other important elements.

Self-reflexivity is a mode of representation that consciously reveals the artifice of the text in order to deconstruct our perceptions of screen realities, revealing screen realism as a carefully constructed representational strategy.

Semiotics, also termed semiology, is a method of studying the social meanings of signs, signification and sign systems. Originally based on linguistics, semiotics has since been applied to cultural artefacts and practices such as advertising, art, clothing, architecture and screen texts. Every aspect of a text's style, form, content and conventions can be understood as signifiers carrying meanings and connotations (signified concepts). In screen analysis, the signs we analyse are the cues and conventions that direct the audience's interpretation of the text via connotations and symbolic meanings.

A **sequence** is a series of connected shots that form a semi-autonomous section of the screen text, such as the credit sequence.

Serials have never-ending storylines that lack resolution in a single episode and resist ideological closure.

Series have self-contained episodes in which the central conflicts and problems are resolved, and the viewer is invited to return to see similar issues resolved in a similar way during the next episode.

Shenguai wuxia pian refers to 'sword and sorcery' martial arts cinema with the theme of chivalry, first popularised in Shanghai films from 1928–31 and originating from *tanci* oral narrative traditions with musical accompaniment, *guzhuang baishi pian* historical period costume dramas and *shenguai pian* fantasy films including magic powers, gods and demons (Teo 2005: 191–2).

A **shift tilt lens**, developed from the swing tilt lens used in still photography, has a shallow depth of field and is used to produce areas of the image that are soft or out of focus while maintaining sharpness in another part of the frame. This draws attention to parts of the image that the filmmaker wishes to emphasise. The optical axis of the lens is normally parallel to the film plane. With this lens, it can be tilted to move it from the perpendicular and rotated on its axis, allowing a subject to be isolated within a particular depth of field.

Shooting ratio is the amount of film shot or video recorded compared with the amount used in the final cut. The shooting ratio depends on the medium (film, video or digital video), the budget, the genre, the director's style, and the cast and crew's levels of experience and competence. With a shooting ratio of 15:1, the cinematographer shoots fifteen times more footage than the editor uses, or the director gets what she or he wants in fifteen takes.

GLOSSARY

The **shooting script** combines the shot list with the script, specifying how each element of the action and dialogue in each scene will be filmed.

A **shot** is one uncut continuous recording of film, video or digital footage.

Shot duration means the length of time a shot is held—that is, the seconds, minutes or frames between cuts.

A **shot list** is a detailed breakdown of the type and style of shots required to give adequate coverage of each scene. Prepared in the pre-production process, it lists every shot that is needed to cover the action in each scene of the script, often planning the order in which they will be shot.

Shot-reverse-shot is an editing technique that shows a pair of shots, usually alternating an image with a shot from the reverse camera angle and position, or a reaction shot showing a character's response to the first image.

Shot size or shot scale, such as close-ups or long shots, refers to the relative size of a subject on screen, the distance of the subject from the camera, and the implied distance of the audience from the subject.

Slash stories are a genre of fan fiction that reworks conventional representations of gender and sexuality by inventing 'homo-erotic relations between fictional characters, most often the male partners commonly found in science fiction or action-adventure stories' (Jenkins 2000).

Soft light originates from a low-intensity light source and casts soft-edged, graduated shadows, or produces shadowless, diffuse illumination.

Sonic overlap is a technique that provides continuity over a cut between two images by continuing sound or dialogue over to the next shot or scene *after* the speaker or source ceases to be visible on the screen.

A **sound bridge** is an editing technique that introduces sound from the next scene or shot *before* the image appears on the screen.

Sound effects refer to noise other than dialogue or music. Sound effects like footsteps and background traffic noise typically enhance realism by focusing attention, establishing location, developing atmosphere, and so forth.

Source music is diegetic background music that comes from tangible sources in the story world, such as radios, or songs that are performed by musicians on screen.

The **speed** of film refers to how the film stock responds when exposed to light: fast film is highly photosensitive and can be used when very little light is available, whereas slow film stocks are more suitable for bright conditions.

Speed ramping is when the frame rate or speed at which the action unfolds suddenly slows down or speeds up, thereby making the action appear superhuman.

Spotting involves careful annotations on the film or television script to identify and place the sound effects and music that need to be recorded and added in post-production. For sound mixers and designers, spotting sheets serve a function similar to that of log sheets for an editor.

A **star** is a person who plays a prominent leading role, eclipsing others with their excellence in some widely recognised way. In film, the star is the actor who plays the main protagonist; in sport, the star may be a champion or the captain of a winning team; and in music, a 'pop star' or a 'rock star' is usually the lead singer or performer in a band. However, playing a leading role and excelling in a professional capacity does not guarantee fame and stardom.

A **steadicam** is a contraption that allows the camera to be steady while also giving the freedom of movement permitted with handheld cinematography.

Stock characters are minor characters whose function in the story is limited to, and often determined by, their job and their costume.

The **story** is the entire narrative, in order, from the earliest motivation or causal factor until the final resolution. The time of the story can far exceed the viewing time.

Storyboards are annotated illustrations of a series of shots, made for the purpose of envisioning and planning how a sequence will be filmed and edited.

Straight cuts are standard editing transitions in which one shot is joined unobtrusively to the next.

Structuralism is a type of narrative analysis originating in linguistics that attempts to disclose the deep structural architecture and patterns like binary oppositions beneath the surface features of a text.

A **structuring absence** is the systematic exclusion of particular identities or features of the world from screen media narratives.

Subjective imagery shows what a character sees in their imagination or their mind's eye (such as flashback, fantasy or dream sequences).

Subjective sound, also known as internal diegetic sound, refers to sounds that are heard in a screen character's inner world, such as audible thoughts, memories, dreams and imaginings.

Subsonics are very low-pitched sounds that reverberate beneath the register that is consciously audible to human perception.

Suture is an editing term that means stitch or splice together so that the cutting point between two shots (the seam or scar) is unnoticeable.

Synaesthesia refers to the evocation of intersensory links, where one kind of sensory experience is perceived, expressed or translated in terms of another sensation.

Synchronous sound is sound recorded simultaneously with the image.

A **synopsis** is a brief summary of what happens in a story.

Telecine is process that corrects for difference in frame rate when transferring movies or programs shot on celluloid from film to a format suitable for video or television.

The **telephoto lens**, also known as a long lens, has a long focal length of 75–500 mm which is suitable for close-ups that are filmed from a distance. Telephoto lenses enlarge the subject while narrowing the field of view and flattening the image, making elements in the background and foreground of a shot seem closer than they actually are.

GLOSSARY

Tentpoling is a programming strategy that attempts to retain viewers on a particular channel by propping up two weaker or newer shows with a strong-rating program in the middle. It is also a film production strategy in which profits earned from blockbusters bankroll smaller projects.

The **third act** of a narrative (the **denouement**) includes the climax of a story, which occurs just before the story ends when the protagonist has a major crisis and faces a serious obstacle preventing them from reaching their goal. The climax arises from this crisis. The third act involves revelations, reversals and significant conflict like a showdown, the outcome of which leads to the resolution. The driving tension that has sustained viewer interest is resolved, the narrative question is answered and new balance is reached, leaving the audience with a sense of unity and closure.

Tempo relates to the speed or slowness of sound or music: accelerated tempos can generate anxiety or adrenaline, whereas a slow tempo can be monotonous or relaxing.

Temporal ellipsis is when time passes in the story world that is not shown to elapse on screen.

Third-wave feminism uses postmodernist, post-structuralist and post-colonial theory to critique the universalism and dualism of earlier feminist thought and reflect on contemporary manifestations of patriarchy and feminism. For instance, drawing on post-structuralism's deconstruction of essentialist concepts of race and gender, it critiques the ideological processes by which 'black' and 'white', or 'man' and 'woman', are placed in oppositional categories. Like postmodernism, postfeminism emerges from late capitalist consumer culture and focuses on the performance of identity, superficial images and consumption, as evident in the popularity of makeover films and shows like *Sex and the City*. Incorporating post-colonial critiques of the effects of colonial oppression, postfeminism celebrates pluralism and difference, acknowledging that patriarchy does not have the same effects on all women.

Three-point lighting is a system that balances the main light source (the key light) with fill light to soften shadows and back light to separate foreground from background.

A **tilt** can be used for both static and mobile framing. A static camera can be tilted up, down or at an oblique sideways angle and locked in position on a tripod to shoot from a high, low or oblique angle. As a camera movement, tilting is a vertical motion, surveying up or down.

Timbre is the tonal quality of a sound. It relates to the ways in which a sound resonates in space and is associated with a characteristic colour, texture or feel.

Tonal montage uses editing to give a scene emotional atmosphere or punctuation, and involves choosing shots on the basis of expressive qualities, scale or evocative lighting, using editing to orchestrate the affective tenor of a sequence.

A **tracking shot**, also known as a **travelling shot**, is a mobile framing technique mounting the camera on tracks, wheels or any device that allows it to move through space and follow the action. 'Travelling shot' is the best term if it is not evident how the movement was achieved, or if it is unlikely tracks were used.

Treatments summarise a storyline in prose form, as part of the script development process. A treatment is a condensed description of the central concept, storyline and character developments in a script, written like a thorough story synopsis or a detailed project outline for the purpose of developing ideas and/or conveying the intended narrative and style to prospective financiers or participants in the production.

Two shot: a shot depicting two people together, usually tightly framed in closer proximity to each other than would be comfortable in everyday life.

The **underscore** is non-diegetic music, usually composed specifically for the production in order to enhance the emotional impact or support the action in a scene.

Uses and gratifications research uses qualitative methods to study how audiences actively engage with media texts, using them to satisfy personal needs or desires. Unlike empirical forms of media effects research, it focuses attention on the practices and powers of the audience in constructing meaning, rather than the power of the industry, artists or texts.

Verisimilitude is the appearance or semblance of truth or realism.

Vertical integration describes a concentration of power in the media industry when a company owns various parts of the production chain— for example, printing press, magazine company, content providers such as photographic databases, the distribution vehicles and retail outlets. For example, the media giant News Corporation owns the website MySpace, the Fox broadcast network and the Twentieth Century Fox movie and television studio, as well as News Limited, which publishes many newspapers.

Virtual actors, also known as 'vactors', or 'synthespians', are digital characters created using CGI techniques.

Voiceover narration is speech that does not originate from a visible source on screen, and that cannot be heard by other screen characters. It is dialogue to which only the audience is privy, and which often seems to emanate from an unseen narrator or from a protagonist's thoughts.

Wide-angle lenses have a short focal length (from 12.5–30 mm) and are good for showing width and depth in a long shot. The wider the angle, the more exaggerated spatial relations become, until objects in the background and foreground seem very far apart on screen and straight lines appear to bend or lean.

Wipes are a form of editing transition in which one shot visibly pushes another out of the way.

GLOSSARY

A **zolly shot** is executed using simultaneous zoom and dolly movements that create a disorienting feel.

A **zoom** is a mobile framing technique in which the image is enlarged or reduced in scale without moving the camera, but by using the camera lens to create the effect of magnification and apparent movement.

Zoom lenses have an adjustable focal length like an 'all in one' wide-angle, normal and telephoto lens which can magnify a subject in the background of a wide-angle long shot until it is framed in telephoto close-up.

bibliography

Abercrombie, N. 1996, 'Television as text', in *Television and Society*, Polity Press, Cambridge, pp. 9–40

Alberoni, F. 2006, 'The powerless "elite": Theory and sociological research on the phenomenon of the stars', in *The Celebrity Culture Reader*, ed. P.D. Marshall, Routledge, New York, pp. 108–23

Allan, B. 2007, 'Music television', in *Television: Critical Methods and Applications*, 3rd edn, ed. J. Butler, L. Erlbaum, Mahwah, pp. 287–324

Allen, R.C. 1989, 'Bursting bubbles: "Soap opera", audiences, and the limits of genre', in *Remote control: Television, audiences, and cultural power*, eds E. Seiter, H. Borchers, G. Kreutzner and E.M. Warth, Routledge, London, pp. 44–55

Almodóvar, P. 2006, '*Volver* online production diary', <www.clubcultura.com/clubcine/clubcineastas/almodovar/eng/diario05.htm> [2 January 2007]

Alpha [magazine] 2005–

Alten, S. 1999, *Audio in Media*, 5th edn, Wadsworth, Belmont

Altman, R. 1987, *The American Film Musical*, Indiana University Press, Bloomington

——2006 [1999], *Film/Genre*, British Film Institute, London

American Mutoscope & Biograph Co. 2006, 'Florence Lawrence: the Biograph girl', <www.biographcompany.com/celebrity/lawrence.html> [26 July 2007]

Anderson, C. 2005, 'Television networks and the uses of drama', in *Thinking outside the box: A contemporary television genre reader*, eds G.R. Edgerton and B.G. Rose, University of Kentucky Press, Kentucky, pp. 65–87

Anker, E. 2005, 'Villains, victims and heroes: Melodrama, media, and September 11', *Journal of Communication*, vol. 55, no. 1, pp. 22–37

Armstrong, R. 2005, *Understanding Realism*, British Film Institute, London

Backstein, K. 2004, 'Flexing those anthropological muscles: *X-Files*, cult TV and the representation of race and ethnicity', in *Cult Television*, eds

S. Gwenllian-Jones and R.E. Pearson, University of Minnesota Press, Minneapolis, pp. 115–45

Badley, L. 2006, 'Danish Dogma: "Truth" and cultural politics', in *Traditions in World Cinema*, eds L. Badley, B. Palmer and S.J. Schneider, Edinburgh University Press, Edinburgh, pp. 80–94

Baron, C., Carson, D. and Tomasulo, F. 2004, *More than a Method: Trends and Traditions in Contemporary Film Performance*, Wayne State University Press, Detroit

Baudrilard, J. 1994, *Simulacra and Simulation*, trans. S.F. Glaser, University of Michigan Press, Ann Arbor

BBC News 2007, 'Germany imposes ban on Tom Cruise', *Entertainment*, 26 June, <www.news.bbc.co.uk/1/hi/entertainment/6240312.stm> [20 August 2007]

Bhabha, H. 2004, *The Location of Culture*, Routledge, London

Bier, J. 1995, 'A nation of hookers', *The Humanist*, vol. 55, no. 6, p. 41(1)

Biressi, A. and Nunn, H. 2005, *Reality TV: Realism and Revelation*, Wallflower, London

Björkman, S., Manns, T., and Sima, J. 1993, *Bergman on Bergman: Interviews With Ingmar Bergman*, trans. Paul Britten, de Capo Press, Austin

Bondanella, P. 2006, 'Italian Neorealism', in *Traditions in World Cinema*, eds L. Badley, R.B. Palmer and S.J. Schneider, Edinburgh University Press, Edinburgh, pp. 29–40

Bondebjerg, I. 2003, 'Dogma 95 and the New Danish Cinema', in *Purity and Provocation: Dogma 95*, eds M. Hjort and S. MacKenzie, British Film Institute, London, pp. 70–85

Boorstin, D. 2006 [1961], 'From hero to celebrity: The human pseudo-event', in *The Celebrity Culture Reader*, ed. P.D. Marshall, Routledge, New York, pp. 72–90

Bordwell, D. 1985, *Narration and the Fiction Film*, University of Wisconsin Press, Madison

——1989, *Making Meaning: Inference and Rhetoric in the Interpretation of Cinema*, Harvard University Press, Cambridge

——2000, *Planet Hong Kong: Popular Cinema and the Art of Entertainment*, Harvard University Press, Cambridge

——2002a, 'Intensified continuity. Visual style in contemporary American film', *Film Quarterly* vol. 55, no. 3, pp. 16–28

——2002b, 'Film futures', *SubStance # 97*, vol. 31, no. 1, pp. 88–104

Bordwell, D., Staiger, J. and Thompson, K. 1985, *The Classical Hollywood Cinema*, Columbia University Press, New York

Bordwell, D. and Thompson, K. 2008, *Film Art: An Introduction*, 8th edn, McGraw Hill, New York

British Film Institute website, 'Film and Television Information—Scripts and Scriptwriting', <www.bfi.org.uk/filmtvinfo/gateway/categories/scriptsscriptwriting> [29 December 2007]

Brooks, A. 1997, *Postfeminisms: Feminism, Cultural Theory, and Cultural Forms*, Routledge, London

Broderick, M. 2001, 'Kubrick's "World of Shit", Murdoch University Pubtalk seminar, Fremantle Hotel, Fremantle, 20 September

Brown, K.R. 2007, *Florence Lawrence, the Biograph Girl: America's First Movie Star*, McFarland & Co., Jefferson

Brown, R.S. 1994, *Overtones and Undertones: Reading Film Music*, University of California Press, Berkeley

Butler, J. 2007, *Television: Critical Methods and Applications*, 3rd edn, Lawrence Erlbaum, Mahwah

Butler, J. 1990, *Gender Performativity*, Routledge, London

Campora, M. 2009, 'Art Cinema in the New Hollywood: Multiform narrative and sonic metalepsis in *Eternal Sunshine of the Spotless Mind*, in *New Review of Film and Television*, vol. 7, no. 2

Carnicke, S.M. 1999, 'Lee Strasberg's Paradox of the Actor', in *Screen Acting*, eds A. Lovell and P. Krämer, Routledge, London, pp. 75–87

Casey, B., Casey, N., Calvert, B., French, L. and Lewis, J. 2002, *Television Studies: The Key Concepts*, Routledge, London

Cawelti, J. 1985, 'The question of popular genres', *Journal of Popular Film and Television*, vol. 13, no. 2, pp. 55–61

CCTV filmmaking, <www.ambienttv.net> [26 June 2008]

Chandler, D. 1997, 'An introduction to genre theory', <www.aber.ac.uk/media/Documents/intgenre/intgenre.html> [11 June 2007]

Chenery, S. 2007, 'Being Angelina', *The Weekend Australian Magazine*, 18–19 August, pp. 16–21

Collins, J. 1993, 'Genericity in the nineties: Eclectic irony and the new sincerity', in *Film Theory Goes to the Movies*, eds J. Collins, H. Radner and A.P. Collins, Routledge, New York, pp. 242–63

Copeland, G. 2007, 'A History of Television Style', in *Television: Critical Methods and Applications*, 3rd edn, Jeremy Butler, L. Erlbaum, Mahwah pp. 253–86

Coulthard, L. 2007, 'Killing Bill: Rethinking feminism and film violence', in *Interrogating Postfeminism: Gender and the Politics of Popular Culture*, eds Y. Tasker and D. Negra, Duke University Press, Durham, pp. 153–75

Cousins, M. 2004, *The Story of Film*, Pavilion Books, London

Cousins, M. and Macdonald, K. 2006, 'John Rouch Interviewed by G. Roy-Leven' in *Imagining Reality: The Faber Book of Documentary*, Faber and Faber, London, pp. 264–267

Crago, M. 2002, 'Just a spoonful of grainy footage: Creating "realism" and authenticity Big Brother style', *Metro Magazine*, no. 133, pp. 108–15

Custen, G. 1992, *Bio/pics: How Hollywood Constructed Public History*, Rutgers University Press, New Brunswick

Dai, J. 2005, 'Order/anti-order: Representation of identity in Hong Kong action movies', in *Hong Kong Connections: Transnational Imagination in Action Cinema,* eds Meaghan Morris, Siu Leung Li and Stephen Chan Ching-kiu, Hong Kong University Press and Duke University Press, Hong Kong, pp. 81–94

Daily Script, <www.dailyscript.com> [3 May 2007]

Dancyger, K. 2007, *The Technique of Film and Video Editing: History, Theory and Practice*, 4th edn, Focal Press, Amsterdam

Dancyger, K. and Rush, J. 2002, *Alternative Scriptwriting: Successfully Breaking the Rules*, Focal Press, Boston

DeCordova, R. 1991, 'The emergence of the star system in America', in *Stardom: Industry of Desire*, ed. C. Gledhill, Routledge, London, pp. 17–29

Dickinson, K., ed. 2003, *Movie Music: The Film Reader*, Routledge, London

Dixon, W.W. 2000, 'Introduction: The new genre cinema', in *Film Genre 2000: New Critical Essays*, ed. W.W. Dixon, State University of New York Press, Albany, pp. 1–12

Doane, Mary Ann 1985, 'The voice in the cinema: The articulation of body and space', in *Film Sound: Theory and Practice*, eds E. Weis and J. Belton, Columbia University Press, New York, pp. 162–76

Dogma Official Website <www.dogme95.dk> [22 September 2007]

Dolly [magazine] 1970–

Donald, James 1989, 'The cinefantastic: Introduction', in *Fantasy and the Cinema*, ed. J. Donald, British Film Institute, London, pp. 10–21

Donnelly, K.J. 2001, *Film Music: Critical Approaches*, Continuum, New York

Dyer, Richard 1998 [1979], *Stars*, British Film Institute, London

——1986, *Heavenly Bodies: Film Stars and Society*, British Film Institute, London

——2002, 'Entertainment and Utopia', in *Hollywood Musicals: The Film Reader*, ed. S. Cohan, Routledge, London, pp. 19–30

——2006 'Stars as images', in *The Celebrity Culture Reader*, ed. P.D. Marshall, Routledge, New York, pp. 153–76

Elsaesser, T. 1995, 'Tales of sound and fury: Observations on the family melodrama', in *Film Genre Reader II*, ed. B.K. Grant, University of Texas Press, Austin, pp. 350–80

Elsaesser, T. and Buckland, W. 2002, 'S/Z, the "readerly" film and video game logic (*The Fifth Element*)', in *Studying Contemporary American Film: a Guide to Movie Analysis*, eds T. Elsaesser and W. Buckland, Arnold, London, pp. 146–67

Ellis, J. 1982, *Visible Fictions: Cinema, Television, Video*, Routledge and Kegan Paul, London

Faludi, S. 1992, *Backlash: The Undeclared War Against Women*, Vintage, London

Feuer, J. 1992, 'Genre study and television', in *Channels of Discourse, Reassembled: Television and Contemporary Criticism*, 2nd edn, ed. R. Allen, Routledge, London, pp. 139–60

Field, S. 2003, *The Definitive Guide to Screenwriting*, Ebury, London

Film Criticism <www.filmcritic.com.au/> [3 May 2007]

Film Reviewing <http://leo.stcloudstate.edu/acadwrite/bookrevpre.html> [3 May 2007]

Fiske, J. 1987, *Television Culture*, Routledge, London

Forbes Magazine 2007, 'Celebrity 100', June

Free TV Australia 2004, *Commercial Television Industry Code of Practice*, 2 July. <www.freetv.com.au/Content_Common/pg-Code-of-Practice.seo> [17 June 2007]

Gallagher, B. 1997, 'Greta Garbo is sad: Some historical reflections on the paradoxes of stardom in the American film industry, 1910–1960', in *Images: A Journal of Film and Popular Culture*, March, <www.imagesjournal.com/issue03/infocus.htm> [25 July 2007]

Gallagher, M. 1997, 'Masculinity in Translation: Jackie Chan's Transcultural Star Text', in *The Velvet Light Trap*, no. 39, pp. 23–41

Gamble, S. 2001, 'Postfeminism' in *The Routledge Companion to Feminism and Postfeminism*, ed. S. Gamble, Routledge, London, pp. 36–45

Gibbs, J. 2002, *Mise-en-scène: Film Style and Interpretation*, Wallflower, London.

Gitlin, T. 1998, 'Postmodernism: What are They Talking About?' in *The Postmodern Presence: Readings on Postmodernism in American Culture*, ed. A.A. Berger, Alta Mira Press, Walnut Creek, pp. 58–73

Gledhill, C. 1991, 'Introduction', in *Stardom: Industry of desire*, ed. C. Gledhill, Routledge, London, pp. xiii–xx

Gorbman, C. 1987, *Unheard Melodies: Narrative Film Music*, British Film Institute, London

Grant, B.K. 1997, 'Introduction', in *Film genre reader II*, ed. B.K. Grant, University of Texas Press, Austin, pp. xv–xx

Grossberg, L. 2006, 'Is there a fan in the house? The affective sensibility of fandom', in *The Celebrity Culture Reader*, ed. P.D. Marshall, Routledge, London, pp. 581–90

Gulino, P.J. 2004, *Scriptwriting: The Sequence Approach*, Continuum, New York

Gwenllian-Jones, S. 2003, 'Web Wars: Resistance, Online Fandom and Studio Censorship', in *Quality Popular Television*, eds M. Jancovich and J. Lyons, British Film Institute, London, pp. 163–77

——2004, 'Virtual reality and cult television', in *Cult Television*, eds Sara Gwenllian-Jones and R.E. Pearson, University of Minnesota Press, Minneapolis, pp. 83–97

Gwenllian-Jones, S. and Pearson, R.E. 2004, 'Introduction', in *Cult Television*, eds S. Gwenllian-Jones and R.E. Pearson, University of Minnesota Press, Minneapolis, pp. ix–xix

Hampton, B. 1970 [1931], *History of the American Film Industry: From its Beginnings to 1931*, Dover, New York

Haupt, A. 2001, 'Black thing: Hip-hop nationalism, "race" and gender in *Prophets of da City* and *Brasse Vannie Kaap*', in *Coloured by History, Shaped by Place: New Perspectives on Coloured Identities in Cape Town*, ed. Z. Erasmus, Kwela Books and SA History Online, Cape Town

Haynes, T. 2002, 'Imitation of Film: Todd Haynes Mimics Melodrama in *Far From Heaven*', interview by Anthony Kaufman, November, <www.indiewire.com> [13 March 2006]

Heath, S. 1981, *Questions of Cinema*, Macmillan, London

Herzogenrath, B. 1999, 'On the *Lost Highway*: Lynch and Lacan, Cinema and Cultural Pathology', *Other Voices*, vol. 1, no. 3, <www.geocities.com/~mikehartmann/papers/herzogenrath7.html> [25 November 2005]

Hickey-Moody, A. and Iocco, M. 2004, 'Sonic Affect(s): Binaural Technologies and the Construction of Auratorship in Rolf de Heer's *Bad Boy Bubby*', *Metro Magazine*, no. 140, pp. 78–81

Hills, M. 2004, 'Defining cult TV: Texts, inter-texts and fan audiences', in *The Television Studies Reader*, eds R.C. Allen and A. Hill, Routledge, London, pp. 509–23

Hjort, M. and MacKenzie, S. (eds) 2003, *Purity and Provocation: Dogma 95*, British Film Institute, London

Holland, P. 1997, 'Production techniques: Sound', in *The Television Handbook*, 2nd edn, Routledge, London, pp. 79–90

Hollows, J. 1995, 'Mass culture theory and political economy', in *Approaches to Popular Film*, eds J. Hollows and M. Jancovich, Manchester University Press, Manchester, pp. 13–36

Holmes, S. and Redmond, S. (eds) 2006, *Framing Celebrity: New Directions in Celebrity Culture*, Routledge, London

Holt, J. 2003, 'Vertical vision: Deregulation, industrial economy and prime-time design', in *Quality Popular Television*, eds M. Jancovich and J. Lyons, British Film Institute, London, pp. 11–31

Horkheimer M. and Adorno, T. 1972, *Dialectic of Enlightenment*, Continuum, New York

Internet Movie Database <www.imdb.com> [7 January 2008]

Jacobs, J. 2001, 'Hospital drama', in *The Television Genre Book*, ed. G. Creeber, British Film Institute, London, pp. 23–6

Jacobs, L. 1968, *The Rise of the American Film: A Critical History*, 2nd edn, Teachers College, Columbia University, New York

Jameson, F. 2001, 'Postmodernism, or the cultural logic of late capitalism', in *Media and Cultural Studies Key Works*, eds D. Kellner and M. Durham, Blackwell, Malden, pp. 550–87

Jancovich, M. and Hunt, N. 2004, 'The mainstream, distinction and cult TV', in *Cult Television*, eds S. Gwenllian-Jones and R.E. Pearson, University of Minnesota Press, Minneapolis, pp. 27–43

Jancovich, M., Lázaro Reboll, A., Stringer, J. and Willis, A. (eds) 2003, *Defining Cult Movies: The Cultural Politics of Oppositional Taste*, Manchester University Press, Manchester

Jancovich, M. and Lyons, J. 2003, *Quality Popular Television*, British Film Institute, London

Jauss, H.R. 1982, *Toward an Aesthetic of Reception*, trans. Timothy Bahti, University of Minnesota Press, Minneapolis

Jenkins, H. 2000, 'Reception theory and audience research: The mystery of the vampire's kiss', in *Reinventing Film Studies*, eds C. Gledhill and L. Williams, Arnold, London, pp. 165–79

—— 2006, 'Interactive audiences? The "collective intelligence" of media fans', in *Fans, Bloggers, Gamers: Exploring Participatory Culture*, New York

University Press, New York, pp. 134–51

Jenson, J. 1992, 'Fandom as pathology: The consequences of characterisation', in *The Adoring Audience: Fan Culture and Popular Media*, ed. L. Lewis, Routledge, London, pp. 9–29

Joyner, J. 2005, 'Iraq group claims U.S. soldier hostage', in *Outside the Beltway*, <www.outsidethebeltway.com/archives/2005/02/iraq_group_claims_us_soldier_hostage/> [30 June 2007]

Kapsis, R. 1992, *Hitchcock: The Making of a Reputation*, University of Chicago Press, Chicago

Kassabian, A. 2001, *Hearing Film*, Routledge, New York

Kasson, J. 2000, *Buffalo Bill's Wild West: Celebrity, Memory, and Popular History*, Hill and Wang, New York

Keane, S. 2007, *CineTech: Film, Convergence and New Media*, Palgrave, New York

King, G. 2002, *New Hollywood Cinema*, Columbia University Press, New York

——2005, *American Independent Cinema*, I.B. Tauris, London.

King, G. and Krzywinska, T. (eds) 2002, *Cinema/Videogames/Interfaces*, Wallflower, London

——2006, *Tomb Raiders & Space Invaders: Videogame Forms and Contexts*, I.B. Tauris, London

Kirsner, S. 2006, 'Dion Beebe, Dean Semler, Tom Sigel, and others on digital cinematography', *Cinematech Blogspot*, posted 16 June 2006. <http://cinematech.blogspot.com/2006/06/dion-beebe-dean-semler-tom-sigel-and.html> [29 June 2007].

Kitses, J. 1969, *Horizons West*, British Film Institute, London

Klevan, A. 2005, *Film Performance: From Achievement to Appreciation*, Wallflower, London

Klinger, B. 1994, *Melodrama and Meaning: History, Culture, and the Films of Douglas Sirk*, Indiana University Press, Bloomington

Krutnik, F. 1990, 'The faint aroma of performing seals: The "nervous" romance and the comedy of the sexes', *The Velvet Light Trap*, no. 26, pp. 57–72

Langer, J. 1999, *Tabloid Television: Popular Journalism and the "Other" News*, Routledge, London

——2006 [1981], 'Television's "personality system"', in *The Celebrity Culture Reader*, ed. P.D. Marshall, Routledge, London, pp. 181–95

Lawrenson, E. 2006, *The Science of Sleep* review in *Sight & Sound*, vol. 16, no. 8, p. 88

Lay, S. 2002, *British Social Realism: From Documentary to Brit-Grit*, Wallflower, London

Lefebvre, M. 2006, 'Between setting and landscape in the cinema', in *Landscape and Film*, ed. M. Lefebvre, Routledge, New York, pp. 19–60

Levi Strauss, C. 1963, *Structural Anthropology*, trans. C. Jacobson and B. Grundfest Schoepf, Basic Books, New York

Lim, D. 2006, 'David Lynch returns: Expect moody conditions, with surreal gusts', *New York Times*, 1 October 2006, <www.nytimes.com/2006/10/01/movies/01lim.html?ex=1317355200&en=fb5663bd7dc96d11&ei=5088

&partner=rssnyt&emc=rss> [28 June 2007]

Lovell, A. and Krämer, P. (eds) 1999, *Screen Acting*, Routledge, London

Lumby, C. 1999, *Gotcha: Life in a Tabloid World*, Allen & Unwin, Sydney

——2004, 'Out of the slipstream', *Griffith REVIEW 5: Addicted to Celebrity*, pp. 109–16

Lury, K. 2005, *Interpreting Television*, Hodder Arnold, London

Lynch, D. and Reznor, T. 2005, 'About the music', interviews with David Lynch and Trent Reznor, <www.geocities.com/~mikehartmann/losthighway/lhsound.html> [25 November 05]

Marks, L.U. 2000, *The Skin of the Film: Intercultural Cinema, Embodiment and the Senses*, Duke, Durham

Marshall, P.D. 1997, *Celebrity and Power: Fame in Contemporary Culture*, University of Minnesota Press, Minneapolis

——2006, 'Introduction', in *The Celebrity Culture Reader*, ed. P.D. Marshall, Routledge, London, pp. 1–15

Martin, A. 2005, 'At the edge of the cut: An encounter with the Hong Kong style in contemporary action cinema', in *Hong Kong Connections: Transnational Imagination in Action Cinema*, eds M. Morris, S.L. Li and S.C. Ching-kiu, Hong Kong University Press and Duke University Press, Hong Kong, pp. 175–88

——2005, 'How film critics work', *Australian Journal of Communication*, vol. 32, no. 3, pp. 2–17

Mayne, J. 1993, *Cinema and Spectatorship*, Routledge, London

Mcdonald, P. 1995, 'Star studies', in *Approaches to Popular Film*, eds J. Hollows and M. Jancovich, Manchester University Press, Manchester, pp. 79–97

McKee, R. 1999, *Story: Substance, Structure, Style, and the Principles of Screenwriting*, Methuen, London

McMahan, A. 1999, 'The effect of multiform narrative on subjectivity', *Screen*, vol. 40, no. 2, pp. 146–57

McQuire, S. 1999, 'Cinematic subjectivity in the new millennium', in *Maximum Vision: Large Format and Special Venue Cinema*, Australian Film Commission, Sydney, pp. 134–46

Mikula, M. 2003, 'Gender and video games: The political valency of Lara Croft', *Continuum: Journal of Media and Cultural Studies*, vol. 17, no. 1, pp. 79–87

Miller, T. 2004, 'Trainspotting *The Avengers*', in *Cult Television*, eds S. Gwenllian-Jones and R.E. Pearson, University of Minnesota Press, Minneapolis, pp. 187–98

Mittell, J. 2001, 'A cultural approach to television genre theory', *Cinema Journal*, vol. 40, no. 3, pp. 3–24

——2004, *Genre and Television: From Cop Shows to Cartoons in American Culture*, Routledge, New York

Mizejewski, L. 2001, 'Stardom and serial fantasies: Thomas Harris's *Hannibal*', in *Keyframes: Popular Cinema and Cultural Studies*, eds M. Tinkcom and A. Villarejo, Routledge, London, pp. 159–70

Morris, M. 2005, 'Introduction: Hong Kong Connections', in *Hong Kong Connections: Transnational Imagination in Action Cinema*, eds M.

Morris, S.L. Li and S.C. Ching-kiu, Hong Kong University Press and Duke University Press, Hong Kong, pp. 1–18

Murray, J.H. 1997, *Hamlet on the Holodeck: The Future of Narrative in Cyberspace*, The Free Press, New York

Napier, S. 2005, 'Anime and Local/Global Identity', in *Anime from Akira to Howl's Moving Castle: Experiencing Contemporary Japanese Animation*, ed. S. Napier, Palgrave Macmillan, New York

Naremore, J. 1988, *Acting in the Cinema*, University of California Press, Berkeley California

Neale, S. 1980, *Genre*, British Film Institute, London

——1995, 'Questions of genre', in *Film genre reader II*, ed. B.K. Grant, University of Texas Press, Austin, pp. 159–83

——2000, *Genre and Hollywood*, Routledge, New York

——2001 'Studying genre' and 'Genre and television', in *The Television Genre Book*, ed. G. Creeber, British Film Institute, London, pp. 1–3

New Weekly [magazine] 2001 (April)

Newcombe, H. 1974, *TV: The Most Popular Art*, Anchor Press, New York

——1976, *Television: The Critical View*, Oxford University Press, New York

New Idea [magazine] 1902–

Nichols, B. 2001, *Introduction to Documentary*, Indiana University Press, Bloomington

Noyce, P. 2001, 'Directors speak: Noyce on sound', *IF (Independent Filmmakers) Magazine* <www.if.com.au/index.html> [28 July 2008]

Olson, M. 2003, 'Turning on a dime', in *Sight and Sound*, vol. 13, no. 10, pp. 12–15

Orr, J. 1993, 'Commodified demons II: The automobile', in *Cinema and Modernity*, ed. J. Orr, Polity Press, Oxford, pp. 127–54

O'Shaughnessy, M. 2004, '*Walkabout*'s music: European nostalgia in the Australian outback', *Metro Magazine*, no. 140, pp. 82–6

Pan's Labyrinth [online production sketches] <www.panslabyrinth.com> [17 March 2007]

Poster, M. 2001, 'Postmodern virtualities', in *Media and Cultural Studies KeyWorks*, eds D. Kellner and M. Durham, Blackwell, Malden, pp. 611–25

Powell, S. 2007, Seminar on editing the television series *24* and other works, Queensland University of Technology, 20 September

Prebble, T. 2004, 'The music of sound', *Metro Magazine*, no. 140, pp. 74–6

Prendergast, R. 1992, *Film Music: A Neglected Art*, 2nd edn, Norton, New York

Preston, W. 1994, *What an Art Director Does: An Introduction to Motion Picture Production Design*, Silman James Press, Los Angeles

Rance, P.T.J. 2005, *Martial Arts*, Virgin Books, London

Real, M. 2003, 'Structural analysis 1: Bill Cosby and recoding ethnicity', in *Critiquing the Sitcom: A Reader*, ed. J. Morreale, Syracuse University Press, New York, pp. 224–46

Robertson Wojcik, P. 2004, *Movie Acting: The Film Reader*, Routledge, New York

Rodman, G. 1996, *Elvis After Elvis: The Posthumous Career of a Living Legend*, Routledge, London

Rojek, C. 2001, *Celebrity*, Reaktion Books, London

Roscoe, J. and Hight, C. 2001, *Faking It: Mock-Documentary and the Subversion of Factuality*, Manchester University Press, Manchester

Rouch, J. 1995, 'The camera and the man,' in *Principles of Visual Anthropology*, ed. P. Hockings, Mouton, The Hague, pp. 79–98

Rowe, K. 2003, 'Roseanne: Unruly woman as domestic goddess,' in *Critiquing the Sitcom: A Reader*, ed. J. Morreale, Syracuse University Press, New York, pp. 251–61

Rubinfeld, M. 2001, *Bound to Bond: Gender, Genre, and the Hollywood Romantic Comedy*, Praeger, London

SandiThom.com 2007, 'Biography,' <www.sandithom.com/07/biography> [3 September 2007]

Schultz, J. 2004, 'Stars, lies and propaganda,' *Griffith REVIEW 5: Addicted to Celebrity*, pp. 7–12

Scott, M. 2006, 'Dion Beebe Interview,' <bonza.rmit.edu.au/essays/2006/Michael%20Scott/Interview.html> [14 July 2007]

Screen Australia 'What is a Synopsis? An Outline? A Treatment?' <www.afc.gov.au/downloads/synopsis_jul08.pdf> [2 May 2007]

Seiter, E. and Wilson, M.J. 2005, 'Soap opera survival tactics,' in *Thinking Outside the Box: A Contemporary Television Genre Reader*, eds G.R. Edgerton and B.G. Rose, University Press of Kentucky, Kentucky, pp. 136–55

Simerka, B. and Weimer, C. 2005, 'Tom Cruise and the seven dwarves: Cinematic postmodernisms in *Abre los Ojos* and *Vanilla Sky*,' *American Drama*, vol. 14, no. 2, pp. 1–15

Simply Scripts, <simplyscripts.com/full_movie.html> [3 May 2007]

Snicket, L. 1999, *A Series of Unfortunate Events: The Bad Beginning*, Harper-Collins, New York

Sobchack, V. 2004, 'Inscribing ethical space: Ten propositions on death, representation and documentary,' in *Carnal Thoughts: Embodiment and Moving Image Culture*, University of California Press, Berkeley, pp. 226–57

Soyoung, K. 2005, 'Genre as contact zone: Hong Kong action and Korean Hwalkuk,' in *Hong Kong Connections: Transnational Imagination in Action Cinema*, eds M. Morris, S.L. Li and S.C. Ching-kiu, Hong Kong University Press and Duke University Press, Hong Kong, pp. 97–110

Stacey, J. 1994, *Star Gazing: Hollywood Cinema and Female Spectatorship*, Routledge, London

——2006 'Feminine fascinations: A question of identification?' in *The Celebrity Culture Reader*, ed. P.D. Marshall, Routledge, New York, pp. 252–85

Staiger, J. 1997, 'Hybrid or inbred: The purity hypothesis and Hollywood genre history,' *Film Criticism*, vol. 22, no. 1, pp. 1–9

Stam, R. 2000, *Film Theory*, Blackwell, Oxford

Studlar, G. 1991, 'Midnight s/excess: Cult configurations of "femininity" and the perverse', in *The Cult Film Experience*, ed. J.P. Telotte, University of Texas Press, Austin, pp. 138–55

Tasker, Y. 1993, *Spectacular Bodies: Gender, Genre and the Action Cinema*, Routledge, London

——1998 *Working Girls: Gender and Sexuality in Popular Culture*, Routledge, London

Tasker, Y. and Negra, D. 2007, 'Introduction: Feminist politics and popular culture', in *Interrogating Postfeminism: Gender and the Politics of Popular Culture*, eds Y. Tasker and D. Negra, Duke University Press, Durham, pp. 1–26

Telotte, J.P. 1991, 'Introduction: Beyond all reason, the nature of the cult', in *The Cult Film Experience: Beyond All Reason*, ed. J.P. Telotte, University of Texas Press, Austin, pp. 5–17

Teo, S. 2005, '*Wuxia* redux: *Crouching Tiger, Hidden Dragon* as a model of late transnational production', in *Hong Kong Connections: Transnational Imagination in Action Cinema*, eds M. Morris, S.L. Li and S.C. Ching-kiu, Hong Kong University Press and Duke University Press, Hong Kong, pp. 191–204

Thomas, D. 2001, *Reading Hollywood: Spaces and Meanings in American Film*, Wallflower, London

Thomas, S. 2006, 'Whatever happened to the social documentary?' in *Imagining Reality: The Faber Book of Documentary*, eds M. Cousins and K. Macdonald, Faber and Faber, London, pp. 419–26

Thompson, K. 2003, *Storytelling in Film and Television*, Harvard University Press, Cambridge

Turner, G. 2004, *Understanding Celebrity*, Sage, London

——2006, *Film as Social Practice*, 4th edn, Routledge, London

Turner, G., Bonner, F. and Marshall, P.D. 2000, *Fame Games: The Production of Celebrity in Australia*, Cambridge University Press, Cambridge

Vanity Fair [magazine] 2007, 'Green Issue' (May)

Walker, A. 2004, '(Re)sounding celluloid: Navigating a cinesonic place in *The Lord of the Rings: The Fellowship of the Ring*', *Metro Magazine*, no. 140, pp. 88–92

Walters, T. 2004, 'Reconsidering *The Idiots*: Dogme95, Lars von Trier, and the cinema of subversion', *The Velvet Light Trap*, no. 53, pp. 40–54

Walton, M. *Storyboards*, <www.cfms.uct.ac.za/storyboard> [3 May 2007]

Wasko, J. 1999, 'The political economy of film', in *A Companion to Film Theory*, eds T. Miller and R. Stam, Blackwell, Malden, pp. 221–33

Watson, P. 2003, 'Critical approaches to Hollywood cinema: Authorship, genre and stars', in *An Introduction to Film Studies*, 3rd edn, ed. J. Nelmes, Routledge, London, pp. 163–83

Waugh, P. 1992, 'Introduction', in *Postmodernism: A Reader*, ed. P. Waugh, Edward Arnold, London

Whittaker, M. and Kennedy, L. 2001, *Sins of the Brother: The Definitive Story of Ivan Milat and the Backpacker Murders*, Pan Macmillan, Melbourne

Who Weekly [magazine], 1992–

Wittgenstein, L. 1978 [1953], *Philosophical Investigations*, trans. G.E.M. Anscombe, Blackwell, Oxford

Wright, W. 1975, *Six Guns and Society*, University of California Press, Berkeley

Yuan, S. 2003, 'Reading the kung fu film in an American context: From Bruce Lee to Jackie Chan', *Journal of Popular Film and Television*, vol. 31, no. 2, pp. 50–9

film credits

3.10 to Yuma (James Mangold 2007)
8 Mile (Curtis Hanson 2002)
21 Grams (Alejandro Gonzalez Iñárritu 2003)
2001: A Space Odyssey (Stanley Kubrick 1968)
À bout de souffle/Breathless (Jean Luc Godard 1959)
Adaptation (Spike Jonze 2002)
The Adventures of Priscilla, Queen of the Desert (Stephan Elliott 1994)
Ae Fond Kiss (Ken Loach 2005)
Æon Flux (Karyn Kusama 2005)
Alexander Nevsky (Sergei Eisenstein 1938)
Alien (Ridley Scott 1979)
Aliens (James Cameron 1986)
Alien 3 (David Fincher 1992)
Alien Resurrection (Jean-Pierre Jeunet 1997)
All That Heaven Allows (Douglas Sirk 1955)
Amelie (Jean-Pierre Jeunet 2001)
American Beauty (Sam Mendes 1999)
American Gangster (Ridley Scott 2007)
American Splendor (Shari Springer Bergman 2003)
Amores Perros (Alejandro Gonzalez Iñárritu 2000)
An Inconvenient Truth (Al Gore 2006)
Arahan (Seung-wan Ryoo 2004)
Assassination of Jesse James (Andrew Dominik 2007)
Babe (Chris Noonan 1995)
Babel (Alejandro Gonzalez Iñárritu 2006)
Back to the Future Part III (Robert Zemekis 1990)
Badlands (Terrence Malick 1973)
Baraka: A World Without Words (Fricke 1992)
Battleship Potemkin (Sergei Eisenstein 1925)
Before Sunrise (Richard Linklater 1995)
Before Sunset (Richard Linklater 2004)
Beowulf (Robert Zemeckis 2007)
The Bicycle Thief (Vittorio de Sica 1948)
Birth of a Nation (D.W. Griffith 1915)

The Blair Witch Project (Myrick and Sánchez 1999)
Blood Diamond (Edward Zwick 2006)
Blue Velvet (David Lynch 1986)
The Boys (Rowan Woods 1998)
Bringing out the Dead (Martin Scorsese 1999)
The Butterfly Effect (Eric Bress and J. Mackye Gruber 2004)
Casino Royale (Martin Campbell 2006)
Charlie's Angels (McG 2000)
Charlie's Angels Full Throttle (McG 2003)
Chicago (Rob Marshall 2002)
Children of Men (Alfonso Cuarón 2006)
Chronicle of Summer/Chronique d'un Été (Jean Rouch 1960)
The Chumscrubber (Arie Posin 2005)
City of God (Meirelles & Lund 2002)
Collateral (Michael Mann 2004)
The Cook, The Thief, His Wife and Her Lover (Peter Greenaway 1989)
Crash (Paul Haggis 2004)
Crouching Tiger, Hidden Dragon (Ang Lee 2000)
Dancer in the Dark (Lars von Trier 2000)
Dark City (Alex Proyas 1998)
The Day After Tomorrow (Emmerich 2004)
The Dead Girl (Karen Moncrieff 2006)
Death Proof (Quentin Tarantino 2007)
The Departed (Martin Scorsese 2006)
Die Hard 2 (Renny Harlin 1990)
Donnie Darko (Richard Kelly 2001)
Doom (Andrzej Bartkowiak 2005)
Dreamgirls (Bill Condon 2006)
The Duellists (Dave Valentine 2007)
Easy Rider (Dennis Hopper 1969)
The Eleventh Hour (Leonardo DiCaprio 2007)
Eternal Sunshine of the Spotless Mind (Michel Gondry 2004)
Executioners from Shaolin/Hung Hei Kwun (Chia Liang Lu 1977)
eXistenZ (David Cronenberg 1999)
Faceless (Manu Luksch 2007)
Fahrenheit 451 (François Truffaut 1966)
Far From Heaven (Todd Haynes 2002)
Fargo (Joel Coen and Ethan Coen 1996)
Fight Club (David Fincher 1999)
Fistful of Dollars, A (Sergio Leone 1964)
Forbidden Lie$ (Anna Broinowski 2007)
The Fountain (Darren Aronofsky 2006)
Fracture (Larry Parr 2004)
Game of Death (Robert Clouse 1978)
Gattaca (Andrew Niccol 1997)
Ghost in the Shell (Mamoru Oshii 1995)

FILM CREDITS

GI Jane (Ridley Scott 1997)
Girl, Interrupted (James Mangold 1999)
The Graduate (Mike Nichols 1967)
The Grand Illusion/La Grande Illusion (Jean Renoir 1937)
Grease (Randal Kleiser 1978)
Grizzly Man (Werner Herzog 2005)
Groundhog Day (Harold Ramis 1993)
Gummo (Harmony Korine 1997)
Hairspray (Adam Shankman 2007)
Harry Potter and the Order of the Phoenix (David Yates 2007)
Hero (Zhang Yimou 2002)
High Fidelity (Stephen Frears 2000)
High School (Fred Wiseman 1968)
High School II (Fred Wiseman 1994)
Hospital (Fred Wiseman, 1970)
The Host (Joon-ho Bong 2006)
Human Nature (Michel Gondry 2001)
The Idiots (Lars von Trier 1998)
Inland Empire (David Lynch 2006)
In My Country (John Boorman 2004)
I Now Pronounce You Chuck and Larry (Dennis Duggan 2007)
In the Cut (Jane Campion 2004)
Irreversible (Gaspar Noe, 2004)
Jarhead (Sam Mendes 2005)
Jesus Camp (Heidi Ewing and Rachel Grady 2006)
Julien Donkey-Boy (Harmony Korine 1999)
Jules et Jim/ Jules and Jim (Francois Truffaut 1961)
Jungle Fever (Spike Lee 1991)
Juno (Jason Reitman 2007)
Kairo (Kiyoshi Kurosawa 2001)
Kenny (Jacobson 2006)
Kids (Larry Clark 1995)
Kill Bill Vol. 1 (Quentin Tarantino 2003)
Kill Bill Vol. 2 (Quentin Tarantino 2004)
Kiss or Kill (Bill Bennett 1997)
Kung Fu Hustle (Stephen Chow 2004)
La Haine/Hate (Matthiu Kassovitz 1995)
Lara Croft: Tomb Raider (Simon West 2001)
Lara Croft Tomb Raider: The Cradle of Life (Jan de Bont 2003)
Layer Cake (Matthew Vaughan 2004)
Legally Blonde (Robert Luketic 2001)
La Jetée (Chris Marker 1962)
Little Fish (Rowan Woods 2005)
Lord of the Rings: The Fellowship of the Ring (Peter Jackson 2001)
Lord of the Rings: The Two Towers (Peter Jackson 2002)
Lord of the Rings: Return of the King (Peter Jackson 2003)

Lost Highway (David Lynch 1997)
Love Actually (Richard Curtis 2003)
The Magnificent Seven (Sturges 1960)
Man with a Movie Camera (Dziga Vertov 1929)
March of the Penguins (Luc Jacquet 2006)
Marie Antoinette (Sophia Coppola 2006)
Match Point (Woody Allen 2005)
The Matrix (Andy Wachowski and Larry Wachowski 1999)
Memento (Christopher Nolan 2000)
Memoirs of a Geisha (John Marshall 2005)
Miami Vice (Michael Mann 2006)
Mission: Impossible (Brian DePalma 1996)
Moulin Rouge (Baz Luhrmann 2001)
Mr. and Mrs. Smith (Doug Liman 2005)
Music and Lyrics (Marc Lawrence 2007)
My Best Friend's Wedding (P.J. Hogan 1997)
My Fair Lady (George Cukor 1964)
The Name of this Film is Dogme95 (Saul Metzstein 2000)
Natural Born Killers (Oliver Stone 1994)
No Country for Old Men (Joel Coen and Ethan Coen 2007)
No Reservations (Scott Hicks 2007)
Nosferatu (F.W. Murnau 1922)
Obsessione (Visconti 1942)
Ocean's 11 (Steven Soderbergh 2001)
Ocean's 12 (Steven Soderbergh 2004)
Ocean's 13 (Steven Soderbergh 2007)
Ochre and Water (Joelle Chesselet and Craig Matthew 2001)
Oh Brother Where Art Thou? (Joel Coen and Ethan Coen 2000)
Once Were Warriors (Lee Tamahori 1994)
Pan's Labyrinth (Guillermo del Toro 2006)
Pi (Darren Aronofsky 1998)
The Piano (Jane Campion 1992)
Pirates of the Caribbean: Curse of the Black Pearl (Gore Verbinsky 2003)
Pirates of the Caribbean: Dead Man's Chest (Gore Verbinsky 2006)
Pirates of the Caribbean: At World's End (Gore Verbinsky 2007)
The Player (Robert Altman 1992)
The Prestige (Christopher Nolan 2006)
Primary (Richard Leacock 1960)
The Proposition (John Hillcoat 2005)
Pulp Fiction (Quentin Tarantino 1994)
Pulse (Jim Sonzero 2006)
Ray (Taylor Hackford 2004)
Rasen (Joji Lida 1998)
Rashômon (Akira Kurosawa 1950)
Red Dust (Tom Hooper 2004)
Requiem for a Dream (Darren Aronofsky 2000)

FILM CREDITS

The Ring (Gore Verbinski 2002)
The Ring 2 (Hideo Nakata, 2005)
Ring 0: Basudei (Norio Tsuruta 2000)
Ringu (Hideo Nakata 1998)
Ringu 2 (Hideo Nakata 1999)
The Ring Virus (Kim Dong-bin 1999)
The Rocky Horror Picture Show (Jim Sharman 1975)
Rome Open City (Roberto Rossellini 1945)
Rope (Alfred Hitchcock 1948)
The Rules of the Game/ La Règle du jeu (Jean Renoir 1939)
Run Lola Run (Todd Twyker 1998)
Salesman (Albert and David Maysles 1968)
The Science of Sleep (Michel Gondry 2006)
Scream (Wes Craven 1996)
The Searchers (John Ford 1956)
Secrets and Lies (Mike Leigh 1996)
Serenity (Joss Whedon 2005)
Seven Samurai (Akira Kurosawa 1954)
The Shining (Stanley Kubrick 1980)
Shutter (Banjong Pisanthanakun and Parkpoom Wongpoom 2004)
The Sick Kitten (George Albert Smith 1903)
Sin City (Robert Rodriguez 2005)
Singin' in the Rain (Stanley Donen and Gene Kelly 1952)
Secret Window (David Koepp 2004)
Serenity (Joss Whedon 2005)
Short Cuts (Robert Altman 1993)
Shrek (Andrew Adamson and Vicky Jenson 2001)
Shrek the Third (Chris Miller and Raman Hui 2007)
Sky Captain and the World of Tomorrow (Conran 2004)
Sliding Doors (Peter Howitt 1998)
Snakes on a Plane (David R. Ellis 2006)
Some Like it Hot (Billy Wider 1959)
Spider-Man 3 (Sam Raimi 2007)
Strike (Sergei Eisenstein 1925)
Sunshine Silence of the Lambs (Demme 1991)
Supersize Me (Morgan Spurlock 2005)
Sweeney Todd: The Demon Barber of Fleet Street (Tim Burton 2007)
Taking Lives (J.D. Caruso 2004)
The Talented Mr Ripley (Anthony Minghella 1999)
Team America: World Police (Trey Parker 2004)
Terminator (James Cameron 1984)
Terminator 2: Judgment Day (James Cameron 1991)
Terminator 3: The Rise of the Machines (Jonathan Mostow 2003)
There's Something About Mary (Bobby Farrelly and Peter Farrelly 1998)
Time Code (Mike Figgis 2000)
Titanic (James Cameron 1997)

SCREEN MEDIA

Titicut Follies (Fred Wiseman and John Marshall 1967)
Touching the Void (Kevin Macdonald 2004)
Touch of Evil (Orson Welles 1958)
True Romance (Tony Scott 1993)
Tsotsi (Gavin Hood 2005)
Twelve Monkeys (Terry Gilliam 1995)
Unbreakable (M. Night Shayamalan 2000)
United 93 (Paul Greengrass 2006)
The Usual Suspects (Bryan Singer 1995)
U-Turn (Oliver Stone 1997)
Valkyrie (Bryan Singer 2008)
Vertigo (Alfred Hitchcock 1958)
Videodrome (David Cronenberg 1983)
The Virgin Spring (Ingmar Bergman 1960)
The Virgin Suicides (Sofia Coppola 1999)
Volcano High (Tae-gyun Kim 2001)
Volver (Pedro Almodóvar 2006)
Walkabout (Nicholas Roeg 1971)
Walk the Line (James Mangold 2005)
Wolf Creek (Greg McLean 2005)
Written on the Wind (Douglas Sirk 1956)
Yojimbo (Akira Kurosawa 1961)
Zodiac (David Fincher 2007)

game credits

Alias (Acclaim Entertainment 2004)
Buffy the Vampire Slayer: Chaos Bleeds (Eurocom Entertainment Software 2003)
Die Hard Trilogy 2: Viva Las Vegas (n-Space 2000)
Doom (id software 1993)
Lara Croft Tomb Raider: Anniversary (Crystal Dynamics 2007)
The Ring: Terror's Realm (Asmik Ace Entertainment/ Infogrames 2000)
The Sims (Electronic Arts 2000)

television credits

24 (Robert Cochran and Joel Surnow 2001–)
Access Hollywood (Ann Lewis 1996–)
Æon Flux (Peter Chung 1991–95)

FILM CREDITS

Alias (J.J. Abrams 2001–06)
American Idol (Simon Fuller 2002–)
Astro Boy (Osuma Tezuka 1963–66)
Australian Idol (Simon Fuller 2003–)
Band of Brothers (Steven Spielberg and Tom Hanks 2001)
Baywatch (Michael Berk, Gregory J. Bonann and Douglas Schwartz 1989–2001)
Beverly Hills 90210 (Aaron Spelling 1990–2000)
Bewitched (Sol Sacks 1964–72)
Big Brother Australia (Mark Adamson and David McEvoy 2001–)
Big Brother UK (Hepworth and Downing 2000–)
Big Love (Mark V. Olson and Will Schiffer 2006–)
Border Security: Australia's Front Line (Grant Bowler, 2004–)
Brothers and Sisters (Jon Robin Baitz 2006–)
Buffy the Vampire Slayer (Joss Whedon 1997–2003)
Casualty (Jeremy Brock and Paul Unwin 1986–)
Celebrity Big Brother UK (Simon Hepworth 2001–07)
Charlie's Angels TV (Ivan Goff and Ben Roberts 1976–1981)
Chicago Hope (David E. Kelley 1994–2000)
Crimewatch (Jeremy Ankok and Steve Bosner 1984–)
Crossing Jordan (Tim Kring 2001–)
CSI (Anthony E. Zuiker 2000–)
Dancing with the Stars (Alex Rudzinski 2005–)
Dark Angel (James Cameron and Charles H. Eglee 2000–02)
Deadwood (David Milch 2004–)
Desperate Housewives (Marc Cherry 2004–)
Dexter (James Manos Jr. 2006–)
Dirty Sexy Money (Craig Wright 2007–)
Doctor Who (Sydney Newman 1963–89)
Don't Forget the Lyrics (Jeff Apploff 2007–)
Drawn Together (Dave Jeser and Matthew Silverstein 2004–)
Dr Phil (Paul Casey and Kathleen Dowdey 2002–)
Entertainment Tonight (Alfred Masini 1981–)
E.R. (Michael Crichton 1994–)
Extreme Makeover (Shanda Sawyer 2002–05)
Firefly (Joss Whedon 2002–04)
Friends (David Crane and Martha Kauffman 1994–2004)
Funniest Home Videos (Vin de Bona, 1990–)
Gossip Girl (Josh Schwartz 2007–)
Grey's Anatomy (Shonda Rhimes 2005–)
Hattori Hanzo: Kage no Gundan/Shadow Warriors (Jôdo Hiramatsu and Kyô Namura 1980–)
Heroes (Tim Kring 2006–)
House (David Shore 2004–)
How to Look Good Naked (Diane DeStefano and Riaz Patel 2008–)
I Love Lucy (Ralph Levy 1951–57)
Jamie's Kitchen (Jamie Oliver and Sandi Scott 2002)

SCREEN MEDIA

Jamie's Kitchen Australia (Jamie Oliver and Tobi Puttock 2006)
Kath and Kim (Gina Riley and Jane Turner 2002–)
Kung Fu (Alex Beaton and Barry Crane 1972–75)
Las Vegas (Gary Scott Thompson 2003–)
Late Show With David Letterman (Rob Burnett 1993–)
Law and Order: Criminal Intent (Dick Wolf 2001)
Lost (J.J. Abrams, Jeffrey Lieber and Damon Lindelof 2004–)
Lost in Space (Irwin Allen 1965–68)
Medium (Glenn Gordon Caron 2005–)
Miami Vice (Anthony Yerkovich 1984–89)
Monkey (Toshi Aoki and Jun Fukuda 1978–80)
My Name is Earl (Gregory Thomas Garcia 2006–)
Neighbours (Reg Watson 1985–)
Nip/Tuck (Ryan Murphy 2003–)
Oprah Winfrey Show (Joseph C. Terry 1986–)
Prison Break (Paul Scheuring 2005–)
Queer Eye for the Straight Guy (David Collins 2003–)
Reaper (Kevin Smith, Michele Fazekas and Tara Butters 2007–)
Rescue 911 (Mark Cole 1989–96)
Roseanne (William Rogers and Roseanne Barr 1988–97)
Roswell (Jason Katims 1999–2002)
Rove Live (Rove McManus 2000–)
Sex and the City (Darren Star 1998–2004)
Six Feet Under (Alan Ball 2001–05)
South Park (Matt Stone 1997–)
Star Trek original series (Gene Roddenberry, 1966–69)
Star Trek: The Animated Series (1973–74)
Star Trek: The Next Generation (1978–94)
Star Trek: Deep Space Nine (1993–99)
Star Trek: Voyager (1995–2001)
Star Trek: Enterprise (2001–05)
Survivor (Mark Burnett 2000–)
The Ali G Show (Sacha Baron Cohen 2003–04)
The Apprentice (Mark Burnett 2004–)
The Biggest Loser (Nathan Taflove 2004–)
The Bold and the Beautiful (Lee Philip Bell 1987–)
The Chaser's War on Everything (Julian Morrow et al. 2006–)
The Green Hornet (George W. Trendle 1966–67)
The Living Soap (Richard Fell 1993)
The O.C. (Josh Schwartz 2003–07)
The Office UK and US series (Ricky Gervais and Stephen Merchant 2005–)
The Path to 9/11 (David Cunningham 2006)
The Shak (Shaheer Azizi 2006–)
The Sopranos (David Chase 1999–2007)
Totally Wild (Stacey Thompson et al. 1995–2002)

FILM CREDITS

Trinny and Susannah Undress (Trinny Woodall and Susannah Constantine 2006–07)
Tru Calling (Jon Harman Feldman 2003–05)
The X-Files (Chris Carter 1993–2002)
Ugly Betty (Fernando Gaitán 2006–)
Veronica Mars (Rob Thomas 2004–)
Walking with Dinosaurs (Haines and James 1999)
We Can Be Heroes (Chris Lilley 2005)
Weeds (Jenji Kohan 2005–s)

index

2 shots 35
24 (TV show)
  audience expectations 224
  editing 95
  time cuts in 117
30-degree rule 109
60 Minutes 246
180-degree rule 107–9
2001: A Space Odyssey 83–4

A Fistful of Dollars 307
A Series of Unfortunate Events: The
  Bad Beginning 143
Abercrombie, Nicholas 172–3, 222
achieved celebrity 254
Act One, see first act
Acting in the Cinema 21
action 17–23
  in mise en scène 2
  shot size and 36
  storyboarding 142
action cinema 119–21, 310–16, see
  also martial arts films
actors, star system, see celebrities; star
  system
Adaptation 128
adaptation from television to film
  281–2

Adorno, Theodor 233–4, 258
ADR 82
Adventures of Priscilla, Queen of the
  Desert, The 45, 46
advertising
  commercial breaks 173
  music in 69–70
  revenue derived from 7
  sound levels increase for 69
  spin-offs from shows 252–3
  sponsorship and endorsements 268
  television based on 100, 175, 208–9
  via star system 252–3
Æon Flux 273–5, 283
  adaptation for US TV 286–8
  cult following 280–3, 286–8
  sexual deviance in 278–9
aerial shots 45–6
aesthetic approach 167, 235–6, 288
affect, waning of 319–20
African-American characters 234
Alberoni, F. 266–7
alienation 285
All That Heaven Allows 6
Almodóvar, Pedro 5, 15, 19
Alternative Scriptwriting: Successfully
  Breaking the Rules 151
Altman, Rick 223–4

Altman, Robert 168
ambient sound 71
Amelie, rhythm in 119
American Beauty 41
'American Dream, The' 13, 17, 167
American Gangster 228
American Idol 246
American Independent Cinema 168–9
American shots 35
American Splendor 191
American tracks 51
amorality 319–20
An Inconvenient Truth 193
anachrony 161
analepsis 161
analogue media, vs. digital xiv
Anderson, Pamela 263–6, *264*
angle 37–9
animation (*anime*) 274, *311*, 323–5
Aniston, Jennifer 259
Anker, Elizabeth 211
antagonists 163, 166
aperture 47
appointment television 298
Arahan 330
Aristotle 230
art department 3–7
art design 1–29
artificiality 318–19
ascribed celebrity 254
aspect ratio 57–61
assembly edits 95
associative montage editing 97
asymmetric flow of media products 326
atmos 71
attributed celebrity 254–5
audiences
  celebrities and 256–60
  for cult media 273–300
  in reality television 208–10
  reactions to genre 224–7
  research into 290–5
  studies of 287

studio audiences 68–9
Audio in Media 87
aural rhythm 117
auteur theory 174–5, 200–1, 230
automated dialogue replacement 82
axis of action 107–9

Babe 219
Babel 156
back light 23, 25
Back to the Future Part III 308
backlash against feminism 312
Backstein, Karen 285–6
Bad Boy Bubby 85
Badlands 306–7
Band of Brothers 206
Baraka: A World Without Words 192
bathrooms as settings 11–12
Baudrillard, Jean 319
Beebe, Dion 32, 53
'Been Caught Stealing' 75
Before Sunrise 186–7
Before Sunset 186–7
Beowulf 180
Bergman, Ingmar 306
best boys 33
Beverly Hills 90210 12
Beyond All Reason: The Cult Film Experience 275
bibliography 354–65
Bicycle Thief, The 27, *27*, 199
Bier, Jesse 268
Big Brother 68, 98, 207
Big Love 57
big print 135
big squeeze 51
binary oppositions 161–8, 231–2
binaural technologies 85
bird's eye camera 39
Blair Witch Project, The 196
blue-screen 57
body text 135
Bollywood 239, 330
boom operation 33–4
Boorstin, Daniel 249

INDEX

bootstrapping 266
Border Security 209
Bordwell, David
  on editing 96
  on genres 222–3
  on narration xii
  on science fiction and fantasy 169–70
Bound to Bond 231
'Brangelina' 251
Bringing out the Dead 83
Brit Grit social realism 201
British Film Institute 152
British New Wave 201
Broderick, Mick 12
Broinowski, Anna 194
Bruckheimer, Jerry 175
Buckland, Warren 320–3
Buffy the Vampire Slayer
  approach to genre 237
  cult following 285, 298
  filming methods 58–9
  musical episodes 75
  sound effects in 81
'bugs' 100–1
bullet-time 55
Buñuel, Louis 115
Butterfly Effect 101–2, 170
buzz track 71

cable television 230
camera work 34–47
Campion, Jane 53
canonical story structure 157
canted frame 39
Carnicke, Sharon 22
Carradine, David 307
cars in road movies 16
Casey, Bernadette 175
casting decisions 20
Casualty 240
category of genre 218
cause-and-effect structure 180
Cawelti, John 236–7
CCTV filmmaking 204–5

celebration of artificiality 318–19
celebrities xx, 245–71
Celebrity and Power 267
Celebrity Big Brother 208
CGI 57
Chan, Jackie 328–9
chanbara 305
channel idents 69
characters
  African Americans as 234
  dialogue reveals 77
  identification with 72, 256–60
  ideologies of 163, 307–10
  names in scripts 136
  social class of 8
  stereotyped 17–19
Charlie's Angels 229, 310
Chaser's War on Everything 206
Chenery, Susan 251
Chiba, Sonny 307
Chicago 106
Children of Men 285–6
children's television 229
Chinese cinema 239
chromakey 57
Chronicle of Summer 200
Chumscrubber, The 278
cinema of social concern 209
Cinéma Vérité 200
cinematography 31–63, 134, 142
CineTech: Film, Convergence and New Media 55
Clark, Larry 196
classical Hollywood realism 188
classical narration 157–9
cliffhangers 100, 173
close ups 35–6, 107
codes of representation 187–90
cognitive theories of spectatorship 288–9
cognitivism 165
colour palette 4–5, 25
comedy
  laugh tracks 68, 82, 99
  mockumentaries 196–7

377

reality television and 206
romantic comedy genre 231–2, 235, 237
sitcom genre 82, 98–9, 235
Commercial Television Industry Code of Practice 229
competitions 207, *see also* game shows
compiled scores 72
complex narrative structures 168–72
composed music 73
composite shots 56
composition 26–7
computer games 179–81, 320–3
computer-generated imagery 57
conglomeration 326
constructed celebrity 255
constructive editing 119–20
contamination of genres 318
content 13, 188, 218
continuity editing 103–13
contrast, lighting for 24
conventions 289
convergence, *see also* narrative structure
  digital games 179–80
  digital technology and xiii–xvi
  globalisation and 326
  multi-platforming 296–7
conversational mode of address 175
copyright 6–7, 134
Cosby Show 232
cosmetics 7
costume 2, 7–9
Coulthard, Lisa 310
coverage 94
Crago, Mowena 207
crane shots 45
Crash 155–6, 159
crash zooms 46
creep zooms 46
Crimewatch 209
critical analysis of *Kill Bill* 303–4
criticism, *see* reviewing
Cronenberg, David 331

crosscutting 101–2
crossover shows 298–9
Crouching Tiger, Hidden Dragon 131
Cruise, Tom 252–3
CSI: Crime Scene Investigation xvi, 57
cues 289
cult media xx, 273–300
  film 277–9
  television 275–7, 279–86
culture 275
  cultural imperialism 326
  cultural studies 292–3
  transcultural influences 303–32
cut-scenes 179
cutaways 106
cutting 95–6

Dai, J. 314
dailies 95
Dali, Salvador 115
dance sequences 75
dangling causes 128–9, 173
Dark Angel 299
Dark City 96
Day After Tomorrow, The 210
de Saussure, Ferdinand 161
Dead Girl, The 168
Deadwood 5, 13–14, 73
decentred experience 174
dedicated channels 297
Definitive Guide to Screenwriting, The 151
democracy 204, 208–10
denouement 127–8
depth of field 47
desire for celebrities 259
Desperate Housewives 222, 252–3
development 127
Dexter 71
Dialectic of Enlightenment 258
dialectical synthesis 115–16, 167
dialogue 75–80
  convincingness of 21
  hooks in 76, 137–8
  in scripts 137

INDEX

on television 68
overlapping 118
realism in 189
DiCaprio, Leonardo 258, 269–70, *269*
Die Hard trilogy 180
diegesis 10
diegetic sound 70–1, 72
digital technology, *see also* technological change
  convergence and xiii–xvi
  digital divide 326
  fan communities and 295–6
  games 179–81, 320–3
  in editing 96–7
  in sound manipulation 84–5
  onscreen graphics 100–1
dilemma-based dramas 176–7
direct address 41–2
direct cinema 191
director of photography 32
Dirty Sexy Money 74
discursive approach to genre 237–9
disintegrative montage 120
dissolution of boundaries 318
dissolves 105–6
Doctor Who 275
docudrama 206–7
documentary film and television 190–5
Dogma manifesto 202–4
'dogs' 100–1
dog's eye camera 39
dollies 44
dolly shots 43
domestic context of television 175–6
Donnie Darko 55–6, 73, 284–5
Don't Forget the Lyrics 73
Doom 322
double exposure 56
Dr Phil 252
dramatic irony 128
dramaturgical space 10
Dreamgirls 223
Duellists, The 204
Dutch tilt 39

Dyer, Richard 259, 261–2, 266

Easy Rider 3
Eckhart, Aaron 250
'economical' style 204–5
edge of frame 33
editing xviii, 93–123
  action sequences 119–21
  edit points 143
  performance and 22–3
  realism in 189
  sound and image 81–2
Eisenstein, Sergei 115, 198
ellipsis 75, 102
Ellis, John 260
Elsaesser, Thomas 12, 320–3
empirical media effects research 291
endorsements, *see* advertising
ensemble hospital dramas 239–42
episodic nature of television 172–3, 241
epistemological issues 190–2
establishing shots 106–7
Eternal Sunshine of the Spotless Mind 7, 10–11, *16*
ethical issues, style and realism 210–13
ethnography 291–2
experiential realism 194–5
exposition 127, 137, 192–3
exposure 47
extra-diegetic world 10, 70, 72
extra-textuality 224
extras 19
extreme close-ups 35
extreme long shots 35
eye level camera 39
eyeline matches 109–12

Faceless 205
fades 101, 105–6
Faking It: Documentary and the Subversion of Factuality 197
fame 250, *see also* celebrities; star system

Fame Games 267
family-friendly material 175
family resemblances approach to genre 236–7
fan cultures 245–71, 294–5
fantasies
  about cult media 294–5
  identification with celebrities 260
fantasy, *see* science fiction and fantasy
Far From Heaven 6
Fargo 50
fast-forward effects 54–5, 121
Federal Communications Commission (US) 282
female experience 177, *see also* gender issues
fidelity 80–1
Fight Club 70–1, 110, *112*
fill light 23–4
Film Performance 22
Film Sound: Theory and Practice 67
film stocks 58
film vs television
  adaptations and 281–2, 287–8
  demands on actors 21–2
  genre in 228–30
  narrative structure 172
  screenwriting 132–3
  sound in 66–71
films, *see also* film vs television
  credits 365–70
  narratives 155–7
  reviewing 146–51, 227
fine cuts 96
Firefly 236
first act 127
first-person perspective 40
first-wave feminism 312–13
fish eye lenses 48–9
Fiske, John 233
Fistful of Dollars, A 307
five star ratings 150–1
'five W's and the H' 148
flashbacks and flash-forwards 101, 169–70

flow-mo 55
flow, on television 173–4
fluorescent lighting 25
focal properties 47–61
focus groups 292
Forbidden Lie$ 194
forced perspective 15
Foreman, George 253
form, realism in 188
formalism 165
formats 57–61
Foucault, Michel 237, 273
fourth wall 42
Fracture 84
fragmented narratives 156–7, 173–4, 320
frames
  frame line 33
  frame rate 58
framing 26–7, 57–61
franchising 296–8
freeze frames 101
French New Wave 200–1
French poetic realism 198–9
Friends
  fantasies about 260–1
  music in 75
  shot patterns 107, *108*
FX 56–7, 210

gaffers 33
Gallagher, Mark 314
game credits 370
Game of Death 319
game shows 82, *see also* competitions
games, family resemblances between 236
gaps 289
gauges of film 58
gaze, ethics of 212–13
gender issues
  binary oppositions and 162
  masculine-coded stories 177
  'musculinity' 312
genre texts 218

genres xix, 217–43
  digital games 179–80
  evolution of 304–5
  hybridity in 221, 304–7
  'inbreeding' 305
  musical 74
  mutation of 304
  reviewing and 150
Ghost in the Shell 323
Gitlin, Todd 222, 317
Gledhill, Christine 250–1, 263, 267
globalisation 325–9
glossary 333–53
Godard, Jean-Luc 201
Golden Harvest studio 329
Gondry, Michel 149
Grand Illusion, The 198
graphic matches 110–12
Green Hornet, The 318
green-screen 57
Grey's Anatomy 240
  commercial breaks 173–4
  genre analysis 239–42
  music in 69–70, 73
  treatment for 131
Grierson, John 191
Griffith, D.W. 103–4
grips department 32–3
Grossberg, Lawrence 258
guest appearances 173
Gwenllian-Jones, Sara
  on cult media 274, 295–6
  on cult television 280
  on immersive engagement 294

halogen lighting 25
hammocking 174
handheld cameras 44–5
hard light 25
Harry Potter and the Order of the Phoenix 220–2
Hate 51
Haynes, Todd 6
HDTV xv
Hearing Film 72–3

Heath, Stephen 263
Heavenly Bodies 261
Hero, The 113, *113*, 307
Heroes 128, 284–5, 298–9
heroes, in binary oppositions 163, 166
Hickey-Moody, Anna 85
high-angle shots 37
High Fidelity 73
high-key illumination 24
Hiller, Jim 234
Hills, Matt 284
Hindi cinema 239, 330
Holland, Patricia 70
Hollywood Antitrust Case 249
Hollywood star system 248–9
Holmes, Su 259
Holt, Jennifer 296
Hong Kong films, *see* martial arts films
'hooks', *see* dialogue; lead sentences
Horizons West 231
Horkheimer, Max 258
horror films 11, 284–5, 330–1, *see also* science fiction and fantasy
hospital dramas 239–42
How To Look Good Naked 208–9
Hunt, Nathan 275
hwalkuk 330
hybridity 221–2, 304–7
hyperdiegetic fiction 284

I Love Lucy 237
iconography 219
identification
  with celebrities 256–60
  with characters 321
ideology
  approach to genre 233
  approach to star system 263–7
  character and 163
  cult media and 277
  masculine-coded stories 177
  reality television and 208–10
  settings and 13
  social change and 307–10
Idiots, The 202–4

illusion of reality 188
image quality 57–61
image-saturation 317–18
immersive engagement 294
In My Country 14–15
In the Cut 38, 54
  camera angles 38
  cinematography 53–4, *55*
  racking focus *52*
Independent Motion Picture Company 248
industry
  cult media in 275–7, 296–9
  genre in 224
inequalities of access 326
Inland Empire xiv, 171
instantaneity 325
institutions and cult media 296–9
intellectual montage 116–17
interactivity 325–6
interconnectedness 326
interdependence 326
interpellation 208–9, 322–3
Interpreting Television 65
intertextuality 219–20, 227, 318
interventional gaze 213
introduction 303–4
Iocco, Melissa 85
Iranian paradocumentary cinema 198–9
ironic hybridisation 307
Irreversible 85
Italian neorealism 199–200

J-Horror 330–1
Jameson, Frederick 320
Jamie's Kitchen Australia 209
Jancovich, Mark 275
Japanese film 330–1
Jarhead 159
Jeet Kune Do style 314
Jenkins, Henry 178, 292–3, 295
Jesus Camp 193
Joiner, David 322
Jolie, Angelina 247, 251, *251*

journalistic mode 230
Julien Donkey-Boy 203–4
jump cuts 109
Jungle Fever 23

Kairo 331
Kapsis, Robert 261
Kassabian, Anahid 72–3
Kath and Kim 197
Kaufman, Charlie 127–8
Kawaii 323–4
Kenny 197
Khouri, Norma 194
kick-flicks, *see* martial arts films
Kill Bill 309, 311, 319, 324
  action sequences 119
  aspect ratio 59–60, *61*
  bogus brands in 7
  sound in 83
  transcultural influences 303–32
Kirsner, Scott 59
Kiss or Kill 109
Klinger, Barbara 262
knee shots 35
Korean film 330–1
Korine, Harmony 196
Kubrick, Stanley 12
Kuleshov, Lev 116
kung-fu films, *see* martial arts films
Kung Fu Hustle 221, 307
Kurosawa, Akira 306–7
kwaito music 74

La Haine 51
La Jetée 219
Laemmle, Carl 248
landmarks in settings 12–13
Langer, John 261, 266–7
Lara Croft: Tomb Raider 315
laugh tracks 68, 82, 99
Law and Order: Criminal Intent 102
Lawrence, Florence 248
Lawrenson, Edward 150
Layer Cake 10–11
Leacock, Richard 191

INDEX

lead-ins 174
lead sentences 148
Lee, Bruce 314, 328–9
Lefebvre, Martin 13
Legally Blonde 25, 26
Leigh, Mike 201
lenses 47–61
Leone, Sergio 306
letterboxing xv
Levi-Strauss, Claude 161
lighting 23–6, 189
limited animation 324
Liu, Gordon 307
Liu, Lucy 310
Living Soap, The 206
Loach, Ken 201
location shoots 6–7, 11
loglines 126
long shots 35
Lord of the Rings xi–xii, 57, 84
Lost 11, 289, 298–9
Lost Highway 3, 87–9
loudness 83
Love Actually 118, 128
low-angle shots 37–8
low-key illumination 24
Lumby, Catharine 246, 270
Lumiere brothers 197
Lynch, David xiv, 87, 171
lyrics of songs 74–5

Magnificent Seven 306
Man with a Movie Camera 198
manga 323
manipulation 192–4
March of the Penguins 192–3
marginalisation 164
marginality 285
Marie Antoinette 4, 8
marketing, *see* advertising
Marks, Laura 86
martial arts films 314, 328–9
  action sequences 120–1
  as hybrids 327
  Kill Bill and 306

Kung Fu Hustle 221, 307
Martin, Adrian 120, 147, 149
Marxism 266
masculine-coded stories 177, *see also* gender issues
masked edits 106
mass culture theory 233–4
match edits 109–13
match on action 110
Match Point 8
Matrix series 11, 306
McCann, Madeleine 255
McQuire, Scott 210
media construction of celebrity 255
Medium 101, 161
medium close-ups 35
medium long shots 35
medium shots 35
melodramas 11
Memento 81, 161
metonymic mise en scène 3
metric montage 116
Mexican cinema 239
Miami Vice 74
microphones 82
midnight movies 277–8
Mikula, Maja 319–20
Milat backpacker murders xii–xiii
mise en scène xvii–xviii, 1–29
Mittell, Jason 218
mixed genres 221–2
Mizejewski, Linda 259–60
mobile framing 47, 144–5
mockumentary film and television 196–7
mode of production of television 174–5
Monican Spies 281
Monroe, Marilyn 261–2
montage sequences 114–17
Moore, Michael 193
More than a Method 21
Morris, Meaghan 329
Moulin Rouge 96, 305
Movie Acting 21

383

MTV-style montage 114–15
Mujahedeen Brigades hoax 185, *186*
mukokuseki 328
multi-camera shoots 37, 97–8
multi-platforming 296–7
multiform narratives 156–7, 171, 181
Murray, Janet 181
'musculinity' 312
music 69–75
Music and Lyrics 224, 237
musicals 75
'must see TV' 298
My Best Friend's Wedding 224–5, 237
My Fair Lady 8
My Name is Earl
  commercial breaks 174
  music in 75
  stereotyped characters 18
  wipes in 106

Name of this Film is Dogme95, The 202
Napier, Susan 324–5, 328
narcissism 258
narrative structure xix, 155–83
  convergence 180–2
  cues and conventions 289
  editing and 101–2
  fragmented 156–7, 173–4, 320
  narrative question 129–30
  realism in 190
  resolution 228–30
  spectacle and 210–11
  Westerns 307–8
Natural Born Killers
  based on *Badlands* 307
  binary oppositions in 165–8
  matches in 111–13
  metonymic mise en scène 3
naturalistic aesthetic 188–90
Negra, Diane 315
neorealism 199–200
neutral angle 37
Newcombe, Horace 230
news footage 213

Nichols, Bill 192–4
Nip/Tuck 280
No Country for Old Men 83
non-diegetic sound 70, 72
non-linear editing 96–7
normal lenses 48
nostalgic classics 277, 279
Nouvelle Vague 200–1
Noyce, Philip 83, 86
NW Magazine 263–5

oblique angle 39
observational mode 193
Obsessione 199
OC, The 12
off-screen space 42–3
off-screen time 104–5
Office of Communications (UK) 229
Office, The 197
omniscient point of view 40–1
Once Were Warriors 118
online fan communities 294–5
open-ended interviews 292
Oprah Winfrey 252
options 134
orientation 127
O'Shaughnessy, Michael 74
over-exposure 47

pace 117
pan and scan xv, 43
Pan's Labyrinth 5
para-social relationships 256
paradocumentary cinema 198–9
Parker, Sarah Jessica 253
participant observation 291
participation in games 321
participatory documentaries 193
Path to 9/11 206
Pearson, Roberta 274
performance 20–3
performative documentaries 194
personification 21
Philosophical Investigations 236
photographic images, realism of 187

INDEX

physical space 10
physicality of sound 83–4
Pi 87
Piano, The 8, 72
Pickford, Mary 248–9
Pink (singer) 258
Pirates of the Caribbean 181–2
pitch 74
pitching a story 126
Pitt, Brad 251
pixels xiv
Plan Américain 35
Player, The 126
plotting 125–53, 160–2
poetic mode 192
poetic realism 198–9
point of view 39–43, 102–3
political economy approach
   to genre 227, 233–5
   to star system 267–8
post-production 94, 99–100, *see also* editing
postfeminism 310–16
postmodernism 316–25
Powell, Scott 22–3, 81–2, 95
power relations 77, 287
pre-production 94
Prebble, Tim 84–5
Preston, Ward 4
Priscilla, Queen of the Desert, The Adventures of 45, 46
Prison Break 69, 115, 168
'Producer's Game' 223
product placement 7, *see also* advertising
production design 3–7
production illustrators 140, *see also* storyboarding
production modes 174–5
program logos 69
project treatments 130–2
prolepsis 161
Proposition, The 14, 48
Propp, Vladimir 162
protagonists 163, 166

pseudo individuality 267
psychoanalysis 289–90
psychogenic fugue 88
public service broadcasters 176
Pudovkin, Vsevolod 116
pulling focus 51–2
Pulp Fiction 156
Pulse 331
Purity Test 281
puzzle plots 168, 180–1

qualitative research 291–2
quantitative research 290–1

racking focus 51–2
Rashômon 307
ratings 290–1
Reading Hollywood: Spaces and Meanings in American Film 10
realism xix
   editing techniques and 103
   realist film movements 197–205
   reality and 185–214
   reality television 205–10
   crime shows 209
   dialogue in 68
   mockumentaries and 196–7
   political economy approach 234
Reaper 130–1
rear projection 56
reception, realism in 189
Red Dust 14–15, *14*
Redmond, Sean 259
reflectionist approach to genre 232
reflexive documentaries 194
remote TV controls 229–30
Requiem for a Dream 42, 49, 81, 115
reviewing
   films 146–51, 227
   television 177–8
Reznor, Trent 87
rhythm 119
Ring Virus 330
Ringu 330
ritual approach to genre 232–3

road movies 11, 15–17, 307
Rocky Horror Picture Show 75, 277, 286
Rodman, Gilbert 256
role models 256–60, 321
romantic comedy genre 231–2, 235, 237
Rome Open City 199
Rope 106
Roseanne 98–9, 237
Roswell 298
Roth, Christine 263–6, *264*
Rouch, Jean 200
rough cuts 95
Rove Live 10
Rules of the Game 198
Run Lola Run 170, 181
rushes 95
Russell, Todd 255

sales pitch 126
Salesman 193
scavenger aesthetic 328–9
scenes
 breakdowns 126–30
 defined 34
 descriptions 135
 scene lines 134–5
 scene space 134
Schultz, Julianne 245
Schwarzenegger, Arnold 246
science fiction and fantasy
 audience expectations 226
 cult media 279–80
 evolved from Westerns 305
 narrative structure 284–5
Science of Sleep, The 148–50
scratch videos 294
Scream 307
Screen Acting 21
Screen Australia 152
screen culture xx
 globalisation and 325–9
 new directions 330–1
 postmodernism in 316–25

screen narratives, *see* narrative structure
screen production 94
Screenwriting: The Sequence Approach 128
scripts and scriptwriting 132–9
Searchers, The 308–9, *309*
second act 127
second-wave feminism 312–13
Secret Window 160
segue 118–19
selective diegetic drop-out 82
self-reflexivity 194
semiotics 161–2, 261–3, 288
sentence structure in reviews 147
sequels, popularity of 181–2
sequences 34, 126–30
Serenity 236, 298
serials on television 172–3, 175–6
series on television 172–3, 241
settings 2, 10–17, 235–6
Seven Samurai 306
Sex and the City 222, 253
sexual deviance in cult media 278–9
shadow and lighting 24
shallow focus 51
Shaw Brothers Studio 329
shenguai wuxia pian 306
Shetty, Shilpa 208
shift tilt lenses 53
shifting focus 51–2
shooting scripts 139–46
shots
 defined 33–4
 duration 117
 listing of 94–5
 shot–reverse–shot pattern 107
 size 35–7, *36*
 storyboarding 143
Shrek series 219, 222
Shutter 331
Sick Kitten, The 103
Silence of the Lambs 77–80, *78–9*, *80*
Simpson, Joe 195
Sims 180, 322–3

INDEX

simulation 317–18
Sin City 57
Singin' in the Rain 67
singles 36, *see also* close ups
Sins of the Brother xii
Sirk, Douglas 6
sitcom genre 82, 98–9, 235
situational stories 176
Six Feet Under 105
Six Guns and Society 231
Sky Captain and the World of Tomorrow 57
slash narratives 294
Sliding Doors 170
slow-motion effects 54, 121
Snakes on a Plane 158–9
soap operas 206, 222
social change 307–10
social class of characters 8
social science approach 290
society, television and 176–7
socio-cultural approach to genre 232–3
soft focus 51
soft light 25
Some Like it Hot 110, *111*
sonic overlap 118
sonic perspective 85
Sopranos 229
sound xviii, 65–90
　bridging 118
　non-diegetic 70, 72
　sonic overlap 118
　sonic perspective 85
　storyboarding 142
　transitions in 117–19
sound effects 80–9
source music 72
South Africa 14–15, 74
Soviet montage 115–16, 198
space of sound 83–4
spatial conventions 106–7
special effects 56–7, 210
spectacle 210–11, 317–18
Spectacular Bodies 315

Spectacular Spectacular 305
spectatorship theories 286–90
speech, *see* dialogue
speed of motion 54–6
speed of sound 83–4
speed ramping 121
speeds of film 58
SPFX 56–7, 210
Spider-Man film series 181–2, 217
spin-offs 223
sponsorship, *see* advertising
sports 177, 254
spotting 84
Spurlock, Morgan 193
stage star system, *see* celebrities; star system
Staiger, Janet 305
Stam, Robert 218
Stanislavski Method 21–2
Star Gazing 263
star system 247–55, 261–8, *see also* celebrities
Star Trek 275, 293, 298
Stars 259, 261
station logos 69
steadicams 45
step outlines 126–30
stereotyped characters 17–19
stock characters 19
story 130–2, 160–2
Story 151
storyboarding xviii–xix, 95, 139–46
storytelling 125–53
straight cuts 105–6
Stratton, David 227
Strike 115
Structural Anthropology 161
structural bias 163–4
structuralism 161–8, 231–2
structuring absences 164
studies of genre 230–9
studio audiences 68–9
studio-based shoots 11
Studlar, Gaylyn 278
style and realism 189, 210–13

subcultural ideology 277
subject (content) 13, 188, 218
subjective imagery 40
subjective sound 71
subsonics 86–7
superficiality 317–18
superimposition 56
Supersize Me 193
suturing 104
symbolic spaces 15–17
synaesthesia 86–7
synchronous sound 66–7
syndication 296
synopses 126–30
synthespians 57

Taking Lives 19
Talented Mr Ripley, The 8
Tarantino, Quentin 94, 307, 317
Tasker, Yvonne 312, 315
tattoos 7–8, 9
Team America 114
technological change, see also digital technology
  cult media and 275–7
  online fan communities 294–6
  television and 178, 229–30
  time-shifting recording 176
telecine xv
telegraphing 128
telephoto lenses 50
television, see also film vs television
  celebrities on 253
  cult shows 275–7, 279–86
  dialogue on 76
  editing for 96, 99–101
  filming options 58–9
  genres in 221, 228–30
  mockumentaries on 196–7
  music programmes 75
  narrative structure in 172–8
  performers on 21–2
  reviewing for 177–8
  screenwriting for 132–3
  shot size in 36
  studio-based shoots 11

television credits 370–3
Television: The Critical View 230
Telotte, JP 273–5, 277
tempo 74
temporal compression 117
temporal ellipsis 75
temporal order 169
tentpoling 174–5
Teo, Steven 327
texts, in cult media 275–7
textual poachers 292
The Adventures of Priscilla, Queen of the Desert 45, 46
The Bicycle Thief 27, *27*, 199
The Blair Witch Project 196
The Butterfly Effect 101–2, 170
The Chaser's War on Everything 206
The Chumscrubber 278
The Cook, The Thief, His Wife and Her Lover 8
The Cosby Show 232
The Day After Tomorrow 210
The Dead Girl 168
The Definitive Guide to Screenwriting 151
The Duellists 204
The Grand Illusion 198
The Green Hornet 318
The Hero 113, *113*, 307
The Idiots 202–4
The Living Soap 206
The Magnificent Seven 306
The Matrix series 11, 306
The Name of this Film is Dogme95: 202
The OC 12
The Office 197
The Path to 9/11 206
The Piano 8, 72
The Player 126
The Proposition 14, 48
'The Purity Test' 281
The Ring Virus 330

INDEX

The Rocky Horror Picture Show 75, 277, 286
The Science of Sleep 148–50
The Searchers 308–9, *309*
The Sick Kitten 103
The Sims 180, 322–3
The Sopranos 229
The Talented Mr Ripley 8
The Usual Suspects
  cuts in 106
  dialogue in 76–7
  sound bridging 118
  stereotyped characters 19
The Virgin Spring 306
The Vow of Chastity 202–3
The X-Files 285, 298–9
theatrical stage design 3
There's Something About Mary 128
thesis statements 304
third act 127–8
third-wave feminism 313
Thom, Sandi 246
three-point lighting 23–4
three-quarter shots 35
Thurman, Uma 313
tilting 43
timbre 87
Time Code 98
time-lapse photography 55
time-shifting recording 176
timing 117
tonal montage 116
top light 25
Touch of Evil 45
Touching the Void 194–5, *195*
tracking shots 43
traditional cohesion devices 170
transcultural influences 303–32
transgression 285–6
travelling shots 43
treatments 130–2
Tru Calling 299
trucking shots 43
True Romance 307
Truffaut, François 201

Truth and Reconciliation Commission (South Africa) 14–15
Tsotsi 74
tungsten lighting 25
Turner, Graeme 162
Turner, Ted 298
TV: The Most Popular Art 230
Twelve Monkeys 102, 219
two shots 35
typecasting 20

U-Turn 16
Ugly Betty 49
  cinematography 31
  colour palette 5
  wide-angle shots 48
  wipes in 106
Unbreakable 163–4
under-exposure 47
under light 25
underscore 72
Understanding Celebrity 267
United 93 211–12
United States, as main source of media 326
US soldier hostage hoax 185, *186*
uses and gratifications approach 293
Usual Suspects, The see *The Usual Suspects*
'Utopia or Deuteranopia' 282

vactors 57
Vanity Fair 269–70, *269*
vehicles, in road movies 16
verisimilitude 20–1
Veronica Mars 12
vertical integration 249
Vertigo 51
vertigo shots 51
Vertov, Dziga 198
video game logic 320–3
video games 179–81, 320–3
video sniffing 205
vilification 164

villains 163, 166
Vinterberg, Thomas 202
violence in video games 321–2
Virgin Spring 306
virtual actors 57
vision mixer 37
visual agency 40
visual culture 303–32
visual metaphor 3
voiceover narration 68, 76, 189
Volcano High 330
Volver 5, 15
von Trier, Lars 202
Vow of Chastity 202–3

Walkabout 74
Walker, Alison 84
Walking with Dinosaurs 191–2
Wasko, Janet 234
We Can Be Heroes 197
Webb, Brant 255
websites
  about celebrities 245–6
  fansites 294–5
  on screenwriting 151–2
Westerns
  approaches to genre 231, 235
  audience expectations 226
  narrative formulas 307–8

settings for 11, 13–14
Whedon, Joss 75, 175
whip pans 43
wide-angle lenses 48
Wing Chun style 314
wipe-bys 106
wipes 105–6
Wiseman, Fred 191
Wittgenstein, Ludwig 236
Wolf Creek 59, 60
  based on actual events xii–xiii
  costumes 7–8, 9
  filming methods 59
  lighting in 26
Woo, John 121
Woods, Rowan 201
Woods, Tiger 268
Written on the Wind 12
wuxia 327–8

X-Files, The 285, 298–9

Yates, Simon 194–195
Yojimbo 306–7
youth culture 328
YouTube 208, 246

zolly shots 51
zoom lenses 50
zooms 46

For Product Safety Concerns and Information please contact our EU representative GPSR@taylorandfrancis.com
Taylor & Francis Verlag GmbH, Kaufingerstraße 24, 80331 München, Germany

www.ingramcontent.com/pod-product-compliance
Lightning Source LLC
Chambersburg PA
CBHW071141300426
44113CB00009B/1046